MEMPHIS STATE UNIVERSITY
00350 1021

REVIEW COPY

THE COMMUNITY BUILDERS HANDBOOK

●

Prepared by the

Community Builders' Council

of

Urban Land Institute

THE EXECUTIVE EDITION

1960

●

URBAN LAND INSTITUTE
Washington, D. C.

First Edition and First Printing 1947
Revised Printing 1948
J. C. Nichols Memorial Edition, and Second Revised Printing 1950
The Members Edition, and Third Revised Printing 1954
The Members Edition, and Fourth Revised Printing 1956
The Executive Edition, and Fifth Revised Printing 1960

Library of Congress Catalog Card Number 60-53545

PRINTED IN THE UNITED STATES OF AMERICA

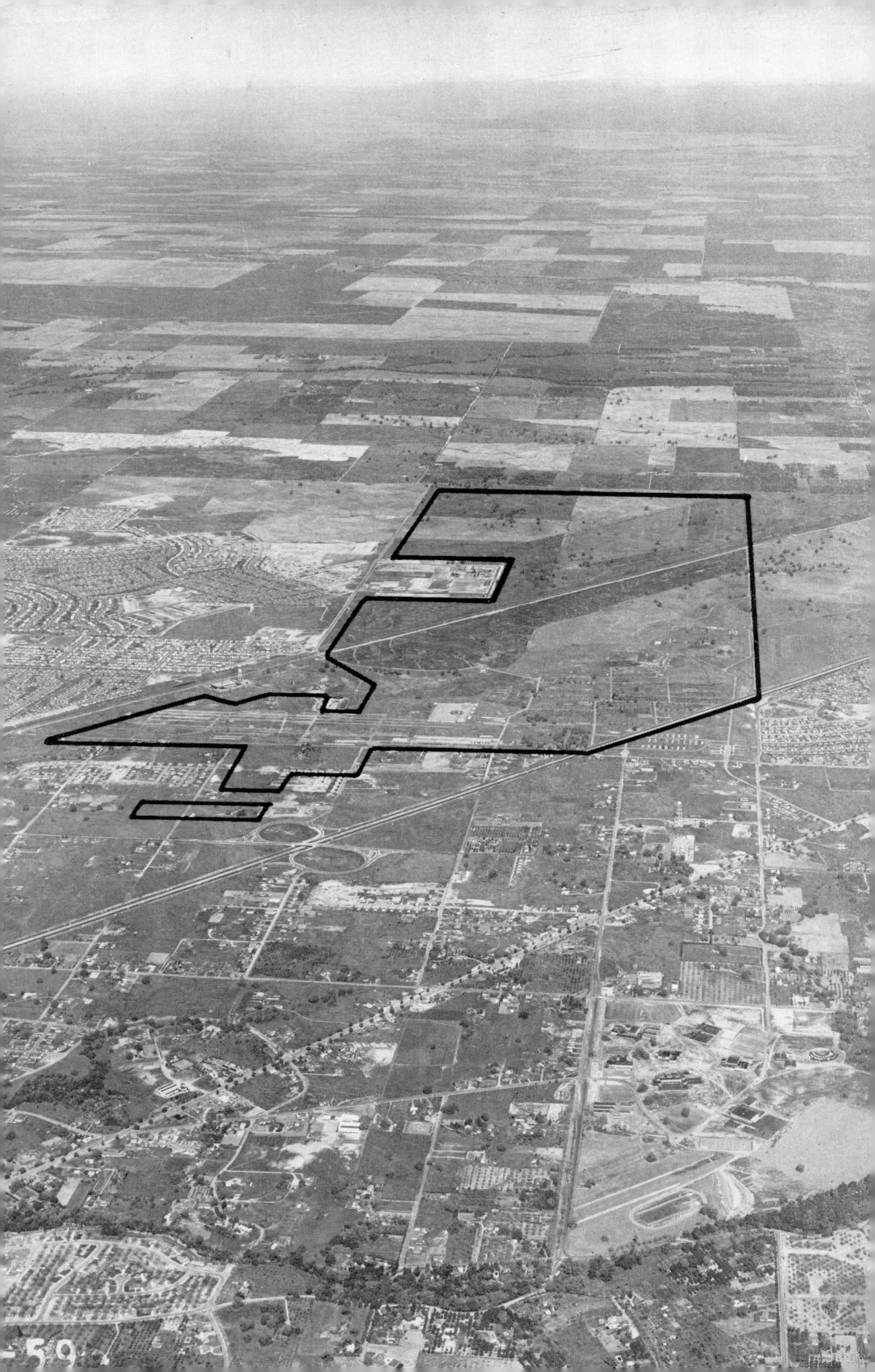
59

URBAN GROWTH

Metropolitan growth problems, including transportation between home and work, lead to consideration of large-scale real estate projects in which employment opportunities and shopping facilities are provided along with residences of varying types. Consequently, the community value of any project depends largely on the quality of planning in the entire metropolitan area and the extent to which the project is in harmony with the development of the metropolitan area itself.

Development of large project areas for a diversity of residential uses, including employment opportunities, shopping facilities, recreational and cultural activities, can make a major contribution to the relief of metropolitan growth problems. A "satellite community" must be examined not only for its land use and land planning concepts and for the validity of its specific balance of uses but also from the standpoint of its investment potential.

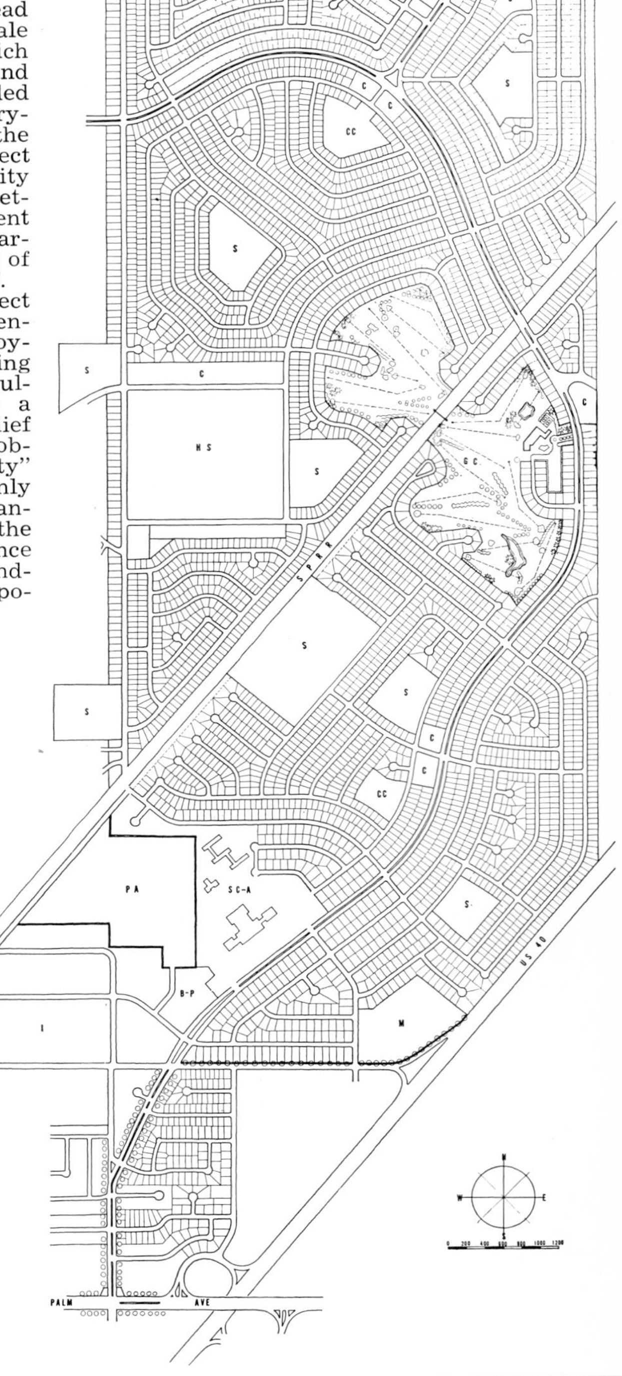

Illustration No. 2

Master Plan, Hillsdale—Sacramento

A David D. Bohannon Organization Planned Community

Frontispiece: **Urban Growth (Illustration No. 1) Hillsdale—Sacramento, from the air**

Foreword to the Executive Edition

The COMMUNITY BUILDERS HANDBOOK first appeared in 1947. Since then two editions and four revised printings have been issued. Like the others this, the Executive Edition, is devoted to practical planning for the sound development of better American communities. To this end, the Handbook includes tested policies for realizing these objectives in new residential neighborhoods and in suburban shopping centers. The Handbook also incorporates methods to apply in protecting the future of these two elements in community development.

The COMMUNITY BUILDERS HANDBOOK is the written work of the Community Builders' Council of Urban Land Institute. It is this Council which gives attention to the residential area being created from raw land and to that more recent phenomenon which has evolved with new residential growth—the integrated shopping center. Other major land usages in urban development fall within the realm of the Institute's two other Councils—the Industrial Council and the Central Business District Council—each spearheaded by a twenty-five member Executive Group.

The Community Builders' Council Executive Group is composed of men recognized for their knowledge and accomplishment in land development, home building, architecture, real estate and analysis, merchandising and shopping center operations. Included in the group are men who have been responsible for many of the nation's noteworthy residential and shopping center projects.

The Council functions through its plan analysis sessions and special studies. In these ways, the Executive Group acts as a valued medium whereby the knowledge of community builders is exchanged, analyzed and advanced. By such unselfishness the group passes on to others the benefits from long and practical experience. This realistic approach to community development is made available through Urban Land Institute's publications and Council meetings.

The Community Builders' Council Executive Group believes that unless we build enduring values in communities we are apt to have great instability and rapid shifts in the character and makeup of our urban areas. Such insecurity creates a tremendous deficit in terms of obsolescence, loss of taxable values and spread of decadence and blight. The group relies on methods and procedures which can stand the valid test of sound land planning, practical expenditure, and proper engineering design.

For the protection of our investment in land, maximum benefits can be realized only through cogent long-range planning. Thus to the developer accrues satisfaction in producing a sound and financially successful project; to the resident, returns an enhancement of his living environment and home investment; and to the community-at-large reverts a well-designed physical development having an enduring taxable base upon which it can depend for continued well-being.

As with other editions, this Handbook follows the basic structure of the original work. But its text and illustrations are revised to augment the references and to bring up to date the happenings and statistical data. The precepts which led to the Handbook's acceptance as a standard working manual remain unaltered. Only details, applications and emphases have been strengthened. These reflect the new trends in community building and the practical experiences as exemplified by the members in the Executive Group of the Community Builders' Council.

We in Urban Land Institute appreciate the wide acceptance which the Handbook enjoys. We feel this recognition is an endorsement of the Council's work and objectives.

BOYD T. BARNARD, *President*
Urban Land Institute, 1960

URBAN LAND INSTITUTE

Officers and Trustees, 1960

Executive Group of the Community Builders' Council, 1960

***Chairman:** Hugh Potter, *Chairman of the Board,* River Oaks Corporation, Houston, Texas

***Vice Chairman:** John C. Taylor, *Chairman of the Board,* J. C. Nichols Company, Kansas City, Missouri

Paul D. Ambrose, Ambrose-Williams & Co., Denver, Colorado

Robert H. Armstrong, *Banking,* Armstrong Associates, New York, New York

W. P. "Bill" Atkinson, Midwest City, Oklahoma

Irving G. Bjork, *Vice President,* Connecticut General Life Insurance Company, Hartford, Connecticut

David D. Bohannon, David D. Bohannon Organization, San Mateo, California

Franklin L. Burns, *President,* The D. C. Burns Realty & Trust Co., Denver, Colorado

W. W. Caruth, Jr., Dallas, Texas

Donald L. Curtiss, Don Curtiss & Associates, New York, New York

Carl Detering, The Detering Co., Houston, Texas

James B. Douglas, *President,* The Northgate Company, Seattle, Washington

*Roy P. Drachman, Roy Drachman Realty Co., Tucson, Arizona

Walter K. Durham, *Architect,* Ardmore, Pennsylvania

L. E. Fite, L. E. Fite & Co., San Antonio, Texas

Robert P. Gerholz, Gerholz Community Homes, Inc., Flint, Michigan

Greenlaw Grupe, Sims & Grupe, Stockton, California

John B. Hollister, *Vice President,* S. S. Kresge Company, Detroit, Michigan

Richard M. Hurd, *President,* Hurd & Co., Inc., New York, New York

Arthur M. King, *Executive Vice President,* Charles F. Curry Real Estate Co., Kansas City, Missouri

John P. Matthews, *President,* John Matthews Co., North Little Rock, Arkansas

Hunter Moss, Hunter Moss & Company, Miami, Florida

John McC. Mowbray, *President,* The Roland Park Company, Baltimore, Maryland

Robert T. Nahas, R. T. Nahas Enterprises, Castro Valley, California

*Maurice G. Read, *President,* Mason-McDuffie Co., Berkeley, California

N. S. Ridgway, Jr., Fritz B. Burns & Associates, Los Angeles, California

Willard G. Rouse, *Vice President,* Community Research and Development, Inc., Baltimore, Maryland

Max Steinberg, *Vice President and Treasurer,* Steinberg's Limited, Montreal, Quebec, Canada

Waverly Taylor, Waverly Taylor, Inc., Washington, D. C.

Angus G. Wynne, Jr., *President,* American Home Realty Co., Dallas, Texas

*J. W. York, *President,* York Building Co., Cameron Village, Raleigh, North Carolina

Boyd T. Barnard, *President,* Urban Land Institute, *ex officio* council member

* On September 29, 1960 Maurice G. Read, Roy P. Drachman and J. W. York were appointed by ULI President Boyd T. Barnard as Chairman and Co-Vice Chairmen, respectively, to succeed retiring Chairman Hugh Potter and Vice Chairman John C. Taylor, both of whom have served since 1950 but who will continue as members of the Council's Executive Group.

Max S. Wehrly, *Executive Director,* Urban Land Institute
J. Ross McKeever, *Associate Director*

Editor of the Handbook, Executive Edition
J. Ross McKeever

Table of Contents

Page

Page

SECTION TWO—PLANNING AND OPERATION OF SHOPPING CENTERS

APPENDICES

List of Illustrations

THE COMMUNITY BUILDERS HANDBOOK

SECTION ONE

Residential Communities

INTRODUCTION

The COMMUNITY BUILDERS HANDBOOK spells out steps needed to insure sound development of new residential and commercial areas. In studying development phases of these two parts in community building, the Community Builders' Council of Urban Land Institute always keeps in mind that a successful subdivision or profitable shopping center is one that meets the tests of present day living applied under practices in good land planning. Under these yardsticks the project must be measured for its relationship to the rest of the community, its realistic planning and its site improvement. To gauge these standards requires proper financing, competent technical service and reference to the methods being used by our most skillful land developers and knowledgeable builders.

The precepts in the Handbook are based on experience and realistic practice under our private enterprise system. Advice and recommendations are given by members of the Community Builders' Council. As quoted in the text, these directives apply not only to smaller, conventional land subdivisions but also to larger-scale operations in which residential neighborhoods are built as communities or wholly new towns. Suggestions pertain to the developer's operations and to the planning commission's regulations. Both agents have parts to perform in the process of community development.

The Handbook is largely devoted to the builder's procedure so that he may graduate from status as house builder to that of community developer. Since he creates new living areas, he must condition his thinking to include livability and long-range value. At the same time, the planning commission in its thinking about zoning ordinances, subdivision regulations and patterns for urban development can benefit from appreciation of the practicalities of community construction—that which is realistic to expect and practical to perform. To this extent the Handbook is also a guide for planning commissions.

Behind the common interest between the developer and the planning commission, there are long-standing considerations which bear upon creating a neighborhood and its larger community. In this interpretation, the development of an environment for complete livability includes the utilities and the facilities which unite the house and lot with their surroundings.

In recent years, changes in the process of subdivision have merged the creation of lots with the building of houses. The practice today tends toward a housing package complete with finished house and its developed lot integrated with paved streets and installed utilities. This practice is here whether the project is ten acres or several hundred acres in size.

Once again, we are experiencing a trend to the development of large-scale residential projects. In these a land developer contemplates transforming several thousand acres of land into a complete community. This practice had only emerged in 1947 when the Handbook appeared. Since then, we have witnessed a period of market change and population growth. These facts necessitate the sharpening of our sights on the principles of land development which make better communities.

As 1947 was ending, the United States had 144 million people. Since then we have reached a total population of more than 176 million. By 1975, the total population figure is expected to be at least 216 million—perhaps 244 million.[1]

In 1950 almost 90 million people, or 57 percent of our total population, lived in the then 168 standard metropolitan areas. These metropolitan areas absorbed 81 percent of the growth between 1940 and 1950 and 97 percent of the growth between 1950 and 1955.

---

[1] Projections of United States population, by age and sex, for 1960 to 1980 have recently been revised by the Bureau of the Census. They were designed to be consistent with high employment and high economic activity.

Present in four series these projections are not meant to be predictions of future size of the population but indicate, rather, the approximate future level and age-sex composition of the Nation's population under given alternative assumptions as to fertility, mortality and net immigration. Following are high-to-low projections for this twenty-year span (in millions):

Year	*Series I*	*Series II*	*Series III*	*Series IV*
1960	182.2	180.1	179.8	179.4
1965	199.0	195.7	193.6	191.5
1970	219.5	213.8	208.2	202.5
1975	243.9	235.2	225.6	215.8
1980	272.6	260.0	245.4	230.8

Illustrative Projections of the Population of the United States, by Age and Sex: 1960 to 1980, may be obtained from the Bureau of the Census, Washington 25, D. C., or at field offices of the U. S. Department of Commerce.

The surprising thing about this fantastic growth is not that it is happening but where it is taking place. If the growth trends in the suburban rings continue to 1975, our 174 metropolitan areas[2] will be 200 standard metropolitan areas. One hundred fifty million people will then live in our major urban areas compared to the 90 million now. As a trend to the suburbs continues, by 1975 the net addition of some 60 million Americans to the metropolitan areas will raise the populations of central cities by only 10 million. The other 50 million will go to suburbia. Of these, 26 million will go into what is now open country—the unincorporated area around the fringes of our metropolitan areas. The remaining 24 million will be in the incorporated places of metropolitan United States.[3]

A projection of physical growth trends gives you an idea of the challenge presented by the job of planning for metropolitan growth and the prospect for the development of many new residential areas.[4] During the 1960's and 1970's we will be in an era of growth, an era of completely new community development and the redevelopment of older existing communities.

Up to 1947 we had a period of tooling-up for community development. Since then we have been sharpening these tools and testing them—even adding to our devices for creating better communities. We must remember that most of our zoning laws date from the 1920's and 1930's. Few of our planning commissions were in any degree effective until the 1940's. Since 1947 we have added the power to condemn property for resale to private enterprise for private use. We have introduced urban renewal and the program for vast new highways. We have added to our means for coping with urban growth but we have not paid strong attention to understanding the problems in urbanization. We have not attempted to guide urban growth with the care and the determination it demands.

Land developers should be active advocates of and participants in the furtherance of comprehensive urban planning programs. The frequent lack of or jumble in zoning, subdivision, building and construction regulations places a serious handicap

---

[2] In 1950 the Bureau of the Census reported 168 standard metropolitan areas. In 1959 the Census reported these had increased to 180. A standard metropolitan area is defined as an urbanized area having a central city of at least 50,000 population.

[3] See *Metropolitanization of the United States,* by Jerome P. Pickard, Research Monograph 2, Urban Land Institute.

[4] See "The Challenge of Metropolitan Growth," by Dr. Philip M. Hauser, *Urban Land,* December 1958. Urban Land Institute.

on the creator of new neighborhoods. When there is an adequate, well conceived and administered planning program for the entire metropolitan area, the developer will not be at a loss to know how his project will fit into the overall framework for the community.

More People are Living in Metropolitan Areas

1900	39.7%
1950	59.0%

More of the Population Growth is in Metropolitan Areas

1900-40	73%
1940-50	81%
1950-55	97%

The Suburbs are Growing Faster than the Cities

1900-50	1⅓ to 1
1940-50	2½ to 1
1950-55	7 to 1

Suburbs will be Bigger than the Cities

	1955	1976
Central Cities	51,023,000	60,000,000
Suburbs	23,281,000	90,000,000

Growth in Number of Standard Metropolitan Areas

1950	168
1955	174
1958	180
1975	200

SECTION ONE

PART I

Preliminary Steps in Community Development

Since 1947 many vast changes have taken place in the United States. Apart from population increases and shifts which have accelerated urban development, science and industry have ushered in the jet age. Discoveries in medicine have brought polio under control. At the same time new products in almost everything Americans use, need or want have been introduced. Real revolutions have occurred in American homes, in people's shopping habits, in their modes of travel, in their recreation and in their goods and services. In these innovations lies the basis for even newer things ahead.[5] To be abreast of existing and emerging markets which have bearing on his operations, the developer must be aware of methods, procedures and practices.

> **I strongly recommend that every developer make a careful market analysis of the needs of his community before he develops a new area for sale.[6]**

In order to heed Mr. Nichols' advice, the following procedures and sources of information are outlined for ready reference by the developer.

A. MARKET ANALYSIS

Subdivisions should be selected to fit a particular market. Purchasing acreage and then trying to find a use for the land puts the cart before the horse. The land developer should first analyze his market and then select his site with its definite use in mind.

---

[5] See "The Amazing Ten Years," *U. S. News and World Report,* December 27, 1957.

[6] The late J. C. Nichols was the dean of land developers. He was the developer of the Country Club District with its Country Club Plaza, in Kansas City, Missouri. Both this residential section and its commercial area are still prototypes for quality in land development. He was chairman of the Community Builders' Council when the Handbook first appeared in 1947 and it is his sage advice, *Mistakes We Have Made in Community Development,* which became the first publication in Urban Land Institute's series of technical bulletins. Mr. Nichols' advice still applies in current development problems and solutions. See Technical Bulletin No. 1, Urban Land Institute.

1. Purpose

Before starting any project, a developer must know what he intends to do and how he plans to go about it. He may be gifted with strong hunches and good horse sense, but he is better equipped when he has definite facts at hand. Then too, he is better prepared when he knows what procedures he has to follow before starting out. For example, when a developer knows who his prospective home buyers are, what their preferences are, what their incomes may be, how many children they have—then he has facts to go on. With definite information about his local market for houses, he is ready to gauge the kind, size, scope and timing of his project. Once he has determined the market demand, his problem consists in finding the site to fit a market rather than the market to fit a site.

2. Sources of Information

(a) Local Sources

Planning commissions, zoning boards and building inspectors offices.—These agencies are good sources for statistics about subdivision activity and the location of new residential construction. Such offices usually compile data about local building permits.

Public utility companies.—To a remarkable degree these companies keep tabs on residential building activity and make forecasts about future demands. Frequently current population estimates and projections can be secured from local telephone, gas, electric, or transit companies.

Research groups and universities.—In many localities committees of the chamber of commerce or the real estate board exist which publish at regular intervals reports on housing and real estate trends. Many such local organizations maintain a research or statistical service on the business, industrial and building climate of the community. Information will vary in degree and accuracy depending upon the local interest or whether there is an active local committee and capable staff.

A number of universities, particularly those having an active bureau of business research, concern themselves with one aspect or another of the building industry. In many instances, such universities play a leading role in the dissemination of local housing and real estate data and information about the economy.

Title insurance companies, savings banks and mortgage companies.—These agencies maintain a detached view of the market. But they may have information about home buyer characteristics.

Newspapers.—Research departments of large metropolitan dailies publish market reports. This source can often provide reliable basic information on the characteristics of people and families in the local trading area.

In many instances statistics about local residential construction are not available or lack uniformity and reliability because of the incomplete or sporadic coverage and manifold sources. Frequently the housing market problem is not so much a question of developing new sources and data but becomes a matter of knowing what the information means and how best to put to use the data which are at hand.[7]

(b) Regional Sources

Several agencies publish city and county data covering most areas within the continental United States. The most prominent organizations in the field are: F. W. Dodge Services, Roy Wenzlick and Company, Dun and Bradstreet, Housing Securities, Inc. In many areas private research organizations and companies compile useful housing reports.

(c) Nation-wide Sources

U. S. Department of Commerce and its Bureau of the Census; U. S. Department of Labor and its Bureau of Labor Statistics are Federal agencies which furnish basic data on population, housing and employment in published form.

The 1960 Censuses of Population and Housing will not be available in final form until 1961. Meanwhile, preliminary findings and the 1950 censuses and the supplementary reports as issued are available. Census reports and publications are available for purchase from the Superintendent of Documents, U. S. Government Printing Office, Washington 25, D. C. Prices vary. Check or money order should accompany any order.

The Catalog of United States Census Publications is issued on a current basis each quarter and cumulated to the annual volume.[8] The catalog is designed to give users of published

---

[7] See *Local Housing Data* by Uriel Manheim, economist. December 10, 1958. Housing Securities, Inc., 250 Park Avenue, New York 17, N. Y.

[8] *The Catalog of the United States Census Publications*, U. S. Bureau of the Census, Washington 25, D. C., Quarterly (cumulative to annual). Contains detailed descriptions of census publications currently issued. Grouped by subjects: Indexed by geographical area and by subject. Subscription $1.25 for four consecutive issues (includes 12 issues of Monthly Supplement which are not sold separately); single copies vary in price.

Census statistics a direct method of locating needed information. All publications are arranged in the catalog by general subject following the organization pattern of the Bureau, namely: 1. Agriculture; 2. Business; 3. Foreign Trade; 4. Governments; 5. Housing; 6. Industry; and 7. Population. An additional section, "8. Miscellaneous," includes general publications, such as Statistical Abstract of the United States (issued annually), not falling within the seven other subject-matter divisions.

The Bureau of the Census publications most pertinent for residential development market analysis purposes are:

Business Statistics

The Census of Business is taken quinquennially. The 1954 Census of Business final reports are available in six separate volumes including retail, wholesale and service trades in summary form for the United States and in area form for states, counties, cities, and standard metropolitan areas. Preliminary reports from the latest or 1958 Census of Business began appearing in the fall of 1959. Most of the statistical bulletins will be published in 1960.

Current reports are issued monthly showing national and regional estimates, by kind of business, of the dollar volume of retail sales, as well as of trends in selected standard metropolitan areas. Central business district statistics bulletins are published for selected large cities with comparable city and standard metropolitan area data for establishments, sales or receipts, and payroll for retail trade, hotels, and theaters.

Housing Statistics

A Census of Housing was taken as part of the Decennial Censuses of 1940 and 1950 and will be conducted again for 1960. A consolidated list of publications of the 1950 Census of Housing appears in the appendix of the annual issue of the Catalog of United States Census Publications. (See footnote 8, p. 7).

Current statistics on housing include quarterly data on vacancy rates and condition and characteristics of available housing vacancies for the country as a whole, urban and rural areas, and inside and outside standard metropolitan areas. Data on rental and vacancy characteristics of housing for local areas result from special sample surveys conducted from time to time.

Until the 1960 Census is available, the 1956 National Housing Inventory provides the first measurements of the Nation's housing supply since the 1950 Census of Housing. The inventory shows the number and characteristics of dwelling units now in existence, as well as the gains and losses through new construction, conversion and withdrawals since 1950.

The subjects covered in Volume I, *Components of Change, 1950 to 1956*, include: 1, occupancy characteristics (occupancy status, color of occupants, and number of persons); 2, structural characteristics (number of rooms, number of dwelling units in structure and year built); 3, condition and plumbing facilities; and 4, financial characteristics (contract monthly rent and value).

Current housing statistics are issued quarterly. The Series H-111 Bulletins pertain to vacant dwelling units by condition and vacancy status for the United States, regions, urban and rural areas, and inside and outside standard metropolitan areas, current quarter compared with same quarter a year ago.[9]

Population Statistics

A Census of Population has been taken every 10 years since 1790, the last being conducted as of April 1, 1960. The 1960 Census will have advance releases available shortly after April of that year.

A consolidated list of the publications of the Census of Population appears in the appendix of the latest annual issue of the Census Catalog (see footnote 8, p. 7).

In the later years between censuses a Current Population Survey is conducted. Through enumeration of a scientifically selected sample of the population, information is obtained currently on employment, unemployment, hours of work, occupation and other subjects. Also available are estimates of the personal and family characteristics of the population, mobility, income, etc.

Estimates of population for postcensal and intercensal dates are prepared, and special censuses of local areas are taken at the request and expense of the local governments involved. Projections of the population are also prepared from time to time.

Current Population Reports are released in series by bulletins:[10]

---

[9] Bureau of the Census, Washington 25, D. C.

[10] Yearly subscription rate for the Current Population Reports (General Population Statistics) is: Series P-20, P-25, and P-27 combined, $2.50. Subscriptions accepted for 1, 2, or 3 years. Available from the Bureau of the Census.

Population Characteristics (Series P-20)[11]
Population Estimates (Series P-25)[12]
Farm Population (Series P-27)
Special Censuses (Series P-28)—taken at the request and expense of the area involved.

In addition to the published data, detailed information in the files of the Bureau of the Census that has been tabulated but not published can be made available, upon request, for the cost of transcribing and reproducing the statistics. Estimates of the cost of such special work are furnished in response to specific requests addressed to the Bureau of the Census, Washington 25, D. C.

The Bureau will undertake projects that involve original collection of data on a reimbursable basis when conditions governing the Bureau's policy concerning special work and services are present. Inquiry can be addressed to the Bureau as noted above.[13]

3. Data Helpful for a Market Analysis

In the market analysis and in a developer's preliminary estimates about the feasibility of a project, data and considerations about the following factors should be included:

(a) Population Growth

The metropolitan region or the entire local area is the unit on which to base an analysis. Rate and direction of population growth applied to suburban trends will indicate the size and location of an outlying project together with the timing of its development.

---

[11] Eight to 10 reports each year. Population characteristics including marital and family status, education, school enrollment, fertility, mobility, age-sex distribution by residence, and number and characteristics of households and families. For United States; in some cases for 4 major regions. Series P-20, No. 90, issued December 1958, contains projections of number of households in U. S. under different assumptions, for selected years 1959-1980. Bureau of the Census, Washington 25, D. C.

[12] Twenty to 22 reports a year. Estimates of current total population, monthly for U. S. and annually for States; mid-year estimates by age, sex and color for U. S. and by broad age groups for States. Various projections of future population for U. S. and States.

[13] To get the full value out of the census data, the special report, *Key to Published and Tabulated Data for Small Areas,* indicates the unpublished material available on population and housing. A similar report based on the 1960 Census will be prepared for use after general findings are available and released. This report is available from the Superintendent of Documents, U. S. Government Printing Office, Washington 25, D. C., or any of the Department of Commerce field offices.

Before calculating the volume of a local housing demand, answers to certain questions need weighing: Is the area growing fast, growing slowly, or is it stagnant? Will there be a decrease or an increase in the demand for housing? At what rate is the community growing? Do not make the mistake of relying on

Illustration No. 3.

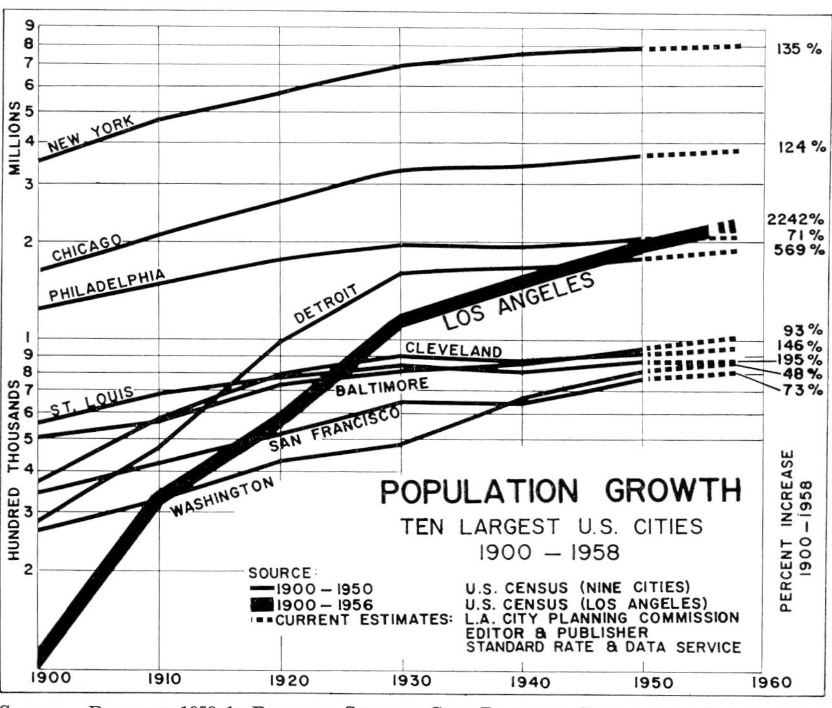

Source: BULLETIN 1959-1; RESEARCH SECTION, CITY PLANNING COMMISSION, LOS ANGELES.

past trends alone. Factors responsible for past growth may have disappeared. It is more likely that new economic factors such as a new basic industry which induces a housing demand, have been introduced.

Current population projections for the United States are designed to be consistent with high employment and high economic activity. Census Bureau figures indicate that by 1975 we will have somewhere between 216 and 245 million people—barring a major war catastrophe. This growth for the United States as a whole is something over 35 percent, but in any individual community it may decline 10 percent or increase 5,000 percent, depending on the local economy and what happens to expand or contract it.[14]

It is important to keep close watch on local economic activity. The introduction of new industry into an area has strong bearing upon factors of community growth, such as employment, purchasing power and family formation. Urban areas owe their growth and prosperity to the fact that they are able to provide employment opportunities. New opportunities mean an expanding population and new housing demand.

A rapidly swelling population means we must have more production to sustain a high standard of living. It means the economy must keep growing to absorb continuing additions to the nation's work force. We are now living at a high level of civilian economy under a partially mobilized "Cold War" atmosphere and we are operating at a level of gross national product which keeps climbing. But should the level of economic activity decline, the rate of growth would slow. Marriage and birth rates, hence the housing market, are closely related to the business cycle.

Birth rates fluctuate with social and economic conditions. Explanation for this is simple. When good times continue, the birth rate will be high. The birth rate in 1950 was 24 per 1,000 population, whereas in 1930 it was 20.6 births per 1,000. In the worst year of the depression, the birth rate dropped to 18.4 per 1,000 population. In 1959 the rate was 24.3 per 1,000. (provisional figure).

Since 1940, people have been getting married younger and they have been having larger families. A surge in the birth rate like that after World War II has repercussions for decades. This reflects on the family formation rates as babies grow to marriageable age. The postwar baby crop will be teen-agers in the early 1960's, marriageable adults by 1970. One thing you can look for is a bulge in our population structure by 1975. This will be an echo of the postwar baby boom. As each age level is reached, the group will cause increases in demand for goods and services. So look at the birth rates past, present and probable to know what to expect in a new homes market. It is useful to know what the population is and what is predicted.

---

[14] See *Metropolitanization of the United States* by Jerome P. Pickard. Published 1959 by Urban Land Institute as the second in its research monograph series.

The total population of the United States, including Armed Forces overseas, was 179,500,000 on April 1, 1960.[15] At the beginning of the 1950 decade the population was 152,552,000.

The average *annual* rate of population increase between 1950-1957 for the United States was 1.7 percent. This rate represents a numerical increase of close to 3 million people per year. As noted earlier the Census Bureau thinks the U. S. population may grow by 57.6 million over the period 1950-1970.[16] If this prediction comes true, the U. S. population in 1970 will be about 208.7 million people. (See also the projections in "Metropolitanization of the United States", footnote 14.)

(b) Regional Changes

On a regional basis, data available in January 1959 indicate a continuing redistribution of population in the United States with Western States showing the most rapid growth and North-

Illustration No. 4.

Average Annual Rates of Increase in Total Population of States: 1950-1957

(Expressed in percent)

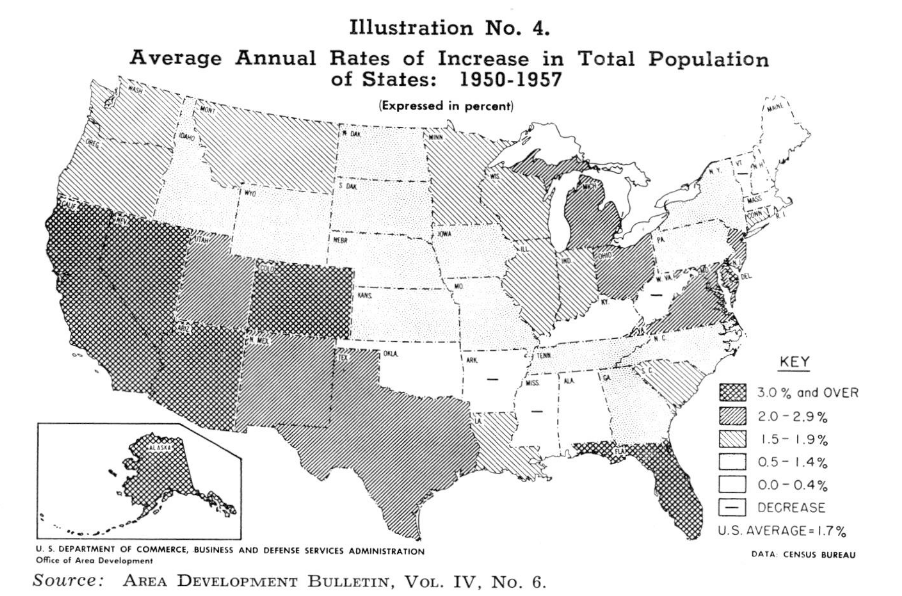

Source: AREA DEVELOPMENT BULLETIN, VOL. IV, NO. 6.

eastern States the least rapid population expansion. Between 1950 and 1957, population of the Pacific Region (Washington, Oregon, California) increased over 26 percent, twice the national average; while the East South Central Region (Kentucky, Ten-

---

[15] U. S. Bureau of the Census. Preliminary population figures as announced June 17, 1960.

[16] U. S. Bureau of the Census. Population Estimates—Series P-25.

nessee, Alabama, Mississippi) with an increase of scarcely 3 percent, exhibited least growth. In terms of numerical gain, however, the East North Central States (Ohio, Indiana, Illinois, Michigan, Wisconsin) surpassed all other regions, increasing by nearly 4.6 million in this seven year period.[17]

Bureau of the Census projections in the past have been conservative. For example, the 1954 Member's Edition of the Handbook carried the statement: "In August 1953, the Census announced that the population had passed 160 million. If this keeps up, the United States will have 175 million people by 1960." A recent projection suggests that our population may rise to 272 million (the highest projection series) by 1980. What this means in terms of housing and other consumer demands, job-making investments and public capital outlays for schools, roads and streets, sewer and water, police and fire protection, etc.—has already been indicated by the high rates of marriages, household formations and births since World War II.[18]

(c) Family Formation and Number of Households

What do population changes mean to the residential growth needs?

Every urban area follows its own economic, demographic and physical characteristics. Even though population growth and the rate of family formation influence residential building levels, population growth in itself is no guarantee of a similar rise in housing demand. Other factors enter in. Such things as local and national business conditions, employment opportunities, income and racial makeup of the population, climate, building costs, land availability, transportation and traffic patterns may create a substantial building volume, but the net gain in population may be small. In projecting residential growth, it is well to take in all economic and social forces, including population trends, which affect a local housing market. Such measurement can be interpolated from the established residential building pattern of a locality.

---

[17] *Area Development Bulletin,* Vol. IV, No. 6. Dec. 1958-Jan. 1959. U. S. Department of Commerce field offices or Superintendent of Documents, U. S. Government Printing Office, Washington 25, D. C.

[18] See "Population Explosion" in *Economic Intelligence,* Vol. XII, No. 2, February 1959. Economic Research Department, Chamber of Commerce of the U. S., Washington 6, D. C.

See also "Residential Growth Patterns in Metropolitan Areas" by Uriel Manheim. *Urban Land,* March 1957. Urban Land Institute.

The type of housing demand in the next few years may be different from the recent single-family type of house now being built in suburbs. The change in part will be due to the age pattern of the population. We are now moving into a situation where there will be a decrease in the number of households between the 30 to 45 age group and an increase in the number between 45 and 55. But there will also be an increase in the number of households over 55 and in the younger age group under 30. From 1965 through 1970 this group may grow about three and one-half times the current rate.[19]

Houses which were satisfactory for older, larger families will not fit the requirements of new young families. The new pattern of demand will require a much larger production of shelter for

Table A.

Average Number of Family Members Other Than the Head and Wife Per Husband-Wife Family, by Age of Head, for the United States: 1958 and 1955

(Average not shown where less than 0.01)

Year and age of head	Average number of family members other than head and wife			
	All ages[1]	Under 18 years	18 to 64 years	65 years and over
1958				
All husband-wife families	1.74	1.42	0.27	0.04
Under 25 years	1.08	0.95	0.13	---
25 to 34 years	2.14	2.03	0.09	0.02
35 to 44 years	2.51	2.28	0.18	0.05
45 years and over	1.22	0.75	0.41	0.05
1955				
All husband-wife families	1.66	1.33	0.28	0.05
Under 25 years	1.08	0.95	0.13	0.01
25 to 34 years	2.04	1.89	0.13	0.02
35 to 44 years	2.26	2.06	0.15	0.05
45 years and over	1.22	0.72	0.44	0.06

[1] Average (mean) size of husband-wife family is two members (head and wife) more than the numbers given in this column.

the older and the younger families. Older families and newlyweds want a less strenuous or different home life from middle-aged couples, who are the main ones with school age children making up the suburban and rural non-farm housing market.

[19] See "Are Urban Land Pressures Easing?" by Robinson Newcomb. *Urban Land,* May 1958. Urban Land Institute.

Apartments, mobile homes, and resort area living can be expected to seize a proportionate share of the coming housing demand.

(d) Average Family Size

The Census Bureau gives statistics for the average family size.[20] During the period 1948-1958, the number of families with two or more children living at home has increased (46% for the decade) and is more than the number with no children or with only one child. The proportion of husband-wife families with two or more children of their own in the home was 32 percent in 1948 and 41 percent in 1958.

The average number of members in husband-wife families *other than the head and his wife* was 1.74 (meaning the average family size was 3.74) in 1958 as compared with 1.66, or an average family size of 3.66, in 1955. (See Table A).

The number of persons per household in 1958 averaged 3.35 for the entire United States, and the range was from 3.16 for the

Table B.

Average Population Per Household and Family, by Color and Region, for the United States: March 1958

Region and color	Average population per household			Average population per family		
	All ages	Under 18 years	18 and over	All ages	Under 18 years	18 and over
United States	3.35	1.20	2.15	3.65	1.38	2.27
White	3.29	1.15	2.14	3.59	1.32	2.27
Nonwhite	3.90	1.66	2.23	4.26	1.97	2.29
Northeast	3.30	1.09	2.21	3.58	1.25	2.33
North Central	3.33	1.20	2.14	3.63	1.38	2.25
South	3.50	1.32	2.18	3.78	1.49	2.29
White	3.38	1.21	2.17	3.64	1.36	2.28
Nonwhite	4.09	1.82	2.26	4.49	2.14	2.35
West	3.16	1.14	2.01	3.54	1.37	2.17

West to 3.50 for the South (Table B). Northeastern households had an average of 1.09 children under 18 years old. Whereas those in the South had an average of 1.32.

Nonwhite households are significantly larger than white households. This fact reflects the larger average number of

[20] Current Population Reports. *Population Characteristics.* Series P-20, No. 88, Nov. 1958. U. S. Bureau of the Census.

children and of lodgers in nonwhite households; a higher proportion of nonwhite married couples and unmarried non-relatives share the homes of others; and the birth rate is higher among the nonwhite population. Nonwhite households contained 1.66 persons under 18, on the average, as compared with 1.15 for white households. White households had an average of 2.14 adults as compared with an average of 2.23 adults for nonwhite households.

(e) Housing Inventory

What housing accommodations are now available?

A local inventory of dwelling units should cover such information as the dwelling type, age, condition and size, vacancy, and rental value. Such survey should take into account the existing substandard housing and any local plans and programs for its demolition or rehabilitation. A local urban renewal program or an interstate Federal highway construction project may eliminate a sizable number of dwelling units from the inventory and create a need for housing of the displaced persons.

Your analysis of the housing inventory and the potential for new structures should include careful inspection of local preferences, prejudices and customs. It should also take into account what new building materials,[21] techniques of construction, methods of merchandising and management are available.

If you plan to produce contemporary, flat-roofed houses in an area where traditional architecture is preferred by the buying public, your market research must take into account ways and means for acceptance of your departure from the ordinary. Similarly, elements like carports or no basements must be weighed before construction. Residential building patterns do not change over night. It takes a while for public taste to become educated to a new style or something that is different. Conversely, it takes an even longer time for public demands to be met by the builders. A check on the local housing offerings will readily reveal what "extras" can be offered which will reveal turning points in the general trend, and any innovations in land planning patterns which may arise. (See footnotes 101 and 128).

---

[21] See *New Housing and Its Materials 1940-56* (Bulletin 1231), Department of Labor. August 1958. Analysis of trends characteristics, facilities and prices of one-family and multi-family housing. Extensive tabulations on types, sizes, facilities, construction materials, plumbing, heating, and other characteristics. Superintendent of Documents, U. S. Government Printing Office.

(f) Occupations

What are the occupations of the potential buyers or renters and the numbers of each?

Basic employment is the key to urban growth and thus the clue to the local market for housing. Basic employment is that which produces goods or services sold outside the local area, thus providing funds through wages and salaries for the purchase of commodities not produced in the community itself. An aircraft plant, an electronic research laboratory typify basic industry. Employees of basic employment industries require services of laundry workers, builders, butchers, grocers, doctors. The ratio between basic employment and service employment in urban places ranges from 1 to 0.8 for small cities (i.e. of 50,000 population) to 1 to 2.1 for the largest metropolitan areas. For each of its own employees, basic industry eventually generates in a community an average total population of six to eight persons.[22]

The non-farm labor force of the United States may grow 35 percent between 1955 and 1975.[23] Along with this increase there may be a greater increase in part-time jobs than in full-time employment. The trends show a dispersion of employment and a higher proportion of plants which are small in size and in number of employees. This trend will accommodate more diversity of employment and will generate more travel trips per capita, perhaps a 40 percent rise by 1975. So in evaluating market prospects for a residential project which is related to the growth prospect for an urban area, particularly in a metropolitan region, take into account the industrial increment, and the increased travel trips from home to work, to shop, to recreation, and the allowances to be made in more parking space at places where each trip terminates. Similarly, consider the pattern the growth might take—whether the development could be a complete satellite community or whether it is to be merely an increment to the existing urban structure.

(g) Incomes

What are the probable incomes of families within the area?

Statistics for the number of families in the different income ranges are needed for comparison with the housing inventory.

---

[22] See "A Metropolitan Area Approach to Industrial Development" by Robert E. Boley. *Urban Land*, Jan. 1958. Urban Land Institute.

[23] "Urban Areas of the Future" by Robinson Newcomb. *Urban Land*, Nov. 1958. Urban Land Institute.

An estimate of the number of families who can afford houses in various price ranges compared with the existing supply and probable demand for a three to five year period gives a clue to your programming for construction. Do not overlook the age grouping, sex and marital status of the population and the family sizes as these do reflect the housing demand in the community.

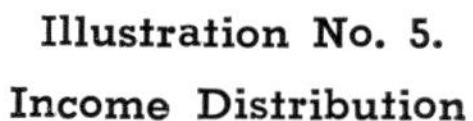

Illustration No. 5.

Income Distribution

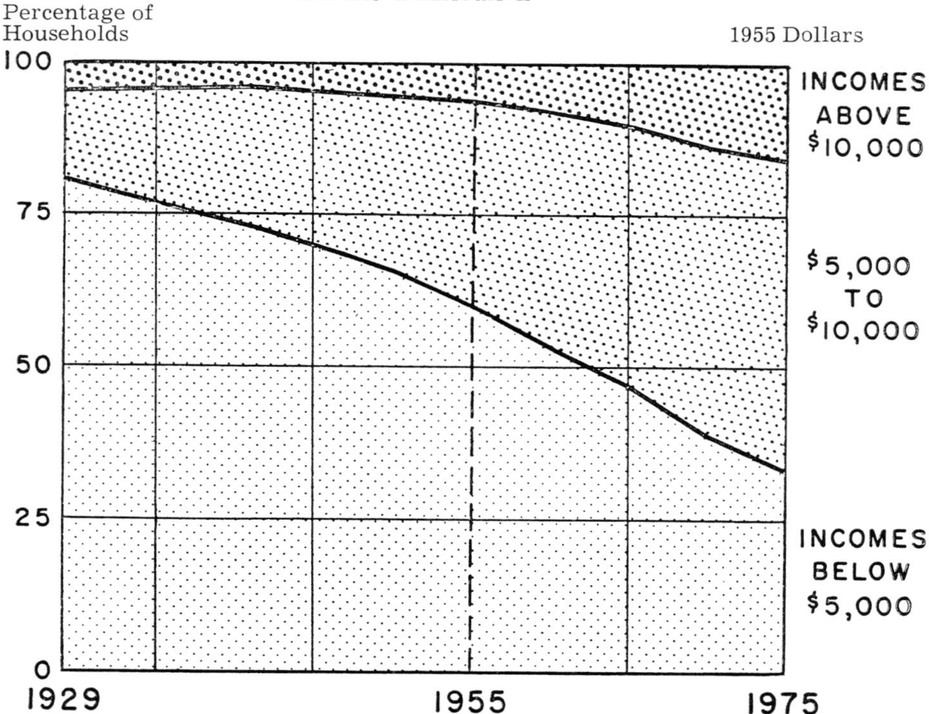

Personal income since the end of World War II and during the past decade has shown a steady rise in all regions of the United States. In 1955 about 60 percent of our 50 million households had incomes of less than $5,000; about 40 percent had incomes above $5,000. The average income, *after taxes,* was about $5,100.

By 1975, over 60 percent of the expected 65 million households may have incomes above $5,000 in contrast with the 60 percent below that figure in 1955. The percent with incomes from $5,000 to $7,500 may increase by one-third; the percent with incomes from $7,500 to $10,000 may about double, and the percentage of those with incomes over $10,000 may more than double. The average income, therefore, may be over $7,000. If this turns out to be true, it should mean that new housing to be built may have average values in 1965 of around $16,000 to $17,000, and in 1975 about $20,000.[24] Illustration 5 projects the income distribution that may be expected in the future.

Illustration 6 shows personal income trends in the United States by regions.

Illustration No. 6.

Personal Income in the United States

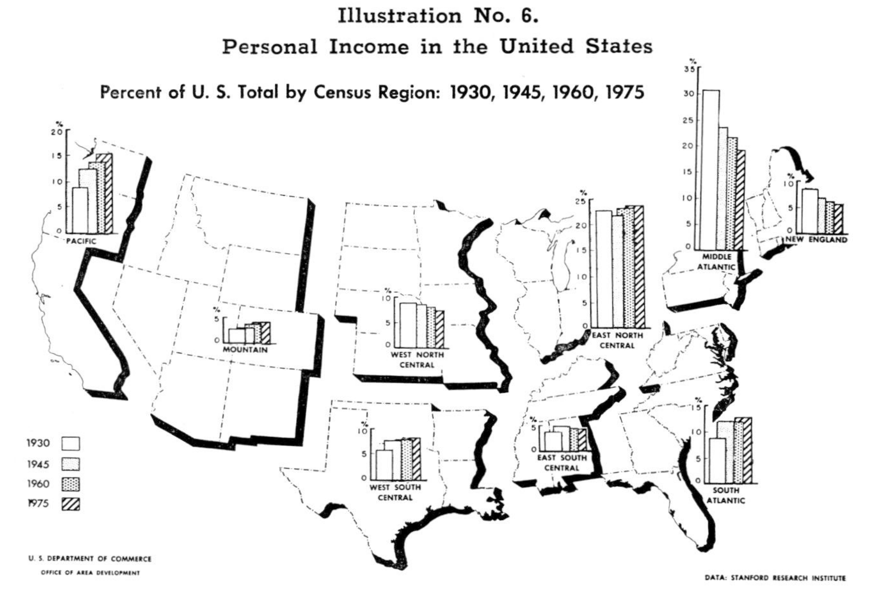

Source: AREA DEVELOPMENT BULLETIN, VOL. IV, NO. 5.

Income distribution is a guide in long-range planning for those responsible in housing analysis, market research, trade area analysis and industrial plant location programs. The ac-

---

[24] "Urban Areas of the Future" by Robinson Newcomb. *Urban Land,* Nov. 1956. Urban Land Institute.

According to Miles Colean, housing economist and ULI Trustee, incomes in constant dollars are climbing close to 2 percent a year, so each year the need for cheap houses will get smaller and the present surplus of cheap houses will get larger: the market for quality houses will get bigger and the shortage of quality houses will get more acute.

By 1980, the average family will have an income well over $8,000 vs. $5,480 in 1957 and $4,600 right after the war (all in constant 1956 dollars). By 1980, nearly 25 million families can qualify through FHA for a $17,000 house and 21 million of those 25 million quality houses would have to be built and sold in the next 21 years. (See *House & Home,* May 1959.)

companying map (Illus. No. 6) shows that the most pronounced increases foreseen between 1960 and 1975 are in the Pacific States and South Atlantic States, while the greatest decreases during that period appear due for the Middle Atlantic and West North Central regions.

Several basic assumptions underlie the estimates shown on the map: Virtually full employment (where unemployment is at the rate of about 4 percent of the civilian labor force); no great change in international tensions and related defense and foreign aid programs; and incremental rather than sharp changes in production, income from production, and geographic income distribution.[25]

As incomes rise, people can demand and can pay for more comfortable and more convenient houses in better developed neighborhoods. As developers learn this, they can provide better quality houses in better communities with longer range values. (See footnote 24).

It must be remembered that between 1947 and 1954 we were catching up with a housing shortage. Since then builders and land developers have met the challenge of providing shelter for a ready market of first-time buyers. Now the market has changed and prospects are improved to help second-time buyers trade up to quality houses.[26]

(h) Construction Costs

At what price ranges can new housing be absorbed? This element in your market evaluation ties in closely with what families can afford to spend for housing[27] and what can be financed through the mortgage market.

To indicate the typical *new-home* transaction (delineated by FHA in terms of medians) insured in 1958 under the FHA program, the following extract from Federal Housing Administra-

---

[25] A copy of "Income Trends in the United States through 1975" may be obtained from Stanford Research Institute, Menlo Park, Calif.

Additional data on personal income are presented in the *Survey of Current Business,* the August 1958 issue of which includes a detailed discussion on "Regional Income Distribution in 1957," available from the Superintendent of Documents, U. S. Government Printing Office, Washington 25, D. C.

[26] See "The Big Change of the 1960's." *House & Home,* Jan. 1959. Time, Inc., 9 Rockefeller Plaza, New York 20, N. Y.

[27] See "How Much House Can You Afford?" *Changing Times,* The Kiplinger Magazine, Oct. 1958. 1729 H St., N.W., Washington 7, D. C.

tion's 25th annual report (for the year ending December 31, 1958) is given:[28]

> ". . . the amount of the mortgage was $12.697, its term about 27 years, the total monthly payment $96.10 (including property taxes and hazard and FHA insurance premiums in addition to debt services), and a ratio of loan to value of 91.5 percent. The property had an FHA estimated value of $14,207, of which about 15 percent or $2,223 represented the land market price. The house was a single-family structure containing 1,092 square feet and provided 5.8 rooms of which three were bedrooms. Customarily, garage facilities of some sort were included, these being reported in almost 3 out of every 4 transactions.
>
> "The prospective monthly housing expense (monthly payment plus cost of household operation and property maintenance and repair) was estimated at $120.87 to be carried by a typical new-home occupant with an annual effective income of $6,803. On the average, about one-fifth of this income was expected to be required for housing expense."

(i) Tax Rates and Assessments

What are the rates and assessments in the adjacent competing communities and how do these levies compare with the public services rendered? How do these levies relate to true market value?

In your market analysis do not overlook the standards of school instruction offered in the school districts in the vicinity of the market area which you are evaluating. Community facilities and services have strong bearing on what you have to offer purchasers or must provide for in your project.

(j) Direction of Urban Growth

In what compass direction or in what segment of the area is building activity taking place? Does this direction indicate the area to explore for the selection of a site?

---

[28] See *25th Annual Report,* Federal Housing Administration. U. S. Government Printing Office, Washington: 1959. For sale by the Supt. of Documents, Washington 25, D. C. Also see annual reports for the FHA housing loan insurance program and for the yearly highlights on the volume and characteristics of mortgage and loan insurance operations and transactions.

For the benefit of those interested in FHA-insured mortgage characteristics by States and Standard Metropolitan Areas, tables containing such data are available upon request from the Division of Research and Statistics, Federal Housing Administration, Washington 25, D. C.

Population spot maps and building permit spot maps will indicate the direction of growth by revealing the extent of active areas and the direction of urban development. (But the character of this growth and whether it is for upper, middle or lower price classes is learned by direct inspection.) These studies compared with the location of places of employment and correlated with transportation facilities, highway routes (both existing and proposed), land use, topography and zoning will help to evaluate quickly the locational characteristics of any contemplated site. Such site locational study will show its relation to regional physical features, facilities and proposals, and will reveal its relationship to competing sites and to the entire urban area.

The local city or county planning commission should be able to help a developer by furnishing him a copy or allowing him to study its data in the form of maps, charts, studies, reports and plans related to the local urban growth and the housing market.

As a final note before beginning to apply a local housing market analysis to local conditions and situations, the residential land developer should remember that urban growth now means expansion into suburban areas whereas, in the past, growth was within the city. With the pattern of urban growth concentrating in and around metropolitan areas, we are entering an era of metropolitan growth problems.[29] In order to select acreage for community development purposes, the developer must more than ever make his plans, develop his programs, reach his decisions and take his action in relation to comprehensive planning programs and land use proposals. For this reason, community developers must understand planning commission thinking and procedures. At the same time, the planning commission must appreciate the practical machinery whereby good planning practices can be carried out as land is developed. Only through mutual understanding and better cooperation between developers and planning officials can there be derived the patterns of land use and development which will create the better communities needed to meet the impacts created by urban growth.

---

[29] See *The Exploding Metropolis* by the Editors of Fortune. 1958. Doubleday and Co. New York.

Illustration No. 7.

Plat of Record

Plat showing needed survey data for final plat of record Hillsdale Unit No. 2

NOTES:

THE MERIDIAN OF THIS SURVEY IS IDENTICAL WITH THAT OF SURVEY AND SUBDIVISION OF RANCHO DEL PASO, BOOK A OF SURVEYS, MAP NO. 94
ALL DISTANCES ON CURVED LINES ARE CHORD MEASUREMENTS
RADII SHOWN ARE CENTER LINE RADII, UNLESS OTHERWISE SHOWN.
ALL STREET CORNERS HAVE A TWENTY FOOT RADIUS CURVE AT THE PROPERTY LINE. DISTANCES ALONG THE STREET FRONTAGES OF CORNER LOTS ARE TO THE INTERSECTION OF STREET LINES PRODUCED.

LEGEND:

SET BACK LINE
PUBLIC UTILITY EASEMENT LINE
GUY WIRE AND ANCHORAGE EASEMENT
1 1/2" IRON PIPE MONUMENT TAGGED "R.E. 2675"

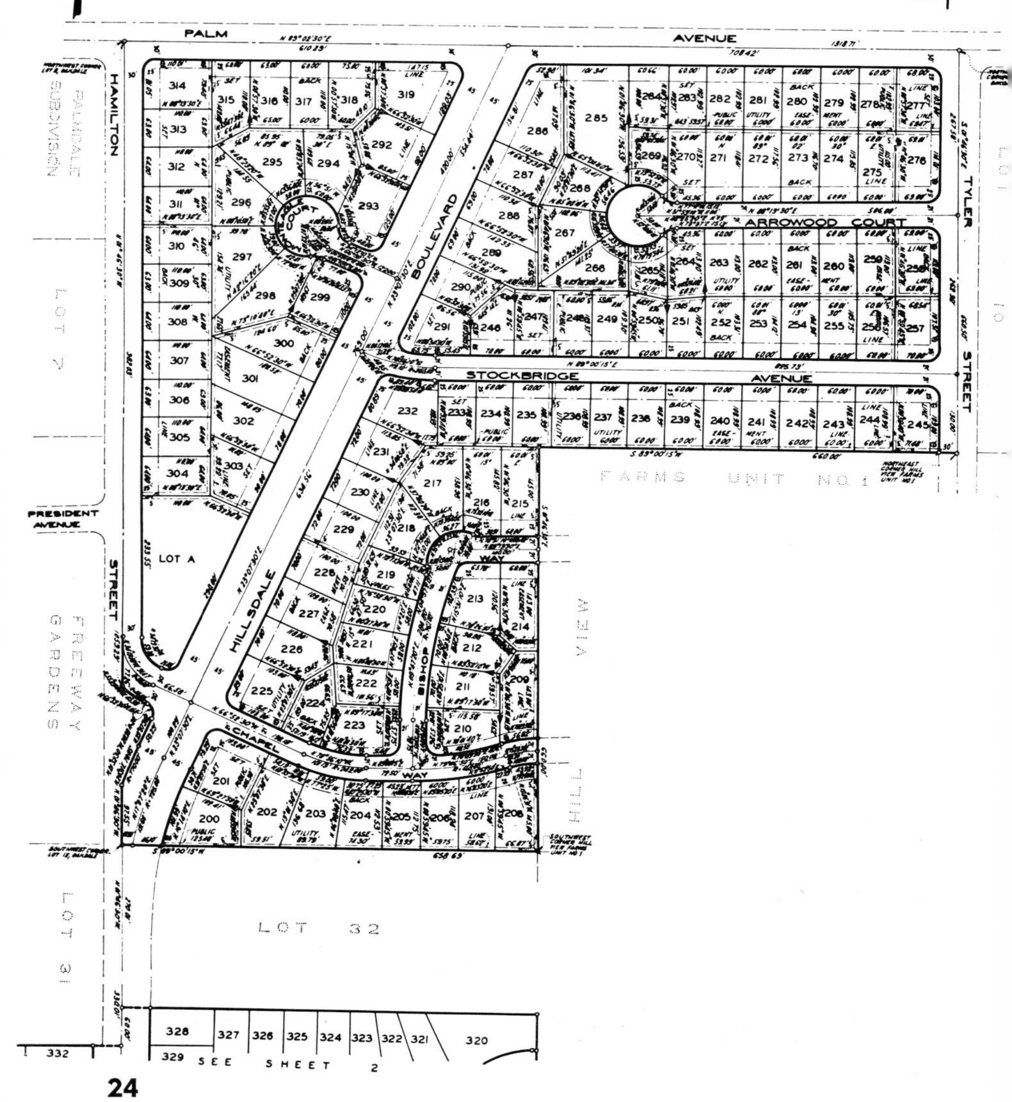

B. TECHNICAL PLANNING SERVICE

No part of any development project can be considered separately. Each step in the preliminaries should be thought out, weighed and fitted together for its relationship to the ultimate, completed project. Before making his final decision, the developer should check out his procedures. In his early site selection investigations he should have exploratory discussions with all the agencies involved so that his path will be smoother and freer from delays and frustrations. By a preliminary checking with the local planning agency, zoning administrator, municipal engineer, building inspector and FHA officer, the developer will pick up useful suggestions and ideas for the necessary procedures in processing his project toward final approval. He should not wait until he has actually purchased his tract of land before he learns what steps are required or what outside factors have to be taken into account.

In addition to preliminary consultation with approval agencies, a developer will find that it pays to get the best technical services available. Before selecting and planning a site, the developer's time and money will be saved by his obtaining technical services. Occasionally several of these services may be offered by one individual or by an office providing for complete services. Competent, experienced land planners, engineers and architects, through skillful treatment can greatly increase property values, decrease construction and maintenance costs, and add tremendously to the appeal and marketability of any development. Benefits from the use of good technical services can return many times their cost. Don't try to save pennies here. Pay a fair fee. You will make money through the ultimate success of the project.

The following topics indicate the technical fields pertaining to land development services:

1. Land Planning, Site Planning and Landscape Architecture

Land and site planning involve matters of site selection and the determination, allocation and location for specific uses of the land. Included are considerations about the topography, means of access and communication, vehicular and pedestrian traffic, open spaces and areas for residential, commercial and industrial uses—all coordinated to produce a unified development which can be built economically, operated efficiently and maintained with normal expense.

Landscape architecture deals more specifically with the treatment of ground forms including selection of plant materials, detailed relationships between buildings and the site, open spaces around buildings, recreation and other use of areas.

2. Engineering

Engineering includes the surveying service needed to establish precise location of streets, lot and building lines and to furnish topographic maps, detailed data and working drawings needed for the establishment of grades, earthworks, street improvements, storm water drainage lines, sanitary sewers, water supply mains, and other public utilities.

Illustration No. 7 indicates the type of engineering survey data usually required on a subdivision plat of record.

3. Architecture

Architecture involves the planning, design and construction of structures.

Successful builders find that the architect is an essential member of their development team. In this era of large-scale land development for residential construction, operative builders must offer purchasers more than a merely well-built structure on a good lot. They must offer an architecturally pleasing house with a good floor plan well adapted to the topographic features of the lot and in good relationship to other houses. Builders are finding that a talented architect also provides them with aids other than a house plan and an elevation design. The architect helps with such added services as site planning, building materials selection, exterior color styling and coordination, interior decoration, professional supervision, and merchandising advice. These extras pay for themselves in acceptable, faster-selling houses.

Yet in the last anlysis, the developer's own vital question is "Will it pay?" This decision cannot be left to the opinion of the planner or the architect, no matter how well-considered their advice may be.

C. SELECTION OF THE SITE

1. Accessibility and Transportation

Lack of good access to an otherwise developable site is a common cause of a project's failure. Highway access and transportation facilities to places of employment, the central business district, shopping centers, schools, churches, and recreation are primary considerations in site selection. With the automobile now the predominant means of transportation to every daily activity, site accessibility becomes very important. Also, the automobile has changed the relationship of transportation between home and place of employment. Location is measured in travel time instead of distance. Walking distance no longer carries the importance it once did.

When travel time (by whatever means) to centers of employment is less than 30 minutes, the site location is good. When such travel time is over 30 minutes but not more than 45, the location is fair. A location requiring over 45 minutes travel time is poor, except for a few of the largest cities where an hour would not be excessive.[30] While proximity to places of employment is not always necessary or desirable, good access in point of time and convenience by both public transportation and private cars will add desirability to any project. Today rapid transit lines, expressways, parkways and controlled access freeways become indicators to areas for growth and development.

---

[30] In 1958, the Planning Council of the Greater Baltimore Committee conducted a survey of journey-to-work habits of persons working in downtown Baltimore. See accompanying Illustration No. 8, page 28.

Transit time—This chart shows how much time Baltimorians spend traveling to work either by car or by bus. According to the figures, the largest percentage of the people spend between 15 and 30 minutes in transit.

Income figures—The chart shows how income groups travel to work. Black lines represent percentage using automobiles; gray lines represent percentage using public transportation.

High points of the survey results are: Over 42 percent of all employees working downtown usually use their cars, while five percent use rail or taxi or walk.

The median time spent in getting to work is 32 minutes. Drivers make it in an average of 28 minutes, bus riders in 39 minutes. The auto commuters travel a longer distance. The average number of persons per car is 1.7, and 61 percent of all work-bound cars contain only the driver.

Lower-income people use the bus more. The median income of all downtown employees is $4,036. The median for bus riders is $3,220 and for motorists it is $5,563. Seventy-four percent of those making $2,500 or less use the bus, while 83 percent of those earning $10,000 or over drive to work.

Source: *Passenger Transport*, Jan. 16, 1959.

Good transit facilities become increasingly important as the price range of dwellings decreases. Complete reliance on the private automobile for transportation to and from places of

Illustration No. 8.

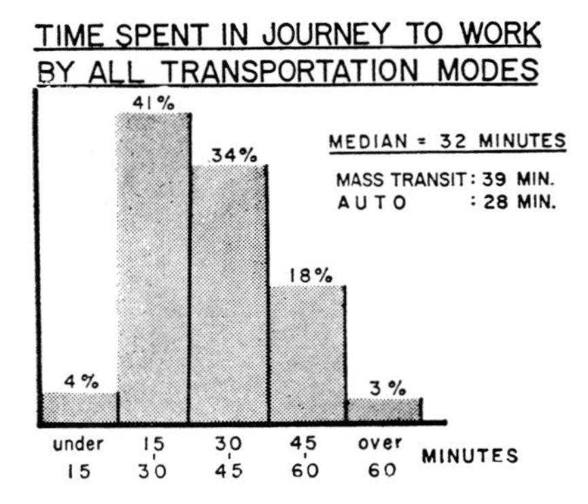

TRANSIT TIME—This chart shows how much time Baltimoreans spend traveling to work either by car or by bus. According to figures, the largest percentage of the people spend between fifteen and 30 minutes in transit.

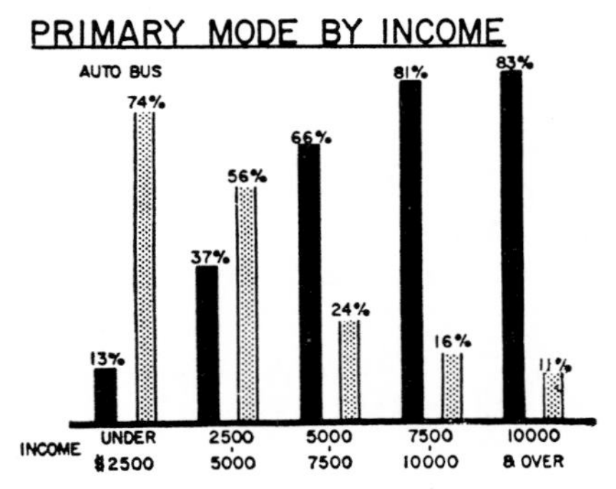

INCOME FIGURES—Chart shows how various income groups travel to work. Black lines represent percentage using automobiles and gray lines represent percentage using public transportation.

Source: PASSENGER TRANSPORT, JANUARY 16, 1959.

employment and shopping is not advisable except perhaps in higher priced developments where more and more two-car families can be expected.[31]

If a low-cost development is under consideration, a site within walking distance to places of employment is ideal. But if the site lacks public transit and is over a mile in walking distance from employment or from shopping, then it is poorly located for a development of low-priced housing construction.

The illustration illustrates the rules of thumb for maximum distances from home to employment and to other facilities.

---

[31] Multicar households have increased at a tremendous rate, growing by 55 percent in the past five years. Motor-vehicle registrations continue to gain and are expected to pass 68,398,000 for 1958. Bureau of Public Roads reports these 1958 figures:

passenger cars	56,975,000	+1.9% over 1957
trucks and buses	11,431,000	+1.8% over 1957.

Source: *Automotive News,* Oct. 6, 1958.

For forecasts of population, motor vehicle registrations, travel, and fuel consumption, see *Public Roads,* A Journal of Highway Research, vol. 30, no. 12, February 1960, published bimonthly by the Bureau of Public Roads, U. S. Dept. of Commerce, Washington 25, D. C.

2. Location and Approaches

Of utmost importance to the success of a residential development is its location within the urban area, the manner in which the major thoroughfare routes approach it, and the character of existing and future growth along these routes.

A "good address" for medium to high-priced projects is especially important. Such projects should preferably be on the "right side" of town. Fighting long established adverse trends may prove difficult and expensive. In low-cost projects, land costs, convenience to work, schools, and shopping, are more important factors than a "good address".

Illustration No. 9.

Ideal Maximum Distances to Daily Activities

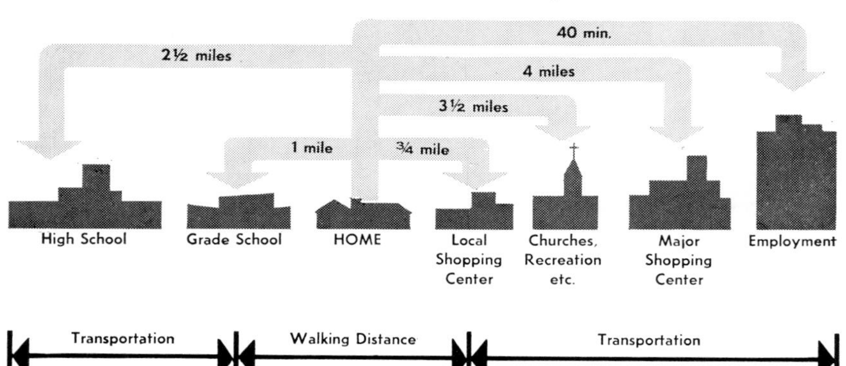

Desirable maximum distances to employment and other facilities within which it is felt feasible or safe to build residential developments. The distance to a high school in some localities may be unimportant because of school bus transportation.

Locational factors that should be considered in the selection of any site include the following:

(a) Trends in past city growth should be carefully studied to determine the direction in which high, medium and low-cost developments have tended to move. It is very difficult to reverse major directional trends. High value development, subject to local factors, will usually continue to move outward from the central district in radial or segmental patterns. Prestige is added to a project if located in the "proper" section of the urban area. Higher priced residential areas have shown the same general directional movement outward from the urban center over the years. When the early fine residential development started northwest from the center, for example, successive outward extensions for the higher cost homes usually continued in the same direction. The trend holds true even when development takes place in suburban areas outside corporate city boundaries. It is usually inadvisable to buck established land development trends, especially when the project is small.

(b) If access to the site is available only over congested routes, or through depreciated commercial, industrial, or residential areas, it will probably be wise not to consider it for a high-price development and to abandon the site in favor of one with more favorable approach routes. It may be possible, however, in some instances to acquire additional land or obtain rights-of-way which will permit an entirely new or improved approach, at least to the general vicinity of the development. Two classic illustrations prove the importance of providing a good approach where none existed previously. In order to secure an improved, direct approach to that now famous high grade residential area of Shaker Heights in the Cleveland metropolitan area, the developers bought a right-of-way from the Nickel Plate Railroad. This cost millions of dollars and of course is an unusual situation that could rarely be duplicated.

In Upper Arlington, a 3,000 acre residential development adjacent to Columbus, Ohio, a strip of land four miles long was acquired to provide a quick and pleasing approach to the central district of the city. In both cases the acquisition of a good approach was a major factor in making the development marketable.

(c) Under the provisions of the Federal Highway Act of 1956, more than 41,000 miles of new interstate freeways will be built for linear connection between established urban centers plus connection to important international boundary and defense points.[32] In the next few years, the highway program will open vast areas that heretofore have not been developed due to poor access. With freeways reaching into these undeveloped areas, complete new satellite communities are feasible. Such com-

---

[32] See *The New Highways: Challenge to the Metropolitan Region,* Technical Bulletin No. 31. Urban Land Institute. See also *Cities in the Motor Age* by Wilfred Owen. The Viking Press, New York. (Both references stem from the symposium sponsored by Connecticut General Life Insurance Company, Hartford, Conn., Sept. 1957).

See also "Highways and Urban Development—Guidelines for Action." Syracuse University, 1959. (Based on the National Conference on Highways and Urban Development held Oct. 5-9, 1958 at the Sagamore Center, Syracuse University).

Illustration No. 10.

THE NATIONAL SYSTEM OF INTERSTATE AND DEFENSE HIGHWAYS

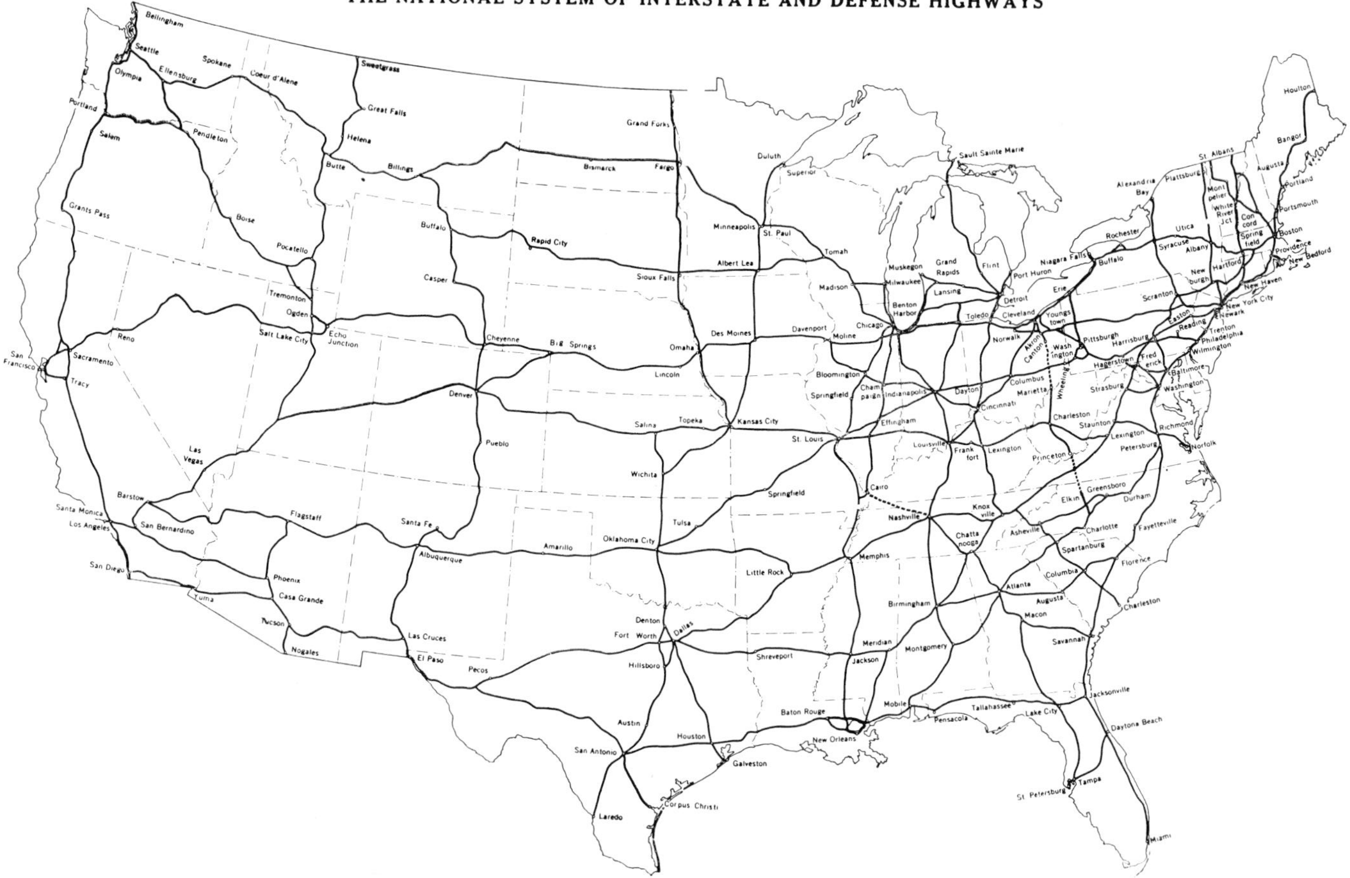

munities can have residential development balanced with employment opportunities in industry and commerce integrated into the new town. Pressures of population growth will bring about this movement.[33]

The highway program also furnishes a great opportunity to set a new basic structure for the future of metropolitan areas. The location of rights-of-way for the new freeways and their interchanges with local access highways becomes a determinant for the kind of development that will take place. By proper advance planning, the highway program can be an asset instead of a hazard.[34]

3. Size of Development

The size of the tract that can be handled financially must be carefully considered before acreage is purchased. Because of taxes and high carrying charges, it is not practical to carry too much acreage at any one time. Many developers have "gone broke" trying to carry too much acreage. Compound interest must always be figured on unsold land and improvements. Where possible, according to Council member Maurice Read of Berkeley, future expansion should be available through long-time options on adjoining areas.

Preliminary sketch plans can be quickly worked out for various proposed subdivision sites which will indicate the approximate number of lot units after deducting streets, parks, and unbuildable areas. Such approximations should then be related to the ability of the developer to sell over a period of time and to carry the costs of land purchase and development.[35]

In the immediate postwar period, a combination of circumstances such as a housing shortage, record family formation and easier mortgage financing led to the rise of the operative builder and his undertaking of sizable projects which moved from raw land to complete communities within a very short time, two years in some cases. Thousand-acre developments such as Lakewood in Southern California, Park Forest southwest of

---

[33] D. D. Bohannon, then President, Urban Land Institute. May 18, 1959.

[34] See "Spacing and Location of Interchanges on Freeways in Urban and Suburban Areas" by Max S. Wehrly. *Urban Land,* October 1958. Urban Land Institute.

[35] Capital gains and losses from real property subdivided for sale are governed by the Federal income tax regulations. For the interpretations of the Internal Revenue Code of 1954, see regulations, section 1.1237. U. S. Treasury Department, Washington 25, D. C.

Chicago, and the Levittowns of Long Island and Pennsylvania were built as single operations to meet local housing needs.

"With a population bulge anticipated for the 1960 decade, a new factor in land development is emerging. This is the formation of numerous large organizations with adequate capital to plan total community projects without governmental assistance. These syndicates represent substantial capital resources and are a factor not present heretofore on a broad national basis. Already extensive tracts of land have been acquired in many metropolitan areas where population growth is expected. These entrepreneurs are far-sighted and are moving well ahead of present demand, but in areas where they expect population pressures to be greatest. Some of these proposed projects represent thousands of acres lying just outside of the present metropolitan area. It is reasonable to believe that in such strong hands the lands will be well-planned and developed as the market demand for the community unfolds. Though as yet unpublicized, this is a trend and is taking place in such growth areas as Florida, California, the Southwest including West Texas, New Mexico and Arizona."[36] Thus, we will see taking place the development of large-scale communities, complete with varied housing types, shopping center, public buildings, schools, churches, parks, and with areas for local recreation including golf courses, swimming pools, ball diamonds and tennis courts.

4. Land Cost

Ordinarily the proposed selling or rental price of the dwelling units, based on careful analysis of the market, should determine the price that can be paid for the land, and not the reverse. In the past an improved lot for houses which would be priced to sell at $10,000 normally could be figured at about 15 percent of the total house cost and could gradually be raised to as high as 25 percent for homes costing $25,000 or over. Now 15 percent of the total cost attributable to land seems to be an absolute minimum in a metropolitan area. For higher priced houses it is not uncommon to find that the land cost runs higher than 25 percent of the total cost. The old rule of 8 percent to 10 percent for lot to building value is obsolete.

In the current period of rising prices and lessening value for the dollar, any rule of thumb that tends to indicate a ratio

[36] D. D. Bohannon, then President, Urban Land Institute. May 18, 1959.

between the price of the house and the price of the improved lot is fallacious. Appraisers once figured that a ratio of retail price of the lots over the raw land cost could be 4 to 1 with profit for the subdivider.

A good clue to current site-value ratio can be gleamed from the annual report of the Federal Housing Administration. FHA's report for the year ending December 31, 1957 has this to

Illustration No. 11.

A DECADE OF EXPERIENCE

The ten-year span—1948 through 1958—discloses a picture of rapidly rising property values and mortgage amounts, larger homes with more rooms, all capped by more liberal mortgage terms. Here are the trends, based on FHA loan characteristics:

	In 1948	In 1958
Median size of homes (sq. ft.)	912	1,092
Number of rooms per home	5.4	5.8
Estimated property value per home	$8,721	$14,207
Average market price of sites	$1,049	$ 2,223
Site-value ratio	11.7%	15.4%
Median mortgage amount on a home	$7,058	$12,697
Loan-value ratio	81.0%	91.5%
Typical monthly mortgage payments	$58.08	$ 96.10
Amortization period	20.1	27.3
Other estimated monthly housing expenses	$20.56	$ 24.77
Housing expense to income ratio	21.7%	20.4%
Income levels	$4,000	$ 6,803

Source: Washington Letter, NAHB. Dec. 14, 1959.

say: "From 1946 through 1957, property values and mortgagors' incomes for both new-and existing-home transactions have more than doubled. For example, land prices for new homes rose from $761 in 1946 to $2,148 in 1957. The sharp increase in land prices is reflected by the site-value ratio which has advanced from 11½ percent in the early postwar period to almost 15 percent in 1957.

"The major factors in the uptrend of property and land values and of home buyers' incomes have been the scarcity of building sites and high development costs, the demand for larger and better equipped homes, the availability of mortgage money, and the general inflation of prices and the rise in personal income characterizing the last decade."[37]

Raw land suitable for subdivision has gone up in price much more proportionately than has the costs for site preparation and construction. The scarcity of improved, vacant lots within cities and the high cost of preparing raw acreage for building in the suburbs warrants the conclusion that prices for improved lots have started on a long-term rise.[38]

So, the Council agrees it is impractical to set any figure as a measure for what a residential developer can afford to pay for raw land. The appraised price of the finished house will determine the price of the mortgage on it. Financing will be geared to local evaluations. Marketability and the ability of prospective purchasers to meet the down payment and mortgage payments will determine what a developer can and will pay for land.

In the matter of land cost for development purposes, David D. Bohannon makes these pertinent observations.[39] "The price of acreage in fast growing areas has accelerated rapidly. The effect of the higher acreage prices for level and near level land suitable for subdivision is bringing about a balance. The balance takes place whereby rugged terrain and rough country can be developed, and is being developed, with building lot prices comparable to lot prices obtained on the high-priced, preferred more level acreage. This finding will vary from area to area, of course, but it is an important land cost factor in that rough land is usualy of little value for agriculture, and hillside development [properly handled] does create desirable residential use.

"Similarly, the law of supply and demand will come into effect. Or to put this another way, the monopoly value of urban acreage will be greatly lessened as substantial acreage becomes

---

[37] 24th Annual Report. Federal Housing Administration.

[38] See *Vacant Land Values in Seattle: 1935 to 1955.* Current Planning Research No. 23, May 1, 1959. City of Seattle, City Planning Commission. This study shows Seattle land values for small-family sites in 1955 were double what they were in 1935. Commercial and industrial sites similarly were included in the Commission's study.

[39] David D. Bohannon, May 18, 1959 in a letter on the subject of the 1959 proposed housing bill.

Table C.
Property Characteristics by Property Value, 1-Family Homes, Sec. 203, 1958

FHA estimate of property value	Percentage distribution	Average: Property value	Average: Property replacement cost	Average: Market price of site	Price of site as percent of value	Average: Calculated area (sq. ft.)	Average: Number of rooms	Average: Number of bedrooms	Percent of structures with garage
NEW HOMES									
Less than $8,000	0.3	$7,659	$8,392	$1,016	13.3	929	4.9	2.8	19.8
$8,000 to $8,999	1.2	8,532	9,166	1,228	14.4	850	4.7	2.7	43.4
$9,000 to $9,999	4.6	9,503	9,971	1,441	15.2	901	4.8	2.9	59.2
$10,000 to $10,999	9.9	10,425	10,968	1,573	15.1	958	5.0	2.9	60.1
$11,000 to $11,999	9.6	11,427	11,874	1,658	14.5	1,014	5.1	3.0	61.4
$12,000 to $12,999	10.6	12,425	12,942	1,794	14.4	1,071	5.2	3.0	67.2
$13,000 to $13,999	11.4	13,414	13,916	1,967	14.7	1,095	5.3	3.0	68.3
$14,000 to $14,999	11.4	14,406	14,953	2,182	15.1	1,127	5.3	3.0	67.9
$15,000 to $15,999	10.9	15,395	15,950	2,377	15.4	1,168	5.5	3.0	68.8
$16,000 to $16,999	9.2	16,393	16,889	2,595	15.8	1,206	5.5	3.0	73.2
$17,000 to $17,999	6.7	17,378	17,905	2,786	16.0	1,272	5.6	3.0	74.3
$18,000 to $18,999	4.8	18,375	18,960	2,985	16.2	1,332	5.8	3.1	80.7
$19,000 to $19,999	3.4	19,357	19,920	3,207	16.6	1,389	5.9	3.2	84.1
$20,000 to $21,999	3.5	20,712	21,283	3,525	17.0	1,444	6.0	3.2	83.6
$22,000 to $24,999	1.9	23,074	23,582	3,924	17.0	1,580	6.2	3.2	86.7
$25,000 and over	.6	27,359	28,331	4,460	16.3	1,653	6.2	3.1	84.5
Total	100.0	14,394	14,921	2,223	15.4	1,138	5.4	3.0	72.7
EXISTING HOMES									
Less than $8,000	4.8	7,086	10,150	1,057	14.9	950	5.0	2.4	47.6
$8,000 to $8,999	6.5	8,401	10,893	1,286	15.3	950	4.9	2.4	59.9
$9,000 to $9,999	8.4	9,376	11,620	1,467	15.6	970	5.0	2.4	65.0
$10,000 to $10,999	10.8	10,373	12,504	1,661	16.0	1,002	5.1	2.5	66.2
$11,000 to $11,999	10.7	11,359	13,297	1,829	16.1	1,021	5.1	2.6	68.2
$12,000 to $12,999	11.4	12,355	14,306	2,000	16.2	1,061	5.3	2.7	70.2
$13,000 to $13,999	10.4	13,359	15,139	2,176	16.3	1,093	5.4	2.8	73.2
$14,000 to $14,999	8.6	14,335	16,052	2,339	16.3	1,125	5.4	2.8	74.2
$15,000 to $15,999	7.5	15,319	17,033	2,547	16.6	1,171	5.6	2.9	75.7
$16,000 to $16,999	6.2	16,335	18,003	2,741	16.8	1,224	5.7	2.9	80.5
$17,000 to $17,999	4.4	17,313	18,952	2,959	17.1	1,269	5.7	3.0	81.7
$18,000 to $18,999	3.4	18,298	20,045	3,165	17.3	1,335	5.9	3.0	86.4
$19,000 to $19,999	2.0	19,284	20,920	3,344	17.3	1,367	5.9	3.1	85.2
$20,000 to $21,999	2.5	20,678	22,464	3,736	18.1	1,455	6.1	3.1	88.3
$22,000 to $24,999	1.9	23,027	24,775	4,105	17.8	1,539	6.3	3.2	90.8
$25,000 and over	.5	26,715	29,146	4,557	17.1	1,731	6.4	3.3	92.0
Total	100.0	13,069	15,045	2,150	16.5	1,105	5.4	2.7	74.9

Source: FHA, 25th Annual Report for the year ending December 31, 1958.

accessible through the highway program. Therefore, excessive acreage price acceleration will force development into the newly accessible areas. In many instances, such areas will be unspoiled and can be planned properly with character and appeal.[40] It is

[40] "One of the most important means we have for forging the future city is the modern highway . . . It can be used to give the city form and pattern, to demarcate land uses and to protect neighborhoods . . . If there is urgency anywhere in our impending task it is this—to bring about effective coordination between highway planning and the city planning of which it is an essential part." Miles Colean in his keynote address, Combined Meeting ULI Councils, Columbus, Ohio, June 11, 1959. See also *The New Highways: Challenge to the Metropolitan Region,* Technical Bulletin No. 31, Urban Land Institute.

therefore apparent that availability of residential sites will be ample for as much expansion as can be projected in the coming decade and beyond.

"I believe investigation will show a tremendous movement of strong money into those areas that show the greatest promise of growth. This, in itself, is strong evidence that there will be no shortage of residential sites and competition will pretty well take care of unreasonable speculation in acreage values."

5. Physical Characteristics of the Site

(a) Topography and Shape of the Site

Moderately sloping sites are preferable to either steep or very level land. As a rule it has been found that improvement costs rise sharply on slopes of over 10 percent. Heavy grading creates settlement and erosion problems. Although the original acreage cost of rough broken land may be less, it will frequently be found to cost so much more to grade and make usable that the final improved lot costs will be higher than if more-expensive but more-level land were purchased. An exception to this relationship between cost of land and cost of lot improvements for steeply sloping sites is found in Mr. Bohannon's previous remarks.[41] For higher priced properties where lots are to be developed at no less than three to the acre, broken topography and wooded areas work out very well. But for low priced homes where lot costs must be held to a minimum, gently rolling and well-drained land is by far the best. Very flat land presents numerous problems in sewerage and storm drainage that may raise improvement costs to a very high figure. Get a topographic survey of the site before you buy.[42]

The shape of the subdivision site should be compact. Irregular boundaries and the presence of utility or railway easements may result in unusable areas and uneconomical street and lot layouts.

---

[41] See also "Hillside Development" by David D. Bohannon in "Practicalities in Residential Land Development." *Urban Land.* January 1959. Urban Land Institute.

[42] U. S. Geological Survey quadrangle sheets, or in certain localities, maps prepared by the War Department, will be of value in evaluating the general location and topographic character of the site. These may be obtained from the U. S. Geological Survey, Dept. of Interior, Washington 25, D. C. U.S.G.S. maps are often also on sale at certain local book stores.

(b) Drainage and Subgrade

A site should have good natural surface drainage. Watch out for marsh or swamp areas or wet pockets which must be drained, frequently at prohibitive cost. Clay-loam, sand, gravel or other porous material affords good soil drainage and economical construction. Sites which have served as dumps or have otherwise been filled, and sites which have underlying rock close to the surface or high ground water, should be avoided. Test holes should be dug in various parts of the property and conditions carefully noted. (See p. 75, Part II, A. Site Information For Planning).

(c) Tree Growth

Existing tree growth on any site is desirable. It is possible to build economically on wooded land by selective clearing, even for lower-priced housing. Too many times handsomely wooded acreage has been deliberately bulldozed down to bare earth before beginning construction. Such denuding destroys for years the increment in value that a stand of trees gives to a residential community. This asset should be preserved despite the temporary disadvantages of having to take some care with trench locations, workmen's traffic between buildings and storage of materials during the course of construction.

Council member John Matthews of North Little Rock says "Choose your trees before you build. Save the best and clear out the undesirables. By indications on the property's topo survey, the best trees can be avoided in locating streets, houses and driveways. While it is a little cheaper to build on treeless land, selling even low-cost houses is much easier with plenty of trees to stop prospective buyers' eyes from sweeping endless distances. Being able to see several blocks at a glance gives any new development that depressing mass housing project look."

The cost of locating and marking the trees is repaid many times over by the value added to each house. Cost of locating the trees on the topographical map is minor as is any additional cost in the clearing operations. Home builder Edward R. Carr of Washington, D. C. in his Virginia suburban community, North Springfield, found that he can save good large trees for no more than it costs to plant a new, small buggy-whip sapling.

Illustration No. 12. Preservation of Trees

Existing tree growth on any lot adds to the value of the house.

Gerholz Community Homes, Inc., Flint, Michigan

Mr. Carr estimates that $200 to $300 is added to the value of each house by his tree conservation technique.[43]

6. Utility Services

No factors in site selection are more important than the availability of water, sanitary and storm sewers, electricity, gas, and public transportation. Not only should the lines for these services be at or near the site but they should also be of adequate capacity to carry the increased load of the new development and future development of the surrounding tributary area.

With tremendous growth of metropolitan areas, now and expected, water supply and sanitation cannot be developed nor handled satisfactorily by individual action of the various communities politically divided by artificial boundaries. The developer of a large-scale community must investigate and calculate more carefully sources for and availability of his water supply and sewage disposal. Not all states have legislation authorizing authorities or districts on a regional basis nor do they all permit privately owned utilities to develop service for a large area.[44]

(a) Water

Public water supply mains at or near the site are the most desirable solution for site selection. Thus, the developer should determine whether it is possible to connect his project with an existing public water supply system. If such connection is possible, then he should investigate with the proper public authorities the capacity of the water system to handle the additional load. With ever increasing consumption of water by municipalities and by industry many existing public supplies

---

[43] See "Accent on Trees." *Urban Land*, July-August 1955. Urban Land Institute.

[44] The Nation's rainfall is not evenly distributed geographically or chronologically. By 1975 our American economy can be expected to use 73 per cent more water than is being used now. So cities will be in competition for water resources. The developer of a large-scale community must investigate and calculate very carefully his source of water supply and its availability. (*Water Use in the U. S. 1900-1957.* U. S. Department of Commerce, Washington 25, D. C.)

Illustration No. 13. The House and Its Lot

Wider lot frontages throughout the country are occasioned by the long, low look in houses with attached carport or garage and by the increase in floor area of the house itself.

Gerholz Community Homes, Inc., Flint, Michigan.

are already operating at full capacity and are unable to meet an additional demand by the development of new residential projects.

If the developer must develop his own water supply, he is faced with an engineering, incorporation and financing problem plus the choice of providing either a central water supply for his development or individual water systems for his dwelling units. Individual wells give water that may vary in quantity and quality, and individual pumps require frequent inspection and maintenance. In some areas small community water companies have been formed by developers. They are usually controlled by state utility commissions or health departments and are much superior to individual wells, but they also add to the problem of development, and are much less desirable than a public water supply.[45] (See also page 164). Cooperative water companies in which the property owners are members generally have not proved successful and are not recommended.

Adjacent water mains should be checked for quantity and pressure to assure normal supply that is sufficient for present and future fire protection.

(b) Sewerage

A public sanitary sewer system to service the site is the best solution to the sewage disposal problem. There are only two other solutions—a private community plant or on-lot disposal. If connection to a municipal system is not immediately available, then check with authorities for possible scheduling of sewer main extensions or look into building your own community system. Only as a last resort should you consider an on-lot system which means individual septic tanks or cesspools. So unsatisfactory are septic tanks generally that regulations governing this installation have stiffened. Also, in many sections of the country, home buyers have a sales resistance against the septic tank.

A community sewer system installed by the developer with a monthly rental charge is superior to individual septic tanks

---

[45] See "Water Systems for Residential Communities," Chapter 8, parts A and B, pp. 60-71, *Home Builders Manual for Land Development.* National Association of Home Builders, 1625 L St., N.W., Washington 6, D. C. Second revised edition 1958.

See also *Individual Water Supply Systems.* Public Health Service Publication No. 24. Supt. of Documents, U. S. Govt. Print. Office, Washington 25, D. C.

and has proved successful in many parts of the country.[46] Provision should be made for its continued operation. (See also page 156).

With public sewers of adequate size adjacent to the site, invert elevations should be carefully checked by the site planner or engineer with all parts of the site to determine whether or not they can be used. Sites lower than the adjacent sewerage system will involve pumping problems requiring future fixed maintenance charges.

(c) Storm Drainage

Surface drainage is better taken care of by a sewerage system separate from the sanitary sewers. It is desirable that either existing storm sewers of sufficient size be available or that there exist streams or valleys into which storm drainage can be discharged. You cannot cut off natural drainage of adjacent land and you may not be able to dump excessively accumulated water on your neighbor or even in any stream or public drain without definite and written permission from the owner or public authority. Do not overlook this point and be sure to obtain the necessary clearances in writing. Don't overlook the greatly increased run-off of water as an area becomes fully developed, including the entire watershed.[47]

(d) Electricity and Gas

These services are normally supplied by private utility companies at their own expense. It is necessary that electricity be available at the site for light and power, also for cooking and heating water in the event that gas is not available. In choosing a site, the location and capacity of all distribution lines in the vicinity should be indicated on study maps. At the start of a residential development, it is common practice for the private utility company to charge the developer for the cost of main extensions and then to refund as customers are added.

(e) Utility Costs

Standards for street location and alignment, street widths, paving, sidewalks, and other utilities should be geared to the type of development which they are to serve. This is a reason-

---

[46] See "Sanitary Sewerage Systems." Chapter 9, *Home Builders Manual for Land Development.*

[47] See "Community Facilities" by Rodney M. Lockwood in "Practicalities in Residential Land Development." *Urban Land,* January 1959. Urban Land Institute.

able statement with which no municipality should take serious exception. For example, this principle has been well recognized in the subdivision ordinance of LaGrange, Illinois, which says: "Whenever streets or alleys are paved or surfaced, such paving or surfacing shall be of a type and strength suitable for the volume and character of traffic to be expected." And yet a number of municipalities make little or no distinction between the width of street and type of paving used on a minor street of single family homes and that serving a traffic-way through an apartment or commercial development. A case in point is one city which requires reinforced concrete pavements or bituminous surface with concrete base on all streets, regardless of the type of development served. Where the developer pays for the installation of streets, he must inevitably pass this cost on to the purchaser as part of the initial price of the house.

Such rigid regulations form a definite deterrent to economical development. To require paving wider or of a type higher than needed for the use it will receive is false economy and an inequity to the developer and purchaser alike. Regulations governing provisions for right-of-way and width and type of pavement should be geared to the function that the street will perform. A short minor street furnishing access to some single-family houses need never have the same width and pavement type as a major arterial traffic flow street.[48]

Another inequity with which the developer is often faced is that of requiring improvements and utilities in excess of those needed to serve the specific area being developed. An example is the case of a developer who is required to put in at his expense a sanitary sewer main larger than required for his particular project in order to serve future development outside of his own project. Such additional expense applies as well to water mains, width of streets and similar items. There are two objections to this type of requirement: One, that the developer, and not the

[48] All too frequently: (1) Street design standards are arbitrarily applied from one city to the next, using commonly accepted dimensions, etc.—rather than developed from scratch on the basis of what the streets are to be used for. (2) Standards, once developed, are all too often applied across the board within any given jurisdiction—without considering variations in the character and density of the neighborhoods served. Thus the streets are often inadequate in high density areas and overbuilt in low density areas—the latter resulting in a waste of land (too much in the right-of-way), an "urban" appearance in what might otherwise be a semi-rural type of development, and an excessively high cost per front foot. See "Notes on Street Cross-Sections in Residential Subdivisions" by Allen Benjamin. *Urban Land,* May 1960. Urban Land Institute.

municipality, is creating new taxable values for the city as a whole to which the city is not contributing; and two, that the developer, and finally the purchaser, is paying for improvements which are benefiting and properly chargeable to areas beyond his development, and which are of no direct benefit to him.

Another aspect to this problem has been emerging in recent years, caused primarily by the pressing need of cities for additional revenue. Many cities now charge a sewer service fee. Thus the developer and home buyer stand the entire capital cost of a utility from which the municipality as a whole derives special revenue.

The Council strongly recommends that where municipalities obtain revenue from water service or through sewer fees, they should amortize the cost of such installations from the revenue so derived. This would substantially lower the initial cost to the developer and purchaser alike. Cities now charging such installation costs to the developer, or which, in addition, assess the home owner, are urged to change their practice.[49]

Regarding the extent to which utilities should be installed at any one time by the developer, Council member John Mowbray of Baltimore warns: "Don't make the mistake of installing street improvements and utilities on too much land in advance of sales. This greatly increases the carrying load, tends to create shop-worn property, and takes away interest, zeal and sales value in opening new areas. Buyers like new offerings."

7. Site Environment

Good environment is basic to good housing. In selecting a site, pay close attention to conditions surrounding the property. All too often developers concentrate so intently on the acreage cost of land and the apparent ease with which site improvements can be installed that later matters are overlooked—such as sales resistance and the cost of minimizing adverse influences from adjacent areas.

(a) Land Use

The site should be reasonably free from the influence of nearby undesirable land uses. If the area is zoned, consult the

---

[49] See *Utilities and Facilities for New Residential Development,* Technical Bulletin No. 27. Urban Land Institute.

zoning map and regulations. (See also page 60). An area zoned for industry is unsuitable for residential development.[50]

Undesirable surroundings such as railroad tracks, cemeteries, poorly subdivided and cheap developments, or run-down commercial and noxious industrial uses must be guarded against as neighbors for residential land uses. Physical buffers such as parks, golf courses, stream valleys and certain types of institutional properties may minimize such bad effects. Buffers of plantings and screen walls can be created, but such corrective measures must be taken into account in the site development cost. Land that can be bought cheaply because of poor surroundings is never a bargain.

Illustration No. 14.

The Most Effective Position for a Sound Screen Is Position C. A Is Fair, and B Is the Worst.

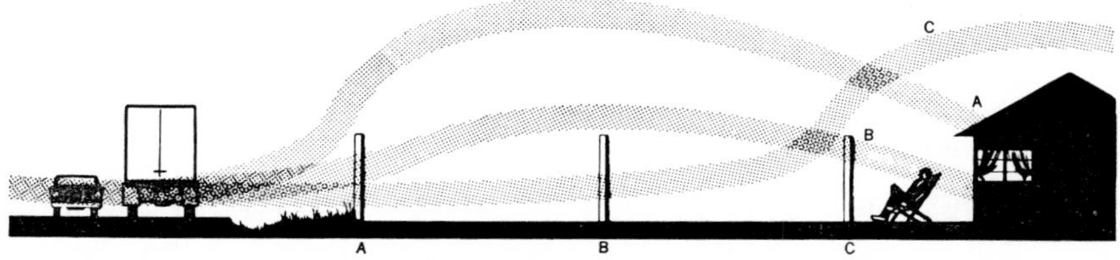

Source: "NOISE, PAYMENT FOR PROGRESS?" SRI JOURNAL, STANFORD RESEARCH INSTITUTE, SECOND QUARTER, 1957.

(b) Traffic Streets

Freedom of the site from the adverse effects of through traffic is highly important. Heavy traffic streets can be as detrimental as cheap developments or commercial and industrial uses. Whenever possible, sites split by existing or potential major thoroughfares should be avoided. Check with your planning commission and highway department on this matter, and, if possible, endeavor to have proposed thoroughfares relocated along the periphery of the community. Any additional land dedicated to the municipality or county to achieve this end may pay big dividends. To avoid interference with sleep and outdoor living, larger, deeper lots abutting heavily travelled thoroughfares are desirable.[51] (See also page 118).

---

[50] See *Prohibition of Residential Development in Industrial Districts,* Technical Bulletin No. 10. Urban Land Institute.

See also "Exclusion of Residences from Industrial Districts." *Urban Land,* February 1960. Urban Land Institute.

[51] By taking advantage of natural or man-made features between the source and the hearer, noise can be reduced. The positioning of a

(c) Dampness, Smoke and Views

A site should be free from smoke and offensive odors. The direction of prevailing winds and of periodic storms and fog is important in many areas. Good views and a pleasing outlook are great assets and should be carefully preserved.

(d) Flooding

Check all low lying sites for likelihood of present and future flooding. No residential development within a flood plain should ever be contemplated. If the site contains sufficient buildable area above flood height, the lower land may be reserved for park and play areas. Frequently land subject to flood can be filled above flood dangers with excess excavation. Again, however, don't underestimate the increased run-off which results as an entire watershed is developed.

(e) Fire Hazard

Proximity to large tanks for the storage of gas, oil, and other inflammable materials should be avoided.

(f) Airports

In selecting acreage for development, pay sharp attention to the property's location with respect to an airport—existing or proposed. Take into account possibilities for construction of new airport facilities and runway extensions or other enlargements.

The local planning commission is a good source for learning about future airport development prospects. Where there is no planning commission, the county engineer should have information about current airport plans. The aviation commission of the state should be helpful also in securing data for any local, long-range civilian airport program.

---

screening wall is indicated in the illustration (No. 14). Shrubbery and trees are practically useless for reducing the magnitude of the sound pressure unless the growth is tall and thick. Screening the noise source from the hearer has a psychological advantage. When the source is not directly connected with danger and is not visible, its annoyance is lessened. Thus, trees and other plants may serve a quite useful psychological purpose. Wind is a factor in the long-distance transmission of sound. In general, it is better to live upwind from the source than downwind. This, of course, should be a factor in residential site location. See "Noise—Payment for Progress?" by Vincent Salmon in *Stanford Research Institute Journal,* 2nd quarter 1957. Stanford Research Institute, Menlo Park, Calif.

(g) Effect of Airports on Residential Developments

The importance of site investigation in relation to an airport comes from possible adverse effect of the airport on the residential development. Adverse influences of airports are based on objections induced by nuisances from noise, vibration, psychological hazard, and personal annoyance. The objections vary according to conditions in different parts of the country and in individual communities. The main factors that govern the degree of adverse effect on immediate and outlying neighborhoods, in any case, are the size, type, use and ownership of the airport and the physical, economic and social aspects of the land in question. But when property lies under a flight pattern or

Illustration No. 15.
Influence of Airports on Residential Developments

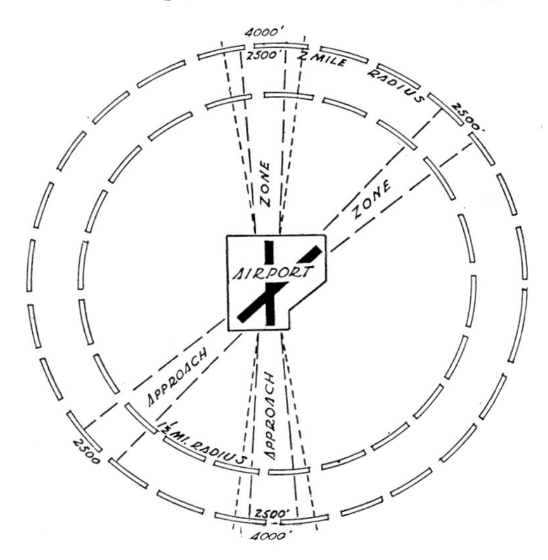

1. Major airports should be no closer than two miles to a residential area.
2. Areas in approach zones and within two miles of limits of major airstrips are definitely objectionable to residential developments.
3. Normal approach at 30:1 glide angle plane elevation at two miles is 352 feet. Generally accepted limit of trespass is 1,000 feet in elevation.
4. Instrument approach at 40:1 glide angle plane elevation at two miles is 264 feet.
5. Width of approach zones at the two-mile radius is 2,500 feet for contact flying and 4,000 feet for instrument flying. (Planes do not always stay within these approach zones.)
6. Zone for protection of aircraft and persons on the ground as recommended by the "Doolittle Report" is shown by Illustration 16.

Source: *Opinion Surveys of Trends on Urban Development and Redevelopment.* Technical Bulletin No. 3, Urban Land Institute (out-of-print).

within zones of plane approaches and take-offs, particularly for jet planes, adverse influences on property are intensified.

The effective "area of objections" to airports should be determined separately for each airport by ascertaining the attitudes likely to be encountered from the market within that community. Furthermore, all land included within a four-mile radius from an airport is not uniformly affected. Land within

Illustration No. 16.

Protective End Zones for Airports as Recommended by the Report of the President's Airport Commission, May, 1952

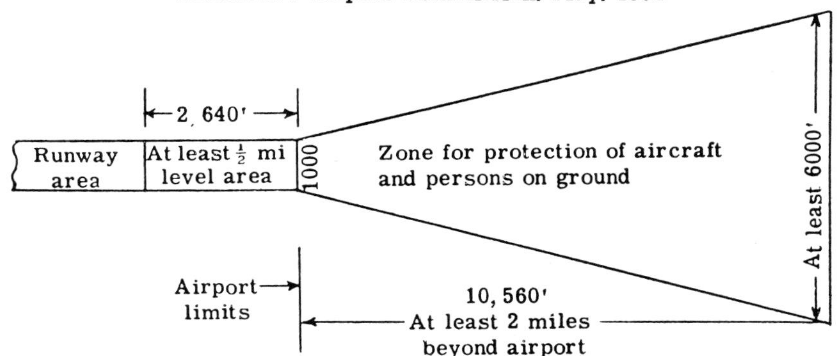

the approach zones in line with the direction of runways is the area most directly affected. However, the path of plane approach to the runways can be shifted from time to time.

Both the FHA[52] and the VA[53] recognize that land beneath the approach zones to runways can be adversely affected. At one time (up to about 1952), FHA refused generally to consider insuring mortgages within a four-mile radius of an airport if the houses were beneath the normal landing and take-off paths. Both the FHA and the VA through their regional offices now consider each case on its own merits for their appraising of residential properties near airports. The implication here is

---

[52] See *FHA Underwriting Manual,* Underwriting Analysis under Title II, Section 203 of the National Housing Act, revised April 1, 1958. For sale by Sup't of Documents, U. S. Gov't. Printing Office, Washington 25, D. C. FHA follows the practices outlined in its Underwriting Manual in which it says: "Locations near an airport may be subjected to the noise and danger of low-flying aircraft. The rating of the feature must reflect the importance of the hazard or nuisance to the user group."

[53] See VA Technical Bulletin 4A-121, dated June 26, 1952, and the illustration page 50.

Illustration No. 17.
Zones of Influence

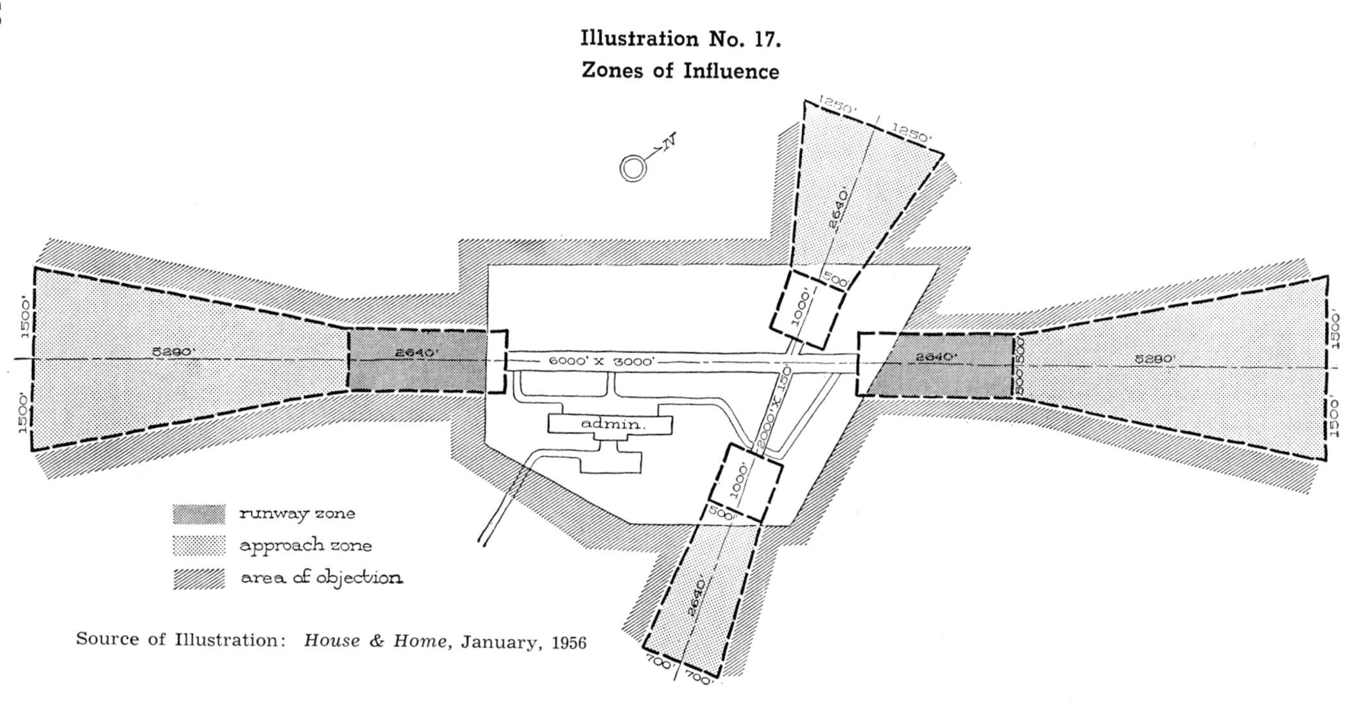

Source of Illustration: *House & Home*, January, 1956

Illustration of zones defined in VA Technical Bulletin 4A-121 dated June 26, 1952 (does not illustrate departures permitted in Paragraph 6 of that bulletin) which explains the principles by which VA regional offices are governed in processing submissions for appraisal within areas defined.

not that the so-called airport nuisances do not affect residential land value adversely but rather that they do not affect it as much as many people once thought.

With the development of air travel, the airport has become an employment generator. Many of these people want to live close to their place of work, so residential developments have sprung up adjacent to airports despite the nuisance factor of noise. Similarly, outlying office building and industrial development has taken place on sites adjacent to airports. Such building development has added value to land adjacent to major airports, particularly. As John Matthews of North Little Rock observes, "Our industry (i.e. homebuilding) seems to have overestimated the airport nuisance all along. With air-conditioning coming into use more generally, homes remain closed summer and winter, further minimizing outside noise."[54]

(1) THE NOISE FACTOR. The factor that *is* severe and that is the major depreciator of residential property values is the noise generated by planes landing and taking off and flying overhead.

The width of the noise area covered by the conventional four-motor, propeller-driven airliner is approximately two miles from each side of the flight path. See Illustration 19, "Range of Transportation Noise". Directly below such plane at two miles from the airport after take-off, the noise level is 105 decibels, loud enough to blanket out conversation. Even at 10 miles from point of take-off, when the plane has climbed to 3,000 feet, the noise level, though of short duration, is 80 decibels—still above talking level. In the case of jets, the noise level and the band covered by their operational noise is about twice that of the conventional plane. Jets with their high-pitched whine have their highest noise level at their start-to-taxi, take-off and landing positions.

(2) AIRPORTS AND JET NOISE. The jet age in the United States was inaugurated in January 1959 when American Airlines flew the first transcontinental jet passenger flight with the Boeing 707. Other air lines now have jets in service.

Commercial jet aviation at civilian and municipal airports in this country is here even though U. S. airports cannot handle

---

[54] See also "The Impact of the Jet Age on Real Estate," Proceedings of the American Institute of Real Estate Counselors. *The Appraisal Journal,* October 1959, pages 455-474 incl.

Illustration No. 18.
Adaptation of Factors Affecting Residential Land Use in Areas Within the Approach Zones of An Airport.

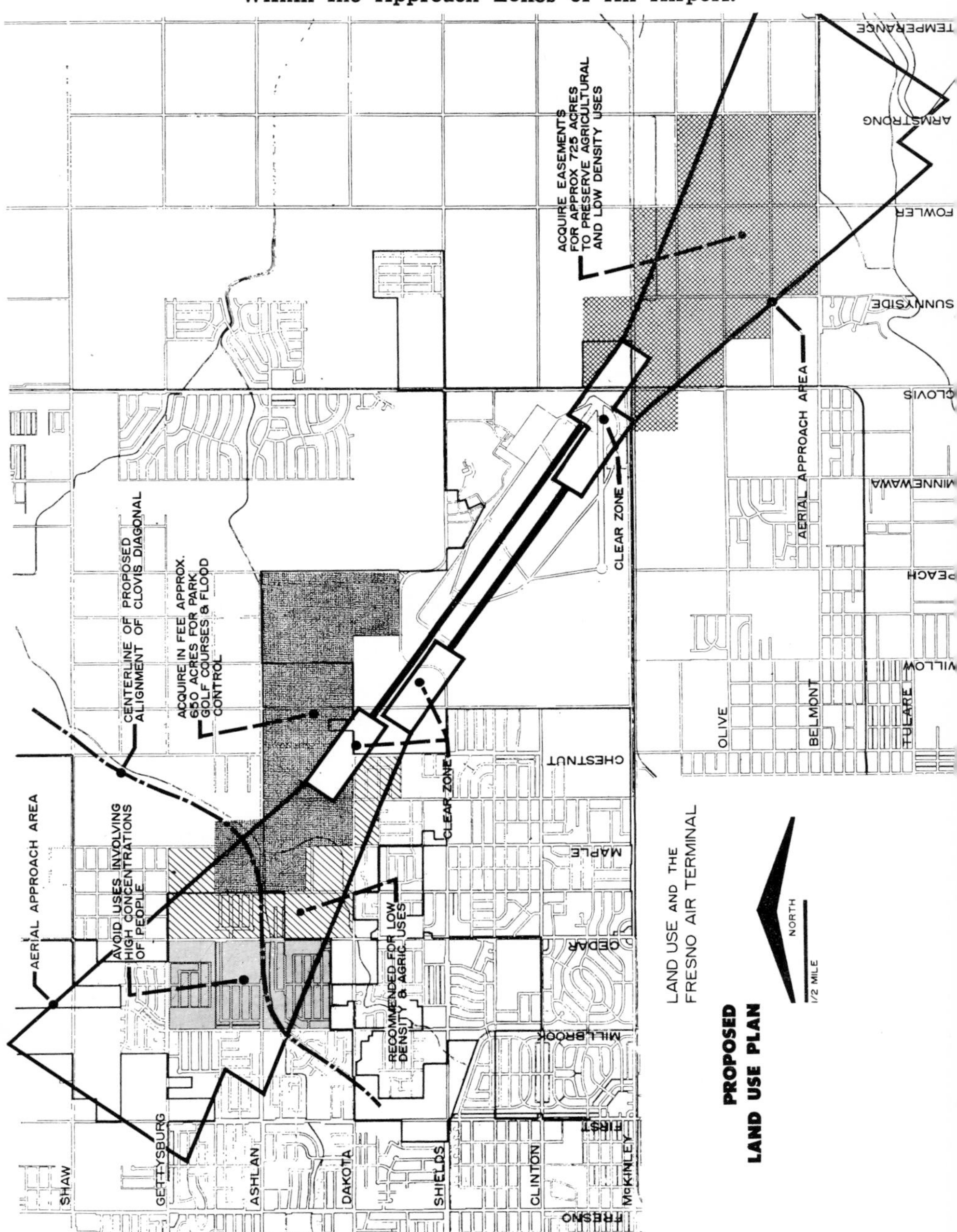

Source: Land Use and the Fresno Air Terminal. A report by the Fresno County and Fresno City Planning Commissions. 2nd ed. August 1959.

Illustration No. 19.
Range of Transportation Noise

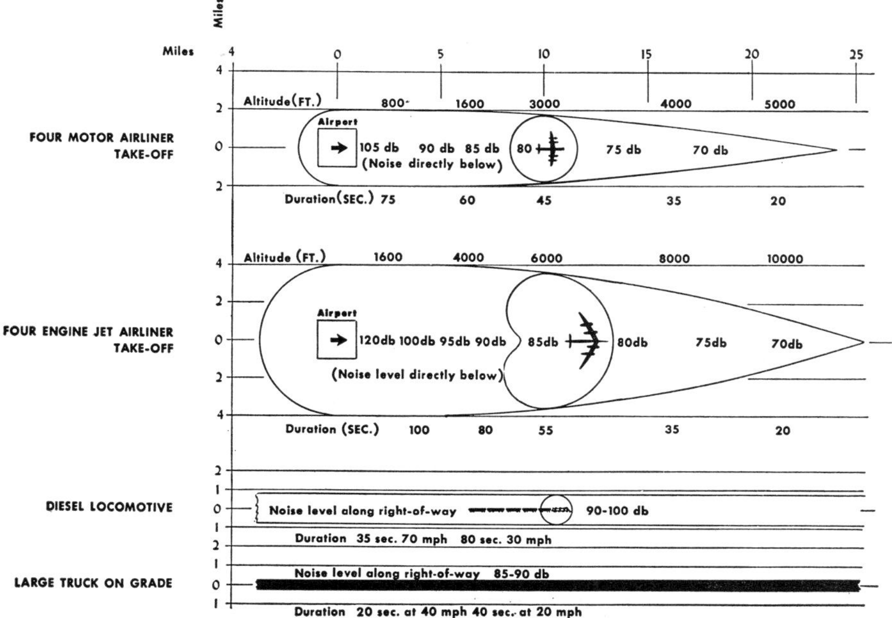

Source: "Measuring Noise in Our Cities," by Dr. H. C. Hardy, Armour Research Foundation, in *Urban Land,* November 1952, Urban Land Institute.

a heavy volume of jet traffic efficiently. Almost every airport requires extensions to its present runways or new runways, wider taxiways, better fueling and lighting facilities and terminal improvements before it can handle jets or the expected growth in passenger traffic.

Big jets, fully loaded, require runways of 10,000 feet or longer. The Federal Aviation Agency has fixed 10,500-feet as the length of airport runways for new aircraft. The Agency does not provide Federal aid to communities for construction of runways greater than this length. But except for a few of our fields, main runways on the country's airports run from 6,500 feet up to 9,000 feet.

The jets will put a real strain on present airport facilities because almost everywhere cities have been caught short by the growth in air travel.[55] In part, the unpreparedness of the

---

[55] U. S. air lines carried more than 49 million passengers in 1958, more than double the 19.2 million hauled as recently as 1950. Predictions are that the number of passengers will soar to 66 million in 1960 and 93 million by 1965.

nation's airports is due to a complacent and mistaken belief in the long-haul, non-stop concept in the operations of jets and that jets will skip most of the United States and fly only to the largest cities on both coasts plus a few large inland cities such as Chicago, St. Louis, Dallas or Atlanta.[56] By 1965, jets can be expected to fly to most major cities of the U. S. Airports will have to cope with the new planes and with nearly twice as many passengers.

Before transoceanic jet flights were inaugurated in October 1958, the Port of New York Authority tested jet operations for noise. As a result the Authory took a firm stand requiring that new jet airliners at New York's International Airport produce no more noise than the largest conventional propeller-driven aircraft using that airport. It is a tribute to the noise suppression work done on the Boeing 707 and the Comet 4 that these aircraft were approved to use the airport at Idlewild.[57]

In the sound measurements taken for these tests the noise of jet take-offs and landings was found to be severe enough to disturb the communities within the flight path. Accordingly, as the Port of New York Authority's noise consultants recommended for Idlewild Airport, fairly restrictive measures should be required in order to introduce the new jet airliners into our present-day airports. From the noise levels measured by those tests, it seems that if we are to continue to operate many of the large airports located in the middle of populated areas without unduly disturbing many of the nearby residents, it will be necessary to impose severe noise control restrictions on jet operations from those fields.[58]

So from what we know now about the inadequacies of present major airports and because of the intensity of jet-whine, it is obvious that the prospective site developer would be well advised to consider carefully the wind patterns and airport locations (both existing and proposed) in locating a new residential development.

---

[56] See "Airports for Tomorrow." *Architectural Forum,* January 1958. See also "Passenger Terminal Building Design Principles," *Architectural Record,* March 1960.

[57] See "Airports and Jet Noise" by Laymon N. Miller, Leo L. Beranek and Karl D. Kryter in *Noise Control,* Vol. 5, No. 1, January 1959.

[58] See "Airports and Jet Noise" (cited above). See also "Noise Exposure in Communities Near Jet Air Bases" by A. C. Pietrasanta and K. N. Stevens, *Noise Control,* March 1958.

(h) Airport Location

No formula for the location of airports which satisfies all aspects of the problem has yet been developed. Close-in locations which have time and accessibility in their favor are the chief offenders from the standpoint of noise, vibration and hazard. Outlying locations tend to reverse these advantages and disadvantages. Looking ahead, it would appear that there are distinct possibilities for minimizing or removing the time and accessibility disadvantages in the larger cities, where it is most important, through the provision of high-speed limited access freeway routes from town center to airport, and in many cases through the introduction of helicopter "limousine" service to and from the central area and the outlying air field. The rapid improvement of the helicopter and recent developments in shuttle and short-haul service in Europe and the United States appears to hold a great deal of promise in helping remove the one major disadvantage of the outlying airport.

A well-designed community plan makes provision for the automobile but at the same time it includes buffers against adverse effects of general traffic and maximum discouragement to heavy traffic volumes on local access streets. Few people want to live next to automobile parking areas and garages, neither do they like heavy traffic near their homes. Had the full extent of the automobile's adverse influence on residential uses been anticipated earlier, a greater segregation of vehicular traffic movement and houses—except for access and servicing—would have been realized than is the case in many older residential areas today. This very factor has been one of the important causes of residential blight.

The physical controls that can be used to regulate the automobile are not feasible with the airplane. So it would seem that rigid regulations, strictly enforced, are the only alternative, and necessary regardless of any reduction of the noise factor.[59]

---

[59] See also *Modernizing the National System of Aviation Facilities* by the Office of Aviation Facilities Planning, The White House, May 1957. Sup't of Documents, Washington 25, D. C.

See also *Small Airports.* Federal Aviation Agency. January 1959. Sup't of Documents, Washington 25, D. C.

8. City Services and Community Facilities

(a) Fire and Police Protection

Careful consideration should be given to the present and potential availability of local fire fighting equipment and personnel. Adequate police protection should be assured either by the municipality or through community organization.

(b) Schools

The presence of elementary schools is one of the greatest drawing cards in new residential developments, for the families with children of pre-school and school age are the ones that form a substantial part of the prospective home-owning market. Even though the provision of schools for a community is traditionally a responsibility of public authorities, the forward-looking developer will consult the local school board to assure the prospective purchasers that there are or will be adequate school facilities in the community.

If you are working in new territory with a very large project, you will find that one school or more will be needed. You will do well by your own interests and by the community-at-large to look into the school situation and to discuss the possibilities of locating a school site within your tract. Mostly, school district lines are drawn by the local school administrative officials. Distances are not the controlling factor in locating schools. Instead the number of pupils which must be taken care of plus the financing available become the more determining considerations.

When distances are too great for walking, school buses are used. "Walking distance," as a maximum, once was considered to be one mile between home and elementary school. But where major highway crossings, existing school service areas and a junior high school system have to be taken into account, the walking distance standard is no longer practical. Even so the accepted principle of a school as the center of the neighborhood within one-half mile radius and located away from any major traffic route still holds. If distances from home to school are substantially greater than one-half mile, school buses or good transit facilities should be available. Distances up to three miles are satisfactory for travel to high schools. In most instances of suburban development the school is no farther away than the nearest school bus stop.

Regardless of whether the locality has an 8-4 or a 6-3-3 system, check school location and construction matters with your local school authorities and planning commission for their relation to your project at the beginning.[60] (See also page 143).

(c) Recreation and Schools

With rising incomes, longer vacations and more holiday weekends, people have more leisure time. Accordingly, space for recreation takes on greater emphasis in site selection for residential development.

Trends in recreation areas are toward a separation of small children's playgrounds and larger recreation centers which include athletic fields, swimming pools, etc., for older age groups. Another trend is toward incorporating these latter facilities with the school site. The building can then be used during off-school periods thus avoiding duplication of indoor facilities such as toilets, showers and gymnasium. Where separate school and recreation boards are established, arrangements for the cooperative use and supervision of the recreation areas during and out of school hours have proved very successful. The resulting economies in land, structures, and maintenance have been substantial.

The Council recommends strongly that school and recreation facilities be contiguous and be used cooperatively and that supervision be provided. Walking distances to recreation areas thus would correspond with those of the school. In any case, usable recreation areas should be within not more than fifteen minutes walking time without crossing major traffic arteries, unless adequate traffic lights or other safety features are provided at these points to protect the pedestrian. Small areas for pre-school children should be provided in addition to the above facilities and maintained by the local government or by a homes association.[61]

School sites, playgrounds and other recreational open space form an important part of community facilities. The *general*

---

[60] With population growth, communities everywhere face impacts on their schools. As background for data on surveys of school needs and future school designs, the following references may be helpful: *School Needs in the Decade Ahead* by Roger A. Freeman. 273 pp. The Institute for Social Science Research, 917 15th Street, N.W., Washington 5, D. C.; *Schoolhouse.* Edited by Walter McQuade, 271 pp. Simon and Schuster, New York, N. Y.

[61] See *Recreation Places* by Wayne R. Williams. Reinhold Publishing Corp., 430 Park Ave., New York 22, N. Y., 1958.

location of school and recreation areas should be determined by comprehensive city planning in relation to the size and population density of the community. The best, most economical time to determine the *precise* location is before or at the time that the land is coming up for subdivision. But as the ownership of parcels seldom corresponds to the neighborhood or community areas, it follows that requiring each subdivider to dedicate a certain percentage of his tract for a school site or playground does not result in obtaining this type of site in the proper size or location. For the same reason, it is unfair to require a subdivider to contribute more than his fair share if the tract should coincide with an appropriate community-wide school or park location.

Consequently, the fair and intelligent method is for the planning commission to designate in a general way by means of its master open space and school location plans the nature and extent of open spaces and school sites, and then, as any portion within the boundaries of a development tract comes to be submitted for subdivision approval, take such steps as will invite the reservation or dedication of open spaces at or about the places designated by the commission's comprehensive planning studies, backed by money adjustment to compensate the owner of a subdivision tract for the excess contributed by him above his fair share.

(d) Waste Disposal and Street Service

Preference should be given to the site which is within an area of public or private refuse collection and, in the north, where municipal or other services supply snow removal and sanding of roadways. Where municipal sewage disposal systems permit their use, the installation of garbage disposal units eliminates the service of garbage collection.

(e) Auxiliary Facilities

Preference should be given to property conveniently served by already established semi-public and private institutions and facilities such as churches, hospitals, movies, and other commercial recreation; banks, laundry agencies, and other shopping service facilities. Remember just because you are developing a few hundred houses you do not necessarily have a demand for a new shopping center. On the other hand, if your project is large and comprises over a thousand new residential units, in your preliminary site evaluation you should think about reserving land for a shopping center project as well as setting aside suitable sites for community purposes such as for schools, recreation and churches. In this case you should be thinking in terms of developing a complete community.

9. Municipal Regulations

(a) Comprehensive or "Master" Planning

Along with other preliminaries before final site selection, you should think about how you will use and develop the entire property and how your ultimate development will dovetail with adjoining subdivisions or with adjacent land use. In other words, "master plan" the entire tract that you are considering. Regardless of the type of project and its development in stages, don't start in piecemeal fashion. Think of it in its entirety and in its relationship to the area surrounding it. Such comprehensive planning of your development is a process similar to the procedure followed by a good city planning commission guided by its professional staff technicians. To give the developer an insight to the planning process the following capsuled version is offered:

"Master plan" is a term with varying shades of meaning in different locations and contexts. Officially, it is the guide for the development of an area—small community, city or region. Legally, its basis is the state enabling act. The plan is advisory and it is prepared by the planing agency and its technical staff. A "master" or comprehensive plan for an urban region or metropolis will differ in degree of detail from one prepared to serve the needs of a small city or town. Regardless of population or extent of the area, a comprehnsive community plan used as a basis for urban growth and development should include no less than the following requisites:

1. A land use plan for the entire area indicating the location and amount of land to be allocated for residential, commercial, industrial, transportation, and public purposes.

2. A circulation plan showing the framework for general locations and types of major routes required for the efficient movement of people and goods into, about and through the entire locality.

Both the land use and circulation plans should reflect careful consideration of:

a. Physical characteristics of the area.
b. Present and probable future trends affecting the economy of the area.
c. Utilities policy recognizing the feasibility of future extensions to existing water, sewer, drainage, power, gas, and other services.
d. Program for community facilities including schools, parks and playgrounds, and other recreational features; health, public safety and other governmental buildings and requirements.

In physical form, a comprehensive master plan should consist of a map, or series of related maps, of the area; presenting in graphic form the information indicated above, together with an explanatory statement. The preparation of these maps should be based upon thorough, intensive and competent surveys and analyses of existing social, economic and physical conditions in the community and of the trends which have influenced development in the past and which can be expected to influence them in the future. Consideration should be given to public and private financial resources; the pattern outlined for the future should be practical and should avoid grandiose or unattainable objectives.[62]

The planning organization responsible for orderly community growth must be realistic in its aims. Nearly always when dissension arises between planners and developers, the fault lies with failure to appreciate each other's viewpoints. Similarly, the problems developers and builders encounter with official plans, zoning ordinances, subdivision regulations and other such aspects of municipal administration frequently arise because there is no broad-scale master planning, or the planning is inadequate, or there is poor administration of planning procedures. So it is very important for developers to understand "planning" aims and for planners to appreciate developers' problems.[63]

(b) Zoning

Zoning originated as a method for protecting existing property values from depreciation caused by intrusion of in-

---

[62] See "Planning before Zoning," *Urban Land,* January 1958. Urban Land Institute.

[63] See also *Real Estate and City Planning* by Richard L. Nelson and Frederick T. Aschman. Prentice-Hall, Inc., 70 Fifth Ave., New York 11, N. Y. 1957.

compatible land uses into established neighborhoods. Early enabling acts and municipal ordinances were defensive in purpose. This limited concept for zoning's objectives still persists in some communities and with many individuals. Recent urban growth has fully demonstrated that zoning based on preservation of the *status quo* does not meet the needs of a growing community. Zoning is a tool of planning and good planning is a prerequisite to good zoning.

Zoning has become a firmly established and accepted form of police power regulation with its almost forty years of experience and favorable legal opinion establishing its benefit and validity.[64] Basically, zoning provides for the division of the municipality into a number of use districts within which the height, open space, building coverage, and more recently the density of population for respective districts are specified.

The Council is strongly in favor of planning and zoning as beneficial instruments in protecting residential neighborhoods against adverse uses and in stabilizing community development and land values. However, many zoning ordinances and maps have been poorly drawn, are obsolete in many respects, such as having too many strip commercial districts, inadequate protection for residential neighborhoods and the like, and are often carelessly administered and amended through uninformed or politically minded city officials and councils. The aggregate result in many cities has been a piecemeal breaking down of comprehensive zoning through isolated ordinance and map changes and unrelated spot zoning with little or no reference to the overall plan for the city. The need for extensive modernization of obsolete codes and procedures in order to correct these and other deficiences is being increasingly recognized and is strongly advocated by the Council.

County zoning, especially within metropolitan areas and urbanized counties, has now come into reality.[65] Another

---

[64] According to the 1959 *Municipal Year Book* (International City Managers Assoc., Chicago) 921 cities stated that they have a comprehensive (use, height, bulk, and area) zoning ordinance. Nearly 46 percent of 875 reporting cities over 10,000 population have revised their zoning ordinance in the last 5 years, 1954-1958. The lag in up-dating their zoning provisions is demonstrated by this percentage figure, even though less than one quarter of the reporting cities have not revised their zoning ordinance within the last ten years—from 1948.

[65] See *Utilities and Facilities for New Residential Development—A Survey of Municipal Policy.* Technical Bulletin No. 27, Urban Land Institute.

desirable recent development is the provision in some ordinances for large-scale community development which will permit a variety of housing types together with a local shopping center and certain other features if carried out as a unit in accordance with an overall community plan.[66] Still another newly evolving concept in zoning is "density zoning." Under density zoning, the provision for minimum lot size would be replaced by a population density of families per acre for the entire subdivision. With density zoning, the developer would have greater flexibility in lot sizes for his housing types.[67] Montgomery County, Maryland, is debating (1959) the institution of such provision in its zoning to encourage land donations for public use, such as schools and parks.

While it is recognized that zoning does not create vested property rights, it is emphasized, however, that due consideration should be given by every zoning board to the economic factors involved in order to avoid confiscation of property values and create confidence in real estate investment and home ownership.

Zoning does not take the place of protective covenants and should not be confused therewith. One is a public police power regulation, the other a private contract. Both are necessary to good communty development. Private covenants are discussed in Part III.

Be sure to check zoning of land adjacent to any contemplated site as well as that of the site itself. Check the possibilities of obtaining zoning revisions if changes appear desirable, such as the inclusion of a local shopping center if justified by tributary population, elimination of string commercial zones and the like. The developer can often render effective service to his community as well as himself by calling attention to and

---

[66] See "Zoning for the Planned Community" by Fred W. Tuemmler. *Urban Land,* April 1954, and "Zoning of Planned Residential Developments" by Goldston and Scheuer, *Urban Land,* March 1960, Urban Land Institute.

[67] The alternative "density zoning" approach for application to vacant or redeveloped land starts with the premise that one of the most important aspects of controlling land use through zoning is the regulation of population density. Therefore "density zoning" envisions residential districts which allow any dwelling type or combination of dwelling types that meet the overall density standards which have been set, provided that the standards for individual buildings of the dwelling type are met. See "An Alternative Approach to Zoning". Philadelphia Housing Assoc. *Issues,* March 1958.

Illustration No. 20.
An Example of a Master School and Recreation Plan.

	SCHOOLS	SCHOOL AND RECREATION	RECREATION: NEIGHBORHOOD	RECREATION: COMMUNITY
EXISTING				
PROPOSED				

PRIVATE SCHOOL AND/OR RECREATION.

Source: General Development Plan, Mount Clemens, Michigan. Geer Associates, Planning Consultants.

Illustration No. 21.

An Example of a Master Thoroughfare Plan.

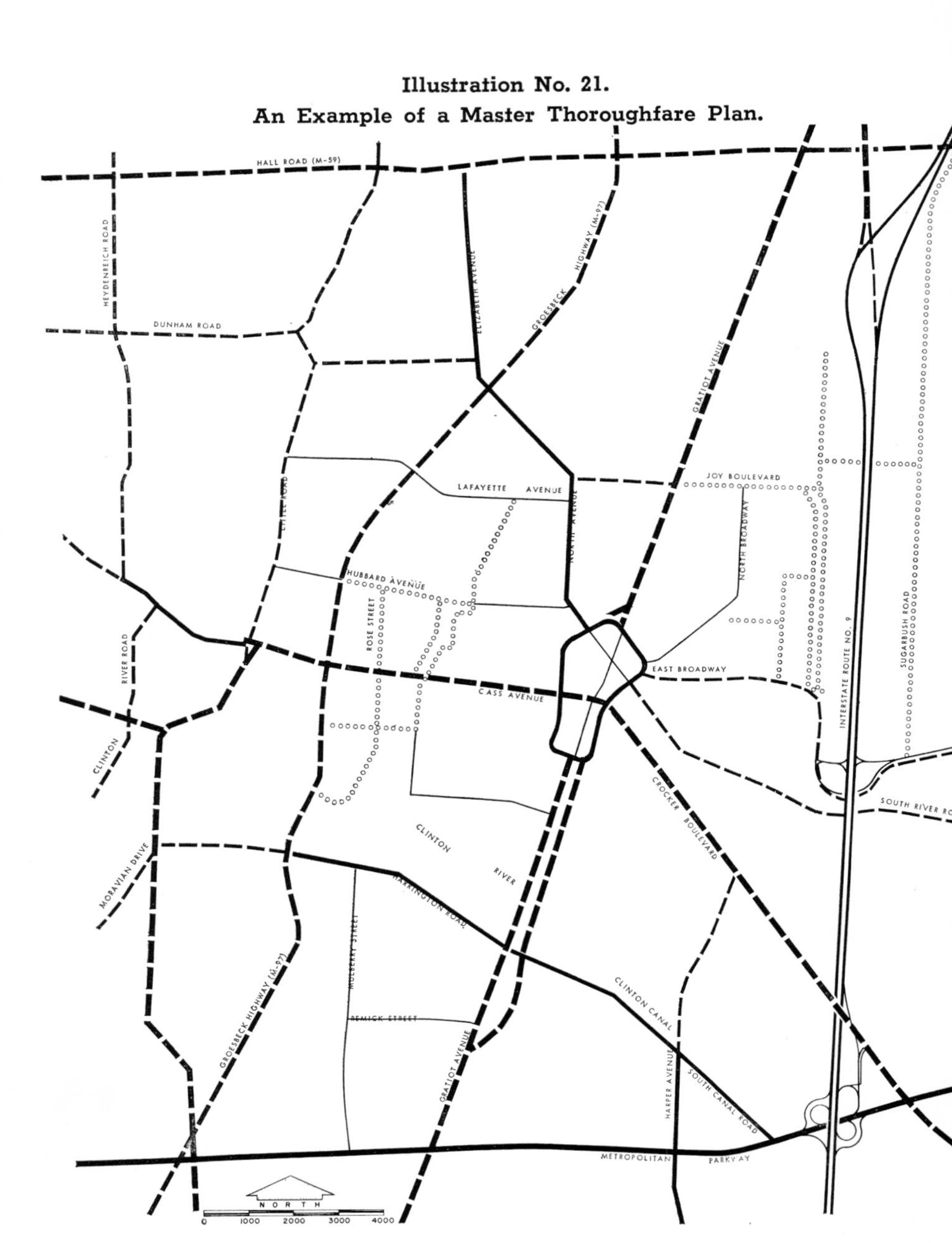

Source: General Development Plan, Mount Clemens, Michigan. Geer Associates, Planning Consultants.

working for the improvement of obsolete or poorly administered zoning ordinances and maps.[68]

(c) Subdivision Regulations

Although more recent than zoning subdivision regulations, under the police power, have also become an accepted method of municipal and county control for the development of land. The business of building a community, and this includes its environs, requires the safeguarding of the interests of the home owner, the subdivider and the local government for assurance that residential land subdivision will provide permanent assets to the locality.[69]

The subdivision of land is both a technical and a business venture with ramifications for the community-at-large. No one has better phrased the purposes and objectives of subdivision regulations than has Harold W. Lautner, one-time assistant director of Urban Land Institute, in his comprehensive study, *Subdivision Regulations*.[70]

"The subdivider of a parcel of land does very much more than sell real estate by a bargain concerning the buyer and the seller alone. The results of his activities are in truth indelibly impressed upon the physical pattern of the community at large. What the subdivider of land does and how he does it are of extreme importance to the general public as well as to the individual. Rarely does a community lay out its own streets. Except in the case of main thoroughfares, most streets are located by the subdivider of land, the community sooner or later accepting these with the lots and blocks as laid out. The subdivider's primary motive in subdividing land is private profit, but the motive of the community, which sooner or later finds itself responsible for the subdivided land as a part of the whole machinery of the city, is public service. The necessity for

---

[68] References: *Simplified Zoning for Small Communities.* Connecticut Development Commission, Research and Planning Division, 475 State Office Building, Hartford, Conn.; *The Why and How of Rural Zoning* by E. D. Solberg, for sale by Sup't of Documents, U. S. Gov't. Printing Office, December 1958; *The Text of a Model Zoning Ordinance, with Commentary,* Fred H. Bair, Jr. and Ernest R. Bartley, Public Administration Clearing Service of the University of Florida, Gainesville, 1958.

[69] See *Suggested Land Subdivision Regulations.* Housing and Home Finance Agency. Reprint. 1960. Sup't of Documents, U. S. Gov't Printing Office, Washington 25, D. C.

[70] Even though this report is now out-of-print and available only in a few public libraries, it remains a standard reference document on subdivision. *Subdivision Regulations* by Harold W. Lautner. Public Administration Service, Chicago. 1941.

coordination of these two desires is evident. The efforts, therefore, of our communities to regulate and guide the subdivision of land are a necessary part of their government and administration. The so-called subdivision regulations are manifestations of direct control of this activity by the community under the police power."

In addition to the comprehensive or "master" plan, both zoning and subdivision regulations are methods for effectuating the proper development of the community. Before embarking on any development plan, the local regulations and approval procedures should be checked carefully, not only for specifications on subdivision design but also for land improvement requirements which are called for.

As in zoning, subdivision regulations in many political jurisdictions have become obsolete in the light of modern subdivision design and land development techniques. In addition, many regulation requirements are excessive with regard to such matters as local street and roadway pavement widths, type and thickness of paving, and other items. The result has been to discourage development within the city in favor of the outlying areas, where in some cases regulations are more reasonable and modern than within the city. In many places, however, subdivision regulations may be absent or wholly inadequate to assure a suitable residential community. There are, of course, instances in the outlying sections where requirements are so severe as to make the construction of modest homes impossible. Cities and counties should study this matter seriously with the view of bringing about more comparable standards between inlying and outlying areas, and to bring their standards into line with modern design and construction.[71]

---

[71] See *Utilities and Facilities for New Residential Development.* Technical Bulletin No. 27, Urban Land Institute.

Subdivision regulations are in use more and more as a device to secure the improvements needed as land is developed for urban use. Specifications included in the regulations reflect the developer's changing role of responsibility for good development.

Installations called for do not always take into account an equitable arrangement for paying the cost of utilities, such as water mains and sanitary sewers. More attention is needed to solving the matter of unfairness in charging immediate projects with installations that benefit territory beyond.

Too frequently adjoining jurisdictions have differing specifications governing land development within the same metropolitan region. In metropolitan areas with many local jurisdictions, all with subdivision approval powers, there is great need for coordinating regulations pertaining to urban growth. There is not enough direct evidence that subdivision plan approval procedures are related directly to comprehensive municipal planning.

All responsible community builders today accept the desirability and necessity of municipal subdivision regulations. Their chief quarrel with these regulations is directed against those municipalities wherein excessive provisions or unreasonable requirements have been adopted as a prerequisite to subdivision approval. Unreasonable provisions include, for example, such items as excessive widths for the roadway pavements on purely local streets in single-family areas; heavy duty construction on local streets; installation of over-sized utilities at the developer's expense to serve property beyond his own development.[72]

Subdivision regulations will usually set up approval procedures and minimum design and engineering standards. In most ordinances the following are included:

1. Submission of a preliminary and a final plan of subdivision for approval prior to legal plat recording. This procedure includes regulations as to plat preparation, fees and costs, time schedules for submission, approvals and public hearings, and dedication of streets and open spaces.

2. Standards and Design Requirements. These regulations establish certain maximum and minimum criteria covering:

a. Streets; their location, width, alignment grades, intersection, use of culs-de-sac, relation to the city street system, alleys (see page 135), easements, etc.

b. Blocks; length, width, cross walks, and utility easements.

c. Lots; size, shape, and minimum dimensions.

d. Open spaces; character, and area required for dedication, if any.

e. Zoning and private covenants and their relation to subdivision regulations.

f. Variations and exceptions.

g. Subdivision names.

---

[72] Under pressures of urban growth many jurisdictions upgrade their requirements under zoning and land subdivision ordinances. This type of action frequently gives rise to friction in community and builder relations. Out of the welter of confusing testimony on a national scale, it appears that the fault basically lies not in the *fact* of regulations but in the *abuses* by those to whom the administration of zoning and subdivision control has been delegated. There is need for education of the public, including public officials, land developers and builders, on the aims and purposes of zoning and subdivision regulations, their relationship to good planning and the results which can be obtained with good planning and zoning.

3. Requirements relating to drafting standards, form of presentation, and information required to be shown on preliminary and final plats.

4. Requirements on grading plans and profiles.

5. Improvements required in the development. These requirements usually include tract and street monuments, street grading, surfacing or paving, curbs, gutters and sidewalks, storm and sanitary sewers, culverts and bridges, water mains, and in infrequent cases, the location of utility lines and installation of gas mains.[73] (See discussion on pages 155-166).

(d) Building Codes

Building codes are mainly concerned with structural requirements, material performances, and arrangement of buildings for health and safety. The codes may touch on site considerations and lotting relative to such items as attached garages, building height, required exits, and other facilities particularly for multifamily and commercial buildings. Be sure to check your building code against the zoning ordinance as its provisions sometimes govern where overlapping regulations occur.

As in zoning, many building codes are badly in need of revision to meet modern building trends. Builders and community developers should take an active interest in securing good building, sanitary, and subdivision regulations. The building codes of many of our cities are obsolete, drawn to favor certain industrial trades and certain types of merchandise, creating unnecessary cost in home construction. Certainly city building codes should permit within the city limits such types of residential construction as are approved today by FHA.

Obsolete codes bar the use of improved, less expensive products and technological improvements. Building costs are increased by endless differences in existing codes that prevent the use of uniform methods and materials. Certainly within the same metropolitan area modern, uniform building codes should be in effect.[74] For this purpose the national codes, such as the

---

[73] Detailed information on modern subdivision regulation practice will be found in *Suggested Land Subdivision Regulations.* Housing and Home Finance Agency. Reprint. 1957. Sup't of Documents, U. S. Gov't Printing Office, Washington 25, D. C. See also footnote 74.

[74] Because uniformity in building codes within an area of multiple jurisdictions is a long-term process, the state building code of North Carolina is mentioned (North Carolina State Building Code. Department of Insurance, Labor Building, Raleigh. 1958. 600 pp. $3). The

National Plumbing Code, prepared by various national construction organizations and other such groups can be adopted widely.

10. Consultation with Local Officials

The Council emphasizes the necessity of advance checking with your local planning commission on matters pertaining to ordinances and codes under its jurisdiction. Check also with the zoning board, the sewer and highway departments, and the building inspector for detailed requirements and procedures; with the school board for extension or location of school facilities; with the health department about stream pollution, mosquito control, sewage disposal, and water supply.

The larger the development, the more important it is that local officials be consulted and their goodwill obtained. This may be done directly, but preferably by working with or through the planning commission.

Before purchasing a site for residential development where Federal Housing Administration mortgage insurance will be drawn upon by the developer, the local FHA office should be consulted. That office's advice about site selection, land planning, and protective covenants will be of great value in helping to avoid costly errors later.[75]

---

new code covers most of the applicable state laws and regulations governing building construction. The new code brings uniformity into the area of building regulations and allows architects, builders, engineers, and developers to practice freely without having to contend with varying requirements in all localities. A standard building code can lower building costs and insurance rates by specifying uniformity throughout a region.

There is a vast difference between subdivision regulations and building codes. The physical components of buildings are manufactured parts subject to standardization under a uniform building code. Subdivision regulations deal with two great variables—land and people—which are not subject to uniformity. There are certain areas of uniformity, however, which can and should be incorporated into subdivision regulations. This uniformity lies in the use of a form for organization of the procedures employed in the administration and enforcement of the regulations—not in uniformity of the specifications. See "A Common Denominator for Subdivision Regulations." Planitorial, *Urban Land,* Dec. 1959, Urban Land Institute.

[75] See *Minimum Property Standards for One and Two Living Units.* Federal Housing Administration. For sale by Sup't of Documents, Washington 25, D. C. These standards became effective April 1, 1959 and mandatory, July 1, 1959. They replace FHA's former Minimum Property Requirements (MPR's). In addition, FHA's Land Planning Bulletin No. 3, *Neighborhood Standards* (separate edition for each FHA insuring office) should be obtained and consulted before proceeding.

11. Methods of Purchasing Land in Large Acreage

(a) General

Where the developer does not acquire all of the land he intends to develop at the start of his project, a plan that sets forth the general scheme of the development should be approved by the owner of the acreage involved, and an agreement entered into setting forth the acreage prices to be paid for the entire property. An owner can usually be shown that it is good business to enter into an agreement with the developer which will insure to the developer the necessary protection and incentive to proceed with a long term program.

David Bohannon of San Mateo, Calif., discusses this aspect of land assemblage in the following statement:

"In most communities, there are holdings of undeveloped acreage which are feasible to develop, but due to the reluctance of the developer to purchase the entire property and the inability of the owner to develop his own property, nothing happens but an accumulation of taxes. Even where the owner of extensive acreage is willing to sell the amount of property which the developer feels he can immediately absorb, it results in poor planning and possible negative effect upon the value of the remaining acreage.

"A community builder and land developer must invest a substantial amount of capital in the preparation of a master plan, in order to insure a sound, well balanced community. To insure the highest use of the land and establish the initial program, he must frequently invest an amount of money entirely out of proportion to the number of acres first subdivided. There is usually an extensive advertising program, as well as physical installations required.

"An owner can be shown that it is good business to enter into an agreement with the developer that will give him the necessary protection and incentive to proceed with a program that may take a number of years to complete. The land owner can well afford to set an arbitrarily low price on a portion of the original acreage, in order to assist the developer in making ends meet through the costly pioneering period.

"First, a master plan that merely sets forth the general scheme of the development should be approved by the owner, and an agreement entered into setting forth the acreage prices of the entire property. The owner must recognize the fact that the initial investment on the part of the developer will increase his remaining acreage value, due to the kind of planning that is undertaken. The owner must also realize that it is to the developer's interest to proceed as rapidly as the market will permit. Since the developer has little control over the market, he must be protected against a possible period of inactivity in which he will have his initial effort and capital frozen for some time.

"It is obviously not to the land owner's interest to freeze the developer out because he cannot meet the requirements of an annual purchase. First, the number of years that it will take to develop the property under normal conditions should be estimated. On a large property, this may be at least ten years and preferably fifteen years.

"It is often argued that the developer should agree to purchase a given predetermined number of acres which normally it would be expected he could absorb. It is proper that the owner have some protection against the freezing of his property when a developer fails to carry out his program. To meet this contingency, the owner should require a relatively small purchase each year in order to continue the option. Obviously, if the developer is inactive, he would not care to purchase additional acreage. Thus, the owner would be released from his agreement. On the other hand, if the developer is in good faith, but finds that market conditions are such that it is not feasible to carry out an active program within any given period, he can protect his investment by making the small purchase required. Thus, when conditions are again favorable, he can proceed with increased effort to place his inventoried property. Without this protection, the developer should hesitate to make the essential investment necessary to establish a project as a complete community development.

"The developer should also be privileged to purchase any amount of acreage he desires, to the end that he may freely carry out his engineering and land planning program. In the event the developer purchases an amount of acreage over and beyond a minimum requirement, he should be permitted to apply the excess purchase to future periods. It is important for the land owner to understand that it is to his interests to give the developer every reasonable protection, as it will encourage the developer in making a far more substantial investment than would otherwise be justified."

In areas where rapid growth is taking place, land owners often believe their pastures and fields should bring selling prices which approximate the ultimate value of improved house sites. Builders are finding that prices have risen out of all proportion to the value of the raw land. As a last resort some developers, confronted with prohibitive land costs, have contracted with the original land owner to share the net profits from the land development.

Essentially the scheme is this: by a "Land Development Agreement," the developer agrees to perform the platting, the laying out, the installation of lot improvements and the promotion of the subdivision. The land owner agrees to accept a percentage of the sale price of each lot with a fixed minimum guarantee. Since the original land owner shares in the profits, he is eager to have the developer undertake the work. Such arrangement for participation in a development gives the original land owner an inviting income spread over a period of time and provides the developer with the land he needs at a price considerably below what he might have had to pay.[76]

---

[76] Walter W. Neller, developer, Lansing, Michigan, has found the Land Development Agreement the best way to soften the hard-boiled, hold-out land owner. Minus legal phraseology, important extracts from the Agreement used by Mr. Neller as his solution to the land acquisition problems are as follows: (Party of the first part is the owner of the land. Party of the second part is the developer.)

> "Second party shall immediately take steps to plat the property above described and to obtain the approval of said subdivision from the necessary authorities . . .
>
> "Second party agrees to save first parties harmless from any expense in connection with the promotion, platting and laying out of said subdivision . . . [and] to pay all costs in installing roads, sewers and similar improvements . . . if made during the term of this agreement . . .
>
> "On sale of said lots, second party agrees to pay net to first parties, twenty-five (25) percent of the sale price of each lot sold, with a minimum of $300 per lot.
>
> "As an additional consideration to first parties, it is agreed that they shall be permitted to select without cost to them two (2) building sites, the same improvements to be installed . . . without cost to first parties.
>
> "Second party shall have exclusive management and right of sale of said lots for a period of ten (10) years . . . any lots remaining unsold shall belong to first parties . . .
>
> "The prices of said lots shall be set by second party . . .
>
> "If second party . . . shall purchase for its own account any of said lots in said subdivision, second party shall pay first parties twenty-five (25) percent of the appraised market value of said lots. or $300 whichever is greater . . .
>
> "Second party shall have the right to determine the time and order in which improvements shall be made in said subdivision and the necessity therefor, the said improvements to be put in as sales of lots and business conditions require . . . "

Under recently enacted Federal legislation, called "The Small Business Investment Act of 1958," the builder-developer has opportunities and advantages in financing a land development program as his own small business investment company. In the past, land-improvement loans have been difficult to obtain except on a very short term basis. If a developer, after putting in utilities and other improvements, did not sell his lots fast enough to pay off any short term financing that he had obtained; he was faced with curtailment of operations or with paying off a loan before he could do so from proceeds. Now, under the Act, he can obtain a straight long term loan from 5 to 20 years. Or he can secure an equity capital loan whereby the small investment company would purchase debenture bonds in the development corporation. At their option, the debenture bonds could be converted into stock of the development corporation.[77]

(b) Options and Purchase Contracts

Purchase contracts should be made to cover relatively long periods. Sliding scale options are very advantageous. In some cases it may be necessary to pay a nominal rent to keep the option alive. The danger of loading up with carrying charges on large tracts cannot be too strongly emphasized. Developers who sign purchase money paper for large acreage create a very dangerous liability.

Do not agree to short time payments on land you buy for development—15 to 20 years is desirable with reasonable release clauses. Many land developers have made the mistake of agreeing to short time payments. If possible, carry future purchases on an option basis with annual payments as small as possible. In purchasing land for future development, try to get payments

---

[77] See "Financing the Small Business Investment Company" by Sylvanus G. Felix and John J. Griffin in *Manufactured Homes, the Magazine of Prefabrication.* March and April issues 1959.

Another innovation in purchasing land and for financing development may be available if and when Congress enacts legislation proposed for FHA insurance of neighborhood development loans for the purpose of aiding the creation of an adequate supply of home building sites with proper land planning and improvements through a "neighborhood development corporation". A bill has been introduced to the 86th Congress, first session. Such new self-liquidating program for FHA insurance of neighborhood development loans would assist in financing the purchasing, planning, improvement and marketing of land as planned and protected neighborhood units.

on principal and interest delayed if you expend certain agreed amounts on installing improvements on unreleased land.[78]

(c) Release Clauses

The developer should be able to release any acreage of lots and streets that he needs. He should avoid tying himself up to releasing large blocks at a time.

Once in commenting on experiences in developing the Country Club District of Kansas City, J. C. Nichols offered warnings which still are timely: "Do not fail to anticipate large increased taxes on land held for future development. This occurs because of greatly increased assessed valuations due to successful nearby developments. Tax assessors should not so penalize land held for future developments, but should assess it at wholesale land value.

"Do not assume that your assessor will not unduly tax your unsold lots in a subdivision. This unjustified increase of taxes has broken more good subdividers than any other factor. Unsold lots in the hands of a developer are still wholesale raw land and should not be assessed as lots until sold for a more intensive use.

"Don't forget that the last lots sold, if carried over a number of years with interest compounded, may not even repay your carrying charges to say nothing of the original cost of land and improvements."

One final word of caution is offered by the Council—before purchasing any site for development purposes, investigate your tax situation and explore all angles, both corporate and individual. Whether or not you can take advantage of provisions in the Internal Revenue Service code for exemption, depreciation, capital gains, etc., may or may not affect your decision to purchase or to proceed.

[78] In the 1955-1960 era of land development we have seen the rise of large-scale developers in Florida, California and the Southwest who are in a position to attract big capital and who can purchase thousands of acres ahead of actual development. By spreading their risks, these large-scale developers can buy materials more cheaply and can afford unusually low closing costs for houses on fully improved lots. By big promotions and big advertising campaigns, these developers move their product quickly, thus making savings not available to small-scale subdividers.

Private enterprise has successfully demonstrated that it can open large land areas for new development if it has large-scale financing for land purchases and community facilities. With wise land purchasing, efficient land planning and timely marketing, the economic soundness of large-scale land development by private enterprise has been demonstrated.

SECTION ONE

PART II

Planning the Development

A. SITE INFORMATION FOR PLANNING

1. Survey Maps

There are four kinds of site data required before site planning and development can be intelligently started. These data cover property lines, topography, utilities, and site location. The first three kinds of information are obtained by field surveys and can often be combined on one map.

(a) Property Line Map

This map should usually be at a scale of 1 inch equals 100 feet and should show the following information:

1. Bearings, distances, curve data and angles of all outside boundaries and of block and individual parcel boundaries.

2. Location and dimensions of any connecting streets along the boundary of the property and the intersection lines of any adjoining tracts.

3. Any encroachments on outside boundaries as determined by survey.

4. All streets, alleys, or easements within or contiguous to the property with deed or dedication reference.

5. Names of record owners or reference to recorded subdivisions of adjoining property.

6. Any corner stones, pipes or other physical boundary markers as determined by survey.

7. All U. S., county, or other official bench marks, monuments or triangulation stations within or adjacent to the property, with precise position and description noted.

8. Computed area of all parcels comprising the property in square feet or acres.

9. True and magnetic meridian on the date of survey.

Permanent stone or concrete monuments should be set at each corner or angle on the outside boundary if not already so established. FHA requirements call for complete information on this point.

(b) Topographic Map

Where the site is rough, well-covered with fine trees, or with steep slopes; separate property and topographic maps are desirable. Topographic maps should show the following data at a scale of not less than 1 inch equals 100 feet:

1. Contours—
   - (a) One-foot interval where average slopes are 3 per cent or less.
   - (b) Two-foot interval where slopes are up to 15 per cent.
   - (c) Five-foot interval where slopes are over 15 per cent.

2. All existing buildings and other structures such as walls, fence lines, culverts, bridges, roadways, etc., with spot elevations indicated.

3. Location and spot elevation of rock outcrops, high points, water courses, depressions, ponds, and marsh areas, with any previous flood elevations as may be determined by survey.

4. Size, variety, caliper and accurate location of all specimen trees worth saving, and outline of all wooded areas.

5. Boundary lines of property.

6. Location of any test pits or borings if required to determine subsoil conditions.

Usually sufficient accuracy can be obtained at a cost saving by employing a stadia or plane table survey rather than a cross section survey in obtaining the above data.

The aerial survey is another method for topographic mapping. This stereoscopic method has become a useful technique for topographic map preparation. The aerial method has the advantages of economy and speed. A photogrammetric engineering company can furnish quickly a contour map of any property after the air photos have been taken. The resultant topographic map will be accurate and completely indicative of the physical features of the site.

(c) Public Utilities Map

It is sometimes desirable where the amount of data would make combined maps confusing to provide a separate map at a scale of 1 inch equals 100 feet showing by type:

1. All utility easements or rights-of-way.

2. Location, size and invert elevations of existing sanitary sewers, storm drains or open drainage channels, catchbasins and manholes.

3. Location and size of existing water, gas and steam mains, and underground conduits.

4. Location of existing overhead telephone and electric service and trunk lines, street and alley lighting with pole locations.

5. Location of any rail lines and rights-of-way.

6. Location of police and fire-alarm call boxes and similar appurtenances.

(d) Site Location Map

This map should be prepared at a smaller scale and with a view to possible later adaptation in advertising the development and should include the following information:

1. Location of site with reference to the principal existing and proposed streets and principal approach or approaches.

2. Location and type of built-up areas in the vicinity.

3. Size and extent of nearby shopping centers.

4. Location and type of employment centers.

5. Location and type of transportation lines.

6. Location of churches, schools, parks, playgrounds and other educational and recreational facilities.

7. Zoning and covenants covering adjacent land and approaches to the site.

8. Jurisdictional boundaries.

9. Mile or half mile circles radiating from the site.

B. PLANNING THE SITE

1. Site Planning

Planning the subdivision, or site planning, involves the determination of the specific uses for definite areas of land and the planning of these areas in such a manner that the structures, the means of access and communication, the vehicular and pedestrian traffic, the open areas for recreation, and the areas for houses or other uses are coordinated to produce a unified development which can be built economically, operated efficiently, and maintained or marketed at normal expense. It is a technique that requires the assistance of a person or persons qualified by training and experience in this particular field. (See Part I, B.) It is upon a well ordered arrangement of land and ground forms that the engineering and architectural features are constructed.

It is doubtful if a development has ever been contemplated which in its plan, as proposed, would secure the unqualified approval of all planners or developers. Compromises must always be made. Only wide experience, thorough knowledge of local markets, topography and conditions related to the environment can provide the basis for compromises. No plans illustrated in this book are presented as "perfect" plans. They represent aspects of good planning and construction practice.

2. Neighborhood Planning

"Let us so plan and build," advises Hugh Potter, "as to create stable values and neighborhoods of such permanent character that they will endure for generations."

Neighborhoods are local communities, in a sense, each with well-defined boundaries and with a focus for community life.[79] Neighborhood is defined as the geographic area within which residents may all conveniently share the common services and facilities required in the vicinity of the dwellings. The Council assumes that for planning purposes the extent of the neighborhood is determined by the service area of an elementary school. The neighborhood unit (see Neighborhood Unit Principles, Illustration 22, page 79) involves the concept of comparatively homogeneous groups of families occuping an area sufficient to provide, among other things, a child population for an elementary school of efficient size.[80]

A complete and self-contained neighborhood unit should have sufficient population to support an elementary school and

---

[79] Neighborhood boundaries are generally set either by natural features — such as topography, stream valleys, terrain, etc. — or by demarcations such as freeways, major streets, railroads, non-residential land uses including industrial, commercial, recreational and other open space uses like cemeteries, golf courses, institutions, etc.

[80] See *Design of Residential Areas,* Thomas Adams. Harvard University Press, Cambridge, Mass. 1934.

Illustration No. 22.
Neighborhood Unit Principles

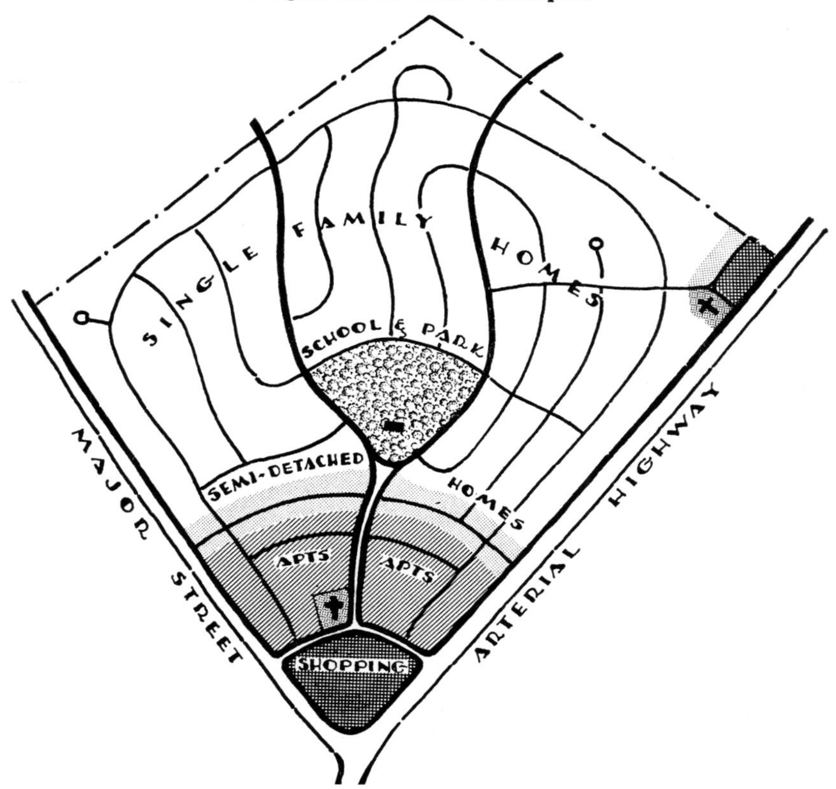

1. *Size.* A residential unit development should provide housing for that population for which one elementary school is ordinarily required, its actual area depending upon its population density.

2. *Boundaries.* The unit should be bounded by arterial streets sufficiently wide to facilitate traffic by-passing the neighborhood instead of passing through it.

3. *Open Spaces.* Small park and recreation space, planned to meet the needs of the particular neighborhood should be provided.

4. *Institution Sites.* Sites for the school and other institutions having service spheres coinciding with the limits of the unit should be suitably grouped about a central point or common, and combined with the neighborhood recreation area, usually.

5. *Local Shopping Center.* If warranted by the population to be served the local convenience shopping facility should be located at the edge preferably at an arterial traffic junction and adjacent to similar commercial districts, if any, of adjoining neighborhoods.

6. *Internal Street System.* The unit should be provided with a special street system, each highway being proportioned to its probable traffic load, and the street net as a whole being designed to facilitate circulation within the unit with good access to main arteries, and to discourage its use by through traffic.

recreation facilities.[81] Its development may provide for local shopping. The unit should be bounded by main traffic arteries and not cut by them. Local streets within the neighborhood should be designed to serve the local needs of residential access and should discourage use of the streets by through traffic. New neighborhood units, whether close-in or outlying, may have a balanced composition of various dwelling types—single-family houses, row houses, two-family houses, garden apartments, high-rise apartments, etc.—at various densities appropriately located for variety in price ranges. Well-planned commercial shopping areas and industrial parks may be established near or in conjunction with several neighborhood units to form a complete satellite community. Soundly planned and properly financed, the new neighborhood units can represent reasonable costs to the home builder, to the home purchaser, to the renter, to the taxpayer and to the local government which services the new areas.

The neighborhood is the basic measurement used by city planners in evaluating elements linked with people and areas for formulating a master or comprehensive community plan. The neighborhood concept is equally valid for guiding the development of new suburban residential land and in redeveloping worn-out central city areas.

The creation of well-balanced, self-contained communities should be the objective of all subdividers and operative builders. For new construction, this can be accomplished more easily when a large tract is under one ownership and one building operation. But the development of a complete neighborhood is not precluded even when there are several small subdivisions in separate ownership in the area. By careful, cooperative planning, these tracts can be integrated into a development that will eventually form a complete community of homes, schools, shops, recreation and other facilities.

The residential land developer should keep the neighborhood concept continuously in mind, both from a standpoint of his own profit and from a sound growth pattern for his city. Isolated or scattered projects for small acreage tracts, or a series

---

[81] With technological changes traditional concepts of the neighborhood built about a community school may come. For example, with any change in physical organization of the school there will be substantial change in neighborhood composition. Since the prevailing use of school buses, the walk-to-school principle has altered the school locational pattern in outlying areas. Similarly, widespread use of closed circuit television may alter the role of the school plant itself.

Illustration No. 23. A Golf Course Subdivision

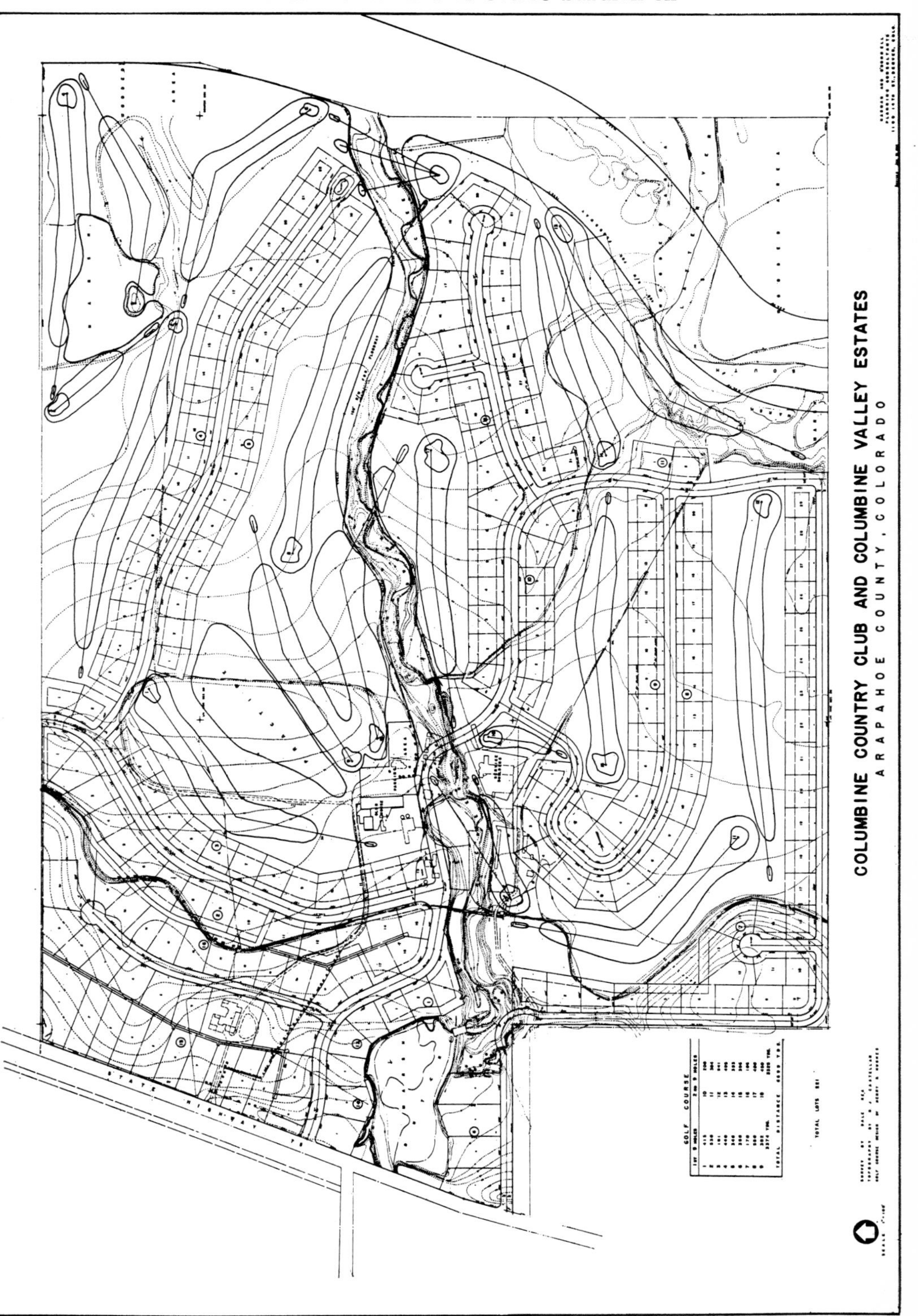

of lots developed with houses strung out along existing highways in rural areas and bearing little or no relation to any neighborhood idea, are a thing of the past. Apart from its wastage of land, this type of urban sprawl is expensive to service and is unsuitable as an urban environment.

It is rare, of course, that a complete and physically integrated neighborhood can be created on less than 200 acres. As this is greater acreage than the average developer can handle, it is recommended that land be selected in or contiguous to a neighborhood already started, or that several operators pool their resources to create the complete community.

This latter method has been used successfully by groups of six or eight small builders to achieve what none could do working alone. By pooling financial resources to buy several hundred or even a thousand acres of land, each cooperating builder can participate in a community development not feasible on an individual basis. Through teamwork the participating builders are assured of a reserve supply of improved lots to build upon without tying up excessive capital in land. Cooperatively, they can hire the best possible land planner to master plan their community. They can afford a top engineering staff and an expert tax consultant to guide their finances. They can buy improved lots on equal terms. They can install the street improvements, water supply, sewage disposal and other community facilities not feasible otherwise. For the small builder, it is a way to solve his problem in finding lots to build upon.

With the growing scarcity of suitable building lots already prepared for house construction in and around large cities and with the high cost in acquiring suitable acrage for development purposes in these areas, the cooperative method of site acquisition, site planning and land preparation represents the practical way for a group of builders to obtain improved lots in a planned and unified community development, rather than in scattered, fragmentary projects.

The neighborhood concept is not limited to raw land development. Planning commissions in their studies for new growth areas of cities or in replanning older sections are using the neighborhood concept as the basis for studies. For example, in Chicago the master plan of land use contemplates the progressive establishment of 59 community units, each containing between 5 and 15 neighborhoods. Their size, type, boundaries and community facilities have been determined on the basis of existing physical barriers and an exhaustive land use survey, and modified in accordance with plans for major thoroughfares, transportation, parks and playgrounds and other physical, social and economic factors.

(a) Effect of the New Highways

The huge interstate system of highways now being constructed under provisions of the Federal Highway Act of 1956 will make vast areas of raw land easily accessible to metropolitan cities.[82] New highways and access roads invite land development, but they do not furnish water supply, sewage disposal and schools. If left unbalanced by such needed development measures, the new expressways can lead to scatteration of small subdivisions sprawled over wide areas without necessary services and facilities. With full-scale planning and a market demand, private enterprise can find the way to create new satellite communities patterned as planned and protected neighborhoods complete with homes served by optimum sized, well-located schools, tied together by an efficient street system and having employment opportunities and shopping facilities in proximity to the residential areas. The development of such projects can contribute to relieving growth problems of the metropolitan city. Consequently, the effectiveness of any such "new town" is likely to depend largely upon the quality of its planning and the extent to which its development is in harmony with the growth of the metropolitan area in which it is located.[83]

---

[82] See *New Highways: Challenge to the Metropolitan Region.* Technical Bulletin No. 31, Urban Land Institute.

See also *Cities in the Motor Age.* Wilfred Owen. The Viking Press, Inc., 625 Madison Ave., New York 22, N. Y., 1959.

[83] For populaton projections and the extent to which urbanization may take place based upon the economy of metropolitan areas, see *Metropolitanization of the United States* by Jerome P. Pickard, Urban Land Institute Research Monograph No. 2, Urban Land Institute. Whether or not our population growth projections coincide with our predictions for the next 40 years, the city with its diversity of people, its complex economic, social and physical structure, its dependence on the national economy, will need to be carefully planned on a regional basis so that the urbanization of the future can be developed along efficient patterns of transportation, water supply, sewerage, public services, etc.

Search for a solution to metropolitan growth problems, including transporation between home and work, leads to consideration of large-scale real estate projects in which employment opportunities and shopping facilities are provided along with residences of varying types. Such terms as "self-contained," "integrated," or "balanced" are used to describe large-scale projects (1,500 acres is a fair measurement of what might be called "large-scale" because at this size land uses other

Illustration No. 24. Belmont—A Realization of Neighborhood Planning Principles

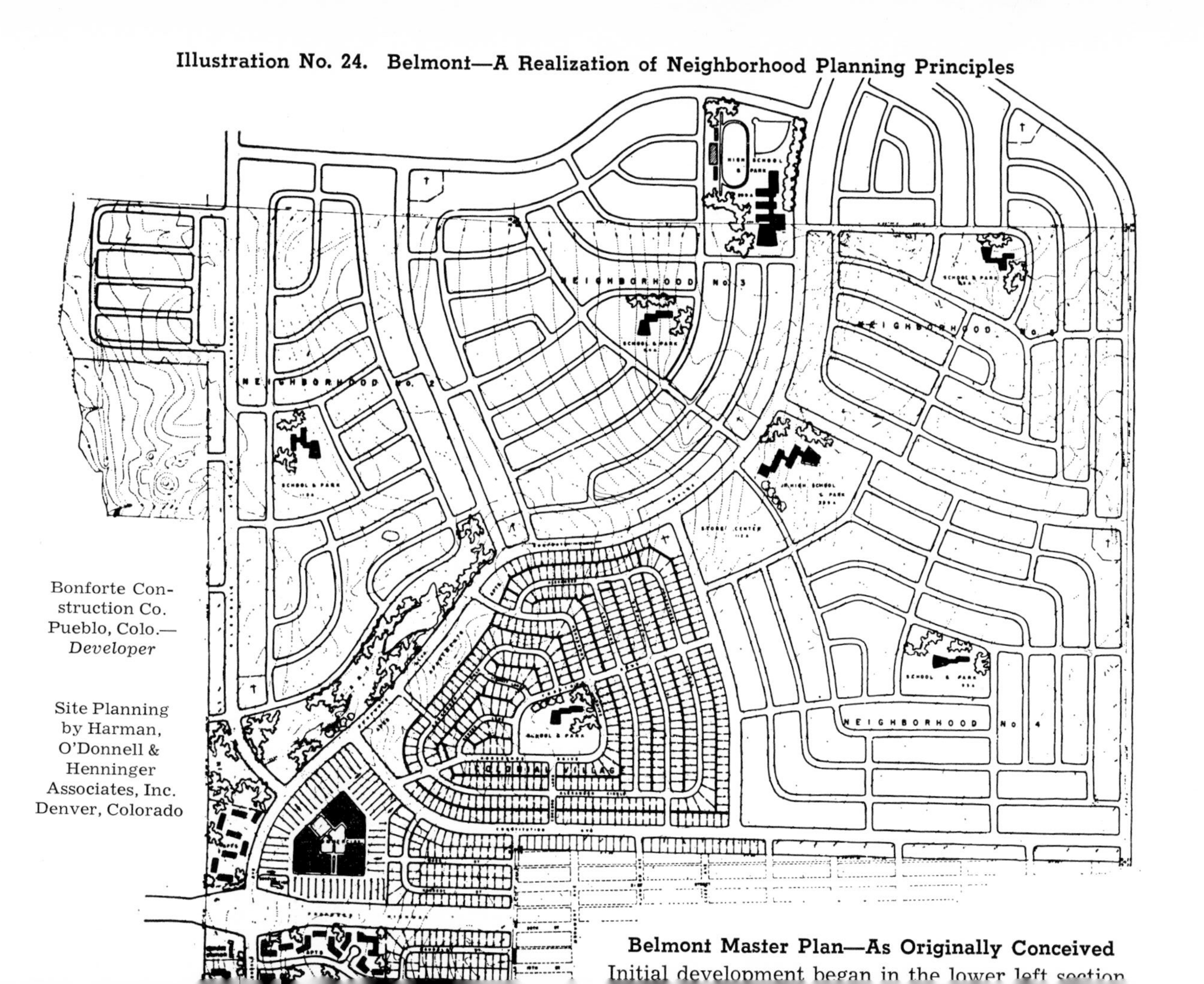

Bonforte Construction Co. Pueblo, Colo.—*Developer*

Site Planning by Harman, O'Donnell & Henninger Associates, Inc. Denver, Colorado

Belmont Master Plan—As Originally Conceived

Initial development began in the lower left

(b) Belmont—A Realization of Neighborhood Planning Principles

To illustrate the principles of neighborhood units as applied to a large-scale community development, Belmont in northeast Pueblo, Colorado, is cited. (See the master plan illustration, page 84, and the plan as constructed, page 86).

The 3,000-acre tract is planned for ultimate development as five neighborhoods, each with a centrally located elementary school combined with park and recreation area. A system of major streets bounds each neighborhood and leads to the main shopping center placed at the entrance to the community from the main access highway. Minor streets are designed to discourage shortcuts and traffic through a neighborhood.

Attention is called to the careful arrangement of land uses in the community plan made by the land planners. A natural valley park is used as a buffer between the shopping center and a neighborhood. Apartments are effectively used as a transitional use between commercial and single-family dwellings.

Construction started in November 1951 in the southern portion. Here approximately 1,600 acres are served by three separate municipal sewer systems. The northerly 1,400 acres await extension of the sewers before development.

Development control of the whole community is retained by the original developer, who built 1,100 homes before turning over subsequent building to other builders who have added another 500 houses to date (1960). Houses built in Belmont vary in price from $10,000 to $40,000. The lowest priced homes are restricted to the eastern and western edges. The highest priced homes are placed on the ridge which runs approximately north and south through the center of the community.

---

than residential must be introduced). Yet these terms allow for misunderstanding of the concept itself. In reality, probably no area less than the complete metropolitan area could be described as reasonably self-contained. Consequently, the community value of any project is likely to depend largely on the quality of planning in the entire metropolitan area in which it is located and the extent to which the development of the project is in harmony with the development of the metropolitan area itself.

Nevertheless, the development of large project areas for a wide diversity of residential uses, including employment opportunities, shopping facilities, recreational and cultural activities, can make a major contribution to the relief of metropolitan growth problems. A "satellite community" must be examined not only for its land use and land planning concepts and for the validity of its specific balance of uses but also from the standpoint of its investment potential. See *Hillsdale-Sacramento, a Panel Study.* Urban Land Institute, 1959.

See also "New Towns for America" by Carl Feiss. *A.I.A. Journal,* January 1960.

Illustration No. 25.
Belmont Master Plan as Constructed to April 1960

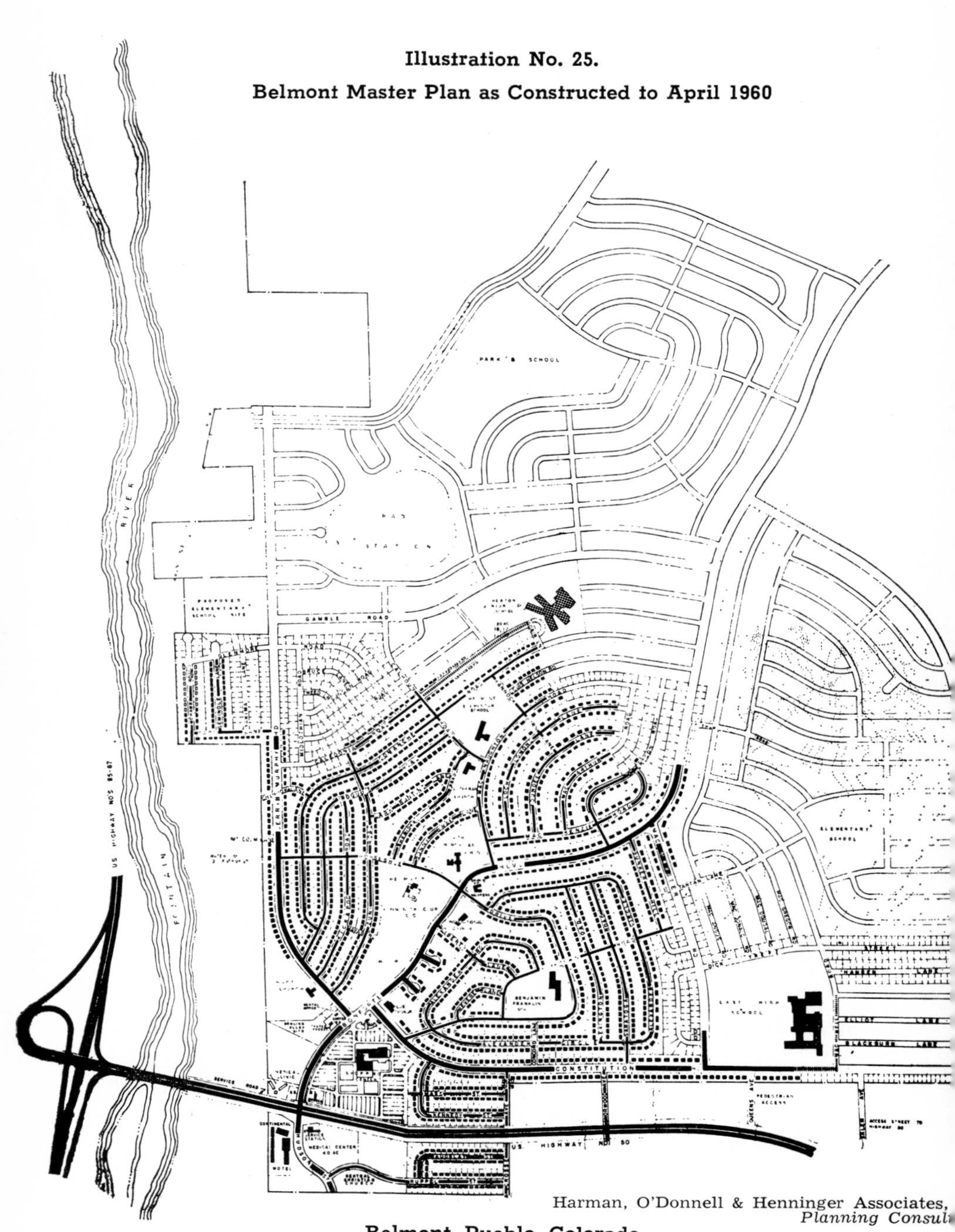

Harman, O'Donnell & Henninger Associates,
Planning Consul

Belmont, Pueblo, Colorado
Extent of development to date is shown in black.

Of the 1,600 acres that are served by existing sewer systems, approximately 800 acres have been developed to 1960, as follows:

Business and shopping area	70 acres*
2 elementary grade schools	20 "
Junior high school	20 "
Senior high school	45 "
Community club	5 "
Park	7 "
5 churches	20 "
Apartments	7.5 "
Unsuable, vacant land	20 "
Freeway right-of-way	12.5 "
Area devoted to housing	573 "
Approximate acreage in use—April 1960	800 acres

* Of the 70 acres in the commercially used area the following division has been made:

Main shopping center	26 acres
Motor hotel area	8 "
Church site	5 "
Medical center	9 "
Service station area (5 stations)	12 "
Streets	10 "
	70 acres

3. Dwelling Density

The total acreage of the site less any unusuable or nonresidential areas multiplied by residential density figures shown in Tables D and E will give the approximate number of dwelling units and thus the population to be accommodated. These calculations can then be checked against your analysis of the market for the project.

Table D
Lot Sizes and Dwelling Densities

Dwelling Unit Type	Lot Dimensions Per Dwelling Unit in Feet	Net Density* Dwelling Units/Acre
Single Family		
Detached houses	100 x 200	2.0
	80 x 160	3.5
	70 x 140	3.3
	60 x 125	4.3
	50 x 100	6.5
Semi-Detached houses	30 x 125	8.7
	26 x 125	10.0
Row houses, two-story	20 x 100	16.3
	16 x 100	20.4
Garden Apartments, two-story		15 - 25
Garden Apartments, three-story		25 - 35
Apartments, multiple story to 12 stories		50 - 85

* Net density represents the number of dwelling units per acre of land within the site, after deducting 25 per cent of the site for allocation to streets, park and recreation areas.

Gross density is computed on the basis of net land area plus area devoted to streets and other nonresidential uses and one-half of bounding streets and one-quarter of bounding street intersections.

Illustration No. 26. Neighborhood Planning Principles Realized (Air View)

Belmont, Pueblo, Colorado—as constructed to April 1960

Bonforte Construction Company, Developer

Harman, O'Donnell & Henninger Associates, Inc., Land Planners

Table E

Lot Areas and Dwelling Densities

Dwelling Unit Type	D.U.'s per Net Acre	Assumed Average Sq. Ft. of Lot per D.U.
Single-family	1	40,000
" "	2	20,000
" "	3	12,500
" "	4	10,000
Two-family	6	6,000
Row house	15	2,600
Garden apartment*	25	1,600
Multi-story apartments*	50	800

* The more intensive the use of land, the greater need there is for recreation space, wider streets and sidewalks, shorter blocks and off-street parking. In multi-family development careful consideration must be given to land coverage and open space needs. High density, multi-family intrusions into single family residential development must be avoided. Apartment buildings must be spaced and located within the project so as to provide transition between residential land uses. The developer of multi-family areas has a responsibility in making such sections of his city fitting, appropriate and serviceable to his community.

4. Price Range and Dwelling Types

Your analyses of the local market and your site location will indicate the price ranges and dwelling unit types to plan for and whether rental units and nonresidential land uses should be included in your project.

Once the construction of homes in any given project was limited to one price class. This restrictive practice has changed. Better balanced and greater stability are obtained by having houses of various price ranges in a single residential community.

A similar change has come about with regard to a reasonable diversity of housing types within the neighborhood. A well-balanced neighborhood plan providing for a variation of housing accommodations will help materially in stabilizing values and in preventing decline by allowing the individual family to adjust its housing requirements to its size, age grouping and income status at any given time and still remain within the community of its choice.

However, in developing a small project of approximately 100 units or less, houses with too great a variance in price range or type should not be mixed. A fairly narrow price variance is undoubtedly the wiser procedure. But in a large-scale project, where a diversified community is being created, a variation in price ranges and in housing types is desirable. It is better to graduate by devoting both sides of a street or a section to each price group with careful transition between.

As John Mowbray of Baltimore observes, "Houses facing each other should be of the same price class and quality. The observer should not be conscious of a sharp transition or values will be adversely affected in the higher priced group. In a large development it is rarely wise to have houses all in one price range. Neighborhoods of low and medium, and medium and high priced houses can be attractively blended if carefully planned. The gradual transition need not be offensive if sufficient care is taken with the architectural design of the houses and careful attention given to site planning."

Based on constant dollars, well designed homes costing 17 to 20 thousand dollars can be blended successfully with those in the 24 to 28 thousand range. Well designed homes costing 12 and 14 thousand are not too wide a variation. Good architectural design and careful site planning make up for variables in sales prices. Finer neighborhood appearance and better street pictures result from careful study of relationships between houses and between houses and their lots. With clean-cut architectural design, well chosen combinations in building materials, and with attention paid to siting houses on the lot for privacy and proper orientation, the net result gives greater marketability than does a wide variation in prices of the houses. Then too, as John Matthews of North Little Rock says, "With the architectural approval covenant coming into more general use, the size and cost of houses in a development becomes less important. A small house in good taste is obviously more desirable next door than a large, expensive monstrosity."

Remember too, under the 1958 Housing Act the FHA down payment to buy a $20,000 house is less than the down payment required to buy a $12,000 house before 1954. Later revisions in the act may cut payments for higher priced homes still lower. With incomes in constant dollars rising about two per cent a year and with FHA requiring no more income to buy a quality house built with maintenance-saving quality materials, the market moves toward better houses built on better lots planned for greater livability.[84]

---

[84] Miles Colean, housing economist. See "The Quality House," *House & Home,* May 1959.

5. Multi-Family Development

Population projections for the 1960's show there will be strong factors at work favoring rental housing units. There will be more young married couples in their early twenties, not yet ready to buy houses. There will be many more older couples whose children have left home and who are ready to give up big houses they no longer need. With longer life expectancy, growth in social security, pension funds and other retirement benefits, more older people will be able to live alone. Single-person households will increase.[85]

Customarily, apartments have been built in cities. With current construction (1960), the trend shows apartment rental units are moving to the suburbs. Where land is too expensive for single-family houses, new construction in garden apartment forms or row houses offers development possibilities for a growing market. Similarly, as urban renewal projects reach land disposition stages (see page 188) the opportunities for rental housing become important to the developer.[86]

(a) Multi-Family Units in the Community Development

As noted previously, recent trends in large-scale residential communities planned on the neighborhood unit principle favor

---

[85] See "Are Urban Land Pressures Easing?" by Robinson Newcomb. *Urban Land,* May 1958, Urban Land Institute.

[86] See "Rental Housing" by Franklin L. Burns. *Urban Land,* January 1959, Urban Land Institute.

See also *Rental Housing, Opportunities for Private Investment.* Louis Winnick. McGraw-Hill Book Company, Inc., New York 36, N. Y.

See also Federal Housing Administration, "Digest of Insurable Loans," "Rental Housing Insurance," and "How to Test Financial Soundness of Rental Housing Properties"; obtainable from your local FHA Office or from FHA, Washington 25, D. C.

See also "Why You Should Look Into Rental Housing," *House & Home,* April, 1958, pp. 103-107.

The shift in housing demand poses problems for home builders and for cities. To satisfy the housing needs of young families, older couples, smaller families and, to some extent, families with lower than average incomes (particularly those displaced in urban renewal and highway construction projects) suggests among other things an increased emphasis on apartments and even mobile homes.

The U. S. Department of Labor and the F. W. Dodge Corp. both are reporting increased interest in multi-family construction. Multi-family construction was important in the days of the "608" program immediately after World War II, but dropped in significance by 1952. In 1956 the percentage of housing starts represented by multi-family units began rising and came to 17 per cent of the total starts in 1958. Part of this increase was due to "tight money" for single-family construction. But apart from the financial factor, the market for multi-family units is rising.

Illustration No. 27.

Example of Good Community Design
Military Housing—Fort Bragg, N. C.

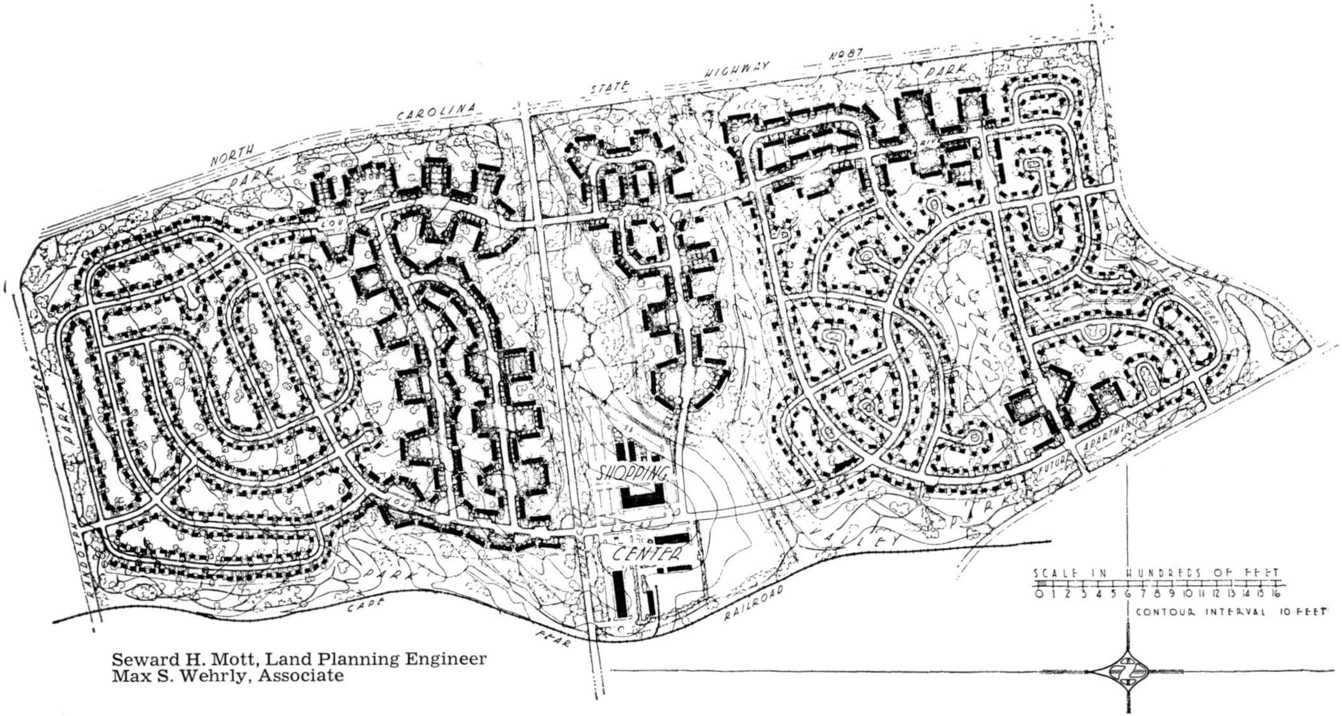

Seward H. Mott, Land Planning Engineer
Max S. Wehrly, Associate

the inclusion of varied types of residential accommodations. Normally, the inclusion of multi-family units, whether in two and three story garden type, high-rise elevator buildings, or row and semi-detached houses, should be confined to projects contemplating a thousand or more units. Such developments are large enough to form complete communities and are typical of urban renewal projects in older, central city areas.

A good location for multi-family units is adjoining the shopping center or grouped on thoroughfare frontage. It is not good planning to scatter them through a single-family area. It is desirable to place a buffer land use, such as a park, school or church between apartments and single-family houses. The use of well designed double houses (semi-detached) between the apartment and single-family areas often provides a good transition. It is usually best to provide for the same type of land use on both sides of a street. The change of use will then be at the rear lot line instead of the street line.

The desirable ratio of multi-family to single-family dwellings will depend on the location of the project, present and future market demand, and local custom. In general, it is desirable to keep the ratio low.[87] Remember local custom and preferences for and against apartments are factors in market demand. Overall standard metropolitan area percentages of total dwelling units indicate that existing multi-family units of all types, as a percentage of all housing units, range from a high of 73 per cent in the New York area to 13 per cent in the Fresno, California, area.

In deciding the amount of multi-family use to build in a residential project, weigh carefully the present-day features of apartment construction which will make them more livable and therefore more rentable.[88] To date, the popularity of apartment housing has suffered because we are accustomed to seeing existing buildings which crowd the land and which have an unimaginative, institutional look. Through good design, it is possible to combine the amenities of suburban houses with the convenience of close-in living. By incorporating the improvements of air-conditioning, sound proofing, larger rooms, adequate wiring, gadget-filled kitchens, ample storage space, outdoor

---

[87] By a "low ratio" is meant 5 per cent to a maximum of 15 per cent of the total gross acreage allocated to residential use within the project (see Allocation of Land Use, p. 102).

[88] See "How to Meet the Big New Market for Better Apartments." *House & Home*, October 1959, pp. 128-185.

terraces, and other appurtenances of the single-family suburban house; new apartments can be built for long-range livability. Frequently the new apartments can have a swimming pool and other club-like features for the exclusive use of tenants. With these improvements, plus low land coverage and attractive landscaping, the architectural appearance of the apartment project holds lures for the suburban-oriented tenant.

(b) Garden Apartments

In outlying communities the so-called garden-type apartment is recommended. Three stories is the maximum height to consider in this type of development which by its very name implies low land coverage and ample open space between buildings. Occasionally a multiple-story building can be introduced into the project to give variety to the development.

The first objective of the investor in rental housing[89] should be to create a property that will retain its market appeal. He must have something that people will want to live in for a long time to come. Otherwise his investment will be unsound, no matter how good or how economical his construction may have been. In order to accomplish this "something with lasting appeal," he must see beyond the average of what is being currently offered. The new project, to be successful, must therefore be not merely as good as its competition; it must be ahead of its time. In specific terms, the principles in rental housing design can be reduced to these:

(1) Low land coverage and plenty of open space.
(2) Privacy and quiet for the individual family.
(3) Adequate and convenient off-street parking for tenants' cars.
(4) Convenient community shopping and recreational facilities.

---

[89] Keep in touch with FHA offices as to current rulings about its Section 207 (rental housing) requirements. For example, in February, 1960, FHA was liberalizing its program to make it easier for sponsors to qualify for mortgage insurance.

Illustration No. 28. Contemporary Apartments

By using larger room sizes, larger windows, by opening apartments to patios and balconies and by adding fences, plantings and swimming pools, among other things, apartments are taking on characteristics of the well-designed house.

Westwood Apartments, Santa Clara, California
David D. Bohannon Organization, Developers

Garden apartments are undergoing transformation in design and are taking on amenities of the individual suburban house. The newest structures (1960) have an attractive, comfortable look. They are losing their impersonal, nondescript appearance.[90]

In land planning the trend is toward lower density with open spaces used to preserve the site in its natural state, using care to preserve existing trees. Where possible, this "garden space" should be kept free of parking with service features carefully grouped. Open space counts for most where there is a lot of it in one place. Small courts and broken-up areas are not only costly to maintain but they do not give the breadth and sweep that is needed to emphasize the impression of open space. The concentration of the open areas in the rear, or off-street side, of the buildings accomplishes this. The open areas provide large private parks for tenants and are free from traffic of any sort. At the same time, the entrance sides of the buildings can be more closely spaced, an arrangement that economizes land where it is not needed and permits savings in paving.

There is a notable trend toward design aimed at giving garden apartments more of the appearance of a well-designed house instead of an institution. By using larger windows and by opening apartments to patios, terraces or balconies, an integration of indoors and outdoors can be achieved. More privacy for individual apartments is obtained by fences, walls and plantings used as screens between patios and between buildings and the street. More apartment units have separate entrances. Interior public corridors are being eliminated in favor of outdoor balcony corridors where the climate permits this form of access. Interior design is being improved by better insulation for noise control, by individual heating and air-

---

[90] See "The New Look in Garden Apartments." *Urban Land,* May 1958, Urban Land Institute. See also "Plan Garden Apartments for People." *House & Home,* April 1959, pp. 129-139. See also "How to Meet the Market for Better Apartments." *House & Home,* October 1959, pp. 126-185.

A new term for garden and high rise apartments built as a large-scale planned development on a large, single ownership tract of land might be "Estate Apartments".

Illustration No. 29. Garden Apartments

In rental housing, the developer must create a property that will retain its market appeal through low land coverage, privacy for each unit, adequate and convenient off-street parking.

Homestead Village, La Grange Park, Illinois
William Joern & Sons, Developers

conditioning, by larger room sizes, bigger storage spaces and better kitchens equipped with garbage grinders, dishwashers, built-in ovens and appliance outlets.

More garden apartments are being equipped with club-like attractions for the tenants, such as outdoor play areas, tennis courts and swimming pools.

To create a garden apartment development with its outdoor and other space attractions means a lower density than apartment projects have provided in the past. Low density as well as low land coverage with a range of from 10 to 15 families per acre is ideal. Not more than 25 per cent of the land covered by buildings in any garden-type apartment project is the absolute maximum coverage—around 15 per cent or less is better. A land coverage of around 25 per cent would result in a little over 20 families per acre for a two-story development, and over 140 families per acre in a twelve-story development. Obviously, no hard and fast rule can be made for density of population in a rental project. What is practical in a suburban area would be impractical in a central city area because of extreme variation in land cost. However, the long-term trend is toward a decline in density throughout our urban areas.

It is now well recognized that the less is the area of streets in relation to the total project area, the better. Limited street areas increase the amount of land for development purposes, decrease traffic hazards, increase privacy and reduce project costs.

Ample off-street parking space *must* be provided. The minimum standard is one parking space per apartment. Additional space for guest parking is practical. The total number of spaces necessary varies with the type of building occupancy and the local conditions. Diagonal curb parking in recessed bays accessible from the access street can be used successfully, if local regulations permit this treatment. From actual experience, the best solution on internal streets which carry no through traffic is to give the street sufficient width to allow diagonal parking on either side of two moving lanes. This arrangement not only provides the maximum amount of parking with a minimum installation of paving but it also places the cars in the most convenient location for tenants and prevents the useless waste of open areas of the property. These private interior parks are the project's best feature, so in arranging the location of off-street parking avoid the use of parking compounds which invade this interior space.

Sometimes, though, simple but well-designed carports in a parking compound are a suitable solution to the off-street parking problem. Under-apartment garages save land on hilly sites, but may raise building construction costs because they require fireproof construction, often with sprinkler systems. The garage problem is interwoven with the parking problem. In most parts of the country car owners no longer consider garages essential and it is almost impossible to make them remunerative. However, where winters are severe, some tenants will insist on garages; in such climates it is advisable to provide a minimum number.

It is essential that every apartment project have conveniently located neighborhood shopping facilities, but it is not always necessary or advisable that these be provided by the development. In fact, where the surrounding conditions are such as to permit more or less unlimited continguous commercial development, the construction of additional shopping facilities may best be omitted. But where the project can control the situation through favorable zoning or natural advantages of location in drawing from a sufficiently wide trading area (see Section Two), a shopping center may be a profitable investment and desirable land use to introduce into the project.

(c) Cooperative Apartments

Another type of multi-family development project suitable for either suburban or in-town locations is the cooperative apartment. A cooperative apartment differs from other types of rental housing only in its opportunities for the investor under FHA Section 213 and in its advantages to the tenant.[91] However, the development plan must be right, there must be a view, and the architectural plan must be good.

Cooperatives have a growing appeal in resort areas. By their elimination of service problems and their supervision during long seasons when tenants live elsewhere, cooperatives have appeal for retired people living on investment income.

In essence, a cooperative apartment means an apartment within a multi-unit building, multi-storied or garden-type, where all the customary apartment services are offered and where

---

[91] See *Cooperative Apartments: Their Organization and Profitable Operation.* National Association of Real Estate Boards, 36 S. Wabash Ave., Chicago 3, Ill., 1956.

the ownership and the cost of operation are shared by the occupants in proportion to the value of the space they occupy.

Most cooperatives have at least half of their costs of construction provided by means of a mortgage. The other half is the equity, which requires no dividends. The dividend comes to the buyer in the form of a lower rent. The result is the assessment or maintenance charge, normally about 30 to 50 per cent under the fair rental value of a similar apartment in a rental building.[92]

(d) Row Houses

The row house has been in eclipse in recent years.[93] There are reasons for this disfavor: The greater flexibility of the automobile for reaching outlying areas, the encouragement of the single-family detached house by insuring agencies, and the higher net income and larger size of families, generally. But the major objection to row houses of the past has stemmed from their drab monotony and lack of good design in their floor plan, architecture and site planning.

These faults combined to bring discredit to an otherwise basically sound and suitable type of housing accommodation. Its success as a sound and stable investment, both for rental and home ownership, has been favorable.

The row house offers a development opportunity for both suburban and in-town sites. With densities of 15 to 20 families per gross acre of site, including access streets, row houses have site development costs lower than comparable garden apartment projects and can have elements of privacy and proprietorship not possible in the multi-family structure.

To create a market demand which the row house is capable of generating, the following items should be included in a row house development:

1. Heightened prestige and desirability factors: For example, "group house" or "town house" are fresher descriptions than is the term "row house".

2. The prestige factor needs backing both inside and out by ingenuity, imagination and design quality on the part of the builder, his architect and site planner.

---

[92] American Society of Real Estate Counselors. Summary of Round Table Discussion. January 24, 1959.

[93] See "Row Houses Emerging as a Popular Mode of Living" by Max S. Wehrly. *Journal of Homebuilding,* October 1959.

3. Rear garden oriented units are essential. With integral garage, entrance and service features placed on the street side, terraces for outdoor living accessible to a fenced or walled garden area or common open space on the rear are needed. Rear service and narrow light wells are taboo. Units must be only two rooms deep.

4. A twenty foot width should be the minimum for today's "open planning". Any width less than 16 feet is obsolete. Lots measuring 20 x 90 to 100 feet in depth will accommodate 22 to 24 two-story units per net acre. This density and lot width accommodates two-story units having attributes of the present-day detached house including integral garage, two bedrooms and bath, front setback and rear garden. An additional half-story containing heating and air-conditioning unit, storage space and a studio room is entirely feasible where basements are omitted. For units with second-story rooms side by side, lot widths of 22 to 25 feet are essential.

5. Party walls must be fully sound-proof. Building lengths should not be long—six to eight units in one building are appropriate.

6. Carefully prepared protective covenants covering exterior architecture, use of house, yard or garden spaces and any common areas are a prime requisite.

In the tastefully designed, fully up-dated, contemporary row house, a new housing type is available to use for problem sites suitably located and for satisfying a growing market demand in the younger and older age group families.

(e) Impacts of Multi-Family Development

Municipal officials and community leaders are wise to examine carefully all aspects of proposed projects which differ in dwelling type from those they are accustomed to seeing. Frequently, zoning debates rage in residential areas where developers seek permission to build apartments. Usually owners of private houses in a nearby neighborhood take opposition to proposed rental housing schemes, thinking perhaps that the new use will "down-grade" their area. It matters little when emotions are involved, what the plans call for. Opposition is generally based on two underlying points: Aesthetics—that single-family houses are superior to all other types; social standing—that people living in apartments or rental units are on a low rung of the social ladder.

Many times the opposition is warranted. But if a project is soundly conceived and designed for extremely low land coverage[94] with broad, open space for landscaping and recreation and with ample off-street parking, then the community must evaluate some of the more "practical" aspects of apartments vs. single-family houses: Which type of project generates greater numbers of school children; in which are public service costs higher, etc.?[95] The answer for the community logically lies in refined planning and zoning regulations adapted to large-scale community development, which require the ample open space, parking and density provisions to insure the site design and architectural appearance in apartments which are becoming increasingly common.[96]

6. Allocation of Land Use

As a preliminary step in designing the street and block layout of the site, numerous sketches will be made by the land planner before the ultimate site plan is determined upon. In these preliminary designs, study of the physical characteristics

---

[94] As noted in the discussion of garden apartments, page 94, land coverage of 15 per cent is recommended.

[95] In its study of Bratenahl Village, Urban Land Institute found the following relationships between children of school age and dwelling unit types:

Single-family	.7 children per d.u.
2 story garden type apartments	.27 " " "
10-12 story high-rise luxury type apts.	.1 " " "

Bratenahl Village, A Report to the Sponsor. Urban Land Institute, 1958.

See also *Municipal Costs and Revenues Resulting from Community Growth.* W. Isard and R. F. Coughlin. Chandler-Davis Publishing Co., Wellesley, Mass.

See also *The Cost of Municipal Services in Residential Areas.* W. L. C. Wheaton and M. J. Schussheim. U. S. Department of Commerce, Washington 25, D. C.

[96] See "Zoning for the Planned Community" by Fred W. Tuemmler. *Urban Land,* April 1954, Urban Land Institute.

See also "Zoning of Planned Residential Developments" by Eli Goldston and James H. Scheuer. *Urban Land,* March 1960, Urban Land Institute.

Illustration No. 30. The Long, Low Look in Houses

Lot sizes generally should be larger to offset the large single-family house being built today. On minor streets in single-family areas and in large lot development, sidewalks may be eliminated without objection.

The Village, Wichita, Kansas
Town and Country Estates, Inc., Developer

of the site, any controls superimposed by peculiar circumstances of access, adjacent uses, comprehensive area plans, zoning, utility rights-of-way (if any cross the site), etc., together with the density of family units and type of dwelling to be accommodated, will make adjustments for the allocation of land use within the site and the area to be devoted to streets, residential sites, recreation, schools, shopping, and such similar elements within the development.

In general, areas allocated to *non-residential uses* within the neighborhood tract should not exceed 35 per cent; 20 per cent is the norm for area devoted to streets;[97] 10 per cent in public open space; 5 per cent in commercial use[98] are other measurements for preliminary allocation of land use. In thinking about the site in terms of lot sizes, street layout, school and other public areas, the land use allocations will be very close to the practical if residential use approximates 60 per cent of the area with the other 40 per cent assigned to other uses, including streets. As indicated, a low percentage of the total area devoted to streets approaches the ideal.

Recreation areas should seldom be less than two to two and one-half acres in extent if they are to be of any great value to the community. Small children's play lots, however, can contain as little as 4 or 5 thousand square feet.

Schools and recreation areas for older children should be internal to the development except where they are designed to serve more than one neighborhood and should be combined as discussed on page 57. Rough land, such as stream valleys not adaptable to building development, will often lend itself to

[97] Area in street allocation, depends on density of development. For a subdivision of single-family houses 25 per cent devoted to street rights-of-way approaches a maximum for efficient use of the site. Of course, innovations in site design or introduction of housing types other than single-family detached houses will alter the standard percentage of the total acreage allocated to streets.

[98] For a shopping center as part of the development, allocation of area for that purpose depends not on an arbitrary "standard," but on the analysis of the market, the trade area, and other factors which set up justification for a shopping center (see Section Two).

Illustration No. 31. The House and the Car

With the common use of the automobile there has been a transformation in the orientation of the house. The motor car approach to the house has created new use for the lot, new design for the house and re-location of its living areas. The street entrance and the service side of the house are the same.

Gerholz Community Homes, Inc., Flint, Michigan, Developer

open space use. Steep hillside sites are not of much value for active recreation areas, however, and school and playground sites should be reasonably level or capable of being made so without undue grading. It is seldom advisable to locate either of these uses directly on a heavily traveled highway. Libraries usually desire an easily accessible location near a main thoroughfare, and form a good buffer between business and residential areas.[99]

7. Block Size and Arrangement

The physical character of the site should have strong influence on the design of blocks, their size and shape. But often local custom and regulations set the pattern. Some cities still require that new streets be continuations of existing streets and that straight alignment be adhered to regardless of topography, function of the street, or integrity of a neighborhood. Such arbitrary regulation forces blocks into rigid patterns for the sake of engineering uniformity and is highly undesirable in planning for a new residential neighborhood.

Experience by Community Builders' Council members finds that block patterns in lengths up to 2,000 feet are practical under proper conditions, though 1,800 feet is more usual. In general, long blocks are practical; short blocks increase street area, raise development and maintenance costs, introduce more traffic hazards. Long blocks normally should lie in the direction of main local traffic flow for convenience in reaching major neighborhood objectives—the school, the bus stop, the local shopping center, etc.

Once, cross walks through a long block were considered desirable; actual experience has proven them impractical. They are disliked by abutting property owners. They are little used, and are difficult and expensive to maintain. Of the cross walk, John Taylor has this to say: "We dedicated and improved several pedestrian ways in long blocks. They have not proved desirable. Only in an extreme case, do we feel they are justified. If such pedestrian ways *are* built, we suggest omission of all adjoining planting. Even so, adjoining home owners fear trespass and vandalism from narrow pedestrian ways near their homes." Similar experience by other members leads to the strong Council

---

[99] For area wide principles which should rightly be considered in library site selection see *The Effective Location of Public Library Buildings* by Joseph L. Wheeler. University of Illinois Library School, Urbana.

recommendation that cross walks be eliminated from single-family residential development, except in very unusual situations.

Use of long blocks eliminates unnecessary cross streets. This can produce up to a 20 per cent saving in street and utility costs over the short block plan and provides more front selling feet. Based on years of satisfactory experience with the long block, the Council urges that municipal authorities revise their subdivision requirements, where necessary, to permit block lengths up to 2,000 feet with proper regard for storm drainage and focal points already mentioned, thereby promoting economies in development and maintenance and greater freedom from intersectional traffic hazards.

From long blocks we derive the so-called "superblock plan" wherein deep blocks are penetrated by a series of short culs-de-sac (see page 131). An adaptation of the superblock scheme is used in garden apartment site plans. In this kind of rental housing development, wherein maintenance is part of the centralized management's responsibility and service, interior block parks with their cross walks are practical. But to adopt the interior park[100] as a principle in block design for single-

---

[100] The superblock plan is frequently referred to as the "Radburn Plan." For a complete presentation of the Radburn Plan and its design principles see *Toward New Towns for America* by Clarence S. Stein. University Press of Liverpool, 1951.

When Radburn, N. J., was built in 1928 it embodied a number of ideas that had older roots. A critical need led Henry Wright, the planner, and Clarence Stein, the architect, to combine these ideas and create the first major innovation in town planning since the garden city concept, the need for a design that would enable people to live with the automobile with a minimum of danger and friction. Mr. Stein in his book (see above) lists the features that made Radburn "a town for the motor age" roughly as follows:

(1) the superblock;

(2) single purpose instead of all-purpose roads, separating storage, movement, collection and other functions;

(3) separation of pedestrian and vehicular traffic, both vertically and horizontally;

(4) the house "turned around";

(5) the park as the backbone of the neighborhood, with open spaces in the superblocks joined as a continuous park.

In a number of later developments, the "Radburn Idea" was evolved further through the elaboration of the form of the superblock and the arrangement of the roads and open spaces, notably in the "green-towns" built by the Resettlement Administration in the late 1930's. Here it was combined more successfully with the garden city and neighborhood unit concepts.

One might expect that the ensuing 23 years would have seen steady progress in these principles of town building, considering the spectacular advances that have taken place in technology, the high level of prosperity that has prevailed through most of that time, the proliferation

Illustration No. 32.
Common Mistakes in Lotting

Existing streets and property lines are often controlling factors. Several common mistakes made in lotting are shown below. If the street can be relocated, it is worth the trouble.

When diagonal streets cannot be avoided:

Lot this way

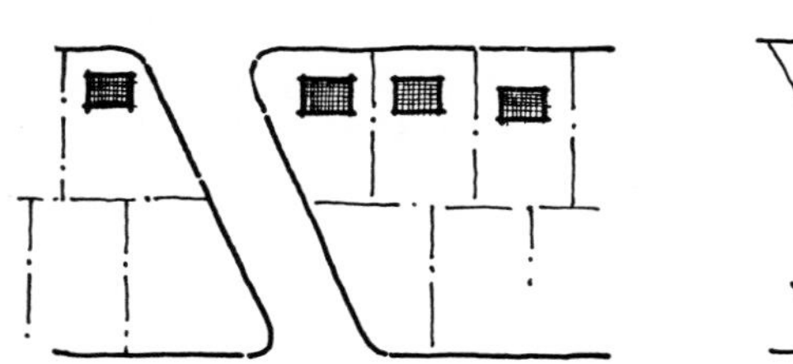

Not this

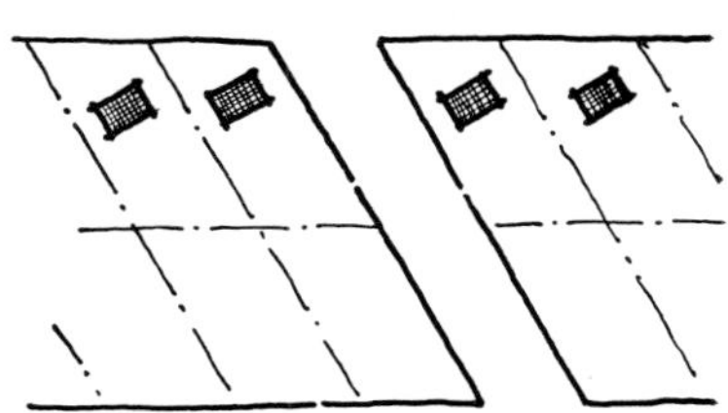

When existing intersecting streets form acute-angled intersections:

Lot this way

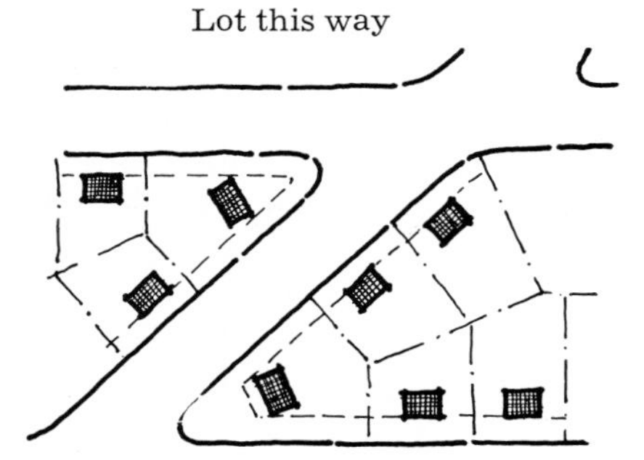

Not this

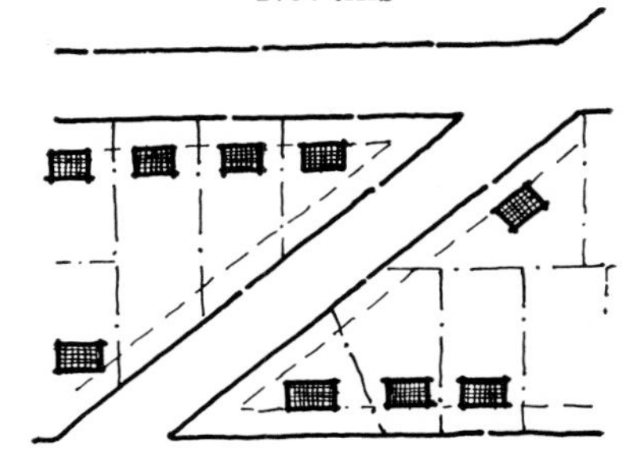

Where future street extensions are not required in corners of the property:

Lot in this manner

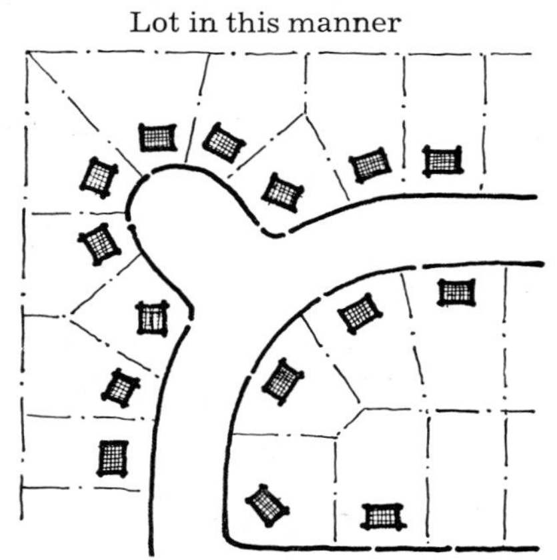

Not this

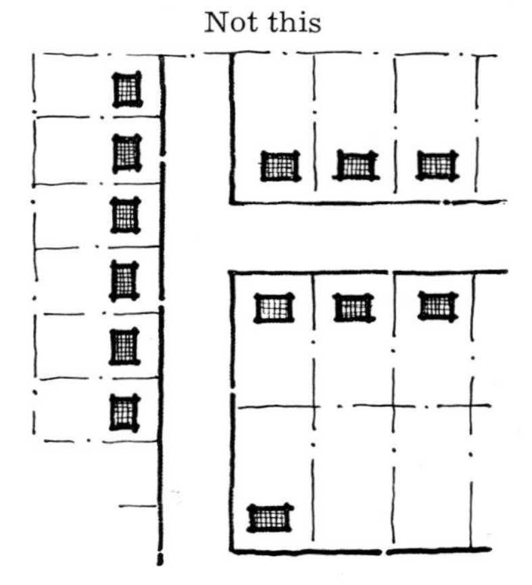

family detached houses built for sale under individual lot ownership is not recommended because of the park maintenance and access problem. Such schemes call for close cooperation and a homes association of the individual families over a long period. Until we have careful analysis and comparisons of all development costs in the superblock plan as against a conventional block development plan its economies may not be borne out. It is hoped that findings for comparative costs of development will be provided by phase two of the NAHB-ULI Subdivision Innovation Study. See footnotes 101 and 128.

The superblock is one of the innovations in land planning. During the 'fifties the single-family house standing on its own lot has been the dominant pattern in residential land development. With rising costs, both for the raw land and for the lot improvements, the price of housing for our growing America continues to go up. Concern about the economics and efficiency of the single-family lot development pattern points to the need for new thinking in anticipation of our housing growth in the 'sixties and after. New and modified patterns and forms of organization for single-family row house and apartment development concepts can be applied to the residential land development when the innovations are justifiable by their economics or by their marketability.[101]

8. Lotting

(a) Lot Size

While minimum lot area and frontage provisions are a function of the local zoning ordinance, specifications for the level of improvements to be installed in new developments come under subdivision regulations.

Lot sizes for single house units vary throughout the country, with local custom acting as an important factor. In the Detroit area, and in many southern cities, lots of greater depth than 100 feet are preferred; while in some West Coast cities, lots 100 feet in depth are the accepted standard. Where the lot and the

---

of suburban growth, but above all the greatly increased impact of the automobile as a dominant force in American life. Instead, while we find such advances in the British new towns and Kitimat, Valingby and Chandigarh (all of which draw heavily on the American new towns of the 1930's), there have been few examples in our own country.

[101] See the research study on innovations in land planning, sponsored jointly by Urban Land Institute and the National Association of Home Builders, to be released as a *Technical Bulletin,* January 1961.

house are sold as one package produced by the developer, shallow lots may be introduced when careful siting of the house and good design are used. Where lots only are developed for sale, larger lot sizes are desirable to allow for purchasers' individual preferences and for custom-built houses. In this latter case, as Council member J. W. York of Raleigh, North Carolina, says: "We think that lot sizes generally should be larger to offset the type of larger house being built today."

In level sections of California, low-priced properties have been developed satisfactorily with shallow lots of no more than 90 feet in depth. In the north, where two-story houses have been customary, the minimum lot size recommended is 60 x 120 feet or 7,200 square feet in area. In the south and west, in warm

Illustration No. 33.

Diagram Showing Good and Poor Lotting Practice

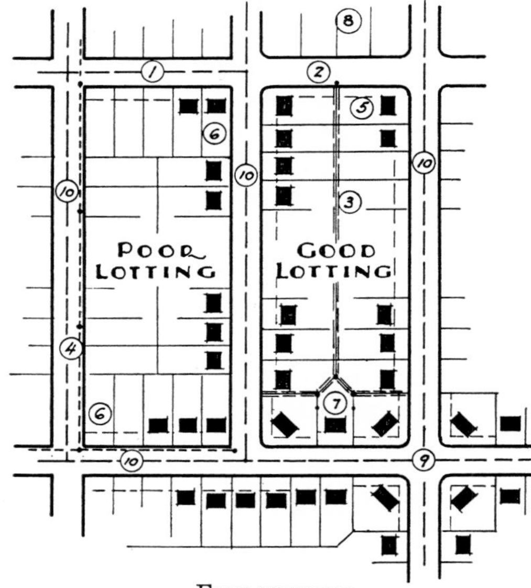

EXPLANATION

1. Excess underground utilities at end of block required.
2. No underground utilities at end of block.
3. Rear overhead utility easement.
4. Street overhead utilities.
5. Increased corner lot width.
6. Corner lots too narrow.
7. Good use of butt lot.
8. Butt lots require extra utilities with bad view down rear lot line.
9. Good lotting at street intersection.
10. Required underground utilities.

climates, or where the one-story house is used, at least a 70 foot lot width is recommended. The wider lot frontage throughout the country is occasioned by the new "long, low look" in houses with the attached carport or garage and by the increase in floor area square footage of the house itself.

In general, lots less than 70 feet wide are not suitable for the true rambler. The "long low" house type may be placed lengthwise on a narrower lot, but this placement is not recommended by the Council unless the house plan and house grouping permits additional open side yard space. Given the same lot depth, land development costs for the wider lot will increase proportionately.[102]

Certain economies can be effected to offset the cost of wider lots without affecting the livability of the subdivision. One-story houses can be placed closer to a street line without the appearance of crowding as long as space between houses is carefully related to room arrangement. This is especially feasible where the living room is in the rear. Again, it is pointed out that, given the same gross floor area, the house with the "long low look" will have larger lot coverage than will the conventional two-story house, leaving less open yard space. This is acceptable to the buyer as long as the total lot area is not decreased. Thus, if a lot area of 7,200 square feet is held, the overall density of the project will not be increased and a lot approximately 70 x 100 will result. While the same lot area can be obtained, there will be normally fewer lots for any given tract of land as more street will be required per lot. So the developer inevitably will be faced with some additional land development costs per lot.

Today, the builder-developer has the opportunity of designing his house type to suit the topography, size and shape of the

---

[102] See *The Effects of Large Lot Size on Residential Development.* Technical Bulletin No. 32, Urban Land Institute.

This study suggests that substantial economies can be achieved by the developer and home owner in large lot districts (i.e., where lot areas are 15,000, 20,000 and 40,000 square feet and above) if the requirements for certain improvements are waived and the standard of certain others is adjusted with lot size in a manner appropriate to low density character of single-family development. For instance, sidewalks, curbing and grass strips, pavement type, or reduction in number of catch basins are adjustments in the specifications which can be made for low-density development. The important element in subdivision approval regulations of the lot improvement standards is that these specifications be flexible for the character of development. A single-family area of 40,000 square foot lots need not be developed with street improvements on minor streets called for by a development at 4 families per acre.

lot which he is creating. Although variation in house types and design are desirable, it is possible to carry diversification too far. Different styles of houses should be carefully coordinated, not just mixed together. Improper relationships between the lot size and the house placed upon it can be prevailing faults decreasing the livability and long-range value of a project. Houses that are too large for their lot produce inadequacies in side yards and other open area, despite their conformance to a specified dimension of the official subdivision regulation. This fault of lot crowding makes it difficult to offer good orientation and use of the lot in site planning.

In lotting it is important to fit the house to the lot and to make adjustment in house placement to take advantage of the natural contours and natural stands of trees on the site. Finer neighborhood appearance results from studying the relationships between houses and between houses and their lots, instead of rigidly adhering to set lot specifications. With carefully selected combinations of exterior materials and with attention paid to sitting the house on the lot to provide privacy and good orientation, the net result is greater benefit to the purchaser, savings in site development costs and greater marketability of the product for the developer.

Under present-day land developer-merchant builder operations, where the total building program is carried out as part of the subdivision development and where the house type can be related to the size and topography of the lot, careful design and layout will permit lots to be 100 feet deep. In such cases, public regulation of lot size (through zoning or subdivision codes) by density of development rather than by dimension enables greater flexibility for the land planner and site developer.

Hillside development is another situation which calls for special consideration of standardized subdivision regulations on the part of planning commissions and land developers.[103] Inflexible imposition on hillside developments of subdivision regulations designed for close-in flat land often makes land development so expensive that the steep land is by-passed or developed improperly. Developers of these special tracts, usually in areas of low density, need leeway in the matter of lot sizes, lot shapes, frontages, rights-of-way, street widths, easements and setbacks. In such developments the most informal development consistent

[103] "Hillside development" is generally defined as being in areas having a natural slope of the ground in excess of 10 per cent.

COMPUTING CHART

TO FIND THE TOTAL COST OF AN IMPROVED LOT (RAW LAND AND STREET IMPROVEMENTS)

COST OF RAW LAND DOLLARS PER ACRE — SCALE A

5,000 — 4,800 — 4,600 — 4,400 — 4,200 — 4,000 — 3,800 — 3,600 — 3,400 — 3,200 — 3,000 — 2,800 — 2,600 — 2,400 — 2,200 — 2,000 — 1,800 — 1,600 — 1,400 — 1,200 — 1,000 — 800 — 600 — 400

TOTAL COST - DOLLARS PER LOT INCLUDING RAW LAND & STREET IMPROVEMENTS

100'X200' SCALE F: 5,800 — 5,700 — 5,600 — 5,500 — 5,400 — 5,300 — 5,200 — 5,100 — 5,000 — 4,900 — 4,800 — 4,700 — 4,600 — 4,500 — 4,400 — 4,300 — 4,200 — 4,100 — 4,000 — 3,900 — 3,800 — 3,700 — 3,600 — 3,500 — 3,400 — 3,300 — 3,200 — 3,100 — 3,000 — 2,900 — 2,800 — 2,700 — 2,600 — 2,500 — 2,400 — 2,300 — 2,200 — 2,100 — 2,000 — 1,900 — 1,800 — 1,700 — 1,600 — 1,500 — 1,400 — 1,300 — 1,200 — 1,100 — 1,000 — 900 — 800 — 700 — 600 — 500

70'X140' SCALE E: 3,300 — 3,200 — 3,100 — 3,000 — 2,900 — 2,800 — 2,700 — 2,600 — 2,500 — 2,400 — 2,300 — 2,200 — 2,100 — 2,000 — 1,900 — 1,800 — 1,700 — 1,600 — 1,500 — 1,400 — 1,300 — 1,200 — 1,100 — 1,000 — 900 — 800 — 700 — 600 — 500 — 400 — 300

60'X120' SCALE C: 2,600 — 2,500 — 2,400 — 2,300 — 2,200 — 2,100 — 2,000 — 1,900 — 1,800 — 1,700 — 1,600 — 1,500 — 1,400 — 1,300 — 1,200 — 1,100 — 1,000 — 900 — 800 — 700 — 600 — 500 — 400 — 300

70'X100' SCALE D: 2,900 — 2,800 — 2,700 — 2,600 — 2,500 — 2,400 — 2,300 — 2,200 — 2,100 — 2,000 — 1,900 — 1,800 — 1,700 — 1,600 — 1,500 — 1,400 — 1,300 — 1,200 — 1,100 — 1,000 — 900 — 800 — 700 — 600 — 500 — 400 — 300

COST OF STREET IMPROVEMENTS DOLLARS PER FRONT FOOT — SCALE B

25 — 24 — 23 — 22 — 21 — 20 — 19 — 18 — 17 — 16 — 15 — 14 — 13 — 12 — 11 — 10 — 9 — 8 — 7 — 6 — 5 — 4 — 3 — 2

— INSTRUCTIONS —

LAY STRAIGHT EDGE ACROSS SCALES "A", "B", "C", "D", "E" AND "F" SO THAT IT CROSSES SCALE "A" AT THE POINT REPRESENTING THE COST OF RAW LAND PER ACRE, AND CROSSES SCALE "B" AT THE POINT REPRESENTING THE COST OF STREET IMPROVEMENTS PER FRONT FOOT. THE READING AT THE POINT WHERE THE STRAIGHT EDGE CROSSES SCALE "D" INDICATES THE TOTAL COST OF AN IMPROVED 70 FT. BY 100 FT. LOT; WHERE THE STRAIGHT EDGE CROSSES SCALE "C" INDICATES THE TOTAL COST OF AN IMPROVED 60 FT. BY 120 FT. LOT; WHERE THE STRAIGHT EDGE CROSSES SCALE "E" INDICATES THE TOTAL COST OF AN IMPROVED 70 FT. BY 140 FT. LOT; WHERE THE STRAIGHT EDGE CROSSES SCALE "F", INDICATES THE TOTAL COST OF AN IMPROVED 100 FT. BY 200 FT. LOT.

EXAMPLE: WHERE THE COST OF RAW LAND IS $1,800 PER ACRE, AND THE REQUIRED IMPROVEMENTS COST $14 PER FRONT FOOT - PLACE THE STRAIGHT EDGE ON SCALE "A" AT $1,800 AND SCALE "B" AT $14.

FOR 4.2 LOTS PER ACRE - 60'X120' - READ ON SCALE "C" $1,270, THE COST OF AN IMPROVED LOT.

FOR 4.3 LOTS PER ACRE - 70'X100' - READ ON SCALE "D" $1,400, THE COST OF AN IMPROVED LOT.

FOR 3.1 LOTS PER ACRE - 70'X140' - READ ON SCALE "E" $1,560, THE COST OF AN IMPROVED LOT.

FOR 1.5 LOTS PER ACRE - 100'X200' - READ ON SCALE "F" $2,600, THE COST OF AN IMPROVED LOT.

- NOTE -

IN THIS CHART APPROXIMATELY 30% OF THE GROSS ACREAGE IS ALLOWED FOR PUBLICLY DEDICATED LAND.

LOT SIZE	NET LOTS PER ACRE
60'X120'	4.2
70'X100'	4.3
70'X140'	3.1
100'X200'	1.5

IN ARRIVING AT THE TOTAL COST OF EACH IMPROVED LOT AN ALLOWANCE MUST BE ADDED TO THE FRONT FOOT COST FOR THE INSTALLATION OF IMPROVEMENTS IN THE CROSS STREETS ON WHICH NO LOTS FACE. THIS ALLOWANCE WILL VARY FROM 12% TO 40% DEPENDING ON THE LENGTH AND WIDTH OF BLOCKS.

AN ADDITIONAL ALLOWANCE FOR RAW LAND COST SHOULD BE MADE WHERE LARGE PARK AREAS ARE DEDICATED.

Source: Federal Housing Administration Data Sheet SA-401.

with good access and proper drainage should be allowed.[104] Steep topography frequently necessitates unusually deep lots or narrow frontages. Very careful site planning is needed to use the land efficiently without excessive site grading.

For modest priced single-family houses lots of too great depth should be avoided, as the excess depth is not used and becomes unsightly through lack of maintenance. Generally, wide shallow lots have better market appeal than narrow deep lots, but the cost of street improvements will be greater for the wider lots because of the increased frontage. (See footnote 102 preceding.) Ordinarily, the old rule of thumb for relation between the depth and width of a lot holds true for single-family detached houses—that is, the lot depth should be twice its width.

Where row houses are developed, shallower lots are acceptable, with lot widths ranging between 16 feet to 25 feet. However, 90 to 100 feet should be a minimum lot depth.

For low and medium priced developments lot width is an important factor in controlling the cost of street and utility improvements for the developer initially and for the home buyer

---

[104] See "Design and Development of Hillside, Large Lot and Resort Subdivisions" by George C. Bestor. *Urban Land,* March 1958, Urban Land Institute.

See also "Practicalities in Residential Land Development" by David D. Bohannon. *Urban Land,* January 1959, Urban Land Institute.

Hillside development requires special site treatment of individual lots, thus indicating a custom type of building operation and site planning. To impose the same specifications as for level land necessitates earth moving operations and transformation of the natural site. So for hillside development it is recommended that special subdivision regulations be adopted by governmental jurisdictions. For these special hillside subdivisions, variations prohibited in general subdivision ordinances are necessary. Driveway easements used by two or three lot owners can be worked out, approved by the regulatory body and made a recorded obligation of future owners without fear of the easement becoming a public maintenance obligation.

For hillside subdivisions, street widths can be lowered safely. For a service cul-de-sac or minor loop street, a 40 to 42 foot right-of-way with a pavement width of 20, 24, or 26 feet can be provided, depending on the length of street and number of houses it is to serve. Where buildable land is limited by steep topography, the width of right-of-way is important. A 20-foot pavement with U-gutters and strategically located streetside parking bays permits roads to fit the topography and to preserve fine specimen trees where a 35- or 40-foot pavement required for flat land would only blast the site and mar the area's charm and natural amenities.

Illustration No. 35. Livability in Land Development

Lots should be planned for more enjoyment of the lan
Open land is what many families move to the suburbs fo

Pine Spring Gardens, Fairfax County, Virgin

Keyes, Smith, Satterlee & Lethbridge, Architects and Land Planne

ultimately as Council member Robert Gerholz of Flint, Michigan emphasizes.

In residential developments beyond the reach of municipal water supply or sewage disposal facilities and where driven wells and septic tanks must be on the same lot, minimum lot areas must be increased to 20,000 square feet to avoid possibility of contamination, nuisance and health hazards. A septic tank sewage disposal system sets minimum lot size. Minimum requirements for septic tank sewage disposal vary widely throughout the country depending on the composition of the subsoil and underlying rock. Minimum standards in such cases are prescribed by the local or state health authority. Be sure to check the governing regulations.

(b) Lot Lines

The laying out of lots should not be done casually or left wholly to your engineer. Careful restudy of lot lines with due regard for topography can frequently result in thousands of dollars increased value by the creation of more desirable and usable home sites. This is more often possible where lots are larger with more flexibility in lot line location, but should by no means be overlooked in close development. Qualities which should be sought in lot layout as determined by lot line location should include:

1. A favorable site for placing the house without requiring excessive grading, footings or foundation walls. The question should always be asked—"Does the lot contain a good house site?"
2. Usable land to front and rear for lawn, garden, etc.
3. Adequate surface drainage away from house location with slopes generally toward the street or rear, with reasonable grade for garage and driveway approaches from the street.
4. Minimum amount of grading, and retention of specimen trees beyond the house location.

Side lot lines should be approximately at right angles to the street or radial to a curved street and, except where dictated by topography on large size lots, should be straight. Rear lot lines

Illustration No. 36. Building for Privacy

Developing the lot for family privacy involves, among other things, the increased use of high walls, fences and planting material. These elements are integral parts of the house and its lot and should not be omitted from the initial project.
Gerholz Community Homes, Inc., Flint, Michigan, Developer

also should normally be straight and avoid acute angles with side lines except under special topographic conditions. Odd-shaped lots are hard to sell. Just a few such difficult lots and hangovers through the years can make your project a financial loss. Streets that intersect at acute angles make poor shaped lots. Such intersections should be avoided. It is desirable that where there are utility easements along rear lot lines, the lot lines be as straight and long as possible in order to avoid an excessive number of manholes, poles, and guy wires at angle points.

As John Matthews of North Little Rock puts the matter of lot lines: "Curved rear lot lines are very questionable. Straight runs at the rear of lots are highly desirable to eliminate excessive guy lines, overhead wires across the rear of lots, complicated fencing and complicated lot surveys."

(c) "Butt" Lots

A so-called "butt" lot is not desirable or economical except where the ends of blocks face lot frontages across a street. As shown by Illustration 33, the butt lot utilizes street frontage and utilities and closes off any unsightly view down rear lot lines from the block opposite.

Corner lots should be from 10 to 20 per cent wider than interior lots in order to provide an adequate yard space on the side street. A 10 to 15 foot differential in building set back between the side yard of the corner house and the front yard of the adjacent house on the same street is permissible depending on lot size. Where 25-foot front yards are required, at least a 15-foot side yard on the street side of the corner lot is desirable. Corner lots approximately square in shape permit diagonal placement of the house and provide both for a transition with the side street, an interesting grouping around the street intersection and an adequate sight distance for automobiles entering the intersection.

(d) Lots Abutting Traffic Arteries

When the property faces a heavy traffic street, there are several ways to protect residences from traffic noise and distraction. Most of these suggestions will increase improvement costs but create more desirable, easier marketable lots. From the traffic point of view it is highly desirable to keep both the number of individual driveways and the number of street intersections with main thoroughfares to a minimum.

1. Lay out deep lots with houses backing on the traffic way and screened from it by fence or wall and planting. To be suc-

cessfully done, the developer should erect the wall or fence and do the planting as part of the site development. This will insure a consistent treatment along the traffic frontage which is essential for appearance and permanency.

2. Face houses toward the highway and lay out a planting strip 20 feet or more in width between the traffic way and an access street to serve the houses. The access street introduces an additional setback from the original property line, thus providing for a buffer against traffic noise and hazard. The lots facing the traffic artery then have a marketability otherwise lacking.

3. Construct short cul-de-sac or loop streets, extending in from the highway with lots laid out so that no houses face directly on the traffic way.

4. Face houses on the highway but with some additional setback, and service them from alleys or rear drives, permitting no individual driveway entrances to the highway. While some developers dislike this type of treatment, it has been successfully handled in a number of developments.

5. Face houses on the intersecting streets with driveways on the side streets, with kitchen and service on the highway side but opening on the rear yard. This, of course, will increase the number of street intersections on the main highway, but is usually less costly, only from the initial development cost standpoint.

Local conditions and preferences will govern the method which will best serve the particular case. See Illustration 37.

9. Building Lines

Building lines may be set by subdivision regulations or by the zoning ordinance. The required dimensions should usually be considered as a minimum and not a standard. In any case, minimum building lines should be included in the protective covenants to assure adequate front yards and building setbacks, and to provide for better relationships among property owners, and between property owners and the community. The size and depth of the lot and character of the street will affect the amount of setback required. Building setbacks also depend upon street width, and may vary from five feet where hillside property is involved to as much as 50 feet or more on major highways to avoid noise, fumes and dirt. Setbacks of 25 to 30 feet from the property line on minor residential streets have become fairly standard. However, where the land developer is also construct-

Illustration No. 37.

Methods of Subdividing Along Heavy Traffic Ways

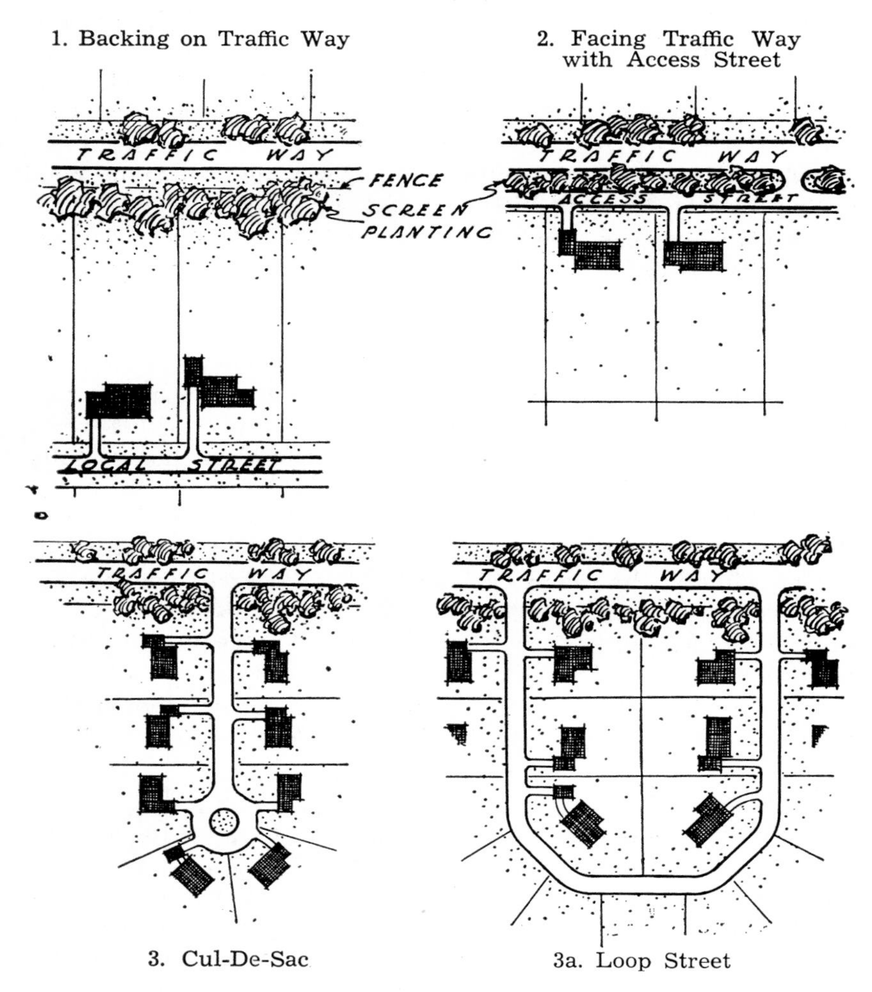

ing the houses, lesser setbacks of 20 or even 15 feet, in some cases, may be used satisfactorily if attention is given to proper house grouping and street width.

Where living quarters are in the rear, lesser setbacks may be entirely satisfactory, particularly where one story structures are involved. Use of the integral curb and sidewalk will also increase the apparent setback of the house from the street; and the lesser setback creates more rear garden space. Economies are also obtained by shortened utility connections, and driveways to attached garages. Garages attached to houses should set back at least 20 feet from the property line to allow for off-street parking in front of the garage or carport.

For greater interest, varied setbacks have been used by placing building lines on alternate groups of lots back 5 to 15 feet. Care should be taken in the arrangement of setbacks. Do not stagger every other lot, but rather try to group the houses, giving consideration to their architecture, the location of drives and service yards, and the alignment of the street. Varied setbacks are not necessary on curved streets, but will help to avoid a monotonous line when used on long straight streets.

Maurice Read suggests that it is the proper procedure to have your land planner and architect make a plan showing the location of each house on a street, possibly with a colored sketch of each house elevation, so that the relationship of the houses to each other is clearly evident. In a large housing project where a limited number of house plans and elevations are used, this procedure will be found invaluable in selecting the house types and the variations in plan and elevation that go well together, not only for the best street "picture" but for the best treatment of each lot.

Regarding corner lot setbacks, Hugh Potter states: "There should be a flexible arrangement for side yard setbacks on corner lots. We have been using 15 to 20 feet with the right of the developing company to reduce it if they so desire."

10. Streets

Location of major streets should conform to the master street plan for the community. This may mean that a few of the more important streets of the community may have to be continued through the development and be of greater width. Other streets preferably should be planned to discourage their use for through traffic by introducing well-spaced T-intersections.

Fire protection should be considered carefully. Plans should be checked with local fire officials for hydrant location, cul-de-sac turn-arounds, access to buildings, etc.

The street pattern should relate properly to the major and secondary street plan and to site terrain. Natural drainage courses or ridges can often be used to advantage as street locations. Avoid a gridiron pattern of streets; it is monotonous, inefficient and costs more money.

Illustration No. 38. Subdivision Planning Standards

SUBDIVISION DATA
TOTAL ACREAGE 24.4
RESIDENTIAL LOTS 101
LINEAL FT. ROADWAY 5200
LINEAL FT. FRONTAGE 6800
PARK ACREAGE 1.1
TYPICAL LOT 60′ x 125′

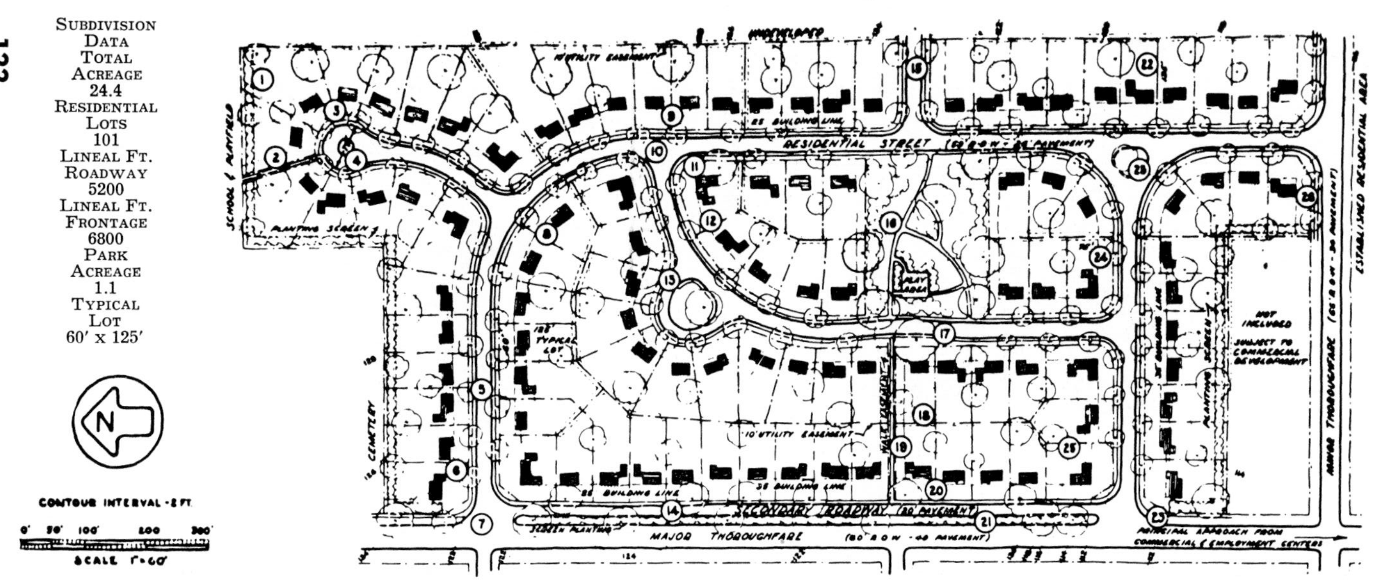

1. 15 foot easement for planting screen to provide protection from non-residential use.
2. 10 foot walk easement gives access to school.
3. Cul-de-sac utilizes odd parcel of land to advantage.
4. Turn-around right-of-way 100 feet in diameter.
5. Street trees planted approximately 50′ apart where no trees exist.
6. Additional building set-back improves subdivision entrance.
7. Street intersections at right angles reduce hazards.
8. Lot side-line centered on street end to avoid car lights shining into residences.
9. Residences opposite street end set back farther to reduce glare from car lights.
10. Three-way intersections reduce hazards.
11. Property lines on 30′ radii at corners.
12. Lot side-lines perpendicular to street right-of-way lines.
13. "Eyebrow" provides frontage for additional lots in deeper portion of block.
14. Secondary roadway eliminates hazard of entering major thoroughfare from individual driveways.
15. Provision for access to land now undeveloped.
16. Neighborhood park located near center of tract. Adjacent lots wider to allow for 15 foot protective side line set back.
17. Pavement shifted within right-of-way to preserve existing trees.
18. Above ground utilities in rear line easements.
19. 10 foot walk easement provides access to park. Adjacent lots wider to allow for 15 foot protective side line set back.
20. Variation of building line along straight street creates interest.
21. Screen planting gives protection from noise and lights on thoroughfare.
22. Lots backing to uncontrolled land given greater depth for additional protection.
23. Low planting at street intersections permits clear vision.
24. Wider corner lot permits equal building set back on each street.
25. Platting of block end to avoid siding properties to residences across street.
26. Lots sided to boundary street where land use across street is non-conforming.

NOTES TO ILLUSTRATION NO. 38

Subdivision Planning Standards

The diagram opposite, prepared by the FHA,* illustrates many of the standards advocated by the Community Builders' Council. Modifications of Items 2, 11 and 19 are indicated by experience. Plan indicates kind of information which should appear on any good development plan.

This subdivision provides 101 desirable building sites for low cost houses. A majority of the houses face east or west and will, therefore, receive sunlight into their front rooms at some time during the day. In the preparation of the plat for recording, lots should be numbered consecutively throughout the entire tract.

The street plan is adapted to the topography and provides for surface water drainage. The number of entrances from the major thoroughfare is limited. The street pattern facilitates the flow of traffic from the principal approach. Curved streets create greater appeal than is possible in a gridiron plan. The long blocks are desirable and reduce expense for cross streets. This subdivision does not require its own system of major thoroughfares. However, recognition is made of the present and planned roadway pattern of the city in which it is located by reservation of a right-of-way for connection to adjacent acreage when it is developed.

A subdivision of this size does not require provision for complete community facilities, such as stores, schools, and churches, necessary in a full-scale neighborhood.

Complete information regarding the site and its relation to the town or city of which it is a part is essential to the planning of a desirable residential neighborhood. Not only is it necessary to have a closed, true-boundary survey but also complete topographical data, including locations of existing trees that are to be preserved. The capacity of storm and sanitary sewers should be known. The adequacy of a safe water supply system and the existence of other essential utilities, and of transportation facilities, are important factors bearing upon suitability of the tract for development purposes.

Residential subdivisions should be located where they will not be adversely affected by industrial expansion and other non-conforming uses. They should be in the trend of residential development of similar type homes. To further assure stability, residential areas should be safeguarded by recorded protective covenants, and the establishment and enforcement of a zoning ordinance governing the use of the property and surrounding areas.

---

* For each of its 75 insuring offices, FHA issues a local Land Planning Bulletin No. 3, *Neighborhood Standards*. It contains:

a. general advice to developers and builders,

b. generalized national Requirements stated in broad objective terms,

c. definite local standards showing typically acceptable methods of meeting the Requirements,

d. more detailed technical data for the guidance of sponsors' technicians.

Street improvements and subdivision exhibits are fully covered in these bulletins. See also *Minimum Property Standards for One and Two Living Units*. FHA.

(a) Street Widths

There is the tendency in many municipalities to require excessive widths for minor single family residential streets. This is reflected in a similar tendency to require excessive roadway pavements. The Council is of the opinion that *minor street rights-of-way in residential neighborhoods of single-family detached houses* should not exceed 50 feet with roadways not greater than 26 feet from face-of-curb to face-of-curb.

In these neighborhoods car parking space must be provided by individual driveways provided on each lot; hence, the 26-foot pavement width is sufficient for slow moving traffic and for one lane of parallel curb parking. Remember, the primary function of the *minor* residential street is that of access to abutting property and not for traffic movement as such. The 26-foot width allows adequate space for car movement in backing out of individual driveways which have proper radii. Provision for two moving lanes *plus parking* requires 33 to 34 feet of pavement, invites fast traveling, increases initial paving costs by 20 per cent, and adds a like increase to future maintenance.

On *major* residential streets which must act as *collector* streets for traffic originating in the neighborhood, on streets adjacent to shopping centers and other focal points, and for serving garden apartment or other multi-family developments, 60-foot street widths with 34 to 36-foot pavement widths are satisfactory.

In summary, street improvements are essential elements in the creation and maintenance of stable and attractive residential areas. In a new subdivision, the required widths of street pavements should be established to provide adequately for traffic and parking needs *based on the functional classification* of each street without imposing excessive improvement costs for either the initial construction or later maintenance.[105]

---

[105] The responsible developer has no objection to installing at his expense such utilities, including street pavement, as are required for the site improvements he needs in creating the residential lots of his own project. However, he does object when excessive demands are made for utility installation, street pavements or assignments of area not for the benefit of his own project. Specifications in the subdivision approval ordinance should be geared to the type, the size and the price bracket of the project with which the developer is working. But if, under specifications of the subdivision regulations, the developer is required, for example, to install and pay for roadways that are to be paved heavier than his project needs, or if he is required to provide trunk sewers or water lines intended to serve areas beyond his immediate project, then the

Pavement widths for streets in a residential subdivision as recommended by the Community Builders' Council are:

36 feet for collector streets;

34-36 feet for minor streets for row houses and *within* a garden apartment development;

26 feet for minor streets of single-family detached houses.

Right-of-way widths, similarly recommended (except for hillside conditions) are:

60 feet for collector streets;

60 feet for *minor* streets within a multi-family development;

40-50 feet for *minor* culs-de-sac and streets of single-family detached houses.

(b) Sidewalks

Many cities require the construction of sidewalks on both sides of the roadway in all residential subdivisions. However,

---

municipality has exceeded the bounds of equity and reasonable requirements.

Oversized utilities or community facilities needed beyond the project are charges against the municipality-at-large or, at the very least, are a proratable charge against the areas to be benefited by the installed conveniences of the immediate project.

Where standards for street widths and paving, sidewalks, and other utilities are not related to the type and density of the subdivision project, such regulations form a deterrent to economical development. There are proper adjustments for scaling improvements to the character of development. For example, a street's *function* should determine the specification for its width and paving. A minor street serving single families differs in function from that of a trafficway serving a multi-family or commercial development.

"The principal point to be made here is that while subdivision specifications are a desirable and necessary form of public regulation when reasonably drawn and exercised, they can easily become excessive in their requirements and an unreasonable burden on the developer and new home owner."

See *Utilities and Facilities for New Residential Development—A Survey of Municipal Policy*. Technical Bulletin No. 27, Urban Land Institute.

As cited earlier, an excellent guide to the form, content, and organization of the subdivision ordinance is found in the booklet, *Suggested Land Subdivision Regulations*. HHFA. For sale by Superintendent of Documents, U. S. Government Printing Office, Washington, D. C. Reprinted 1957.

on minor streets in single family areas, two sidewalks are frequently unnecessary and in open development of large lots of 100 foot frontage or more, sidewalks may be eliminated without objection. The Council questions whether sidewalks contribute to the safety of children as accidents usually occur when they run into the roadway or emerge from behind parked cars. Sidewalks tend to encourage use of the street for play rather than off-street areas such as the rear yard or a playground. The Council recommends a sidewalk on at least one side of the street, in general, *except* in large lot, low density or open development, as noted. In special situations such as along a school frontage two sidewalks are needed.

On major residential streets that serve as collectors of traffic from minor streets, as approaches to the school, bus stop, shopping center, and other focal points of the community, and where densities exceed five families per net acre; sidewalks are usually needed on both sides of the street.

Four-foot sidewalks are sufficient on minor streets, although sidewalks three feet six inches in width have proved entirely satisfactory where combined with rolled curbs. Greater widths are unnecessary except where leading and adjacent to shopping centers and other focal points. In any case, all utilities such as poles and fire hydrants should be kept out of the sidewalk width.

The integral sidewalk and curb is suitable for minor and for collector streets, although its use in northern climates complicates snow removal. For this reason, such construction is objected to by city engineers. In the snow belt area sidewalks should be at least three feet from the curb if there are no trees between the sidewalk and the curb. If there are street trees, the distance should be at least seven feet. Driveway aprons which break the sidewalk level are an objectionable feature of the combined sidewalk and vertical curb, but can be obviated

Illustration No. 39. Street and Lot Improvements

Use of vertical curb integrated with sidewalk. The respo
sible developer has no objection to installing at his exper
such utilities, including street pavement, as are required
the site improvements he needs in creating residential l
of his own project. He does object when excessive demar
are made for utility installation, street pavement or assig
ments of area not for the benefit of his own project.

Westwood, a project by David D. Bohannon Organization, San Mateo, Califor

GREENWAY DRIVE

by the use of the rolled curb. Settlement is one feature to watch in the construction of the sidewalk continguous to the curb. This may be avoided if the sidewalk subgrade is thoroughly prepared prior to placing.

(c) Rolled Curbs

Rolled curbs (see illustrations 40 and 41) are favored by the majority of the Council and have been universally accepted in many parts of the country. They provide a pleasing unbroken street line, do not require expensive curb cuts for driveways such as are necessary with the straight curb, and are one of the most practical cost reducing items in street consideration. The objection has been made that the rolled curb encourages automobile parking on the sidewalk or grass strip. This has not been found valid by Council members who have used it. But on steep grades the rolled curb is impractical and is not recommended in hillside development.

The rolled curb can be easily and quickly laid by use of a steel template with only front and back forms. At street intersections, curb returns with a radius of 15 feet are recommended. At such points, the rolled curb should be warped into a straight curb. This discourages corner cutting by automobiles and avoids the danger of a pedestrian's slipping on a sloping surface at the crosswalk, especially by women wearing high heels.

(d) Car Clearances

Concern has been expressed by the Council over the tendency among automobile designers to reduce the ground clearance and increase the overhang of cars. The result is that some cars cannot clear ordinary changes in grade such as driveway aprons, rolled curbs, commercial garage ramps, and streets in hilly areas, without damage to the car. It is recommended that developers investigate new car clearances when

Illustration No. 40. Street and Lot Improvements

Use of the rolled curb and planting strip between curb and sidewalk.

Lakewood, North Little Rock, Arkansas
John Matthews Company, Developers

Illustration No. 41.

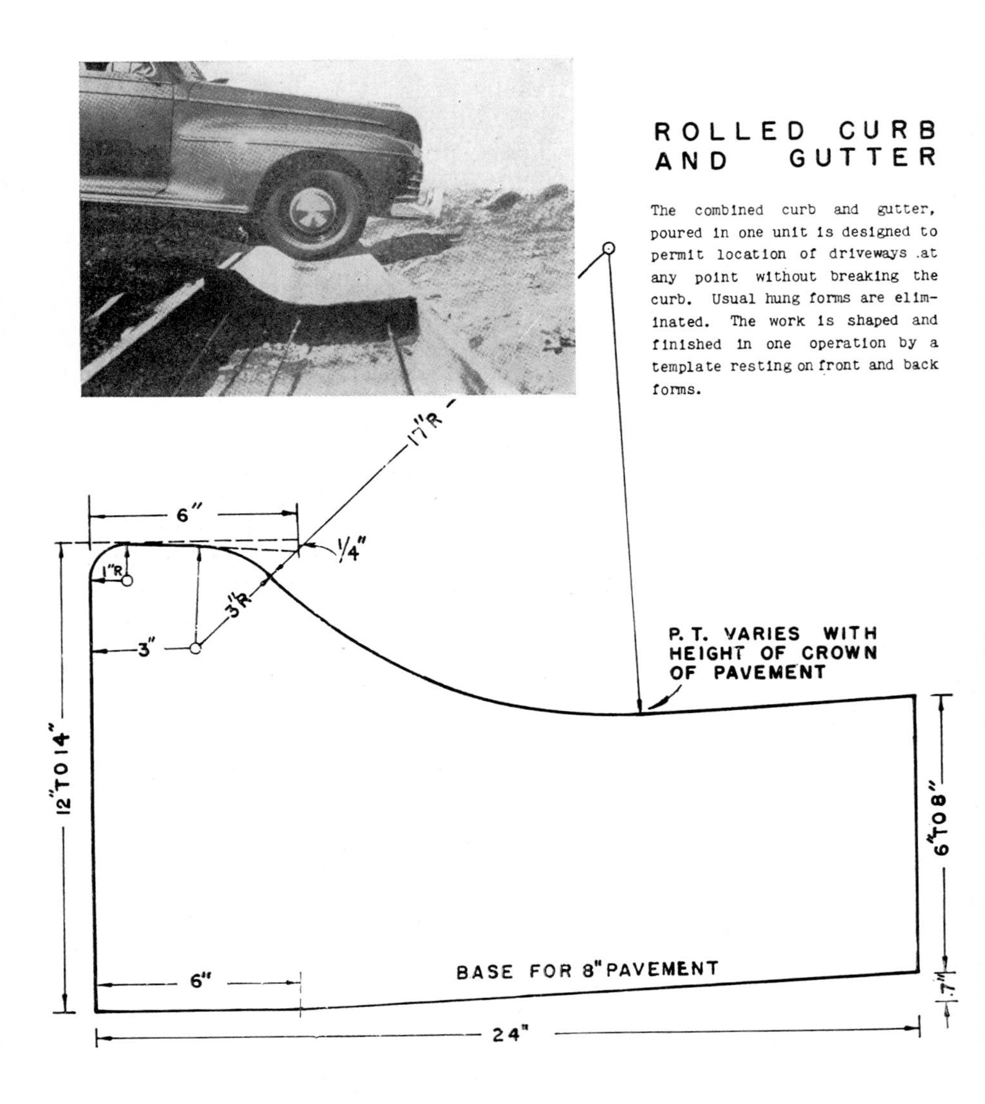

ROLLED CURB AND GUTTER

The combined curb and gutter, poured in one unit is designed to permit location of driveways at any point without breaking the curb. Usual hung forms are eliminated. The work is shaped and finished in one operation by a template resting on front and back forms.

Illustration No. 42.
Rolled Curb

laying out new areas and advise residents in their developments of car models in which this difficulty is to be encountered.[106]

(e) Culs-de-Sac and Loop Streets

Culs-de-sac are dead-end streets with a turn-around for cars. Culs-de-sac are one of the best street types to use in single-family development because of the privacy offered to the houses

---

[106] According to the U. S. Bureau of Public Roads, today's cars (1959 models) will not scrape their bumpers if the sag in vertical curves has a 75-foot minimum radius. The underbody will not scrape if the crest in vertical curves has a minimum radius of 45 feet. The testing staff of Ford Motor Company recommends a vertical sag of at least 90 feet. This requires not more than 5 per cent change in slope between any two 10-foot chords. Thus, the ramp over a 6-inch curb should be at least 10 feet long. Another recommendation decreases the curb height from 6½ inches to 5½ inches across the driveway and sags the walk grade by one inch.

As shown by the accompanying illustration 43, L. A. Bauer, expressways engineer, Cincinnati, Ohio, feels that the safest way to design these critical driveways and roadways is to make a model study. He makes a model cutout of one of the longest cars (1959 model):

Over-all length	19 feet
Wheelbase	133 inches
Rear bumper clearance	12½ inches
Front bumper clearance	9 inches
Underbody clearance	6 inches
Front wheel to bumper	35 inches
Rear wheel to bumper	60 inches

His procedure to avoid trouble is first to design the driveway or roadway to available standards; next, plot the profile on a natural (2:1) scale; third, slide the cutout model over it and make the needed adjustments.

Illustration No. 43.
Critical Clearances Applied to Vertical Curb

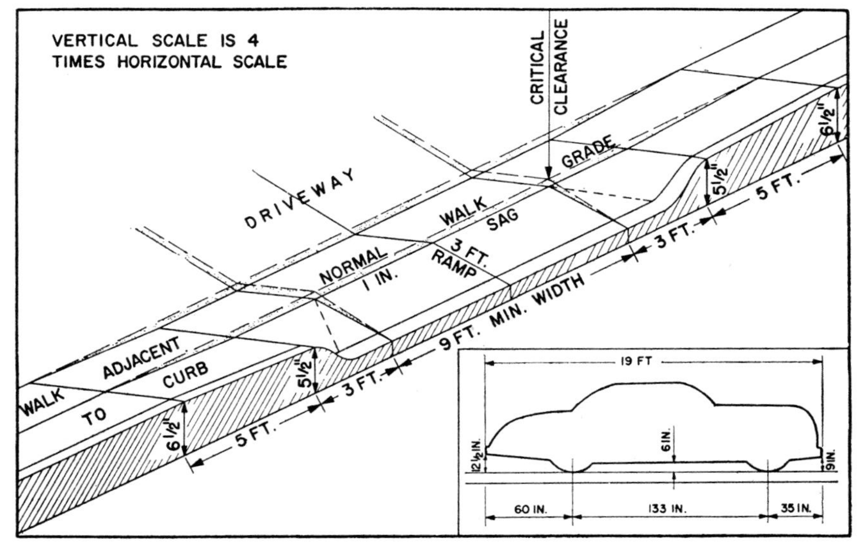

Source: The American City, April 1959.

so served. On this point, David D. Bohannon of San Mateo, California, says: "These are the most desirable locations in the entire subdivision. We get a premium price for cul-de-sac lots for the obvious reason that they provide the house sites most desired by our customers." He continues to say: "Many cities in California are trying to discourage subdividers from planning developments with cul-de-sac streets—apparently because the postman and some other delivery men and the fire department don't like to double back."

Culs-de-sac streets are satisfactory when they are not over 500 feet in length and have a turn-around at the end with a minimum radius of 40 feet from the center of the circle to the outer curb. Any more than 20 single-family houses served by a cul-de-sac lengthens the dead-end travel and induces motorists to pull into a private driveway instead of waiting to reach the turn-around at the street end. Pave the entire turn-around circle. A small grass plot in the center is useless, expensive to install and maintain and is apt to be unsightly.

There is objection, however, to overuse of culs-de-sac in any one subdivision as they then present problems of sewerage and drainage, dead-end water mains and refuse collection. Such

Illustration No. 44.
Culs-de-Sac and Their Uses

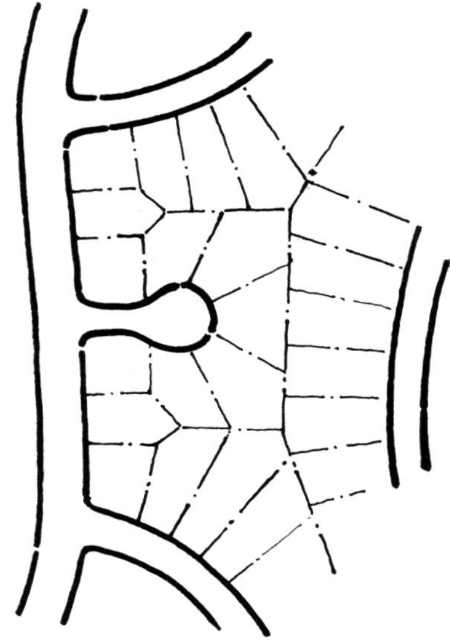

a. Proper Lotting for Single Family Houses on Culs-de-Sac.

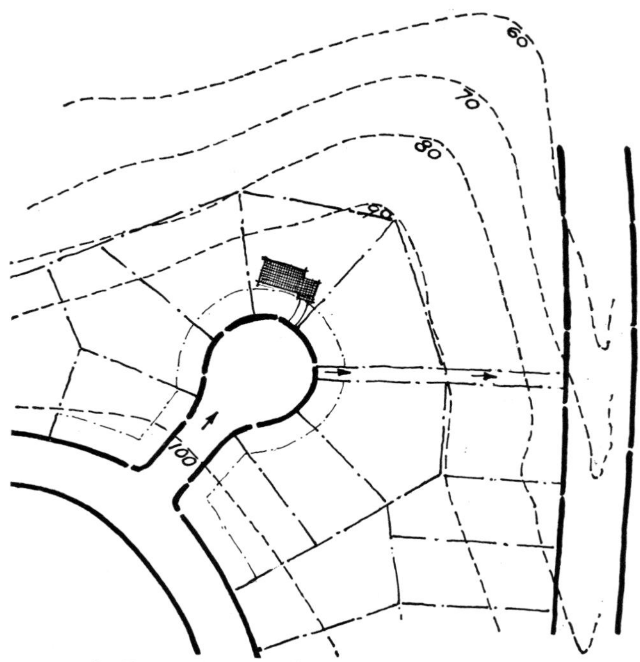

b. Downhill Conditions for a Cul-de-Sac.

Illustration No. 44 (continued)

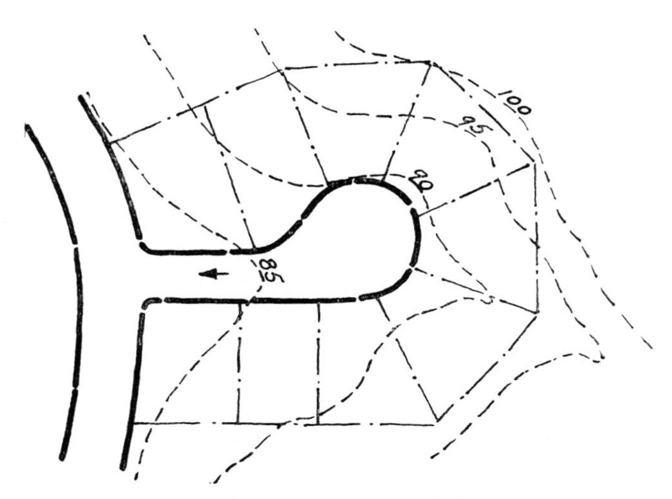

c. Uphill Conditions for a Cul-de-Sac.

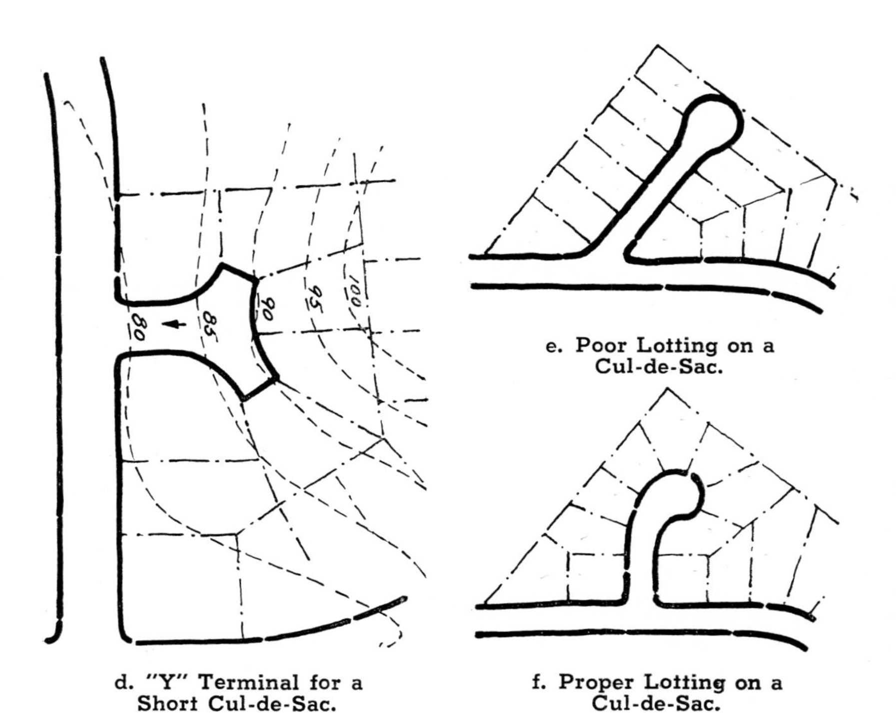

d. "Y" Terminal for a Short Cul-de-Sac.

e. Poor Lotting on a Cul-de-Sac.

f. Proper Lotting on a Cul-de-Sac.

objections can be overcome when the minimum standard for the turn-around area is 100 feet from outer curb to outer curb. The fire department can then maneuver easily. Part of the water pressure trouble can be met by limiting the cul-de-sac length to 500 feet, as recommended. Objections to dead-end water mains can be solved if the main is placed in a property line easement at the rear of the property lines instead of in the street; or if two culs-de-sac are paired, with water mains to serve both streets looped by means of cross-property easements.

In multi-family, or even intensive single-family developments, where a considerable volume of traffic is generated, use of culs-de-sac is questionable as they require all entering traffic to turn and leave by the point of entry, thereby approximately doubling the local traffic volume. The use of the Y or T "back-around" can sometimes be used to advantage on short culs-de-sac where a small number of lots are served. Excessive grading to provide for the circle can thus be avoided.

In many cases loop streets can be used to good advantage as they do not have the objectionable features of the cul-de-sac, but do contribute to privacy and discourage through traffic. Loop streets and culs-de-sac can also be used to advantage to pick up groups of lots in odd corners of the property, in the center of excessively deep blocks, or where topography or natural features make a normal street pattern difficult. A skilled land planner will not limit himself to a fixed pattern or stereotyped repetition of street and block treatment. Each development is a separate problem requiring not only adjusting the plan to the topography but recognizing local customs and market preferences.

(f) Alleys

Alleys in present-day single-family or two-family residential neighborhoods are no longer desirable nor considered necessary. A rear property line easement is preferred to an alley where needed for power lines or sewer rights-of-way.

The disappearance of the alley from the residential neighborhood, particularly from those areas that are being newly created on raw land in the suburbs, is one of the advances which have been made in land planning during the motor age. With the common use of the automobile there has been a transformation in the orientation of the house. The street entrance and the service side of the house are the same. The motor car approach to the house has created a revolution in the use of the lot, the design of the house and the location of the living areas. We no longer need a front and a rear.

The alley for access to garages in rear yards and as a right-of-way for rear service has been eliminated in the planning and development of new neighborhoods. Return to an alley form of platting is a retrogression to the outmoded scheme of gridiron street and block pattern. The old gridiron pattern of residential development is expensive, unadaptable to topography, unattractive, detrimental to creation of neighborhood values, and archaic.

It is true that in certain sections of the mid-west, where land is flat, subdivision regulations in some communities still call for alleys. By continued custom in these places utility lines and servicing does take place in alleys. But this custom is "old hat". In older sections of existing communities that were built during the earlier "trolley car era" of land development, alleys are in existence. But perpetuation of this outmoded form of utilitarian access is needless for new single-family areas.

In row house or multi-family developments, alleys or rear service drives may be necessary for refuse collection or to provide access to off-street parking facilities and for fire protection. Always, in commercial areas, rear access is necessary for loading and unloading purposes. *If provided,* alleys should be 20 feet wide and be paved for the full width. A lesser width makes commercial alleys inadequate for passing, backing, and for building access by trucks. Greater width encourages their use for parking and even induces some traffic movement. Alleys should normally enter streets at right angles. Dead-end alleys are never desirable, but when they may occur an adequate turn-around space is required.

(g) Intersections

Fairly sharp curb radii of not more than 15 feet at intersections on minor streets are desirable rather than longer

Illustration No. 45. A Cul-de-Sac and Its Privacy

Culs-de-sac are one of the best street types to use in singl family development because of the privacy offered to hous so served.

David D. Bohannon Organization, Develop

radii which permit high automobile speeds in turning corners thereby endangering pedestrians. The amount of street paving is also reduced with resultant savings in paving costs. Acute angle street intersections should be avoided where at all possible. They create excessive roadway paving, are traffic hazards, and create block shapes which are difficult and uneconomical to lot.

Illustration No. 47.
Street Jogs—and Cross Traffic.

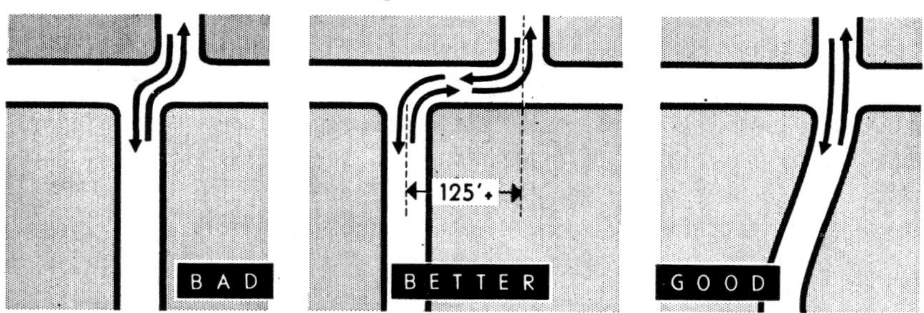

Source: SUGGESTED LAND SUBDIVISION REGULATIONS, HHFA

Similarly, slight jogs at street intersections are undesirable. Intersections can be staggered if the distance between center lines is at least 125 feet, as shown by illustration 47. But it is better to curve the street as it approaches the intersection in order to effect a right angle alignment when the street is to be continuous. However, for minor, interior streets to discourage through traffic and to encourage safety, it is best to use T intersections. For the safety feature of the T or three-way intersection see illustration 61, page 209.

By building traffic safety into residential neighborhoods, we provide not only for safe street traffic movement but we also achieve good land subdivisions. High standards for traffic safety are compatible with characteristics of street layout which make for livability in residential areas. Effective results in

ustration No. 46. A Cul-de-Sac and Its Advantages

A cul-de-sac street can be used to good advantage to pick up groups of lots in odd corners of a subdivision, in the center of excessively deep blocks, or where topography or natural features make other street patterns difficult to develop.

David D. Bohannon Organization, Developer

long-range preservation of property values can be obtained readily through proper original design and layout.[107]

(h) Driveways

Driveways too commonly have little or no radius at their intersection with the curb or street pavement. However, proposals made by some traffic engineers to use curb radii for driveways up to twelve feet are entirely unsound. Such returns would not only be costly, but would require wide park strips between curb and sidewalk, occupy from ½ to ⅔ of the roadway frontage of the ordinary 50 to 60-foot lot, and invite excessive speeds in approaching or leaving individual driveways. Eight feet is considered the minimum driveway width with a 3 to 5-foot transition radius at the curb. Use of the rolled curb makes the provision of curb returns unnecessary.

Strip or ribbon driveways with a central grass panel have not proved satisfactory as they are difficult to maintain, become unsightly, and decrease construction costs very little if any. It it better to provide a full 8-foot paved driveway to the garage or carport that can double as an entrance walk to the house; but if it does this double duty, then the width should be 10 feet in order to permit a person to pass a car parked on the driveway without his having to walk on the grass.

(i) Planting Strips Next to Curb

Planting strips, where curbs and walks are separated, should be at least seven feet wide if street trees are to be planted. Five-foot strips are too narrow for proper tree growth. Tree roots eventually tend to heave sidewalks where narrow strips are used. The Council recommends planting street trees back of the sidewalk where root growth will not be restricted, unless adequate planting strips are provided.

---

[107] There are rules for safety as a factor in street design for a residential subdivision: (1) Use three-way, instead of four-way, intersections; (2) use curved streets; (3) minimize access roads; (4) eliminate continuous streets, particularly between two major access highways; (5) break continuous collector streets; (6) avoid irregular intersections such as multi-legged intersections of more than four legs, Y-types where two legs meet at acute angles, jogs in intersection alignment where the legs are too close together to operate as separate T intersections, adjoining four-way intersections too close to operate independently, and hidden intersections where visibility is limited by buildings, trees or shrubbery.

See "Subdividing for Traffic Safety" by Harold Marks, Traffic Survey Engineer, Los Angeles County Road Department. *Urban Land,* October 1957. Urban Land Institute.

Illustration No. 48.

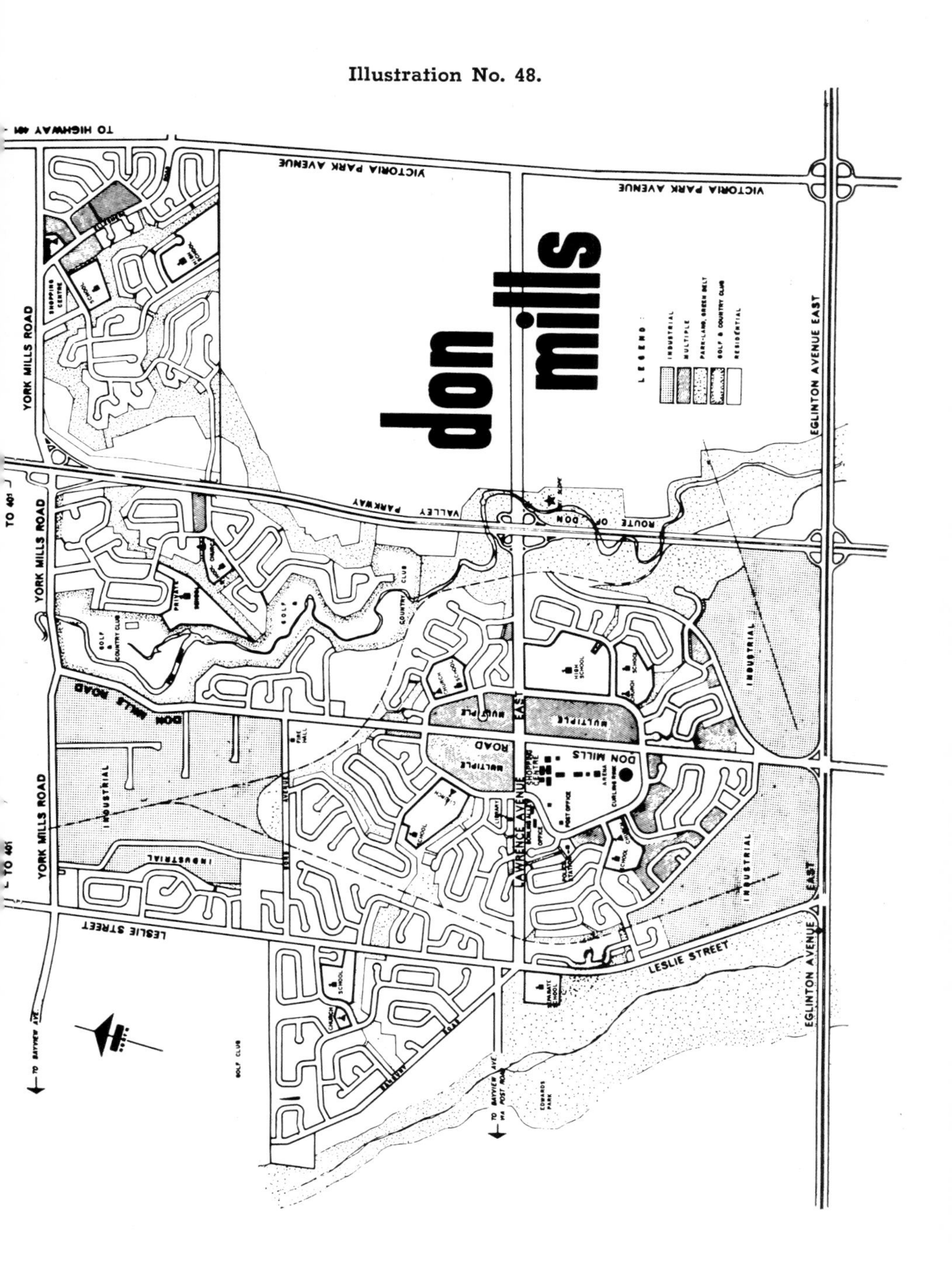

Illustration No. 49.

Photo by Photographic Survey Corp. Ltd.

Air View of Don Mills Looking Northwest From Eglinton Ave. and Don Valley Parkway

11. Street Improvement Costs

The cost of local improvements per lot will vary in different sections of the country and will also depend upon local requirements. In recent years costs have varied so widely and fluctuated so rapidly that any tabulation of average cost data is of doubtful value. Also improvement requirements vary so widely that no listing of items to be included in cost quotations is practical.

The illustration (p. 113) shows a method of computing the total cost of an improved lot after raw land cost and street improvement costs are known. It should be noted that front foot costs should be expressed in terms of "selling" feet, i.e., to include in the cost per front foot of land to be sold, the costs of side street construction, plus the cost of any improvements abutting frontage to be dedicated for park, playground, or other open space use.

12. Community Facilities

School and church sites should receive careful attention when establishing the general development plan for a residential project. In locating schools, walking distances are no longer controlling factors; instead, site area and number of pupils which a school must take care of are criteria. When distances are too far for walking, school buses are used or children are delivered by a parent.

(a) School Sites

The school's location should be selected after consultation with the local school district officials. (See also the earlier discussion of schools as a factor in site selection, p. 56.)

From the developer's standpoint, an elementary school should be accessible from all sections of his project. However, as a universal rule, sites selected should not front on a major thoroughfare because this would expose the children to hazards of heavy traffic and the school to traffic noises. In the case of an expressway with grade separations and parallel service roads, these difficulties are eliminated somewhat. Location on a main traffic artery is not recommended. It is also poor policy to place the school in the choicest section of the development area. Noise from student outdoor activity is a somewhat adverse factor unless the playground is well insulated from adjoining houses. (See Council members' comments on pages 144 and 147.)

School sites with ample playground of at least 5½ to 7 acres for elementary and 10 acres or more for high schools are standard specifications.

The Council recommends that locations for school sites and their sizes be checked with local school officials because standards vary, other than the 5 acres minimum for elementary schools. As an illustration, a national education group is setting 5 acres for each 500 pupils with an additional acre for each additional 100 students; 10 acres for each 1,000 pupils with an additional acre for each 100 students; high schools, minimum 8 acres, and ranging up to 35 acres in site area.

Sidewalks should be constructed on both sides of streets leading directly to the school.

Certain principles for site planning are applicable to any school: (1) Each building should be attractively set back within the site to provide for landscaping and to secure insulation from the street and for adjacent properties. (2) Each school should be provided with appropriate amount of space prepared for faculty parking and for space and access needed in connection with maintenance and operation. (3) Elementary schools, especially, should be provided with a drive to a sheltered building exit. The drive should be of a design suitable to facilitate safe movement of vehicles of parents bringing children or picking them up. There is greater need at high schools for student parking, and for patron parking at athletic events and other community activities held at the school. Schools served by bus transportation should have bus parking space.

In planning the school site in relation to the surrounding neighborhood, it is not necessary or even desirable to have the school grounds surrounded by abutting streets. In fact, as J. W. York of Raleigh says: "We feel that school sites should *not* be surrounded entirely by streets and we do not feel that it is objectionable to have residential lots abutting school grounds." As to the advisability of having streets on only one or two sides of school sites, John Matthews of North Little

Illustration No. 50. Protective Covenants

Attractive home neighborhoods are not assured of contir ing appeal and stability unless protective covenants preve inharmonious or injurious future use of individual properti

Street scene in Maryvale, Phoenix, Ariz
John F. Long Home Builders, Inc., Develo

Rock adds this note: "We no longer donate land to school districts. Better planning results when sites are sold instead of donated. This seems a simple solution to a serious problem in meeting a board's site requirements. By purchase of sites, school boards will take a realistic view of all factors including the safety of the children, and the high cost of providing surplus streets and sidewalks plus more land than a school needs or can care for."

In certain sections of the country a developer is well advised to reserve a kindergarten site adjacent to school grounds, play areas or parks. If several alternate kindergarten sites are reserved in the original platting, then those of the community interested in establishing this community facility on a private basis are provided for. Surplus sites can be marketed later as residential home sites.[108]

---

[108] School authorities are generally agreed that optimum elementary school enrollments range between 480 and 720 pupils, requiring from 16 to 24 classrooms.

In estimating the number of school children generated by residential development the following information is offered: Check the ratio of school population to total population from current Census reports, or from a direct school census for your area (see footnotes, page 10). The ratio will range between 14 and 25 per cent. The U. S. Office of Education, Department of Health, Education and Welfare, Washington 25, D. C., estimates .7 of a school age child per family for the preliminary estimates of pupil education in Federally affected areas. This Office also issues a report, "Statistics of State School Systems", based on findings of the Biennial Survey of Education. Check for the latest circular. Usually it gives summary statistics for public elementary and secondary education by states, including school-age population and total population.

In its panel study, *Bratenahl Village,* Urban Land Institute found the following figures useful in estimating school population for planning purposes (repeated here for the reader's convenience):

In single-family development ______	.7	school-age child per unit
In garden apartment development __	.27	" " " " "
In high-rise, luxury apartments __	.1	" " " " "

See *Bratenahl Village, A Panel Study.* Urban Land Institute, 1958.

Illustration No. 51. Hillside Development

Hillside development requires variations from general subdivision ordinance specifications. Inflexible imposition of regulations designed for relatively flat land makes development of steep land so expensive that it is either bypassed or badly scarred. For low density, developers of hillside tracts need leeway in lot sizes, street widths, lot shapes, frontages, and setbacks.

Street scene in San Mateo, California
David D. Bohannon Organization, Developer

(b) Church Sites

In planning a large-scale residential development, reserve several church sites. Churches today require on-site parking and a site necessarily must be from 3 to 5 acres or more in area.[109] Because of the automobile parking problem, churches without sufficient on-site parking have proved undesirable neighbors when located on a residential street. Activities are going on continually in a modern church.

It is a responsibility of church administrators to decide on the membership standards which they expect their churches to achieve. Otherwise, there can be no basis for deciding how many sites must be reserved for church in any one neighborhood. There are differences in membership standards from one section of the country to another and between various major faiths and denominations. Taking extreme examples, one of the more radical sects may be expected to operate normally with 100 constituents, while an urban Roman Catholic parish may consist of five to ten thousand persons.[110]

From his experience in community development, John Matthews has this advice to offer about church sites: "We find it advisable to have a variety of sites from which churches may choose. Church boards have as many different ideas about what constitutes good location for a church as individuals have in selecting a home site. This means designating on your plan more church sites than will ever be needed as such. These must be planned so they may later be subdivided into residential plots or used in some other way after all the various denominations which church a neighborhood have made their site choices.

"Suburban churches are apt to be so prosperous there is danger in over-churching new neighborhoods. The National Council of Churches recommends new churches be given assurance by developers that additional sites will not be offered until two or three thousand new residents have moved into an area, or until it appears that all existing churches are reasonably well established."

---

[109] A Roman Catholic parish site needs enough land for a rectory, convent, school and playground, in addition to customary minimum needs for the church and its off-street parking—10 acres is indicated.

[110] Many urban churchmen believe that a church of about 500 members is the optimum size of a neighborhood institution, while a downtown church, to support a diversified staff and program, may need 1,500 to 2,000, or even more. See *Church and City Planning* by Robert C. Hoover and Everett L. Perry. Bureau of Research and Survey, National Council of the Churches of Christ in the U.S.A., 297 Fourth Avenue, New York 10, N. Y.

Even so, in designating church sites, a developer should consider the eventual structure as it will become a terminus to a view which will be created for the street picture.

Church sites adjacent to shopping centers have been found satisfactory where they act as a buffer between residential and business uses. However, when a church site is adjacent to a shopping center, the parking space of the shopping center should not be counted as that needed for the church's own requirements; otherwise, the church parking can impinge upon the shopping center during shopping hours.

(c) Recreation Areas

The accelerated rate of leisure time and the increasing incomes available for expenditures on games and sport demand expanded private and public facilities for recreation including playgrounds, parks and open spaces of all types and at all levels.

It is the consensus of the Council that play areas are needed in a residential area. However, difficulty is experienced in managing and maintaining them. The solution lies in whether the municipality-at-large will own and operate the area, or whether it will be maintained and managed by a local homes association. (See Part III, Section One.)

The type and size of the recreation area for the development also depends upon the type of development being created. An in-town apartment development requires space for children's active play not needed in an open type of single-family house development in an outlying area.

The desirable size of a playground varies with the population composition of the neighborhood.[111]

The following are minimum desirable sized playground areas for various populations, exclusive of school sites:

Population	Size (acres)
2,000	3.25
3,000	4.00
4,000	5.00
5,000	6.00

[111] As a guide, see *Recreation Areas—Their Design and Equipment.* Second Edition. By George D. Butler. The Ronald Press, 15 East 26th Street, New York 10, N. Y.

For space standards see *Guide for Planning Recreation Parks in California.* California Committee on Planning for Recreation, Park Areas and Facilities. State Printing Office, Sacramento 14, Calif.

Playgounds of less than two to two and one-half acres are of little value except for pre-school children's play lots. Five per cent of the gross area of a project is considered about the maximum amount of land a developer can afford to *dedicate* for park and recreation purposes. (This is not to say that 5 per cent of an area is all that is *needed.*) If additional land is desired by the city it should be acquired by purchase. A child should have to walk no more than one-half mile to a playground under ideal location conditions.

A complete recreation area should be large enough to provide most of the following features:

A section for pre-school children.
Apparatus area for older children.
Open space for informal play.
Surfaced area for court games such as tennis, handball, shuffle board and volley ball.
Field for softball and group games.
Area for story telling and quiet games.
Shelter house with toilet facilities.
Wading pool.
Corner for table games for older people.
Landscape features.

A good location for playgrounds is at or near the school site. Some unsatisfactory experience with playgrounds has been vandalism in destruction of ornaments and equipment, and difficulty in selling adjacent houses. Adequate supervision should thus be assured either by the municipality, developer, or homes association if the areas are to be retained as assets to the development. The importance of this matter is reflected in the following resolution of the Council:

RESOLVED, That the Community Builders' Council of the Urban Land Institute strongly favors the establishment of publicly or community dedicated children's playgrounds in connection with all residential development and that insofar as possible, they should be combined with or contiguous to the school site in order that duplication of facilities will be avoided; and that such playground facilities will receive proper and continual supervision by the public authorities having such matters in charge.

(See Part III for problems of management).

Interior block playgrounds are considered undesirable by a majority of the Community Builders' Council. A few members have found them satisfactory. It is generally felt, however, that the provision of playgrounds is a community obligation and that most of the unsatisfactory experience could be overcome by proper location as well as better supervision.

As indicated earlier, there are several methods in effect for obtaining land for community facilities through the process of subdivision approval and as provided for in subdivision ordinances. These methods are: Requiring the developer to dedicate a site; to hold a site in reserve for a stated length of time and to sell the requested site at a negotiated market price; to offer the site as a donation; or to pay a fee for each house.

Among these direct specifications, the method by which the developer is required to dedicate for public use a site based upon a stated percentage of the area in his subdivision is inequitable for the developer *and* the municipality. Similarly, payment of a fixed fee per house does not assure that either the community-at-large or the immediate subdivision will benefit from any site so obtained. It is better that the regulation state that the subdivider shall hold in reserve, for a stated time, land which may be needed for park or recreation purposes. During this interval (six months to a year, perhaps), the land so reserved should be referred to the proper public agency for acquisition by it at a negotiated market price.

Recreation areas in their size and location should be related to the neighborhood and to the city plan. If a specification in the subdivision regulation calls for x per cent of the area being subdivided to be dedicated or assigned to public purpose, the result is apt to be scattered patches of land improperly located in relation to access and for use by the public.

Properly, the acquisition and location of recreation areas and school sites should be determined by comprehensive city planning. By relating population density and age groups of the community to the accepted standard for the size and type of area needed, recreation areas and school sites can be located in a general way. The best, most economical time to determine the precise location is before or at the time the land is coming up for subdivision. But as the ownership of parcels seldom conforms to neighborhood areas, it follows that requiring each subdivider to dedicate a certain percentage of his tract for a playground (or other park or school purpose) does not result in getting a site of proper size or location. For the same reason, it is unfair to require a subdivider to contribute more than his fair share if his tract should coincide with the appropriate location and the proposed size for the area indicated by the city's master plan.

Consequently, the fair and intelligent method as recommended by the Community Builders' Council, is for the planning commission to designate in a general way the nature and extent of open spaces and school sites and then, as any portion of the proposed site comes to be submitted for subdivision approval, take such steps as will invite the dedication or reservation of open spaces at or about the places designated by the commission's comprehensive planning studies backed by money adjustment to compensate the owner of a subdivision tract for the excess of area contributed by him above his fair share.[112]

13. Landscape Planting

A well designed planting scheme will contribute to the beauty of a development and will serve a useful purpose as well. Undesirable views can be screened out and noise diverted by properly located walls or screen plantings of shrubs and trees.[113]

Existing Growth. Healthy existing trees on the development site should be saved whenever possible. A good tree will add greatly to the value of a lot. Road and building locations should be checked on the ground after staking, but before clearing the site. This permits changes in road location to save good trees. During construction, trees and roots must be protected from damage.

Street Trees. Planting of street trees is a desirable, standard practice. Straight streets should have regularly planted trees except where building groups indicate different treatment. Narrow streets may have trees on one side only, preferably on the south or west side for effective shading. Long curves are most effective with trees on both sides or on the outside of the curve. Narrow streets, short streets, or those with one side higher than

---

[112] See *Utilities and Facilities for New Residential Development.* Technical Bulletin No. 27. Urban Land Institute.

To save scenic areas, preserve open country against our spreading cities and to channel urban growth into patterns for livability, see *Securing Open Space for Urban America: Conservation Easements* by William H. Whyte, Jr. Technical Bulletin No. 36. Urban Land Institute.

See also *The Law of Open Space* by Shirley A. Siegel. Regional Plan Association, Inc., 230 West 41st St., New York 36, N. Y.

[113] See also Sections 1207-1208, *Minimum Property Standards for One and Two Living Units.* FHA.

the other are best planted in an informal manner. Trees are commonly planted too close together. Fifty to sixty feet has been found better than 25 to 30 feet, depending on the variety and growing habits. See also the note about width of planting strips, page 140.

In higher priced developments splendid effects may be secured by plantings of single varieties of flowering trees such as hawthorn, dogwood, flowering crab, cherry, etc. During the flowering season they will attract hundreds of visitors and prospective buyers to the property.

Other Tree Planting. In garden apartment development, trees can be concentrated in groups at the ends of buildings, breaking long vistas and giving shade in contrast to sunny lawn areas. Low branched trees may be planted along back lot lines to reduce noise and give privacy to dwellings. Trees should be grouped in order to preserve as large open lawn areas as possible.

Good soil and drainage conditions are necessary for good tree growth. Where the existing conditions are unfavorable, use fewer trees but provide them with good soil and effective protection. It is always better to plant trees on a fill if well compacted and made with good soil than on a cut where the tree will be planted in subsoil.

Few varieties of trees already established will stand fills of more than a few inches over their roots or cuts which remove any substantial amount of the root system. In general, the spread of the root system can be roughly determined by the spread of the branches, although different species vary from this rule of thumb. Tree wells up to several feet in depth have sometimes been found satisfactory under favorable conditions. At best they can only serve to prevent fill against the trunk and for a limited radius around it. Fill around trees is always hazardous as the feeder roots which grow close to the surface must have air and drainage. Certain types of trees such as oaks and beech will nearly always die if filled around. Before filling, a layer of coarse gravel or broken stone to the depth of 6″ to 8″ should be spread on the surface over the feeder roots. This assures air and drainage. A tree-well built a foot or more from the tree trunk and extending to the old ground level should be provided to keep the trunk from rotting. Vertical tiles are sometimes set at intervals above the feeder roots down to the level of the gravel or broken stone fill to provide additional air circulation.

Shrubs. Shrubs and evergreens should be used in large masses only when required for practical reasons such as to prevent erosion on slopes or as a ground cover or a screen. Most shrubs should be planted as individual specimens or in small groups. Do not plant too close to buildings, and allow ample space along walks to permit normal growth without crowding. Shrubs or flower beds in the middle of lawn areas should be avoided. Use only hardy varieties. Protective covenants should require future owners to remove any high planting at street corners which creates traffic hazards.

Protective Plantings. Plantings of shrubs and trees can be effectively used to screen out objectionable views and also to absorb and deflect noise.

To screen out noise along a highway frontage, see the method described earlier, page 46. A railroad along a property line can be screened effectively by use of heavy shrub planting and 6-foot cedar or other type of closed fencing as noted by footnote 51.

Hedges. Hedges may be used in connection with play areas and at a few strategic points in the site plan, such as street corners where they must be kept low, and along project boundaries. Preference should be given to species that have an acceptable appearance and height without continuous trimming or pruning. In apartment projects low hedges along walks are effective in controlling foot traffic, and create a neat and harmonious appearance.

Vines. Vines are usually easy to maintain and may be used liberally on masonry walls, especially blank end-walls of buildings. Vines reduce noise, glare and heat radiation. However, they should not be used on frame construction because of the resulting damage to supports and buildings. Vines of various types are useful for ground cover in shady areas and to protect banks against erosion. Grass should seldom be planted on steep banks or terraces.

Lists of plant materials are often misleading and do not take the place of advice from your landscape architect and nurseryman as to the best varieties for any particular local soil and climate. Get the effect you need from well-chosen plantings. Remember, selection of plant materials is important. Well-chosen plants, properly placed and installed in well prepared soil, will go a long way toward merchandising your development.

C. STREET AND UTILITY CONSTRUCTION

Following briefly are engineering considerations generally incorporated in the engineer's plans and specifications.

1. Project Grading Plans

These plans consist of fixing approximate building floor elevations and finished grades for project streets, drives, walks, and other site areas. To be economical, plans should attain a reasonable balance of cut and fill, and avoidance of fills which will add to depth of building foundations. The existing ground level should be retained wherever possible near trees which are to be preserved.[114]

In general, lawns should slope toward streets or other hard surfaced areas which provide surface drainage directly into public streets, or to natural drainage channels. In general, earth banks should not exceed a 3 to 1 slope. Such slopes should be sodded or preferably planted with ground cover or shrubs. On long steep slopes sod should not be used because of difficulty of maintenance.

Before completing the grading plan, check over the individual lot's drainage provisions and watch out for drainage from adjoining areas. Remember water runs down hill; provide for grass gutters or storm drains. Lawn areas should have a pitch of not less than one inch in 10 feet to avoid puddles.

2. Hard Surfaced Areas

Selection of pavement types must be based upon a study of the nature of the subgrade, climatic conditions, comparative costs, probable wheel loads, character of project, and cost limitations. Street paving specifications should be such that they will be accepted in dedication by the municipality.

Bituminous bound paving is almost universally used by developers unless the municipality requires concrete. A good base reduces maintenance. The small extra cost of an 8-inch base compared to a 4 or 6-inch base is well worth the difference. A bituminous bound top course, either plant mixed or sprayed on

---

[114] See "Lot Improvement Requirements." MPR Revision No. 56, FHA.

See also "Land Development for Buildings on Fill." FHA's Data Sheet 79, applicable to certain areas where special requirements are in effect to prevent differential settlement, landslides and other occurrences which might damage dwellings, streets, or other improvements.

hot, is common and satisfactory in practice. Where macadam or gravel pavement is used, a 6 to 8 inch rolled base with 1½ to 2-inch ready mixed or bituminous penetration top is standard practice in projects for lower cost houses.[115]

To avoid glare and minimize unsightly discoloration from oil and grease on a concrete pavement, it is usually advisable to darken the surface with a light bituminous dressing, or to mix color compound, usually lamp black, with the concrete prior to placing.

There is objection to high road crowns. For bituminous bound roads ⅜ inches per foot is found to be satisfactory. This gives a 5-inch crown in a 26-foot roadway. Gravel roads require a higher crown. On concrete roads a flatter crown is satisfactory.

Curbs and gutters are a necessary part of street construction. In very open estate development, however, it may be possible to utilize cobble stone or wide shallow grass gutters if slopes are favorable and proper maintenance is assured.

Sidewalks should generally be constructed of concrete. Gravel or cinder sub-base is not necessary for walks except under the most unfavorable soil conditions. Steps in sidewalks should be avoided wherever possible, but stepped ramps may be permissible where slopes of over 15 per cent are encountered. If used, they should have a tread of not less than 5 feet to permit alternating the foot at each step, with a 5 to 6-inch riser. Where the sidewalk is laid along the curb, precaution should be taken against uneven settlement of the two elements. Sidewalks crossed by driveways to garages may require greater thickness or reinforcement, although this is usually not necessary if the subgrade is properly compacted.

3. Sewage Disposal

Wherever possible public sewer systems should be used. The next choice is a community sewer system rather than individual disposal methods. Sewage disposal by septic tanks and tile fields for each dwelling should be resorted to only when absolutely necessary. Individual disposal requires an area of considerably

---

[115] See also *A Study of Double Bituminous Surface Treated Residential Streets.* Publication #508. Special Report by Building Research Advisory Board. Building Research Institute, 2101 Constitution Ave., Washington 25, D. C.

See also *Inverted Crown Residential Streets and Alleys.* Publication #509. B.R.A.B. (as above).

larger dimensions than the normal suburban lot in order to provide for an adequate disposal field. However, this is not the only consideration. Sites for the disposal fields should slope away from the house, and should be kept free of trees and shrubbery to insure action of sunlight. The type of soil and subsoil conditions will affect greatly both the area needed and the possibility of polluting nearby surface water or wells. The effluent from disposal fields located on hillsides has been found coming to the surface at considerable distances from the field where it originates. Wide variation in the use of water by individual households, ranging from 30 to 150 gallons per person per day, makes proper design of such installations very difficult. Any use of garbage disposal units with septic tanks means doubling the capacity of the septic tanks and frequent attention to their working order. All of these considerations and others militate against the use of septic tanks.

It is virtually impossible to adapt septic tanks to all of the varied conditions of soil and usage to be found within any given development. Even where conditions are favorable, in a residential community the maintenance of individual septic tanks, after a few years use, frequently becomes a difficult problem. Where they must be used, be sure to call in the State Board of Health and be prepared to conduct percolation tests as these will have a direct bearing on the final lot dimensions required. Also bear in mind that disposal fields may have to be abandoned after some years. Reconstruction of septic tank systems is very seldom practical or satisfactory. In any case, proper design and construction are absolutely essential.

Where the extension of public sewers is not possible, it is recommended that a small central community system be used. Several such systems have been developed in recent years and have been used in many community projects with considerable success. Among the leading companies which have developed community treatment plants for projects ranging in size from 25 to 1,000 homes are: Chicago Pump Company, Chicago; Dorr-Oliver Company, New York City; Hays Process Company, Waco, Texas; Yoemans Brothers Company, Melrose Park, Illinois.

Where small private companies have been organized to operate a community treatment plant, the installation should be supervised by a professional engineer. Rodney Lockwood, home builder-land developer of Detroit, offers this advice: "Unless you have a very large tract with 1,500 or more homes where you can put in a complete sewage treatment plant with adequate numbers of clarifiers and trickling filters, you will be in constant friction with the health authorities over the operation of the plant. In my experience, most small plants which are offered to developers of the small subdivision are very difficult to operate efficiently. The effluent does not come out with the degree of purification which is required. They take a lot of care and labor to operate efficiently. The result is, you end up polluting the natural water course into which the effluent is discharged." [116]

The argument is often made that it is cheaper to install septic tanks than to provide a central plant. This may be true at today's costs if only the question of initial cost of construction is considered, as the cost of sewer connections, mains and plant has increased to a greater extent than that of septic tank installation. However, if all factors are considered, both the developer and the home owner may find they have lost money by septic tank installation. As already mentioned, lot sizes must usually be greatly increased for the septic tank. This may mean that instead of providing a normal suburban lot ranging from 10,000 to 20,000 square feet or perhaps less, a lot of two to four times this amount will be required to provide a satisfactory septic tank and disposal field. Here market demand for acreage lots is involved, with relation to the cost of raw land and possible increase in other improvement costs including grading, water, streets, etc., weighed against the selling price of the lot. Within a relatively few years public sewers may be extended to the neighborhood and connections required in the interest of public health. In this event, the cost of the septic tank installation is lost completely as lines are usually in the rear yard and cannot be converted. With a central system, however, the cost of laterals and house connections is not lost as they should, wherever possible, be designed to connect with the new sewer main without change. Thus the only loss to write off is the treatment plant which may have some salvage value while septic tanks do not. The plant itself may be taken over at part of the public system when it is installed.

The community plant may cost even less to install than a septic tank subdivision. It is impractical to state what a series of septic tank installations will cost under today's prices and for all types of soil conditions. Similarly, a central treatment plant

---

[116] See "Community Facilities" by Rodney M. Lockwood. *Urban Land,* January 1959. Urban Land Institute.

will vary according to the cost of the land which must be set aside for isolation purposes; the increment in number of lots obtainable from the density suitable for the project; the potential for expanding the installation to serve other developments, etc.[117]

However, to illustrate, *even without current accurate cost figures,* the net results of the two systems would be about as follows for a 30-acre subdivision:

WITH SEPTIC TANK	
Maximum desirable density: one to two families/net acre; 24 to 48 families.	
Septic tank installed	$190/unit
Total for Septic tank	$190/unit
Salvage with public connections	none
Cost to be written off/unit	$190

WITH CENTRAL PLANT	
Desirable suburban density: 4 families/net acre; 120 families.	
Sewer mains	$112/unit
House connections	100/unit
Plant prorated	148/unit
Total for Central Plant	$360/unit
Salvage of mains and connections	$212/unit
Plant—2%	3/unit
	$145

Contrary to popular opinion, individual septic tanks require frequent attention and continued maintenance if they are to operate properly and avoid nuisance conditions. They should not be considered as other than temporary installations under even the most favorable conditions.[118]

In an area unserved by public trunk sewers and where natural conditions and approval authorities permit their use, the sewage lagoon is a possible alternative, temporary method of sewage disposal for a project up to the size of 200 single-family houses. The lagoon is not universally acceptable nor is it adaptable to all localities. Land cost is a factor as is limitation on the size of the area to be served and the urban character of the area.[119] Where installed in the Kansas City Metropolitan Area,

---

[117] In the article by Rodney M. Lockwood referred to earlier, for a 500-house development the septic tank installation costs are cited as $350 per dwelling unit; the treatment plant as $160 per unit on the bases of $75,000 for the plant and $100,000 as the value of the assigned land at a $5,000 per acre price.

See also "What You Need to Know About Sewage." *House & Home,* February 1958, pp. 116-123; and "Sewage Treatment Plants for Small Builders." *House & Home,* March 1956, pp. 172-177.

[118] In all sections of the country the trend is toward stricter regulations governing septic tank installations, including larger tank sizes and more careful soil tests. Tanks and tile fields have to be large enough to take the flow from washing machines and garbage disposers. See *Manual of Septic Tank Practice.* U. S. Public Health Service. Gov't Printing Office, Washington, D. C.

[119] See "Sewage Lagoons." *Urban Land,* March 1957. Urban Land Institute.

the sewage lagoon is used as a temporary, low-cost facility until a local watershed development has progressed to the point where trunk sewers and permanent sewage treatment works can be financed by general bonds.

For orderly growth and proper development of an unserved section of a metropolitan area, there is need to set up long-range planning for stage development of public sewers and treatment plants. Incalculable service to the community-at-large results from a sound master sewerage plan where the plan is effectuated by a public authority on whatever jurisdictional basis and financing method are best adapted to the circumstances.

If you plan carefully and overlook no short or long-range opportunity to hook up to public sewers, chances are you will save yourself the cost and trouble of putting in risky septic tanks or tying up capital in community systems. You can also offer the home buyer city sewers at savings to him.

However, in planning the sewer system, the developer should investigate carefully the following points:

1. Is the existing system to which connections are to be made of adequate capacity? Is it a separate, or a combined sanitary and storm water system? (See below).

2. What is the basis upon which the city charges for the installation of sewers?

(a) Are they charged entirely to the developer?

(b) Is total or partial recovery of the initial cost possible?

(c) Can a special sewer improvement district be set up covering the area to be developed?

(d) How are costs allocated where mains and trunk lines must be constructed through the development to serve property beyond its borders?

3. Is a permit to discharge surface drainage into natural water courses required by the local or state government? *Be sure* to check this point as it may save you trouble and expense later.

Illustration No. 52. Floor Plans and House Types

The front porch has disappeared. With the re-orientation of the house and its service features, the porch, or its counterpart the patio for outdoor sitting, has moved to the garden side of the house for greater degree of pleasantness and privacy.

Gerholz Community Homes, Inc., Flint, Michigan, Developer

In general, the sewer lines should be located within street rights-of-way but not necessarily under roadway paving. The system should be coordinated with other utilities and located to avoid existing trees.

The size of house connections to sewers should be not less than 6 inches to avoid clogging; all lateral sewers should not be less than 8 inches. Normally, sanitary sewers should not be laid in the same trench with water supply lines. However, it is possible in some cases, where permitted by the local authorities, to combine the lines in a double-shelf trench which will contain the sanitary sewer at the bottom and the water line on the shelf.

Surface water and storm drainage connections to sanitary sewer systems should be avoided.[120]

4. Storm Sewers

Except in open type of estate development, underground storm sewers will usually be required. Connection with the existing city system is always desirable. However, it is sometimes possible to retain certain natural drainage channels into which storm sewers can discharge, particularly if it is a perennial stream valley which can be dedicated as a park. Check carefully the possibility of flooding during periods of heavy storm water discharge and establish park boundaries accordingly, bearing in mind that the development of upstream property as well as your own will greatly increase the runoff from roofs, paved areas and open lawns.

As indicated above, in some localities it is customary to combine storm drainage with sanitary sewage. But for economic reasons, it is an increasing practice to separate sanitary sewerage from storm water drainage because of the otherwise excessive

---

[120] In the near future, the principle of water-borne sewage may become obsolete. It is not beyond the realm of possibility that nuclear heat may someday reduce sanitary waste to an innocuous ash in the matter of minutes. Already a sewerless toilet is a first small step in the field of water conservation. Either of such developments would revolutionize sanitary waste disposal and subsequently land development concepts. See "The Self-Contained House," Planitorial by M. S. Wehrly, *Urban Land,* July-August 1956. Urban Land Institute.

Illustration No. 53. Yard Space

Builders are realizing importance of yard space. New houses with living rooms to the rear lend themselves to intelligent site planning for more enjoyable indoor-outdoor living.

Gerholz Community Homes, Inc., Flint, Michigan, Developer

size of pipe for a combined system and the overload placed upon the sewage treatment plant. In planning a new subdivision, the street plan and the storm drainage plan can dovetail if the land planner will consider carefully the engineering aspects of storm water collection in designing the street layout on the basis of topography rather than on any preconceived pattern.[121]

5. Water Distributing System

Mains should be located in the street, preferably in the park strip between walk and pavement, or where curb and sidewalk are contiguous, back of the sidewalk. Fire hydrants should be readily accessible, protected from traffic hazards, and located so as not to obstruct walks or parking.

A convenient rule of thumb in estimating the number of fire hydrants required is as follows: One hydrant per 400 to 500 feet of street, or approximately the square footage of the area of the property divided by 200,000. Where buildings are large, closely grouped, and inflammable, one hydrant per 300 to 400 feet is desirable.

As with sewers, a central water supply is always preferable to individual wells. As areas build up, individual wells become increasingly undependable both as to supply and water quality. Initial construction and subsequent maintenance of a central supply will usually be found less expensive and far more satisfactory. Many small private water companies are rendering satisfactory service.

In general, the same points as those listed under sewers should be checked including capacities and pressure of existing mains for both domestic service and fire protection, basis of municipal charges, and allocation of costs. The requirements for any new system should, of course, be checked with the city, county and state authorities.[122]

To form a private water company for the purpose of serving a new community development in an outlying area where the nearest public water supply may be as far away as three miles, under most state laws it is necessary to obtain incorporation papers for the proposed utility company, a franchise from the

---

[121] See "Community Facilities" by Rodney M. Lockwood. *Urban Land,* January 1959, referred to previously.

[122] See "What You Should Know About Today's Well-Water Systems." *American Builder,* June 1959, pp. 166-167.

local jurisdiction to lay mains in the projected streets, obtain permission from a water control board to drill a test well after offering proof of need, submit evidence of proper and safe construction and just and equitable safeguarding of other water supplies. Plans for the well and distributing system must be approved by the state board of health and the rules, regulations and rates must be approved by the public utility commission. So there are a lot of official steps, including public hearings, which a developer must take in forming a private water company to serve a new development where no existing public water supply and distribution system exists.

From experience, it has been found that one full-time worker should be able to take care of ordinary maintenance, repairs, meter reading, billing and collecting for 500 customers.

6. Pole Lines and Gas Service

It is generally desirable to keep pole lines out of the street. Pole lines are unsightly and interfere with street trees. It is better to place poles on easements along rear lot lines. In some areas public utility companies insist upon street location, and in some instances, due to topography and views, it may be desirable to locate them on streets. Poles placed on rear easements have proved highly satisfactory and are recommended in preference to street location as they are less unsightly and can be more readily screened by planting.

While all utilities' minimum easement width requirements for pole lines are not identical, a 10-foot width for pole lines with 5-foot easements along two adjacent parcels is the minimum requirement. Poles generally do not straddle lot lines or corners, but are placed on one side or the other to avoid interference with fences, walls or property stakes. Easements for anchors and guys are usually 4 feet wide, generally 2 feet on each side of a property line, with the length dependent on the height of the pole to which they are to be attached; normally, the length is not less than 30 feet. Continuity of easements from block to block is preferred for providing access from the publicways along rear or side lot lines.

A common easement area for both pipe line and pole line facilities is generally not compatible without a wider easement and a well-defined location for each facility. If some unusual condition makes such common use absolutely necessary, the pipe line trench should be located at the outer edge of a wider easement with the pole and pipe line separated by at least 4 feet.

Early consultation with the utility companies is important so that the utility can engineer its installation consistent with the tract layout, lot arrangements, and other pertinent factors; and so that the easements for public utility purposes can be recorded before individual parcels are conveyed to owners, and to expedite installation of the facilities.[123]

Underground wiring until recently has been too expensive for utility companies and land developers to consider except in special cases. However, there is a trend developing among bigger utilities for underground wiring because of new savings in once prohibitive costs brought about by new cable laying methods and by new types of direct-burial cables. Furthermore, power companies find that underground wiring is less costly to maintain (overhead storm damage and tree trimming is eliminated); is more adaptable to curvilinear street layouts; is easier to amortize; is helpful in promoting bigger electrical loads through use of home equipment and appliances. Telephone companies find this underground wiring eliminates paying rent on power poles. So check into the possibility of underground installation of power lines. The complete disappearance of overhead power lines is a long awaited improvement in community appearance.[124] Furthermore, power and phone lines can be in the same trench when at least 12 inches of packed earth lies between.

Gas mains are usually placed in the street right-of-way between pavement and sidewalk, or between sidewalk and property line. Gas lines and power lines *do not mix,* however.

---

[123] "Public Utility Services in Subdivisions" by A. W. Althouse, Southern California Edison Co. (An unpublished paper.)

[124] See "It's Time to Take a New Look at Underground Power and Phone Lines." *House & Home,* August 1959, pp. 112-117.

Illustration No. 54. Outdoor Living, House and Site United

In lotting, it is important to fit the house to the lot and mak adjustment in house placement to take advantage of natur grade conditions and shade trees on the site. Finer neigh borhood appearance results from studying relationships be tween houses and between houses and their lots, instead rigidly adhering to set lot specifications.

Pine Spring Gardens, Fairfax County, Virgin
Keyes, Smith, Satterlee & Lethbridge, Architec

D. HOUSE PLANNING FOR OPERATIVE BUILDERS

For the housing market of the 1960's, whether it is the first-time buyer or the buyer who is trading up to a better home as his income rises, the quality offering in the house, the lot and the neighborhood will be the keynote as we find better ways of land planning and home building.

1. Floor Plans and House Types

In any project it is necessary to plan the house to fit its site. A house that is right for a 100-foot lot seldom makes sense on a 50-foot lot; a house that is all right on a flat lot may be all wrong on a sloping lot. Even though unit plans are necessary in a large-scale project, particular attention must be given to variations of the basic unit to take advantage of lot conditions, views, trees, and orientation. The tract house takes on characteristics of mass production unless the builder appreciates marketability and employs his architect to correlate the technique of home building and the elements of good design.

Today's home buyer wants a house that offers something extra, and he wants a house that doesn't look like every one in the block. He wants privacy within and without—one area for living, another for sleeping, another for play, for eating, for cooking, and for formal entertaining. This upgrading in demand puts pressure on the building industry to use new materials and new techniques. To meet the challenge of rising costs while offering a better product, means that the housing industry will move further toward assembly line methods and factory-made parts while relying on the architects to produce designs which incorporate good taste and livability with savings made possible by using standard components in the structure.

The present-day house plan calls for easy indoor-outdoor living, open floor plans zoned for privacy. Other features of contemporary house plans include separation of the entry hall from the living room. The living room accessible to the outdoors, the extra bathroom, back-to-back plumbing, bigger and more efficient closets, larger kitchen with more counter space

Illustration No. 55. Indoor-Outdoor Living

Present-day houses call for indoor-outdoor living with easy access from the living room to the out-doors.

Pine Spring Gardens, Fairfax County, Va.
Keyes, Smith, Satterlee & Lethbridge, Architects

and proper wiring for appliances, the kitchen convenient to the front door, more conveniently located storage space—are all standard in better house plans. In addition, new products and new techniques made possible by the growing support in research are introduced into the housing field, first in custom units then into volume building as market demand is reached through marketing methods.[125]

Despite the changes which research and marketing may bring about in the future house plan and housing production, in 1960 we have a housing product that is vastly superior to that presented in 1950: Builders produce better plans and better construction with assembly-line production and prefabricated parts. They offer houses with built-in luxury features even in "low-cost" houses—kitchens with extras, handsome cabinets, wall ovens, work counters, dish washers, home laundries. This equipment becomes part of the "package"—thanks to the change in real estate mortgage provisions.

Central air-conditioning or adequate wiring for individual room units is common. The modern furnace unit makes provision for future addition of coils so that the heating system can also be used as a cooling system. All air-conditioned houses in subdivisions are built. Where the community water supply is limited in its quantity, regulations, such as use of individual recirculating units, are necessary to make sure water is not wasted. Without a water recirculating unit in the house air-conditioning system, water is wasted unless an installation is added to use the overflow water in a lawn sprinkling system.

Where lower cost houses are built by one operator, the number of house types for level sites should be kept to a minimum, but every effort should be made to avoid monotony resulting from any extended duplication of units. Varying setbacks from the street and a selective grouping of one and two-story houses can be successful in creating architectural interest.[126]

---

[125] In the coming decade materials and equipment that go into a house will change, though the external appearance may not be radically different. Aluminum, structural tile, plastics, composition panels are some materials which will come into broader use. Internal changes will be movable partitions, molded bathrooms, plastic pipes, spray-on acoustical ceilings. Electronics will change lighting, the heat pump and solar energy may change heating and cooling radically.

[126] "Architectural interest" does not mean variety in exterior appearance just for the sake of difference. Remember, in mass housing it is relationships between buildings and judicious selection of colors and materials which count—architectural conformity is better than inconsistency.

2. Building for Climate and Privacy

Orientation of the house and interior room arrangement should be given careful consideration as they are affected by sun and prevailing winds. An all glass wall with a western exposure will place a heavy burden on the air-conditioning system unless the window wall is shaded by an overhanging roof. In parts of the country having extreme temperature ranges, insulation of walls and roofs is important for its comfort and maintenance aspects.

Plan your lots for more enjoyment of the land. The open land is what many families move to the suburbs for. A big window-wall opening the house to the outdoor area is the cheapest living space that can be added. All this takes is a little more thought for paving, landscaping, fences, and lighting.

Developing the lot for privacy involves, among other things, the increased use of high walls, fences, and planting material. These elements are essential and integral parts of the house and its lot and should not be omitted from the initial project. Closely related to the subject of privacy under urban conditions is the process of making the most of favorable features of location, temperature, climate, topography, and native tree growth prevailing on any site and minimizing the adverse factors.

Incorporating privacy and "climate control" into community development will influence directly the depth, width, and shape of lots in subdivision design, as well as the later provisions in the protective covenants. The difference in arrangement of a house type on its lot, the architectural and landscape treatment to provide enclosures for privacy, may make it difficult to mix contemporary type houses with conventional styles except where lots are in the acreage category or at least 100 feet wide. However, do not forget the fact that a row house on a 25-foot lot gives more privacy than does a house of the same area set in the middle of a 50-foot lot with narrow, unuseful side yards.

Orientation of the house to the street is important. If quiet areas of a house, such as the bedrooms, *must* be on a street side, they should present as solid a wall as possible to the street. The most open side of the living area should face into the lot. Where one side of a living room must be on a street side, its wall should set as far back from the street as is practical.

Trees and shrubs can break up and help block street noise. A high hedge is effective. Trees close to the street are more effective in controlling noise than trees close to the house. Patio or yard walls at least four feet high do an even better job of cutting street noise when placed close to the house than do trees or shrubs. Block, brick, adobe or stone walls are more effective than wood walls because of their greater mass.[127]

Location and direction of streets to take advantage of, or for protection from, prevailing winds must also be considered. David D. Bohannon emphasizes that the developer must provide fences and landscaping initially and retain architectural control over additions or alterations if best results are to be assured.

3. General

(a) The "long, low" house or ranch type house mixed in with two-story dwellings has been found objectionable in some areas in the north, not in others. On this point, Hugh Potter says: "Where the building sites are large and there are many trees or abundant planting of shrubs, we no longer restrict any street to either one or two-story houses." However, John Mowbray of Baltimore finds that architectural conformity is preferable.

(b) Mixing of homes with kitchens on the street side next to homes with kitchens on the garden side is not considered objectionable. However, it is not desirable to mix front and rear refuse collection in the same area. Where kitchens are on the front, it is recommended that the service entrance open on the side yard as there is objection to such entrances directly on the front. If you have alleys, check with the sanitation department on its collection requirements.

(c) Rental housing should never be intermingled with single-family detached houses for sale.

(d) It is recommended that storage space be provided in garages even where houses contain basements. Provision of storage space in the garage for tools, garden furniture, and similar articles is desirable. In single-car garages it has been found feasible to add 5 to 6 feet to the length of the garage for this purpose. This is preferable to widening the garage as this may require a greater lot width. If a carport is substituted for a garage in the house plan, outside storage closets are essential.

(e) In general, where garages are to be provided, the attached type is recommended. Although construction costs may

---

[127] "How to Control Noise in the House." *House & Home*, April 1958, pp. 128-137.

be somewhat greater, offsetting savings may be effected in shorter driveways, integral construction, and width of lot permitted by the attached garage. The attached garage with direct access to the street is preferred to one placed on the side or rear, because of the great amount of paving required to maneuver a car in getting in and out. Garages in the rear yard detract greatly from its use for garden and outdoor living.

The carport in many areas is more popular than is the garage. More houses are being designed with a use of a larger percentage of their front or public yards for off-street parking. Less grass and more off-street parking is becoming a trend for front yard usage.

(f) The front porch has disappeared. With the re-orientation of the house and its service features to the access street, the porch, or its counterpart the patio for outdoor sitting, has moved to the garden side of the house where it is better related to pleasant living and a greater degree of privacy.

(g) Builders are gradually realizing the importance of thinking of yard space in terms of the public front yard; private rear out-door living yard; and a smaller service yard.

New houses with the living rooms to the rear lend themselves to intelligent site planning for much more enjoyable indoor-outdoor living.

E. PLANNING FOR SPECIAL TYPES OF LAND DEVELOPMENT

Principles and practices for single-family and apartment development are presented on the preceding pages. These are practical rather than theoretical considerations applicable primarily to residential aspects of community building. Irrespective of design patterns into which new residential growth may be taken by innovations in land development[128] and by emerging

[128] Innovations in land development for residential use is the subject of current research (1960) by Urban Land Institute and National Association of Home Builders. The study seeks to find quality, reasonableness and planning technology for application to even better subdivisions than we produce today. Findings will be presented by other ULI publications.

The study involves the general review of land planning concepts and innovations having applicability to the residential use of land. The review is designed to catalogue concepts already developed over several decades and to give background for evaluating new ideas. For example, we need to explore concepts that provide for variations from the orthodox method of land planning such as (1) contour or topographic planning with its recognition of natural land forms; (2) the superblock with

forces in the national economy, science, engineering, transportation and communication; pronouncements by the Community Builders' Council have the underlying objective of building better communities through private enterprise applied with integrity, intelligence and understanding on the part of the entrepreneur, the technician, and the public official.

Changes in U. S. living dictate land development for other than conventional residential use. Resort type subdivisions, golf-course subdivisions, motels, mobile home courts are variations in residential land development. Other special types of land use deserving attention by developers are the marina, the urban renewal project, the industrial park, and the shopping center. So important and specialized is the latter that the Community Builders' Council devotes the second part of this Handbook to the shopping center. Before presenting its guidelines for the planning, development, and operational phases of that element in community design, notes about some of the other special situations are offered.

1. Resort Type Subdivisions

The trend toward resort type real estate development is increasing in the United States. An analysis of the housing inventory shows that about 50,000 vacation homes were built each year from 1950 to 1956. In 1959 it is estimated that more than 75,000 vacation houses were built. There is a trend toward two-home ownership similar to two-car ownership. The market for vacation homes will keep on growing because when rising incomes and longer vacations are matched with greater ease of travel, an inevitable change results in the way people use their leisure time. One of the biggest changes is the building of a vacation

---

its claims of economy and increased amenity; (3) the "garden" apartment with its combination of superblock and topographic advantages in the siting of multi-family dwellings; (4) the geometric principle with its utilization of aerial-lineal projections; (5) the double and triple building line with its multiple use of street frontage, etc.

The application of zoning by density rather than by specification of lot dimension will be given serious consideration. While the study is progressing, already a new concept in residential land planning is emerging—the cluster layout which groups house sites around access courts, with the remainder of the tract left in its natural state. Cluster layouts would thus preserve the rural character of the land by preserving natural features undisturbed. The "common" land could then be owned and maintained by a homes association or municipality. By the clustered building sites, preliminary findings indicate that development costs might be reduced drastically.

Illustration No. 56

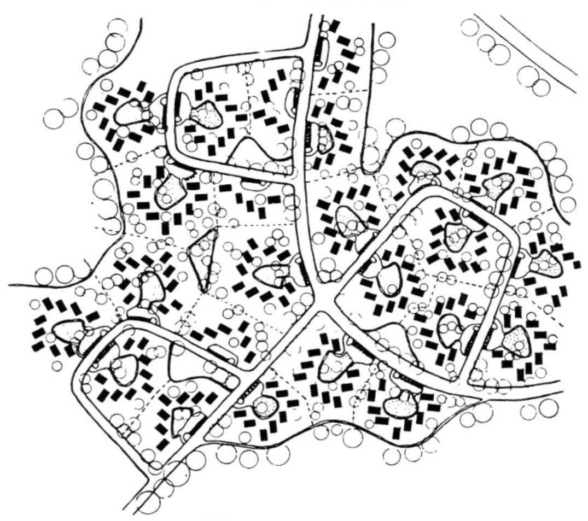

a. The Cluster Plan

Innovations in Land Planning

See also footnote 128, page 173.

The cluster plan provides for less street and public improvements. The cluster method assumes a portion of the land placed in public open space use and a density in the developed portion of a tract greater than that of conventional single lot zoning. For success, the cluster plan would seem to make a neighborhood property owners association necessary for the maintenance and administration of the open park areas. To date (1960) no examples of the cluster type subdivision exist yet the type of plan offers great possibilities for study and analysis.

Source: NAHB-ULI Subdivision Innovation Study, in preparation October 1960. Plans shown are from student work Yale University School of Architecture and Planning. Elbert Peets, instructor.

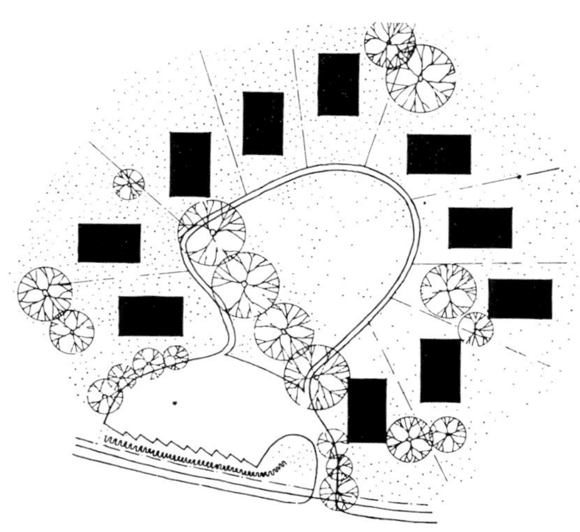

b. Detail, The Cluster Plan

home on hills or lakes or beaches only a few miles or a few hours drive on the new highways, or a short airflight, from home.

With jet plane travel, all parts of the world are no farther than 48 hours away. Thus, in the United States areas devoted to recreation will be competing with resort areas everywhere. The rise in spendable personal income and increased leisure time will create an increasing demand for the resort or retirement type of real estate development.

The physical layout of a resort type subdivision depends upon the physical character of its geographic and topographic nature. The roadway cross-section and the facilities and utilities to be included should be suited to the location. In hilly or mountainous areas, streets or roadways would be similar to those for other hillside subdivisions, see page 112. Elsewhere the street cross-sections would be developed according to their type of use rather than to standardized specifications. In a low density area, the streets in the subdivision should be of a semi-rural type to avoid what otherwise might be an urban appearance.[129]

2. Golf Course Subdivisions

Apart from growth in demand for golf facilities, the golf course as open space offers a practical setting for adjacent high quality home sites. The residential site plan should have as its first objective the incorporation of subdivision design standards for the size of lot, streets, and utilities based on the special open character of the development. Secondly, maximum benefit from the course can be derived when as many lots as possible are platted alongside the fairways, greens and tees, provided the houses are sited properly on the abutting lots. Advantages of view can be taken by siting the houses so that their large glass areas face the course. But the house should not be located opposite an elbow bend of a fairway between a tee and green on a "dog-leg" hole, nor on a direct line of approach shots behind

---

[129] Areas of seasonal dwellings pose another problem; the streets should be designed the same as if the area were occupied the year round, with space for curb parking, sidewalks, etc., reserved for in the right-of-way. Then, if the area were later converted to a year-round neighborhood: (a) there would be adequate right-of-way width, etc., to allow wider pavement, walks, curbs, and the like; (b) catch basins should be located at the proper distance to serve the wider roadway; and (c) the cost of these deferred improvements could be recovered through betterment assessments. See "Notes on Street Cross-Sections in Residential Subdivisions." Allen Benjamin. *Urban Land,* May 1960. Urban Land Institute.

greens. A partial solution against overshot or mis-shot balls landing on private property is to establish a sparse line of trees along the fairways and greens to a depth of 20-40 feet. Trees act as a barrier between the course and the houses yet allow residents a clear view of the course. Trees, however, should not be closer than 20 yards behind a green. Another protective device is to fence the course. This method, though, is expensive to install and maintain, and interferes with the view.[130]

It is generally better to lay out the course before establishing the home sites adjacent to it. Not only does this allow for a visible selling feature but it is also easier and more economical to build a course before rather than after houses are built. Also, in this way maximum benefit from natural features can be incorporated in the course. The acreage available, considering the overall project, determines the golf course size. Fifty acres for a 9-hole course and 110 acres for 18 holes are minimum requirements. For better courses, 80 acres and 160 acres are recommended. Golf authorities agree that the ideal distance for a 9-hole course should measure over 3,000 yards, probably around 3,200 yards. A good average length for an 18-hole course is 6,500 yards. Fairways, generally, should be 60 yards wide. Width depends on length of the hole and type of terrain. The shape of greens depends upon the length or strategy of a particular hole; sizes vary from 5,000 to 8,000 square feet.[131]

Several alternative methods for operation are available to golf course-residential community developers: Homes association; dedication to the community; retention and operation as a separate enterprise; lease; sale.[132] In determining whether to operate as a strictly private or semi-private club, check the latest Internal Revenue Service provisions—clubs that solicit public patronage may lose their tax-exempt status on revenue. Similarly, changes in certain provisions in the excise tax laws apply to exemption for capital improvements.

---

[130] See "Developing Golf Course Subdivisions." G. H. Crabtree, Jr. *Urban Land,* September 1958. Urban Land Institute.

See also illustration No. 23, page 81, and illustration No. 57, page 185.

[131] For complete information about golf course planning, etc., see: *Planning and Building the Golf Course.* National Golf Foundation, Inc., 407 S. Dearborn St., Chicago 5, Ill. This Foundation also provides free consultant services to individuals or groups seriously considering the development of new or additional golf facilities, whether they be private clubs, commercial, or municipal.

[132] See "Developing Golf Course Subdivisions," cited above.

3. Motels

The motel industry developed in response to the needs of motor travelers for convenient lodging close to a highway. The motel evolved from the tourist cabin class of overnight accommodation to a building type calling for distinctive services and swank facilities mostly directed to the motorist.

Stimulated by prospective and rumored investment returns, a land developer is apt to think of the motel as a use for highway-oriented property.[133] He is well advised to think twice. Travel patterns can change. As the interstate highway system begins to function, the motel on a local access route to an interchange point will experience differences in the composition of passing traffic. As travelers' habits have altered, so has the motel industry shifted its operations and level of accommodations.[134]

Land development for a motel is one aspect; the inn-keeping is another. So tricky is the latter problem that a novice developer should lease it to a professional operator. Site selection and site planning are the elements more pertinent to land development and building construction.

According to motel men, a site near an airport is the best location for a motel. The next best location is near a big city, on a highway unlikely to be bypassed for some years; or better still, near an interchange point in the interstate system. The worst location is one entirely dependent on highway business (see footnote 133). Another location eminently suitable for the new motor hotel[135] is the downtown area adjacent to the retail core. Remember, a site next to a main-line railroad or under the approach zone to an airport requires added insulation for noise.

Site planning considerations reflect several operational provisions. About 50 units is minimum for efficient operations. But additional units can be handled by about the same amount of management plus a few more maids to service the added units. When the facility reaches 200 or 300 or more units, it becomes a "grand motel", in motel language. Basic site design considerations are: visibility from the highway; easy access from the high-

---

[133] See "The Motel Free-for-All." *Fortune,* June 1959.

[134] See "The Development of the Kansas Motel Industry and the Kansas Highway System" by Clinton Warne, *Kansas Business Review,* February 1959. Center for Research in Business, University of Kansas, Lawrence.

[135] Motor hotel indicates the facility is motorist oriented by supplying hotel type services. The convenience, comfort and advantages of a motel are combined with the completeness of service of a hotel.

way; a control lobby; parking close to the units. Other site design features relate to services and guest facilities: individually controlled air-conditioning and heating for the units; lounges; playgrounds; swimming pools; switchboard; a top quality restaurant; and a competent service station and garage close by. For source information about planning, construction, and operation the footnoted references are offered.[136]

4. Trailer Parks

Since mobile home living has become so popular[137] in resort areas particularly and elsewhere, the trailer park or mobile home

---

[136] Motel Market and Sales Analysis:

American Motel Magazine, 5 S. Wabash St., Chicago, Ill. (Ask for latest year.)

Motel Industry:

"Let's Begin at the Beginning—Readers' Service Kit." Alice L. Patterson.

American Motel Magazine. (Covers financing, location, operating ratios, etc.)

Feasibility Analysis:

"So You Think You Want to Own a Motel." *Changing Times,* December 1956. 1729 H St., N.W., Washington 6, D. C.

Operations:

"Motel Income Up—But Expenses Slash Profits." *Tourist Court Journal.* Temple, Texas. July 1959. (A trade publication to check periodically).

Appraisal:

The following articles have appeared in *The Appraisal Journal.* 36 So. Wabash Ave., Chicago, Ill., under dates as indicated.

"An Approach to the Appraisal of Hotel and Motel Property," pp. 280-288, April 1958.

"Significant Trends in the Motel Industry," pp. 228-238. April 1959.

Design:

"Motor Hotels," pp. 203-238. *Architectural Record,* Building Types Study, April 1958 and July 1960. (Also other architectural magazines, such as *House & Home, Architectural Forum,* publish motel designs from time to time.)

[137] See "The Motionless Mobile Home" by J. Ross McKeever. *Urban Land,* April 1960. Urban Land Institute. See also *Mobile Home Parks and Comprehensive Planning* by Ernest R. Bartley and Frederick H. Bair, Jr. Public Administration Clearing House, University of Florida. 1960. This report presents principles and references for location, regulation, operation, and site design of trailer parks.

court[138] is a distinct type of land development project. As such, it offers an investment potential, provided the "park" design is "good" and the management and maintenance are properly proficient. A good park would have nine or ten sites to the acre—not 18 or 20 crowded in to boost the operator's revenue. However, in order to create acceptable residential character in the development of a trailer park, high standards must be followed so that the mobile home court will be a pleasant place to live and not just an overcrowded barracks tucked on a piece of land improperly located.

Planning principles involve the following:

(a) Underground water supply and sewerage to each lot or mobile home "stand".

(b) A layout providing for cluster or angle arrangements of the stands—not a grid pattern of streets or access drives with trailers placed at monotonous right angles.

(c) A density of 9 or 10 units per acre. FHA's minimum specifications for spacing between units work out to a density between 10 and 14 units per gross acre with the necessary allowange for common areas, access drives and parking. Lot sizes should approximate 2,450 square feet, with 3,000 square feet for large units. FHA calls for 150 square feet per unit as recreation space; 200 square feet per unit is better.

(d) Landscaping is necessary to create livability and a vegetative buffer strip surrounding the property.

(e) Access drives and parking bays within the park should have a good macadam surface, while the trailer stands and patios should be concrete. Needed near the entrance from the highway are an office structure with service facilities, etc.; a play area, drying yard, tenant lockers. A swimming pool is an extra feature for making the park a better place to live.

---

[138] See *Minimum Property Requirements for Mobile Home Courts.* FHA. Obtainable from any FHA regional office.

See also: "Trailer Parks: The Wheeled Suburbs." Frank Fogarty. *Architectural Forum,* July 1959; "The Appraisal of Trailer Courts." Wm. J. Randall and C. W. McCready. *The Appraisal Journal,* January 1959.

Information about design, a trailer park ordinance, etc., may be obtained from Mobile Homes Manufacturers Association, 20 N. Wacker Drive, Chicago 6, Ill. and the Mobile Home Educational Program, B-4 South Campus, Michigan State University, East Lansing.

5. Marinas

A marina is a service facility for boat owners. The developer of a waterfront subdivision or community can make a well planned marina a positive and real asset to his development. The development aspects include both the off-shore and on-shore uses.[139]

The rising popularity of boating and the increase in boat ownership has not seen a corresponding increase in mooring facilities. Also, with more boats, owners want more facilities, such as a restaurant, sleeping accommodations, and merchandise available at the marina. For this reason, marinas are becoming a more conventional type of commercial venture. It is reported that a well managed marina with extensive commercial facilities can return as much as 10 per cent on investment compared with a return of 1 or 2 per cent on a basic marina.

Most marinas are developed by a municipality with private operation of the leased facilities. Cities in Florida typify, perhaps, the direction and method by which localities provide facilities. But marinas for almost any waterfront community are added lures for home owners who are boat owners.

The marina is a strong device for preserving part of a shore line for recreation. The nature of the shore will govern the marina site basically, but pleasure boat owners prefer a marina in a residential or park area. They also want it separated from docks that serve commercial fishing and charter boats. A standard is one automobile parking stall for each boat mooring space.[140]

6. Community Swim Clubs

In localities where there is no water frontage, a community swimming club as part of the recreational facilities will act as a

---

[139] For planning and development see *Marinas—Their Planning and Development,* by C. A. Chaney. Technical Bulletin No. 14. Urban Land Institute.

See also "Building Parking Space for Boats." *Engineering News-Record,* April 2, 1959.

See also "New Type Boating Yards Cater to Owners, Too." *Business Week,* July 16, 1960.

[140] Throughout the country, thousands of apartment dwellers would like to own a boat, but they don't know where to park it. Lack of waterfront facilities suggests a dry land marina. Such installation could combine the aspects of a huge parking lot and a boating supermarket and would include storage sheds for customers' boat and trailer rigs storage, with office and showrooms for boats and accessories, parking lot and service area for an owner to work on his rig.

focal point for the whole neighborhood. Such a recreation center can be a great asset for encouraging sales within a residential project. Theoretically, there are no limits to the number of families involved—they may range from a dozen to 2,000. But most clubs want to be big enough to build a full-size pool for a moderate price per family, yet small enough to avoid overcrowding. Many such groups thus limit membership to about 300 families living in the immediate vicinity, or perhaps in one or two adjoining subdivisions.

To estimate the size of pool needed; up to 15 per cent of the member families may be using the pool on any one day. There will be three times as many non-swimmers as swimmers, so the shallow end of the pool is generally designed at least three times as long as the deep end. Active swimmers require 27 square feet per person. Ten to 15 square feet per family is about right for the pool surface, including wading pool. Thus the size for 300 families would be 3,000 to 4,000 square feet of pool; for 400 families, between 4,000 and 5,000 square feet.

About 80 per cent of the pool should be between three and five feet deep and the deepest point (8½ feet or more) should be some ten feet from the deeper end and 60 feet or more in length overall. Wading pools should be separate and should have nearby benches for mothers to sit and sun while supervising their youngsters. A rectangular, L- or T-shaped pool is best. Oval or free-form pools are not satisfactory for community pools; they cannot be used for swimming meets, water polo, etc. Three to five acres of land is needed for a 300 or 400-family project. Aprons should exceed water area by about 50 per cent and should include facilities for both shade and seating in the non-active areas around the pool. But don't size the pool for peak days. It will look deserted with a normal attendance. The pool can be overcrowded on a few occasions without arousing resentment.[141]

---

[141] For community swimming pool standards, several references are available:

Recreation Areas, Their Design and Equipment. 2nd Edition. Prepared for National Recreation Association by George D. Butler. The Ronald Press Company, 15 East 26th St., New York 10, N. Y. 1958.

Recommended Practice for Design, Equipment and Operation of Swimming Pools and Other Public Bathing Places. American Public Health Association, Inc., 1790 Broadway, New York, N. Y. 10th Edition. 1957.

Proposed Minimum Standards for Public Pools. National Swimming Pool Institute, Harvard State Bank Building, Harvard, Ill. 1958. The NSPI also issues *Minimum Standards for Residential Pools.* 1959. 9 pp.

Playgrounds, tennis courts, and picnicking facilities can be part of the project. This makes the pool appeal to diversified family interests. Play areas should be fenced off from the pool area.

Swimming pools generate noise and confusion. For this reason alone the pool should be located so that there is a buffer area between the club and close by residences. An ample parking area is essential, with a buffer between it and any adjoining houses. Avoid locations where excavation is difficult although the site must be accessible to utility connections.

Community swimming pools have been developed for memberships of over a thousand families, with an initial membership fee of between $150 and $250. In this larger type, the membership fee is set high enough to pay for the entire initial cost of installation, and in some cases the cost of the site is included in the computation.

An annual fee to cover operating costs and produce some profit, plus amortization of the investment, is usually charged. This annual fee is usually between $10 and $25 per family. One cost-of-operation figure is $5,000 for a 300-400 family membership facility; another shows an average between $6,000 and $10,000. Any operational figure is meaningless, however, because the figure would be dependent on a manager's salary, amount of service provided, income from vending machines, etc., plus the number of months the pool is in operation.

There are several ways for a land developer to include a pool in his project:

Build and operate the pool for profit, just as you would a shopping center, with residents and non-residents eligible for membership. Encourage the home owners' association to organize the pool. You can donate the site or subsidize part of the cost. The home owners association would need the developer's help in organizing the project and contracting for its construction. This is the most common and fastest growing method. In some instances, the developer sets up the homes association under a charter and bylaws. This gives the association powers of assessment up to a stipulated amount per year to undertake specified community functions including the maintenance and operation of recreation areas held by the association for residents within the development.

Do not give privileges of the swim club with the sale of houses and lots. Make joining the club a similar procedure to joining any other club. This will prevent any house buyer from automatically becoming a swim club member. Typical forms of homes associations, charters, and bylaws are found in the appendices.

7. Industrial Parks

Although not a part of residential neighborhoods, industrial parks or planned industrial districts are just as important a segment of a community as are residential and commercial areas. When properly located and carefully developed, industrial parks are definite assets to the community because of the stimulating effect they have on the local economy. Interest in industrial development, once largely confined to area development groups, railroads, industrial realtors, has spread to private land developers. This interest should not be so much in the profit potential of such venture, but in housing and commercial demands which an industrial park can be expected to stimulate.

An industrial park is an exclusive type of planned industrial district designed and equipped to accommodate a community of industries, providing them with all necessary facilities and services in attractive surroundings. A planned industrial district may be further described as a suitably located tract of land subdivided and promoted for industrial use by a sponsoring managerial organization. In this sense, industrial district connotes a restricted use of improved land over which there is a proprietor who devotes himself to the area's planning and development.[142]

The industrial park concept has precise attributes: it is attractive land, subdivided and developed according to a comprehensive plan for occupancy by a community of industries, with streets, track leads, drainage, and other utilities immediately

---

[142] See *Planned Industrial Districts.* Technical Bulletin No. 19, Urban Land Institute (a new edition being readied for release early 1961). See also *Organized Industrial Districts,* U. S. Department of Commerce, 1954; *An Analysis of Organized Industrial Districts,* Stanford Research Institute, January, 1958.

Illustration No. 57. A Golf Course Subdivision

Maximum benefit from the open space of the course can be derived when as many lots as possible are platted alongside the fairways, greens and tees, provided the houses are sited properly on the abutting lots.

Columbine Country Club and Columbine Valley Estates, Arapahoe County, Colorado

Van Schaack & Co., Denver, Developers

Harman, O'Donnell & Henninger Associates, Inc., Land Planners

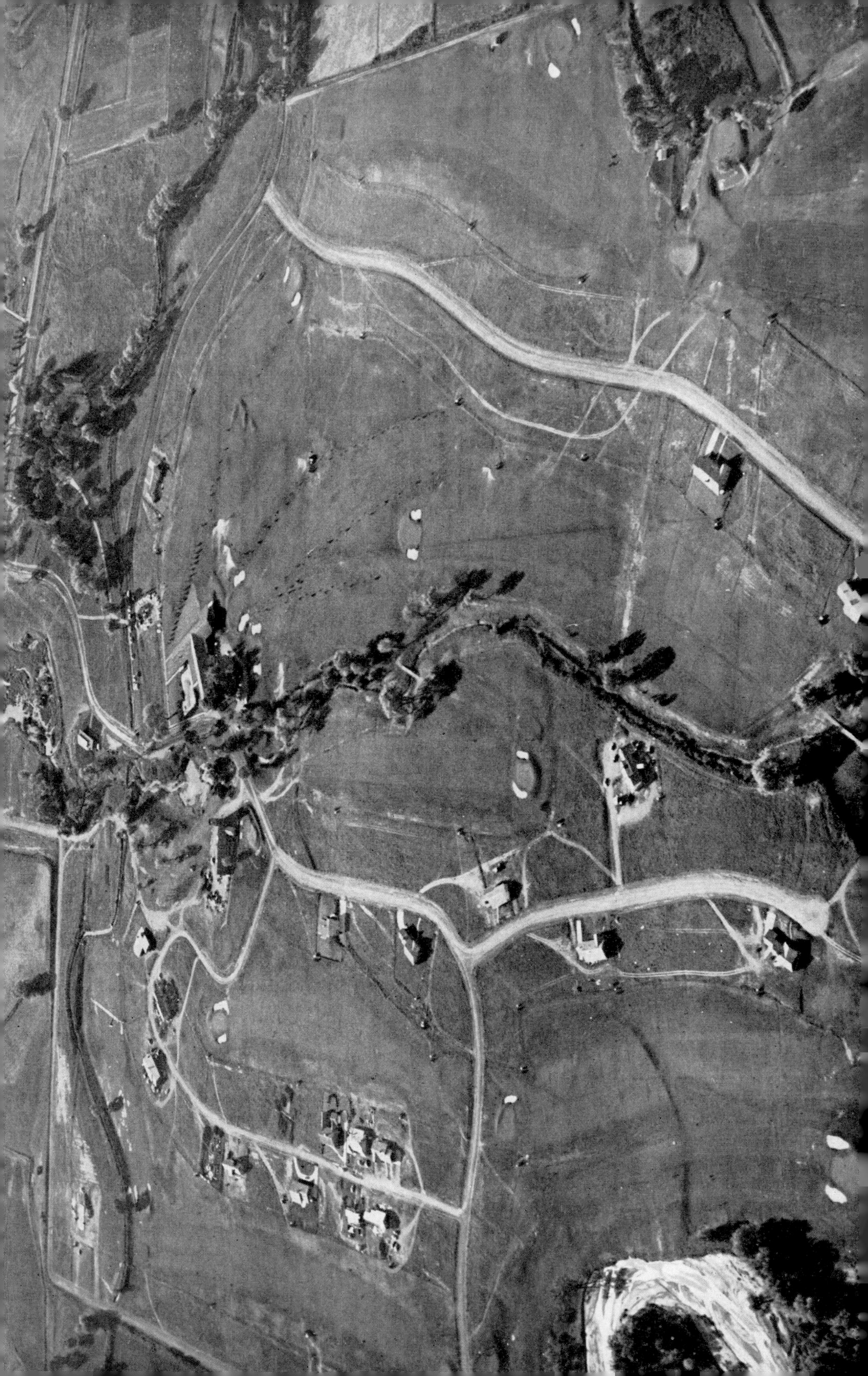

available and with ample room for employee parking, loading, and future expansion. Effectively, the plan maintains control over the area through covenants (more protective than regulations found in modern zoning ordinances) to insure both the developer and the tenants against nuisances, neighborhood deterioration, and other undesirable conditions which could affect adversely the value of their investments.[143]

There are development principles for planned industrial districts which should be followed by the developer:[144]

(a) A careful analysis of the tax situation as it will apply to the developer should be made in order to establish an operating procedure whereby the developer will be eligible for the most favorable tax treatment obtainable under existing federal and state regulations.

(b) A survey of the current industrial structure and the potential for types of industries most likely to settle in a planned industrial district at the proposed location. Layout plans and promotional efforts should be based on results of the survey.

(c) Thorough study of engineering problems and development costs should be made before installing any improvements. Such study should consider these points: (1) facilities and utilities for industry must be larger than those installed in commercial or residential development; (2) development costs are in

---

[143] See "Industrial District Development for Home Builders," *Urban Land,* June 1958; see also "Effect of Industrial Parks on the Community." Robert E. Boley. *Urban Land,* November 1958. Urban Land Institute.
See also "The Role of the Railroads in Industrial District Development." George W. Cox. *Urban Land,* February 1958. Urban Land Institute.

[144] See footnote 143, and see also "Planned Industrial District Development Principles" and "Limited Access Highways and Their Effect on Industrial Expansion and Development." *Urban Land,* December 1959. Urban Land Institute.
See also *Visitacion Property and Crocker Industrial Park, A Report to the Sponsor,* a panel study by ULI Industrial Council. Urban Land Institute, November 1958.
See also *Industrial Estates—Tool for Industrialization* by William Bredo, Stanford Research Institute. The Free Press, Glencoe, Ill. 1960.

Illustration No. 58. A Planned Industrial Park

When properly located and properly developed, industrial parks are definite assets to the community because of their stimulating effect on the local economy.

New England Industrial Center, Route 128, Boston Metropolitan Area
Cabot, Cabot & Forbes Co., Developers

direct proportion to property depths—the shallower the site depths, the higher the cost of development and the greater the loss in gross area.[145]

(d) In planning the advance layout, flexibility is the most important consideration. Consequently, the developer should resist outside pressure to have an advance subdivision layout put on record. To have the streets dedicated immediately, ties the developer to a preconceived plan which may make it impossible to adjust the layout to fit the requirements of future prospects.

(e) The streets in an industrial park should carry only that traffic connected with the operations of the district's tenants. *An arterial highway through a planned industrial district should be deliberately avoided.*

Apart from the pros and cons of dispersed or decentralized industry, the land developer needs an active interest in planned industrial district developments, regardless of whether or not he plans to build such district, since the widened economic base created by new industries means increased demands for residential and commercial developments.

8. Urban Renewal

Essentially, urban renewal is an enlightened, long-range federal assistance program to help cities rebuild their worn-out areas.[146] Urban redevelopment initiated by the Housing Act of 1949 was substantially broadened and extended to include conservation, rehabilitation, and reconstruction by the Housing Act of 1954.[147] Since then, urban redevelopment, as a term, has been urban renewal.

---

[145] Industrial districts range in size from less than 100 acres to several thousand acres. Almost three-quarters of the 300 districts surveyed in 1958 are less than 400 acres in size and about 40 per cent are smaller than 100 acres.

No specifications about lot size, street pavement, off-street parking ratios, trackage curvatures, etc., are cited here because of great variations for specific industrial types. Any such citation could be misleading. See references cited in preceding footnotes.

[146] Urban Land Institute has long had a close interest in urban renewal, having studied and recommended legislation for redevelopment of urban areas. Such legislation was later sponsored and introduced in Congress by Senator Robert F. Wagner in 1943 and was known as the Wagner Bill, S1163, 78th Congress, 1st Session.

[147] For a fuller treatment of the development of urban renewal legislation and for some of the problems which confront operation of the program, as well as for its far reaching implications, see *The Challenge*

Urban renewal is often thought of as a program to clear unhealthy slums, to provide better living accommodations for city dwellers and to replace cluttered, unsightly, and obsolescent downtown business and industrial areas with new land uses appropriate to the central city location. But it is difficult to isolate central city problems and developments from those in the suburbs. Suburban areas do not have the widespread slums and blight which are found in the central sections of most cities. However, urban renewal means blight prevention as well as elimination; it also means development and maintenance of sound, healthy communities. These things are as much needed in the suburbs as they are downtown.

Under the present renewal program and sequence of steps toward offering a cleared site for redevelopment purposes, land is sold by the local municipal agency for redevelopment at its appraised value for uses specified in the urban renewal project plan. The difference between the cost of acquiring the land plus the cost of clearing the site and the lower price obtained later by sale or lease to private developers is the federal write-down (two-thirds of the net cost). One effect of this land cost write-down is to put central city land in a reasonably competitive relationship with outlying land.

Land developers have an opportunity to participate in the rehabilitation and reconstruction projects made possible by the urban renewal program[148] and by the FHA program for mortgage insurance under its Section 221 for new buildings in the redevelopment area, both residential and commercial.[149] While the redevelopment phase of urban renewal is still in its infancy,

---

of Urban Renewal by M. Carter McFarland. Technical Bulletin No. 34, Urban Land Institute.

For an outline as to how the program is officially performed, see "An Outline for Urban Renewal" by Philip W. Kniskern. *Urban Land*, May 1957. Urban Land Institute.

For another clear and precise explanation of urban renewal and how resources of federal, state, and municipal governments can be used with local citizen participation to carry out local programs, see *ABC's of Urban Renewal* by Urban Renewal Division, Sears, Roebuck and Co., Chicago 7, Ill. 1957. 25 pp. illus.; see also "Community Organization for Citizen Participation in Urban Renewal." HHFA. Sup't. of Documents, Gov't. Printing Office, Washington 25, D. C.

[148] See "How Localities Can Develop a Workable Program for Urban Renewal." HHFA.

[149] See *"221"—The Program Nobody Knows*. Metropolitan Association of General Improvement Contractors, 1522 Connecticut Ave., N.W., Washington 6, D. C.

the interest shown in the program by private redevelopers has been substantial. As the program progresses and as participating cities reach the stage in the program where cleared land is offered to bidders, there will be increasing investment opportunities for private developers to build the volume of redevelopment housing, commercial and industrial projects which our cities need for revitalization of worn-out areas.[150]

[150] A factor in the urban renewal plan for a project area is the degree of high-rise apartment development to be included in residential re-use areas. It is conservative to assume that with high-rise units the redeveloped areas will re-house as many families as are displaced by the project. In terms of lot areas, street areas, school and other public areas, etc., the redevelopment plan for residential re-use requires special approval procedures. See "Zoning of Planned Residential Development" by Eli Goldston and James H. Scheuer. *Urban Land,* March 1960. Urban Land Institute.

SECTION ONE

PART III

Protecting the Future of the Development

A. PROTECTIVE COVENANTS

1. General

Protective covenants are contracts between the land subdivider and the lot purchaser expressing agreement covering use of land. They are contracts between private parties. Through this instrument, all parties seek to gain certain advantages—the subdivider to aid his land development program and the purchasers to protect their investments. Strict enforcement of suitable covenants gives best assurance to each lot owner that no other lot owners within the protected area can use property in a way that will destroy values, lower the character of the neighborhood or create a nuisance.[151]

Sometimes called private deed restrictions or deed and agreement, protective covenants from many years of experience have proved to be an essential instrument in maintaining stability, permanence, character, and marketability in community development. Properly prepared for legal soundness, these covenants contribute to the establishment of the character of a neighborhood and to the maintenance of value levels through the regulation of type, size, and placement of structures, lot sizes, reservations of easements, and prohibition of nuisances and other land uses that might affect the desirability of a residential area.

Protective covenants are not to be considered as taking the place of public regulations such as zoning. Both types of regulation are essential and are not necessarily overlapping. Zoning protection is based on governmental exercise of police powers which are considered the minimum necessary in maintaining and promoting public health, safety and general welfare. Protective covenants are private contracts. Being private contracts, protective covenants can go beyond the regulations enforceable by public authority and can go much further in meeting the needs for protecting amenities inherent or built into any particular type of community development.

---

[151] See "Protective Covenants," Land Planning Bulletin No. 3, Data Sheet 40, revised 4/59. FHA.

Protective covenants should provide enforcement provisions, be recorded in public land records, and be made superior to the lien of any mortgage that may be on record prior to the recording of the protective covenant.

For any development, protective covenants should take the form of blanket provisions which apply to a whole area rather than being separate covenants in each deed. Basic restrictions should be made a part of the recorded plat. If, in addition, certain further special provisions are found to be necessary for any particular properties, then they should be added to the individual deeds between developer and purchaser.

Covenants should be drafted and be checked for conformance to state statutes by legal counsel thoroughly qualified in this particular field. Some attorneys specialize in this work and should be retained to pass on the legal aspects. However, the details of the requirements and protection to be covered should be worked out in collaboration with the developer and the land planner. Generally, the final form should not be framed until the sponsor has obtained preliminary subdivision analysis by FHA, if the subdivision is so underwritten, or until the project development plan has been set. By first spending the time and energy necessary to abtain a good physical plan for getting a subdivision started on the right foot, then protective covenants can follow as safeguards naturally.

The covenants recommended by the FHA have been used satisfactorily in thousands of subdivisions and have been approved by the title companies and mortgage investment institutions.[152] They should be considered as minima. In high-priced developments, or those having special characteristics, more detailed controls are usually desirable.

2. Specific Controls

The protective covenants, if reasonable and if maintained, can be enforced. Zoning is political and can be changed. Private restrictions and zoning are the two ways whereby the character of development can be controlled. The precise wording of any such private restrictions cannot be written by the Council. What could be properly legal in one state may not be sustained by courts in another. Aside from the practical matter of items to include in the covenants, the matter is largely one of phraseology for conformity to state law.

---

[152] See Appendix A for sample clauses as used by FHA, 1960.

The following lists what is customary and is recommended as items to be covered in blanket covenants (see Appendix B for suggested forms and clauses):

(a) Control of land use, including restrictions as to type and design of dwellings.

(b) Architectural control of all structures including fences and walls. This control, sometimes called an approval of plans clause, is the strongest means the land developer has at his disposal in controlling the kind of houses built in his subdivision. It is particularly useful when the land developer sells lots to other builders or when custom building of houses by individual purchasers takes place. Some developers retain control over the house color, building material, or architectural style. Specified controls are important in group or attached houses.

Architectural control is best accomplished by the developer's first establishing his own architectural control committee or plan review board, then passing on this control to others as indicated by item 4, "Enforcement," which follows on the next page.

(c) Minimum sideyard and setback regulations, including location or prohibition of accessory buildings.

(d) Control of minimum lot size.

(e) Prohibition of nuisances and regulation of "for sale" or other signs.

(f) Restriction of temporary dwellings and any placement of trailers on the lot.

(g) Limitation of size of structure through a minimum cost or area clause, or both. The inclusion of cost restrictions is debatable, particularly in a period of increasing or irregular construction costs. Where such a restriction is included, it may be advisable to relate the required minimum cost to an authoritative price index such as the United States Bureau of Labor Commodity Index. This has been done by David Bohannon in California. Probably the most simple and effective method is the specification of a certain minimum habitable floor area, exclusive of garages and basements. Such a restriction is capable of direct interpretation, is less open to controversy, and can be used alone or in conjunction with a minimum cost limitation if necessary. Some developers depend entirely on architectural control for maintaining standards of cost, size, and character.

(h) Reservation for utility easements; usually five feet on either side of the rear or side lot line.

(i) Other clauses which may be found desirable or necessary can be added to the above depending on local custom, character of the development, and type of market. Many developers control the grading plan of individual lots, the elevations of first floor building levels, and location of drives and garages.

In a resort area subdivision, the keeping of horses and maintenance of bridle trails can be a special clause. Similarly in a golf course subdivision matters of planting and fencing along the golf course property lines can be regulated for the protection of both home owner and course player.

3. Effective Period

Some covenants are drawn up with a definite termination date, but opinion favors covenants which run with the land, subject to revision by a stipulated percentage (not less than a majority) of the property owners at the end of a 25 to 40-year period, and with provisions for automatic extension in the event no action is taken by the owners at the time specified. It is recommended that any action to be taken by the owners should be required to precede the termination date by at least 5 years. This permits considered action and prevents pressure being brought to bear by any individual who might benefit by an immediate change. No one should have the right to remove general covenants before the end of the minimum period. However, some developers insert provisions retaining minor rights of deviation within certain limits, such as building line adjustment.

4. Enforcement

Unless adequate machinery is set up initially for proper enforcement, covenants may become ineffective through nonobservance and violation. It is always advisable to provide for the establishment of an organization which will take over this duty as one of its functions. Control by the developer of the affairs of such an organization should be passed on to the residents as rapidly as possible. One exception to this is to be found in the enforcement of architectural control which should normally be retained by the developer as long as he has a stake in the community. The establishment of a proper community organization is discussed in the following section under Homes Associations.

In evaluating the type and extent of the protective covenants to place on any particular development, the experience of the

J. C. Nichols Company of Kansas City still applies: "Don't make the mistake of placing restrictions on too large areas in advance of knowing your demand. This may result in some land carrying higher restrictions than later demand will justify. If you use minimum cost restrictions, we recommend a lower general base restriction on a subdivision, adding additional cost restrictions as may be justified when individual sales are made and areas become established with higher cost homes. Always, of course, you should retain approval of architectural design of all structures, including fences, walls, etc. Some developers depend wholly on architectural control and do not set up minimum costs, and perhaps this is a better method.

"In the early days of the Company we made the mistake of restricting land only as it was sold. Today we file a restriction on each area as it is platted subjecting all the land therein to our basic restrictions (setting forth any areas reserved for shops, schools, churches, etc.). Everyone who buys in such subdivision has an injunction right against any violation of restriction. We do not believe it is fair for a developer to place individual restrictions on each lot as it is sold, and not commit the balance of his unsold land."

B. MAINTENANCE AND HOMES ASSOCIATIONS

In developments where adequate public maintenance of park areas, streets or other facilities is not available, it is advisable for the developer to establish a property owners' maintenance association, which may be a home owners' association or other acceptable community maintenance organization, with adequate powers to provide maintenance and to assess the benefiting property owners at a reasonable rate and to administer such assessments. Establishment of a property owners' association is also advisable to provide an effective means of obtaining adherence to protective covenants. The architectural control device may become part of the responsibilities of the association.

The development company initially is the owner of all property within the development. It proceeds to set up the association as part of the covenants or under articles of incorporation executed by the company, in which the company names five to seven persons (usually company officials) to act temporarily as directors, or officers, until their successors are elected. These successors should be resident owners of property within the area covered by the covenants. The association needs a charter from the state to operate as a maintenance organization.

The value of homes associations in community development is indicated in the following statement from the J. C. Nichols Company: "We made the mistake in not setting up homes associations in our properties in the Country Club District at the very beginning, with power to assess 'land' for neighborhood service. We now have 19 such associations, all functioning in an excellent manner under one common staff, and every lot is sold subject to a land assessment for such associations. We even subject our unsold land, where street improvements are in, to this assessment. (This assessment is not on improvements). These associations create neighborhood responsibility through the years, supply many needs and services, and go far to maintain values.

"Homes associations can be of great value in enforcing protective covenants, and in working with public officials.

"The question of care of vacant lots in a subdivision can be solved by an effective homes association with real powers. Be sure to give your homes association broad powers to meet all future and changing needs."

Procedures for a developer's setting up and putting a homes association into operation are somewhat dependent upon the type of community, the intended character and price range of its houses and whether or not municipal services are available. Usually the developer offers a printed brochure or leaflet which describes the charter and by-laws of the association, including its membership and assessment provisions. Later the association can issue its own rules and regulations, particularly for use of any recreational facility or area under its administration. Among homes associations which have been outstandingly successful over the years are those found in the Country Club District of Kansas City; the Roland Park developments of Baltimore; St. Francis Wood in San Francisco, California; San Lorenzo Village, Alameda County, California; Forest Hills Gardens, Long Island, New York; Park Hills, Berkeley, California; Lakewood, North Little Rock, Arkansas; Blue Ridge and Ennis Arden in Seattle; Wilmington Park, Savannah, Georgia, etc.

1. Powers and Duties

These articles set forth the purposes and duties of the association which may include:

(a) Maintenance of streets, parks, and other open spaces until such activity is taken over by public authority or in lieu thereof.

(b) Maintenance of vacant, unimproved and unkempt lots.

(c) Refuse collection, street sweeping, snow removal, police and fire protection, and maintenance of water and sewer mains and sewage disposal systems until taken over by public authority or in lieu thereof.

(d) Payment of taxes and assessments, if necessary, on all property held by the association for general use of the community.

(e) Approval of architectural and site plans for new construction. Most developers have found it better to retain control over architectural design, planting, etc., during the active development period. In some cases this function has been turned over to an "Art Jury," membership of which is determined by the company. This method probably insures a more consistent degree of good design than by giving the functions to the homes association, the members of which may be swayed by special interest in the purchase or in the effect which the new house will have on their own particular property. Control over this function may be assigned to the homes association after almost all land has been sold by the developer.

(f) Enforcement of private covenants and restrictions.

(g) Determination and collection of annual charges or assessments which become liens against property in event of nonpayment. In this connection, the Council urges the importance of filing the covenants prior to the sale of lots in order that they may be a prior lien over any later mortgages.

(h) Dispersal of funds collected for maintenance, taxes, or other proper charges levied against property of the association.

(i) Acquisition or disposal of property in the interests of the association, either by purchase, sale, or dedication to a public authority.

(j) Borrowing of money, if needed, for the proper conduct of the association's affairs.

(k) Performance of other proper functions in the interest of the association and the community such as maintenance and replacement of street trees, erection of street signs, operation of a community information office, etc.

Again, comments of the J. C. Nichols Company of Kansas City are quoted for their pertinence to the matter of the organizational setup of a homes association:

"In our early charters we made the serious mistake of limiting the total tax per square foot, and some associations cannot levy over a mill per square foot under their charters. Others have the right by a vote of the majority of the owners attending a meeting called for that purpose to raise it to a total not to exceed two mills. With our present day high costs, the associations with any limitation are in grave difficulty, and several of them are trying to meet the situation by asking for voluntary additional annual contributions to the homes association. This results in a few of the owners refusing to pay; consequently, a number of our associations have had to give up some of their essential duties. We do not believe it will slow down sales to have the charter provide that the assessments can be increased by a vote of the majority of owners attending a meeting called for that purpose, and we certainly should not require that it has to be a majority of all home owners.

"In our association the man owning a big tract has no more votes than a man owning a small tract except that the small tract owners must comply with the minimum lot width permitted. In other words, a man could not divide a lot into several small ownerships and get additional votes. And, even though our company might still own half the land in a subdivision, we only have one vote. This has worked all right over some forty years."

2. Resident Control

Rules and regulations as to the number of directors, eligibility or method of selection, voting power of members, and modifications of the by-laws are set forth when the association is formulated. Membership is usually limited to resident owners and persons purchasing a home site for their personal use. (See notation page 199 about offering club membership privileges as part of the sale of a property within the development).

Voting power can be determined by the association or can be based on the number of square feet of land held or contracted for, or upon the number of building sites so held by the association. The latter method provides an orderly relinquishment of control over the community to the home owners themselves. This is a highly desirable objective. Experience has shown that those associations which have been most successful have had community responsibility turned over to the residents as rapidly as possible with the minimum of control retained by the development company except in the early stages. In some cases the incorporation of the association is left to the discretion of the members. However, incorporation is desirable especially where public services are being performed and power is given to collect and disburse money.

By-laws governing the association which provide the usual specifications as to membership, voting rights, property rights, corporate powers, elections, powers and duties of directors and other officers, conduct of meetings, and amendments may also be established initially by the company, although this may be left to the association to develop.

John Matthews, developer of Lakewood in North Little Rock, makes the following suggestion about resident control of the property owners association: "Our feeling is that the operation of a property owners association" (or a community club, for that matter, when such features are part of the community's facilities) "should be turned over to residents as soon as possible.[153] But title to the land in private parks should not be released by the developer until about 95 per cent of the subdivision has been sold. This retention is not only a necessary safeguard for the developer's investment and for his recapturing control in an emergency but it is also a safeguard for the investments of the majority of home owners in new areas, which conceivably could be jeopardized by radical minorities.[154]

---

[153] John Matthews elaborates: "Early in our experience we found that membership in the property owners association (or home owners association) should be voluntary rather than mandatory on buying property in the subdivision."

[154] "Assuming the recreational facilities are attractive features of the development and that their annual membership dues are reasonable, 85 to 95 per cent of those eligible will voluntarily join the home owners association. A much more congenial association for the members will result and many headaches will be avoided if the inevitable small percentage of nonconformists are not forced to join.

"By retaining title to the recreational facilities until 95 per cent of the property is sold, your association will like the arrangement because you will be paying ad valorem taxes and carrying liability insurance on the recreational areas. Also, if you should deed these areas, control could get into the hands of the wrong clique. For example, a homes association in California passed a rule that only veterans could belong. Other associations have wrongly permitted the sort of commercial recreational development not appropriate for a residential community.

"We think you should carry this big stick but speak softly, staying in the background as much as possible. Your property owners association will not manage and maintain the recreational areas exactly like you would, but, being closer to the problem, the association will probably do a better job. If you insist on dominating the association, as many developers do, you may get permanently trapped in this profitless and time consuming ordeal that you cannot do as well as the residents themselves." John Matthews.

Ownership of the park areas by a homes association raises the real estate tax issue. The assessment and taxes due on such private recreational land use may prove to be a real burden to the membership.

It has been found that an association comprised of between 500 and 750 families is large enough to operate financially and small enough to retain a close neighborhood interest.

3. Maintenance and Operation

Some developers have established contractual relations with the association whereby they furnish the maintenance and community services.[155] This method has the advantage of relieving the association of operational details and the developer, being directly concerned as a partner in the welfare of the community, will usually furnish better service at less cost than would some concern with no direct interest.

Several large community builders have retained control of maintenance and assessment collections in lieu of setting up a homes association. While this method is used successfully and has certain advantages in insuring consistent maintenance of the community assets, it does not provide the degree of resident participation which seems desirable and makes it difficult in the future for the developer to divest himself of these responsibilities should he desire to do so. Ability to assign these functions should always be assured.

Instead of a homes association, River Oaks (Hugh Potter's development in Houston) has a maintenance fund provision in each deed which levies an assessment of not to exceed two mills per square foot upon all site owners, including the River Oaks Corporation itself on the sites it still owns. The River Oaks Corporation acts as Trustee in the collection and disbursement of the funds. The operation of the maintenance work is under the direct supervision of a capable engineer. Many highly

---

[155] The tract developer provides for the levying and collecting of a maintenance fund. Then, during the early years of the project, aids in collection of the money. During this phase he may even provide free stenographic, clerical, and, in some cases, actual maintenance service together with personnel, not charged to the association.

As the community grows and as its residents begin to take an active interest in the area, the operation of the association is gradually turned over to the community residents themselves. Finally, the developer steps out of the picture completely. Inasmuch as the residents should accept the interest and responsibility of maintaining their own community through the medium of a well organized and operated association.

desirable services are rendered to the residents of River Oaks under this maintenance fund at a surprisingly low cost.

4. Recreation Areas and Clubs

Recreation facilities for a community development are one of its greatest assets—not only for the young people but for the adults as well. The modus operandi for providing these facilities should rest initially with the developer. Relinquishment to resident control, however, should be insured at the earliest moment (see footnote 155). Ownership and operation of the recreation areas may be either part of the homes association's activities or separated therefrom.

Apart from the method of operating the facilities, attention to their location and the site planning of the adjacent residential properties is an important element in their later acceptance or rejection by the residents. For example, if the location of a community swimming pool and its appurtenances is not considered in the planning stage, the noise and confusion from the outdoor activity could affect adversely the value of adjacent residences.[156]

An excellent example of how the homes association operates its recreational facilities as a club is that of the Lakewood Property Owners Association in North Little Rock, Arkansas. For some of its experience as recounted by John Matthews, the developer, see the footnote.[157]

---

[156] See page 181 for planning features of a community swim club. A solution to the swimming pool noise problem is locating it in a 10 or 15 acre park.

[157] Another aspect to consider in operation of a local community swimming pool by a property owners association is this: "If you intend to have swimming facilities, we would not build a bath house. A small wash room facility is needed, but we think it much better for the residents to dress at home and walk, drive or bicycle to the pool" (or beach, if the community has a waterfront). "This eliminates the necessity for a large maintenance budget by the property owners association and lends a festive informal air to the subdivision.

"Our swimming facility pays its own way, including the salaries of four lifeguards. Members of the Association swim free but if they bring guests, the fee is 50 cents per day per guest. When there is a party with twelve children who do not live in Lakewood, that means $6.00 to help pay for lifeguards, etc. On some days, guests' fees amount to as much as $150.00.

"Over 1,400 families live in Lakewood. About 85 per cent belong to the Lakewood Property Owners Association, paying $18.00 per year, per family, in dues. This produces a satisfactory annual budget." (When the community is finished it will have about 4,500 families. Lakewood

An older example of how a homes association may be set up and operated as a club is found in the experience of Blue Ridge near Seattle, Washington, Hugh Russell, developer. The community consisted of 500 medium-priced home sites of which about 25 per cent were built on at the time the club was established. Several tracts of land amounting to approximately 15 acres, and including several stream valley parks, a waterfront, and a club house site, were deeded by the developer to the club which had been previously incorporated.

The developer also constructed a complete club house building which was furnished and equipped by the members, and two concrete tennis courts which could be used for various activities throughout the year including ice skating, outdoor dancing, etc. Total costs involved including the land, tennis courts, club house, fencing, site improvement, and incidental expenses including incorporation, amounted to approximately $65 per lot. Membership dues, originally set up at $24.00 per year per family, were subsequently determined to be about half that amount and have been on this basis ever since. The development is now completely sold and is thus able to operate on a budget about five times as great as that originally established with no increase in family dues.

Provision of facilities such as those described above will often cost the developer no more than an extensive advertising and publicity campaign, and will create a sustained value which will continue to pay dividends for many years in the future. As John Matthews points out: "People have more leisure today but the average family is still on a limited budget. By working together in an association where the developer provides the land and helps the residents install capital improvements, a family can enjoy life far more than in a typical subdivision

---

is fortunate in having two lakes for recreation—one for swimming, the other for boating).

"We (the developers) are still helping with the installation of capital improvements for recreation and are pretty well able to get the Association to spend money for those improvements we think best for the community since we only match funds on projects we like.

"The LPOA operates its recreational facilities and program under the direction of a physical education major with the assistance of several college boys and girls as instructors. One maintenance man works under him all year long. In summer, another is added. Through the part-time instruction program, children of Lakewood learn to swim, to play tennis, baseball, football, etc. This turns out to be a super baby sitting arrangement, very popular with the children and the parents."

where no private recreational facilities or recreational program is provided.

"By featuring your recreational facilities in advertising and giving your salesmen something unusual to show prospective buyers, we believe the extra expense and effort are justified." The reason why most persons purchase a home in a new community is to raise a family in the right environment and to offer all the family members advantages within the family means. Not to recognize this fact is a common shortcoming in many developments.

While initial establishment of homes associations, clubs, or both, is highly desirable, it is possible in many cases to organize such groups in already developed communities. Experience also shows this type of organization is not peculiar to high cost developments. It could form the working basis for any community development and can be adapted to meet particular conditions. Many associations also function as a social nucleus in sponsoring community functions, events, and celebrations. It provides a framework for collective effort within the neighborhood which otherwise is often very difficult to obtain effectively.

C. MAINTENANCE IN APARTMENT DEVELOPMENT

One of the prime rules for apartment maintenance is "don't economize on construction at the expense of maintenance."

Be sure your outdoor areas are private; put fences around patios and landscaped areas. Use a central terrace and swimming pool to tie together several buildings in an apartment group development.

Provide apartments with the same appliances that are being offered for the single-family house market locally. If you don't provide individual apartment dishwashers and washer-dryers, at least provide the space for them; provide laundry rooms equipped with automatic washers and clothes dryers so that tenants are not inclined to want to hang anything out of doors.

In a garden-type apartment, one of the greatest maintenance items is the out of doors clothes drying nuisance. To solve the problem, either plan the development so that no individual tenant yards can be seen from the access street or provide special areas equipped with standard type clothes poles and drying lines from which all articles must be removed by a specified hour (an enforcement problem for management); or install the proper indoors clothes drying facilities, particularly in multi-story buildings.

Based on his experience as developer of garden-type apartments, in the Washington area, Gustave Ring's remarks about grounds maintenance problems are worth noting: "No matter how many sidewalks and paths are planned, they are never quite enough to take care of the short cuts tenants like to make. By providing play and park areas and enforcing regulations, it is possible to keep some of the traffic off the lawns. In planning playgrounds it is always advisable to keep them as far removed from the streets as possible. Mothers will encourage their children to attend the play areas more frequently if they are removed from danger. On the other hand, it is not desirable to have them too far away from the apartments.

Garbage and trash collection can be another maintenance nuisance problem in apartment projects. Garbage disposal is easily solved by the installation of sink disposers, providing best quality appliances and brass plumbing are used, or by wall chute incinerators in high-rise buildings. Trash collection is another matter. Problems of trash collection to be considered are as follows: area to be covered; men necessary to do the job; the best type of equipment to use for efficient collection; and the distance the pick-up has to be carried to a truck.

In the type of garden apartment layout where there are front and back public entrances, trash collections must be made from carefully screened receptacles placed close to the rear entrance to serve several tenants. Then collections can be made by hand or mechanized trucks. In the newer row type of garden apartment design where private terraces or patios face a courtyard, private park, or swimming pool area, there is no "back entrance." In these cases specially designed compartments must be provided for, accessible from the entrance side of the building. The matter of service for trash collection must be planned for in the planning stage of the development. The means for collection can set the layout of the building.

Illustration No. 59. Merchandising the Project

A well designed nameplate as a distinguishing marker a the entrance to the development is useful for merchandisin purposes and for later identification of the community.

David D. Bohannon Organization, Develope

Westwood
CHOICE OF THE VALLEY
planned and built by –
David D. Bohannon
Organization

you saw it on NBC TV
now see it here
HOME
homes
MODEL-OPEN DAILY 2-9 PM

D. SELLING THE PROJECT

1. Merchandising Methods

In addition to the establishment of a sales organization scaled to the size of their operation, developers have found several successful methods for selling houses and lots in a new subdivision. More builders are today working with established realtors or real estate companies. Listed here are ideas which various Council members have used to advantage:

(a) A well designed nameplate as a distinguishing marker at the entrance to the development is useful for merchandising purposes and for later identification of the community in the public mind. Such entrance features should be modest and designed to blend with, or to designate, the character of the community. Once elaborate gateways and entrance features were thought necessary, but experience proved that too much money could be so spent and often sales of adjacent lots were deterred.

(b) A well delineated map of the project can be prepared as part of a sales brochure. Such published maps enable a prospect to identify the location of the development and the houses and lots and their price tags within the development.

(c) A display of each house type built as a demonstrator model complete with interior furnishings and its landscaped lot. These houses can later be sold.

(d) An on-site display room showing placards and samples of the materials used in the project. These can be cut-aways of actual construction. These devices are to show the quality of materials, the soundness of the construction and the choice of design or materials which are available to prospective buyers of houses in the development. But unless this type of demonstration is geared to a full-fledged advertising and promotion program, the displays are costly to maintain.

(e) A sales office equipped to perform the services of buying a home and to answer the questions raised by the uninformed home buyer. Libraries of magazines and books on house and

Illustration No. 60. Model Home for Merchandising the Project

A display of each house type as a demonstrator model complete with interior furnishings and landscaped lot is a useful way of stimulating public interest and sales in the project.

Westgate, Flint, Michigan
Gerholz Community Homes, Inc., Developer

garden architecture, and brochures on steps in financing a home available for distribution are effective ways to stimulate interest of prospective home buyers. Systems of cards can be developed to show all business that can be performed for a client including insurance, loans, legal work, architectural services, appraisals, payment schedules, etc.

(f) Any poor or less desirable lot should be built on first by the developer. As the J. C. Nichols Company says: "Don't make the mistake of building houses on your best lots in a new subdivision just to get it started. It is desirable to build on the areas which may be difficult to sell as vacant lots. Try to make the poorest property the best in your subdivision. Be sure to maintain signs on all property reserved for non-residential uses. Informing the customers about the location of a shopping center site, a church or a school may save you a lot of grief later."

If the developer is offering only vacant lots which buyers themselves are to build on later, price cutting of hard-to-move lots is a questionable practice. It is preferable to make the lot more attractive by added planting or landscaping.

(g) It is desirable to offer landscape planting plans together with types of plant material which grow well in that climate. As part of the sales price of the property it is desirable to include a presentable offering of well-chosen and well placed shrubbery.

(h) As incentives, the developer's staff employees can be helped to build their own homes through an offering of the lot at cost. Prizes, bonuses, or other inducements to salesmen have proved good practice. It is good to have as many of your people as possible living in your developments.

(i) Sales commissions can be based on a sliding scale percentage which increases with the amount, volume, length of service, or combinations of these. Weekly reports should be required from salesmen at sales meetings.

(j) Regardless of the size of a subdivision, only as many houses or lots as the market will absorb rapidly should be readied and offered for sale. This provides a constant supply of new merchandise, stimulates salesmen, and creates a demand because houses in your subdivision are always scarce.[158]

---

[158] John Matthews endorses this system of merchandising small groups of lots: "Preview sales are desirable because with a smaller investment the developer is enabled to get lots on the market quickly. A second opening announcement or sale can then be held after all community facilities are installed and the paving is completed."

2. Modernizing Old Subdivisions

Previously platted and partially improved subdivisions which have only scattered dwelling construction within them present different problems difficult to solve. Replanning is often difficult due to absence of unified ownership of the tract, presence of some utilities and street improvements, or long legal delays. (Essentially, urban renewal and its procedures is another form of modernizing wornout areas.)

In some cases, changed circumstances create a market demand for a refurbishing an old subdivision which has become blighted either through bad planning, scattered development, sub-standard construction, or other adverse influences. Various methods can be employed to re-establish such old subdivisions. They include:

Replatting groups of lots to obtain a better street plan or wider lots; on vacant parcels, building new houses for sale; sale of vacant lots to adjoining property owners; rehabilitation through repainting and modernizing of old outmoded houses to bring back values; furnishing financial aid to the owner of a shabby house if he will agree to clean up or paint up his property; group meetings of the residents to stimulate new interest in the area as a place to live; removal of high, overgrown planting or replanting where none exists; provision of a small park or playground.

Older, built-up in-town areas laid out with a gridiron pattern of streets can be modernized also. A basic provision is relatively

Illustration No. 61.

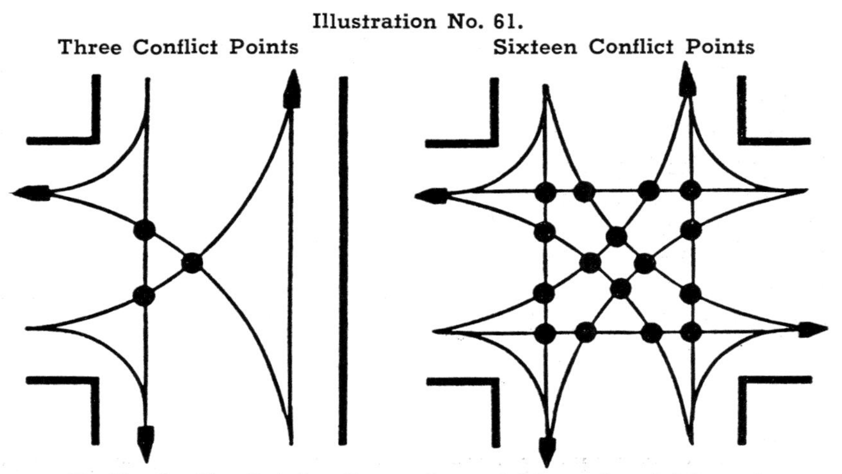

Traffic Conflict Points—Comparison of 3-legged and 4-legged Intersections

Illustration No. 62.

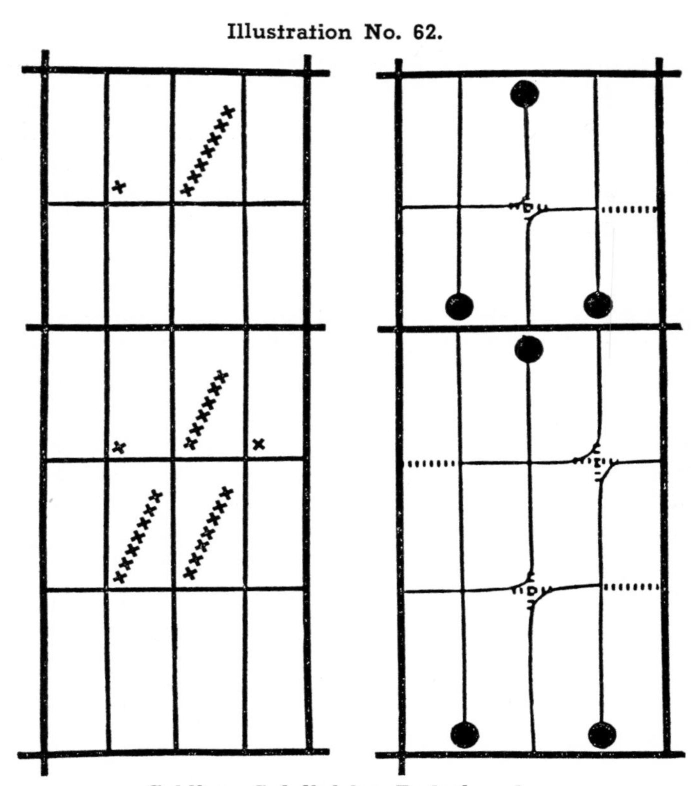

Gridiron Subdivision Redesigned

NOTE: Each x represents one accident during a 5-year study period.

simple—all streets within the area need not be continuous. By vacating some streets, by closing off others to form culs-de-sac and elbows, as shown by the illustration, it is possible to transform a gridiron subdivision into a limited-access type where heavy traffic is prevented from passing through the area. From the economic standpoint, the municipal cost of changing the street pattern by diverters and turn-arounds can be repaid by increased home values. To create such improvement takes leadership from a community improvement association, and cooperation by a municipal government.[159]

---

[159] See "Subdividing for Traffic Safety" by Harold Marks. *Urban Land,* October 1957. Urban Land Institute.

SECTION TWO

Planning and Operation of Shopping Centers

INTRODUCTION TO SHOPPING CENTERS

In presenting an extensive discussion of shopping centers in its Handbook on community development, it should not be assumed that Urban Land Institute's Community Builders' Council places emphasis unduly on outlying commercial development. Rather it should again be made clear that the Council devotes its attention to the land development field, primarily as it relates to use of raw land. But there are specialties. Hence, industrial land use matters fall to the Institute's Industrial Council; central city development and urban redevelopment to the Central Business District Council. Because the planned commercial use, typified by the shopping center, has emerged as an element integrated with sound community development, the Handbook includes basic precepts for shopping center planning and operation.

Realizing that the ultimate success of any new neighborhood depends upon the prosperity of its shopping facility, the Community Builders' Council since its inception in 1944, has focused upon shopping center development. In this time, the Council has built up a considerable body of experience through exchange of information by its Executive Group members, who themselves are the originators, developers and owners of shopping centers. Thus, this section of the Handbook presents principles that have evolved from practice and experience. By such presentation, the Council is simply trying to arrive at the best guide to help others in the complex shopping center field.

Even though the principles for good development remain constant, variations in their application appear in actual practice. Hence, any specifications cited are guides—not rules. These guides are the concepts in shopping center planning and operation which have grown out of practical experience. Some are emphasized; some may be modified; others can be denied; still others can be ignored. In shopping center planning, leasing and operation—for every firm statement there can be a firm exception.

1. Definitions.

At the outset, it is necessary to clarify the difference between *shopping center* and *shopping district. Shopping center,* as a term has precise meaning. As used by the Community Builders' Council, *shopping center* means: A group of commercial establishments, planned, developed, owned and managed as a *unit,* with off-street parking provided on the property; and related in its location, size and type of shops to the trade area which the unit serves.[160]

This definition is standard. It eliminates from the shopping center concept miscellaneous collections of individual stores standing on their separate lot-parcels strung along street frontages or clustered in a contiguous area—with or without incidental off-street parking. These are shopping *areas* or retail shopping *districts.* Shopping centers on the basis of their planned layout and unified operation differ from shopping districts even though both complexes are commercial areas for retail selling purposes in general notion.

Because the shopping center is a fairly new land use development, many of its components have not been referred to uniformly. But certain terms have standard usage. To clarify the interpretation in practice by the Community Builders' Council, the terms are defined on pages 215-219.

---

[160] Other criteria by which the shopping center can be judged relate the parking space provision to the building unit. In setting the relationship between the parking and the structure confusion in statistics often comes about because different factors can be used to denominate the ratio—such as gross building area, gross floor area, or gross sales area. Hence, ratios between the number of parking spaces and the building unit are not always comparable. To avoid any misunderstanding in statistical analyses, the Council has decided that *gross leasable area* is the uniform factor to employ in all cases. See also subsequent definitions, pages 217-218.

Illustration No. 63. A Present Day Shopping Center

The shopping center is a group of commercial establishment planned, developed, owned and managed as a **unit** with off street parking provided on the property; and related in it location, size and type of shops to the trade area which th unit serves.

Hillsdale Shopping Center, San Mateo, Cali

David D. Bohannon Organization, Owners/Develope

Photo: Moulin Studios, Courtesy, David D. Bohannon Organizatio

KAPIOLANI BOULEVARD
Free Parking
Thrifty Drugs
Cooke Trust Company
Liberty House
Dator Jewelers
Hub Clothiers
Rigs
Kress
Chas. Brewer & Company
National Dollar
Home Insurance
American Factors
Castle & Cooke
Bishop Trust
Alexander & Baldwin
Bishop Bank
Young Hotel Building
Dillingham Building
Theo H. Davies & Company
FREEWAY

(a) Types of Shopping Center

As the shopping center evolved, three distinct *types* have emerged, each distinctive in its own function: the neighborhood, the community, and the regional. In all cases the shopping center's type is determined by *its major tenant.* Neither the site area nor the building area is the determining factor.

The Neighborhood Center—provides for the sale of convenience goods (foods, drugs and sundries) and personal services (laundry and dry cleaning, barbering, shoe repairing) for day-by-day living needs.

It is built around a supermarket as the principal tenant.

In size, the neighborhood center has an *average* gross leasable area close to 50,000 sq. ft. and it can range from 30,000 sq. ft. up to as much as 100,000 sq. ft. For its site area, the neighborhood center needs from 4 to 10 acres. It normally serves a trade area population of 7,500 to 40,000 people[161] within six minutes driving time.[162]

This is the smallest type of center.

The Community Center—in addition to the convenience goods and personal services of the neighborhood center, provides a wider range of facilities for the sale of soft lines (wearing apparel for men, women, and children) and hard lines (hardware and appliances). It makes more depth of merchandise available—variety in sizes, styles, colors, prices.

---

[161] The number of people needed to support a shopping center of *any* type is a variable, not a fixed measure. Factors of income level, disposable income, dilution by competition, plus changing methods of merchandising and store sizes—all enter the calculations. Because of such variables the standard of 1,000 families, formerly cited as the bare minimum support for a neighborhood center, no longer holds. See *A Re-examination of the Shopping Center Market.* Technical Bulletin No. 33. Urban Land Institute.

[162] Research by Voorhees, Sharpe and Stegmaier, as reported in ULI's Technical Bulletin No. 24, *Shopping Habits and Travel Patterns,* showed that shoppers will not travel farther than this for daily convenience needs, normally.

Illustration No. 64. The Shopping Center and the Central Business District

The regional shopping center with its array of merchandising comes close to reproducing the shopping facilities and customer attractions once available only in central business districts.

The Ala Moana Shopping Center in comparison with the Central Business District of Honolulu, Hawaii.

Ala Moana opened in October, 1959, and includes 677,340 sq. ft. of net rentable area and 4,292 parking spaces.

Hawaiian Land Company, Owner/Developer

It is built around a junior department store or a variety store as the major tenant, in addition to the supermarket. It *does not have* a full-line department store, though it may have a strong specialty store.

In size, the community center has an *average* gross leasable area of about 150,000 sq. ft., but the range is between 100,000 sq. ft. and 300,000 sq. ft. For its site area, the community center needs from 10 to 30 acres or more. It normally serves a trade area population of 40,000 to 150,000 people.

This is the type of center which is most difficult to estimate for size and pulling power. Because some shopping goods are available, the shopper will compare price and style. This complicates sales volume predictions and opens the way to competition from other centers. The shopper is more erratic in her shopping habits for clothes and appliances, but she will generally go to her favorite supermarket for her household's daily needs.[163]

This is the intermediate or "in between" type of center.

The Regional Center—provides for general merchandise, apparel, furniture and home furnishings in full depth and variety.

It is built around a full-line department store as the major drawing power. To add even greater depth and variety for comparative shopping, *two* department stores (or even *three*) may be included in the tenancy.

In size, the regional center has an *average* gross leasable area of 400,000 sq. ft. Regional centers range in area from 300,000 sq. ft. up to 1,000,000 sq. ft. or more. The department store normally occupies about one-third to one-half of the total gross leasable area. The regional center needs at least a population of 100,000 to draw from. It is generally designed to

---

[163] If population increases in the trade area can be predicted substantially, the prudent developer of a community center will plan to have adequate land available for expansion. When the growth in sales volumes warrants and the drawing power justifies additional apparel shops and services, the community center often can be enlarged to regional status by the introduction of a full-line department store.

In a large metropolitan city, the community center is vulnerable to competition. It is too big to live off its immediate neighborhood trade and too weak to make a strong impact on the community. The development of a strong regional center, with the pulling power of its department store, can hurt the community center even though the two centers are located several miles apart.

In cities of 50,000 to 100,000 population, the community center may actually take on the aspect of a regional center because of its local dominance and pulling power even though such center's tenancy does not include a full-line department store.

serve a trade area of 100,000 to 400,000 or more people. In site area, the regional center needs at least 30 acres or more.[164]

The regional center provides complete comparison shopping facilities in depth and variety. Because of this characteristic, its customer drawing power is based on its capacity to offer complete shopping facilities. This attraction extends its trade area by 10 to 15 miles or so, modified by the factors of competitive facilities, travel time over access highways, etc.

The regional is the largest type of shopping center. It comes closest to reproducing the shopping facilities and customer attractions once available only in central business districts.

Indicators for Types and Sizes in Shopping Centers *

	Neighborhood	*Community*	*Regional*
Leading Tenant (basis for definition)	Supermarket or Drug Store	Variety or Junior Department Store	One or two full-line Department Stores
Average Gross Leasable Area	50,000 sq. ft.	150,000 sq. ft.	400,000 sq. ft.
Ranges in GLA	30,000-100,000 sq. ft.	100,000-300,000 sq. ft.	300,000 to over 1,000,000 sq. ft.
Usual Minimum Site Area	4 acres	10 acres	30 acres
Minimum Support	7,500 to 40,000 people	40,000 to 150,000 people	100,000 or more people

* The precise characteristics under these indicators do not hold rigidly. Often elements change because of the treatment required to make necessary adaptations or adjustments for the characteristics of the trade area, nature of competition, and variations in site location.

Note

Other definitions needed for the language of shopping centers refer to areas and to parking usages. Most frequently used for descriptive and comparative purposes are these:

(b) Areas

Site area—The gross land area of the property within the property lines; expressed as that area in square feet against which real estate taxes are levied ordinarily (including not only land held in fee but also that which may be under lease).

[164] Site areas over 80 acres begin to get too vast for pedestrian distances. On such sites, other commercial land uses may be introduced—such as office buildings, medical units, motor hotels, etc.

Building area—The ground area covered by the enclosed structure or structures.

Gross floor area—The total floor area of all buildings in the project, including basements, mezzanines, and upper floors. It is the figure best used in quoting building costs. Abbreviated as **GFA.**

Gross leasable area—The total floor area designed for tenant occupancy and exclusive use, including basements, mezzanines, and upper floors, if any; expressed in square feet and measured from the center line of joint partitions and from outside wall faces. It is all that area on which the tenants pay rent; it is the area producing income. Abbreviated as **GLA.** This is the figure now used in expressing relationships and in making comparisons for statistical analyses. As it includes the actual *sales* area, GLA is the true generator of traffic and parking requirements.

Sales area—The gross leasable area *minus* the tenant's storage space.

Common area—The total area within the shopping center that is not designed for rental to tenants and which is available for common use by all tenants or groups of tenants. (Parking and its appurtenances, malls, sidewalks, public toilets, truck and service facilities, etc.).

(c) Parking Usages

Parking area—The space devoted to car parking, including on-site roadways, aisles, stalls, islands, and other features incidental to parking.

Parking index—The number of car parking spaces made available per 1,000 sq. ft. of GLA. The parking index is the standard comparison to be used in indicating the relationship between the number of parking spaces and the gross leasable area.

Parking ratio—The relationship between space allotted for the parking and the space occupied by the building. This ratio is useful only in preliminary planning stages; it is not an accurate indicator of the amount of parking provided for in relation to the center's tenant composition. Too many variable factors such as layout and appurtenances of the parking area, differences in using GFA, GLA and sales area, etc., as the denominator, affect the comparison. Hence, the parking index is the better standard for expressing relationship between the parking and the commercial structure. Parking ratio is often calculated inaccurately on the basis of a relationship of square feet of parking as related to the square feet of GFA, and expressed as a ratio of 3 to 1, for example.

2. Distinguishing Features

Once we understand the general definition and terminology used in shopping centers, then we can appreciate its distinguishing features and elements. In outline, the following component parts distinguish the shopping center as a *building type* and merchandising complex:

a. A site that is suited to the type of center which the market analysis has justified; located for easy access from the trade area and arranged properly for retail selling and parking use.

b. A building composition that is an architectural unit and not a miscellaneous assemblage of stores.

c. An on-site parking arrangement that allows for ample entrance and exit and for minimum customer walking distances between the parked car and the store building.

d. A service facility that separates goods delivery movement from customer circulation and eliminates servicing from the public's awareness.

e. A tenant grouping that provides for greatest merchandising interplay among the stores.

f. An agreeableness in surroundings that lends an atmosphere for shopping in comfort, convenience and safety—weather protection, foot traffic separated from vehicular traffic, landscaping, quality in design—characteristics not associated with the usual commercial district.

Each element must be translated to fit conditions and circumstances peculiar to the climate and geography of the site. The interpretations, adaptations, and innovations in these basic features are what must be dealt with in planning, developing, and operating a successful shopping center.

In putting together these basic physical elements in the present-day pre-planned shopping facility—either in an outlying suburban area or in a central city urban redevelopment area—there are steps that the developer must take during the long interval between the time he conceives the project and the stage when he opens the center as a commercial reality.[165] See Steps and Stages in Shopping Center Development, page 234.

3. Evolution of the Shopping Center

Shopping centers are recent developments. The present-day complex began as an experiment to go with suburban living and the daily use of automobiles. The automobile accounts for the phenomenon that is the shopping center.

The shopping center grew out of the first Sears' and Ward's stores, which were built outside of downtown locations and the early free-standing grocery markets, which were erected on a lot with some places to park customers' cars off the street. The early experiments evolved from a single unit into a series of stores under one owner-management. Then, later, the series took on clear characteristics as the early try-outs became successful practices.[166]

---

[165] The planning and building of a shopping center is usually thought of as a real estate and construction problem; the larger the center, the more complicated the problem. It is true that shopping center development has many of the entrepreneurial elements of a real estate venture; but from the way in which the present-day shopping center has evolved, actually its planning, leasing, construction and operation is a merchandising project, basically.

[166] Even before the springing up of markets with some customer parking located on the lot, the earliest "shopping center" venture was that of The Roland Park Company in Baltimore. There, at Roland Avenue and Upland Road, Edward H. Bouton, the president, built in 1907 an architecturally unified building for stores set back from the street. *(Continued page 223.)*

Illustration No. 65. The Evolution of Shopping Centers

Country Club Plaza, Kansas City, Missouri, begun in the early 1920's by the late J. C. Nichols, was one of the first suburban commercial developments planned with unified architecture, center-wide management policies, landscape treatment and provision for customer car parking. This center has had over 35 years experience and provides many of the guidelines in leasing, management and promotional practices which today are principles in shopping center development and operation.

Photo: Courtesy, J. C. Nichols Co., Owners/Developers

The first planned shopping center developments started in the 1920's. The late Jesse Clyde Nichols began developing the suburban Country Club Plaza in Kansas City, Missouri, with its unified architecture, management policies, landscape treatment and provision for customer car parking. In 1937, Hugh Potter started his River Oaks Shopping Center in Houston, using the "modern" style of architecture and cantilevered canopies for the first time. Meanwhile, Shaker Square, near Cleveland, was built with traditional architectural flavor.

In 1931, the late Hugh Prather of Dallas pioneered with the first unified commercial development having its stores turned away from the access street. Highland Park Shopping Village in the Dallas area can be called accurately the prototype of shopping centers—with unified stores built on a single lot surrounded by parking space for customers. Others built in the 'twenties and 'thirties as strip stores having off-street parking in front or at the sides are the evolutionary developments of stores designed for the automobile age. The evolution was too widespread to single out one specific project as the first shopping center other than pointing out Edward H. Bouton's first concept

---

To convert this open space from providing for horse-drawn carriages to parking for automobiles, required only paving the front grass area and the carriage drive.

Mr. Bouton, the developer of Roland Park, pioneered in many other ways: He initiated protective covenants, "zoning" for a specific use, setback requirements, architectural control, flexible restrictions, wider lots, extensive landscaping by the developer, maintenance funds, and civic responsibility on the part of the developer. He gathered other developers at his Roland Park home for discussion of these advances in subdividing land and advocated the integration of commercial facilities to serve nearby residential areas. There, at Mr. Bouton's home, such community builders as J. C. Nichols and Hugh Potter received inspiration and guidance. Here, too, were sown the seeds that ultimately blossomed as the Community Builders' Council of the Urban Land Institute.

llustration No. 66. The Evolution of Shopping Centers

River Oaks Shopping Center was started in 1937 by Hugh Potter using "modern" architecture and cantilevered canopies for the first time. The two semi-circular buildings shown in lower foreground of photo were placed on either side of a main street, thereby proving the axiom "do not divide a shopping center site by a through street". But the center was provided with sufficient site area so that building expansion could take place as the high-income trade area grew. River Oaks Garden apartments are adjacent, thus illustrating the advantage of close-by, supporting population. To the apartments have been added air-conditioning, master TV antenna and swimming pool.

River Oaks Shopping Center, Houston, Texas
Photo: Courtesy, River Oaks Corporation, Owners/Developers

at Roland Park (see footnote 166), Mr. Nichols's later applications in Kansas City, then Mr. Potter's arrangement of principles in Houston, and Mr. Prather's revolutionary departure at Dallas.

The development pioneers of the 'twenties and 'thirties created the pattern for the merchandising concept that is the shopping center of today. The upsurge in construction started in 1940, then became a wave of such building after the end of World War II.

During the 1950's, the growth of Suburbia and the increased use of the automobile induced the rise in shopping center construction as the new plant to serve the new market. In the '50's the successful practices led to tested principles of procedure in shopping center planning. The decade of the '60's will see a similar evolution take place in management methods and operation.[167] Experience will indicate the patterns.

4. The Shopping Center and the Downtown District

Development of commercial real estate in the suburbs is nothing new. Even before the common use of the automobile, at least 65 per cent of the total retail trade in cities over 750,000 population was conducted outside the central business district.[168] Larry Smith observes: "The extent of commercial development in the suburbs is closely related to the population size of the city. It is characteristic for food to be sold in the neighborhood close to where people live. It is also characteristic for clothing to be sold in the central business district."

Consequently, the growth of retail trade outlets in the suburbs is related to the growth of the city. From the urban growth since 1945, smaller cities are moving into larger city classifications. Because larger cities have always had a greater development of suburban retail trade, a taking on of normal characteristics of the larger city has created an impression of a

---

[167] An accounting of the actual number of shopping centers in existence is not vital. It is more important to know what role shopping centers play in our economy, what elements make shopping centers successful, what practices lead to their survival. No census of centers exists but an educated guess by the Executive Editor, *Chain Store Age*, places the number close to 4,500 centers of all types in operation by the end of 1960.

Already, shopping centers have become a new "industry," as evidenced by the formation of International Council of Shopping Centers, a trade association to promote the interests of owners and managers.

[168] See "Commercial Real Estate Relationships—Downtown and Suburban" by Larry Smith. *Urban Land*, March 1956. Urban Land Institute.

See also *Suburban Downtown in Transition* by Pratt and Pratt. Institute of Research, Fairleigh Dickinson University, Rutherford, N. J.

flight to the suburbs. In metropolitan areas where the population in the central city has shown less increase percentage-wise than in the suburban areas, the real forces of population growth are being misunderstood. Too often this shift is referred to as decentralization when, as a matter of fact, it is new urban growth.[169] With the new pattern of urban growth, shopping centers come into being by reason of the increase in suburban population and the resultant increase in purchasing power located there, rather than by reason of any flight of downtown business.

(a) Appreciating Downtown

Downtown is slow to adjust to changing conditions. Because of its multiple ownerships in small parcels, its conflicting interests, its failure to achieve unified action, downtown development lags behind rapid suburban development. Suburban properties, because of their control by single owners in large tracts, lend themselves to comprehensive development within a short two or three year period.

Downtown has strength. Several detailed research studies have uncovered shoppers' attitudes which show downtown's advantages and disadvantages.[170] Advantages are: better selec-

---

[169] Preliminary findings from the 1960 Census as released by the Bureau of the Census in June 1960 show that several metropolitan central cities, such as Philadelphia, New York, Washington, D. C., have lost population in their central areas. This fact reinforces current urban renewal efforts to revitalize worn-out central city areas. As this effort progresses during the 1960 decade, downtown areas may see a return of close-by purchasing power now being diluted by lower income population occupying in-town areas formerly devoted to higher income occupancy.

[170] Among these are: *Shopping Habits and Travel Patterns,* Technical Bulletin No. 24, Urban Land Institute; "People's Attitudes Toward Downtown Providence," *Urban Land,* November 1956; *The Shopping Center versus Downtown*—a motivation research on shopping habits and attitudes in three cities—by C. T. Jonassen. The Ohio State University, Columbus.

Shoppers have shown unmistakably in study after study that about 75 per cent of those who express a preference for shopping downtown do so on account of the better selection of merchandise and the pricing policy of the stores. Parking, attractiveness of the shopping facilities, and avoidance of traffic congestion, generally speaking, will account for less than 25 per cent of the reasons for shopping for comparison type merchandise in any particular location. Therefore it appears that the central business district will have to depend on its business from two groups: (1) persons residing near to or working in the central area; (2) shoppers from the entire metropolitan area who want comparison in complete lines and assortments. The buying power of a metropolitan city justifies an inventory of merchandise for discriminating shoppers. The central location which is also the hub of transportation is the logical area for these stores.

tion of merchandise; wider range in prices; more frequent bargain sales; better access to public transportation; more opportunities for meeting friends from other parts of the city; better eating facilities; and more errands that can be accomplished on a single trip. At the same time, downtown's trouble is the parking problem and the care of children during a shopping trip.

Knowing about these attitudes should make it possible for merchants and property owners to act in contending with the rise in suburban trends. Whether downtown's magnetism will continue depends on its ability to safeguard its wide selection of goods, concentrated pedestrian purchasing power, and customer loyalty.[171]

(b) Enabling Downtown to Compete

To capitalize on its strong position, Downtown must promote its shopping advantages and it must make physical improvements. Creating order, stronger merchandising units, related and attractive parking facilities, improved mass trans-

---

[171] In recent years there has been a tendency toward contraction of the number of property uses in the area occupied by the central business district. This trend comes from the elimination of many activities which properly do not belong within the CBD—light manufacturing and warehousing, for example. Downtown's function is this: It is the focal point of community life. It is the transportation focus of the city. It expresses the city's personality and by it the city is judged and evaluated. The intensive section, or its core, should be occupied by major department stores, stores of various other retail types, office buildings, banks, theaters, hotels and restaurants. Adjoining this core and acting as an anchor for the whole downtown area should be the semi-public and public buildings—governmental, educational and cultural centers—clubs, museums, auditorium, music hall—a list by no means complete but indicative of the types of uses that are properly functional in a central business district that is the focus for community life. For example, see selected ULI reports to the sponsors of a CBD study, such as Syracuse, Denver, Detroit, Grand Rapids, Indianapolis, Columbus, etc.

See also *The Changing Economic Function of the Central City* by Raymond Vernon. Committee for Economic Development, New York 22, N. Y.

Illustration No. 67. A Present Day Central Business District

Downtown as a shopping district has strength, but to capitalize on its strong regional position Downtown must promote its shopping advantages and make physical improvements. Creating order, stronger merchandising units, related and attractive parking facilities, improved mass transportation and adequate access will give downtown its heaviest weapon in competition for the customers' dollars.

View of Downtown Flint from ULI Panel Stud

portation, and adequate access will give downtown its heaviest weapon in competition for the customer's dollars.

Among the required physical improvements are: General freedom from congestion; ample, well appearing off-street parking places having suitable walking distances and reasonable storage charges; free-flowing traffic ways for more convenient access; better and faster mass transportation; attractive, modernized buildings; attention to the amenities, including the elimination of garishly illuminated, cluttered, oversized signs; unnecessary noise and impediments to easy pedestrian circulation.

Established older business districts must initiate positive action[172]—for both physical improvement and positive promotions.[173] Otherwise the planned regional shopping center, with its good range and depth of goods for comparison shopping and with its facilities for easy marketing and customer appeal, may become a direct challenger for the lead position in local retail volumes.

5. Judging the Shopping Center Potential

A shopping center does not in itself generate new business; it distributes existing business. As each new center opens, its

[172] As stated in ULI's report to the sponsor of the Syracuse CBD study: "The central business district should be a glorified shopping center—if such can be conceived—capable of having all those facilities that make a shopping center an attractive place to do business and to shop. The following suggestions are made: Immediately proceed to eliminate drabness, unsightliness and shabbiness—facelift structurally good but unattractive buildings where feasible. See that adequate parking is provided and made secure for the future. Seek dramatic action whether this action be by construction of major new buildings, or by other means devised."

[173] See *Conservation and Rehabilitation of Major Shopping Districts* by R. L. Nelson and F. T. Aschman, Technical Bulletin No. 22, Urban Land Institute; also *Downtown Idea Exchange*, published twice monthly by Downtown Idea Exchange, 125 East 23rd St., New York 10, N. Y.

Downtown improvements and promotions need not conflict with interests of its own merchants who have stakes also in the suburbs. Downtown merchandisers must acknowledge geographical diversification. Competition between these units as well as with their rivals should be encouraged. In automobiles, manufacturers' lines strongly and bitterly compete with each other; so in retail selling, the downtown merchants can pit their downtown stores against their suburban outlets and pamper neither.

llustration No. 68. The Reason for Shopping Centers

The growth of Suburbia since World War II and the rise in automobile ownership and use are the reasons for the merchandising complex which is the shopping center.

Photo: Courtesy, Harman, O'Donnell & Henninger Associates, Inc., Denver

business volume comes in part from the central business district and in part from other suburban shopping areas. Until the increases in population and the readjustments in shopping habits catch up, additional retail facilities are justified only by actual increments in population and purchasing power.

Each new center must be justified on the basis of the need of the area which it is designed to serve. Without fully taking into consideration the competition both existing and planned, a new center will find itself in competition with all existing facilities now serving the population, as well as with any new shopping centers which might be built in the meantime to serve the same population.

This last observation raises the issue of competition between shopping centers. It also raises a danger signal for competing centers which seemingly are justified, but are basing their supporting purchasing power on duplicate statistics. Each new center must be justified on the basis of purchasing power available to it and by gauging the nature of its competition.

6. A Note of Caution

The fact remains that there is just so much spendable income in any municipality or locality. Whether there are too many shopping centers or whether overdevelopment of retail facilities is taking place depends on how thinly the total available spendable income of the community may be divided. Conditions and circumstances indicate that no arbitrary answer can be offered for the arithmetic number of shopping centers that are justified. This conclusion is reached because commercial development follows along with purchasing power. The growth of the suburbs and the redistribution of commercial areas in urban renewal, plus the changing methods of merchandising and the great convenience of shopping by car, lie behind the phenomenon of the planned shopping center.

Yet shopping centers can be overdone. The concept has caught on to the extent that nearly every entrepreneur wants to develop a shopping center. In some cities of the country, construction has gone ahead so fast that shopping centers represent a highly competitive business. In such places, the competition is between centers themselves, not between the centers and the established neighborhood or downtown retailers. This fact about competition, combined with high capital costs, means that the developer is allowed to make few mistakes if he hopes to survive. The philosophy that "if a little is good, then a lot is better" does not apply when it comes to putting too many stores or shopping centers too close to each other in one area.

In the rulebook of the Community Builders' Council, *caution is the first principle of procedure.*

Before beginning actual construction of a shopping center, regardless of its kind or size, there are a multiplicity of things to bear in mind. David D. Bohannon summarizes from his own experience the items that need particular double checking:

"You need sufficient buying power in the supporting territory to draw upon. Check your figures—the present high construction costs can mean a capital investment out of all proportion to your possible return. Be sure you have good planning and competent leasing. In my experience, other main factors affecting the success or failure of a shopping center are: the distance from competing centers or from areas zoned as commercial which may later become competing centers; the adequacy of public transportation; the amount of walk-in-trade; the access to good highways that will bring business to the center."

Concern for the welfare of the community and caution for the safe investment of capital are reasons why the Council issues a note of caution about overbuilding shopping centers. Financially successful shopping center development cannot go ahead faster than the community's ability to absorb the increased space for retail selling.

Echoing Mr. Bohannon's judgment, just cited, are the words of advice from other Council members.

About feasibility: "You must have detailed evaluation of your trade area potential. You must employ skilled advance planning and lease negotiation with reliable tenants. You must follow these preliminaries by sound management and strong customer attraction for the eventual successful operation of your center."

About location: The Council urges care in the selection of site for nearness to competition. The distance from a competing center is always important. Easy access by automobile; public transportation; available walk-in-trade, etc., should be given careful study. The possibility of future nearby competition should be weighed carefully. The assurance of continued growth in the number of families in the area to be served by the shopping center should be conservatively estimated. The buying power per family should be considered. The difficulty of competing with the well-established downtown business district or with business sub-districts throughout the city has a critical bearing on the success of your center.[174]

About size: To prospective developers of large regional centers, Waverly Taylor puts the Council's advice tersely: "Don't make them too big! By sheer size you can create congestion just as bad as you are trying to avoid. Without easy parking, on-site circulation can break down. A center too large for the site can produce a congested area with problems rivaling those in central business districts."

John C. Taylor expresses thoughts on the case in point: "There is no magic formula on how large a site should be. There is grave danger in too many small centers. These will not survive in less favorable times. Size depends solely on proper analysis of the market and on trade area evaluation."

About centers in general: The Council offers this observation: "No longer can luck or early venture substitute for deliberation and design. Where trade habits are already established, the new shopping center's ability to capture customers depends on careful, advance analysis, planning, and leasing followed by continuous management and promotion.

---

[174] *Mistakes We Have Made in Developing Shopping Centers* by J. C. Nichols. Technical Bulletin No. 4. Urban Land Institute.

SECTION TWO

PART I

Planning Preliminaries

Planning for the construction and later operation of a shopping center includes much more than high hopes and good intentions. There are essential preliminaries through which the undertaking must go before it ever reaches its construction stage. The development procedure has moved from being a simplified bit of site selection and construction to a task involving careful market research and evaluation, negotiation, planning, leasing and promotion by a team of experts.

To indicate the extent of teamwork involved in solving the complexity of problems in developing a shopping center, the following lists the technical experts customarily drawn upon by the developer, particularly for the development of a large regional type of center. (For the neighborhood or community center, depending upon the location or complications of the project, the developer might rely wholly upon the market analyst, the competent architect and a leasing agent, in some cases):

Market analyst
Traffic engineer
Architect-Engineer
Site planner
Real estate or leasing broker
Lawyer
Merchandising consultant
Landscape architect

In reality, these experts cannot work independently but must act as a team, each knowing about the responsibilities and contributions of his collaborators.

In shopping centers, the experienced developer knows that there is no substitute for informed judgment—his own and that of his team; the amateur only assumes that his project has potentials.[175] On this point, David D. Bohannon is quoted: "The

[175] See "A Quick Look at Shopping Centers" by Bruce P. Hayden, Secretary, Mortgage and Real Estate Department, Connecticut General Life Insurance Company; a Planitorial in *Urban Land*, February 1959. Urban Land Institute.

value of experience in planning, construction, leasing and management gained by my organization from our first shopping center project in 1945 was inestimable in developing other centers, particularly our large regional center of Hillsdale."

A. STEPS AND STAGES IN SHOPPING CENTER DEVELOPMENT

In putting together any shopping center project there are preliminaries through which the undertaking must go before it reaches its actual stage of construction. The precise order of procedure will vary. The actual timing will change to meet exigencies of local conditions and circumstances. Even though one phase melds into and overlaps with others, each decision is distinct enough to be called a step in the required procedure. Although the order of progression may vary, the major decisions called for are these:

1. Feasibility and Economic Analysis

The first decision is whether the project is feasible. The measurement of the project's possibilities and potentials is the point of departure and is the exploratory stage.

This economic analysis determines the type and size of the project which may be built initially or eventually. It measures the trading area and judges the spendable income. It evaluates the competition and the buying power that may be attracted to the center. It indicates the trend of growth and future prospects. It estimates sales volume potentials and rental returns as a basis for planning the project. This exploration establishes whether cost will unbalance the income.

The project's ultimate success will depend upon the care taken to evaluate the market for the new center with due consideration given to competition and the availability of key tenants.

A center must fit its trade area; a center too small for the sales potential invites later development of a competing center; a center built too large either falters or is an unprofitable investment.[176]

[176] The economic analysis is a job for an expert in that field. The analysis doesn't take the place of a developer's sound judgment, but by its arithmetic it does show on paper whether the new center is justified.

Here, the Community Builders' Council offers another word of warning: "Statistics supporting one center should not be duplicated to show that a second, similar center within the same trade area can be built." This caution seems obvious, but the event has happened all too often.

2. Site Evaluation

The next step in the exploratory stage of the development is a decision about the site. If a site is already owned by the developer, then the decision must be based on proof that the site is a suitable location for a center of the type and size contemplated by the economic analysis. If a site must be found, then acquired, in a location justified by the market survey, the decision must be based on relating all factors of site suitability.

Among the factors that must be weighed to qualify the site as suitable for a center are these:

a. Location. The site must be easily reached over roads with enough unused traffic capacity to avoid future congestion; not located on a cloverleaf intersection on limited access expressways. By automobile, the site must be easy to enter and safe to pull out from. A site serviceable by bus transportation draws customers without cars. A site close enough for walk-in trade has customers already at hand.

b. Size and Shape. The site should be all in one piece, undivided by highways and free from dedicated streets; no grading complications; sufficient site area for the type of center intended, with room for the required parking and for an expansion of buildings and parking.

c. Local Conditions. The site should have adequate utility services available to it, favorable zoning and neighborhood sentiment must be obtainable.

At this stage, the characteristics of local zoning should be carefully investigated. Even though municipal authorities are becoming more familiar with the principles of shopping center site planning and the necessity for permitting commercial use in large areas as contrasted with narrow strips, any problem in obtaining zoning permission for shopping center use can be time consuming. See also Favorable Zoning, pages 260-265.

If more than one site is being analyzed for suitability, each should be checked carefully, as one undoubtedly will have more advantages than the others. The cost of the land need not be a prevailing factor in site selection—though it may be in site acquisition. The fact that land cost is low in a certain location should not lead to a false assumption that a shopping center placed there will be successful. At a higher price for land, a strategic location may enable drawing the maximum sales volume potential of the trading area, thus spelling out the difference between success and failure.

3. Site Planning.

With feasibility determined and the site selected, the project can enter its preliminary planning stage. The preparation of a preliminary site plan goes along as the next step toward interesting key tenants and arranging for the project's financing. In this stage the project begins to take form for its eventual adaptation to the physical characteristics of the site and to the potentials of the trade area.

Site planning calls for designing the site layout to obtain the basic features which distinguish shopping centers, physically. Elements of the site layout are:

a. Parking in adequate amount, arranged in basic patterns (angle, perpendicular, herringbone) for ease in getting from the access highway to the stall and for reasonable walking distances from the parked cars to the shops. The act of parking should be simple and trouble-free.

b. Complete separation of customer traffic and circulation from truck service traffic.

c. Circulation within the site area to prevent customer cars from pulling onto boundary or access streets should they shift parking places while shopping at the center.

d. Arrangement of store locations for relative compactness of stores, for distribution of their pulling power, and for eliminating poor store locations and difficult parking situations.

e. Selection of a pattern for the building arrangement that will best achieve greatest interplay among the stores.

f. Attractive areas for pedestrian customers only.

Professional site planning and engineering studies proceed toward architectural planning while negotiations for the next development stage go forward.[177]

---

[177] At this point a developer is well advised to check his thinking and that of his technicians by submitting his preliminary site layout plans to the Community Builders' Council for review and analysis. This plan analysis service, referred to in the Foreword, is a way whereby a developer who is also a Sustaining member of Urban Land Institute can receive the benefit of advice from a group of practical men who themselves own and develop shopping centers. Write Urban Land Institute for details of this service in membership.

4. Leasing and Financial Negotiations

With a preliminary site layout determined, the negotiation stage in the development is reached.

While the negotiations for securing the key tenants are not susceptible to rules of procedure, the getting of firm commitments from good tenants precedes the firming up of commitments for financing the project and the preparation of final detailed construction drawings. Leases to smaller tenants can follow along after major leasing and financial planning are settled agreements. In this negotiation stage, a prospectus in attractive brochure form makes a valuable exhibit for visual aid in selling the economic analysis, the site's advantages and the preliminary planning to interested tenants.[178]

5. Architectural Planning

The final planning stage follows as the project negotiations are being firmed. Sketches prepared in earlier site planning stages often change radically as leasing and financing details are concluded. Final architectural plans and working drawings incorporate changes and depend upon details arranged under leasing negotiations—basements, storage areas, store fronts, interior finish, etc.

Major details in the architectural planning stage are the structural solutions, the exterior unity, the center-wide conveniences, the decisions on weather protection by collonades or canopies, covered malls, air-conditioning, sign design, provisions for expansion—all come in for finalizing before the letting of contracts for construction.

6. Operations and Management

The eventual construction and pre-opening stage naturally follows after leasing negotiations and the site, architectural and engineering plans are firmed. The letting of contracts for utilities, site preparation and building construction culminate the efforts of the many months of study, negotiating and hasseling covered by the stages before Opening Day.

---

[178] The tenants selected must be good merchandisers who can offer a variety of goods and services for completeness in the center. Branches of key downtown stores and well-known local names will help create customer pull to the center. Do not lean too heavily on national chain stores for tenants.

With construction under way, the management stage begins in earnest. Before tenants move in and opening day arrives, a merchants association and management operation is set up for obtaining cooperation among all the tenants for the benefit of the whole center. The element of management varies according to the type of center, but in any case the management should be a merchandise-minded organization of high executive ability having vision, energy, perseverance and responsibility, which is interested in long-range investment and not quick turnover. Good management can work toward overcoming any mistakes made in the planning and leasing of the center. But little can be done if the mistake was made in site selection or in overjudging the market.

The preceding steps make up stages in shopping center development. Included are the tangible ingredients. In summary, these are location, layout, design, parking facilities, special features, tenants, and management operations. All are ingredients that blend together to attract the shoppers. The way these parts are handled and the method of treating the details often make up the intangible items—such as atmosphere and customer appeal.

Omitted from the notations are the interpretations, the adjustments, the innovations that must be considered and evaluated to apply the ingredients to the specific site and to the local conditions: The proportions used and the extras added will give the blended flavor for the distinction and success of the shopping center.

lustration No. 69. A Shopping Center That Provides Services Once Found Only Downtown

More than anything else, this Center proves that careful advance planning, sufficient buying power in the trade area, together with enough site area for expansion as growth takes place, skillful use of topography, taste in architecture, and careful leasing and management practices make for a successful shopping center operation.

Essentially the site plan incorporates multi-tenant buildings and single tenant structures arranged on blocks surrounded by on-site parking. The arrow, lower left foreground points to location of the multi-level parking structure added in 1960.

Cameron Village, Raleigh, N. C.

Photo: Courtesy, J. W. York, President, York Building Co., Owners/Developers

B. MARKET ANALYSIS

The steps and stages through which a shopping center project must go before the ingredients are ready for the construction and pre-opening stages start with its market analysis. Even before a site is selected, the first decision to be made is whether the project is feasible. (If the site is already owned by the developer, then the site must be analyzed for its suitability as a shopping center.)

Once, shrewd guesses, keen hunches, and a fair amount of entrepreneurial know-how could be taken as good enough basis for building a shopping center. Not so any longer. With strong competition in the field plus complications of high construction costs, tightened financing, and well defined site qualifications; the development of a shopping center is now a technical operation requiring the combined services of the development team—as mentioned earlier. To justify the project, analysis of the supporting evidence must be made. And the analysis is a job for the expert in that field. As J. W. York, owner-developer of Cameron Village Shopping Center in Raleigh, N. C., has said: "Anyone planning to build a center who wouldn't employ expert help shouldn't be building a center at all."

The analysis preliminaries will tell the investor-developer whether there is a demand for additional shopping facilities. Study will show whether new facilities will answer a need growing out of increased population and purchasing power, or whether new facilities will merely compete with existing retail districts.

On this point, Larry Smith, Urban Land Institute trustee, economic analyst and real estate consultant of Seattle, is quoted: "There is a vast difference between a shopping center and a piece of ordinary commercial construction. Ordinarily, the building of a single store represents a small addition to the total retail floor space of the total business community. Mostly this means no addition at all, but a simple replacement. As a result the sales activity of the new tenant brings about little disturbance to the existing equilibrium."

A new shopping center may be equivalent to adding the retail space of a small city to the existing facilities. Where there has been no great new population growth, the existing retail space, presumably, is fairly adequate. In such a situation before developing a project, the entrepreneur must be sure the community can absorb the increment in retail selling space. Then he must make sure that the project will be well located, properly planned and profitably operated.

Remember, the shopping center is a manifestation of retail selling space increasing along with population and purchasing power. The shopping center is also a new departure in merchandising tied to new buying habits, shopping attitudes and travel patterns.

1. Use and Value

The market analysis is used to discover economic facts about the sales volume potential of the location. It is used to uncover how the project may fit the prospective market. It is also used in negotiations with tenants and financial institutions.

The scope and degree of the required investigation is indicated by the following factors: Population, income, purchasing power, competitive facilities, accessibility; and other related considerations—such as shoppers' buying habits and preferences. The number of potential customers living within a natural trade area will be counted. The territory to be drawn from will be indicated by study of access roads, with its limits set by factors of distance and travel time. The type of retail outlets needed, or wanted, will stem from study of the supporting population's income and composition. A gauge of these people's spendable income against the total volume of business done in existing retail areas will show whether there is purchasing power available to a new center. The proportion of this spending to be drawn to the center will depend upon the customer pull to be created. This estimation will point to the size of the operation to plan for. The character of the prospective trade will indicate the quality level at which to aim the tone of the development.

To indicate the value of having a market analysis prior to starting a shopping center development, the words of a vice president of one of America's largest insurance companies are repeated: "They are worth their cost and make an invaluable document for approaching tenant prospects—and a market analysis is required to secure a loan!" [179]

---

[179] At a Community Builders Council plan analysis session held in the fall of 1959, Hubert D. Eller, chief appraiser, Equitable Life Assurance Society of the U. S., spoke about what financial institutions look for in shopping centers. His remarks relate to the use and value of a market analysis. In summary, he said six basic questions would be asked: (1) *"Why is this center needed?*—We would want to know the pulling power of the center you intend to develop, the population of the area

2. Making a Market Analysis

To re-emphasize what has been said, the determination of the immediate and ultimate size of a shopping center is a matter that must be given careful, detailed study. To this point, the Community Builders' Council has frequently advised developers: "A center without definite buying power should not be built—even though it is impossible to state mathematically just how many families you need to support a shopping center." The Council has also advised: "Centers should be located from their market findings and the location should be such that another center cannot come too close in the future." Also: "A market analysis is a job for experts."

---

including density and direction of growth, the economics of the city including the income groups and purchasing power. We will ask for an economic survey—it may not be a *must* for a small center, but it will be necessary for a regional or community center. (2) *Is this the best possible location?*—We must know about the site, including its prominence in the development pattern of the metropolitan area, its accessibility, its relationship to highways, public transportation and walk-in population. We must know the population within reasonable driving time. We must know the social and shopping habits of the population. (3) *Is this a sound design and layout?*—We must know about soil conditions and grading problems. (4) *Do you have the right tenants?*—We want to know whether the market requirements are being satisfied by the department store, the variety store, the apparel stores, the food stores, and all the supporting service stores. At this point we want to know about the related problems and the developer's leasing policy and actual lease provisions. (5) *Is this center insulated against competition?*—We must know about competitive sites, their availability or the monopolistic position of your site. You must satisfy the lender that the center will command success and discourage similar competitive projects. (6) *Is this an attractive long-term investment?*—This question will be answered by the financial institution and will be based on the lender's own appraisal report."

In connection with the last question, Mr. Eller enlarges: "Most shopping centers must be considered when they are in the planning stage, so we must work from plans and specifications. We must double-check cost estimates and be sure that these contemplated outlays include all site improvements, including utilities, paving, driveways, walks, landscaping, fees, profits, commissions, promotions and financing, in addition to the structures. (Sometimes developers ask what cost items are recognized by the lender.)

"The lender will check the income from tenants and the costs of operation including taxes. Taxes are difficult to estimate; experience indicates that taxes increase every year, particularly in the fourth or fifth year of the center's operation. The lender must appraise the value of the property as a long-term investment based on projected net income. This is difficult when we are dealing not with a known site but only with prospective plans and specifications for its improvement. Parenthetically, forecasts of income are nearly always valid; but in estimating expenses, in practically all cases the expenses of operation exceed our forecasts.

"The answer to the final question—*Should we finance this center?*—is one which varies in each individual case and which depends on due consideration of all the above factors."

This advice is to be heeded. Even so, it is well for the developer to know something about the scope and extent of the investigation which the expert market analyst must pursue on behalf of the project.[180] The detail and coverage will vary, particularly for the large regional center.

a. Trade Area. The term "trade area" is normally defined, "that area from which is obtained the major portion of the continuing patronage necessary for steady support of the shopping center." As said before, new shopping centers cannot create new buying power. They can only attract customers from existing districts or capture the increase in purchasing power that accrues with growth of population. Hence, it is necessary to determine first the extent of the area from which the center can be expected to draw customers. Naturally, this trade area varies with each type of merchandise. Families buy food and sundries, to a large extent, within their own immediate neighborhood. They go considerable distances to buy furniture and clothing. So estimating boundaries for a trade area is determined by careful accounting of shoppers' habits, location of existing competition and access by highway and public transportation.

Within the trade area tributary to a shopping center, the strongest influence will be exerted closest to the site. This influence diminishes gradually as distance increases. To take account of this condition, "trade area" is usually divided into three categories or zones of influence. (For a neighborhood center, usually no breakdown of the trade area is necessary; for the community, the first two categories apply; for the regional center all three categories are used.)

The primary trade area—the close-by, the "walk-in" area, and the area which has daily convenience stores no closer than

---

[180] As references see also: Chapters 17, 18 and 19 in *The Selection of Retail Locations* by Richard Lawrence Nelson. F. W. Dodge Corporation, New York, N. Y.

Part I in *Shopping Towns, USA—The Planning of Shopping Centers* by Victor Gruen and Larry Smith. Reinhold Publishing Corp., New York, N. Y.

A Re-examination of the Shopping Center Market by Homer Hoyt. Technical Bulletin No. 33. Urban Land Institute.

"Analysis of the Earning Capacity of a Shopping Center" by Larry Smith, pp. 305-320, *The Appraisal Journal,* July 1959. American Institute of Real Estate Appraisers, Chicago 3, Ill.

"Economic Potential of Proposed Shopping Center" by Larry Smith, pp. 69-87, *The Appraisal Journal,* January 1959.

"Estimating Productivity for Planned Regional Shopping Centers" by James W. Rouse. *Urban Land,* November 1953. Urban Land Institute.

a site under investigation. For convenience items like food and personal services, it is likely that business will come largely from population with 5 minutes driving time.

The secondary trade area—the area which may have local convenience stores but with no important soft line (apparel) and hard line (hardware, appliances, etc.) stores or shopping goods (furniture, high-ticket clothing) stores with more convenient access than the site. Driving time can be set at 15 to 20 minutes or within a 3 to 5 mile radius.

The tertiary or fringe trade area—the area from which customers may be drawn because easier access, greater parking convenience and better merchandise are offered even though other shopping goods stores or department stores may be present. Driving time to the site from this area can be set up to 25 minutes.[181]

The trade area is related to factors of access by highways, driving times, the existence of natural or man-made barriers—such as topography, rivers, railroads, buying power, and competition. Allowance must be made for routes, present and proposed, and for the type of streets and thoroughfares which will serve the project. For example, a car driven on an expressway will travel three times the distance in a given time period as compared with a car driven on a congested, signal-ridden street.

---

[181] It is important to differentiate between geographic distance and travel time. As shown by Voorhees, Sharpe and Stegmaier in their study, *Shopping Habits and Travel Patterns* (Urban Land Institute Technical Bulletin No. 24), the movement of shoppers in an urban area is largely controlled by the *competitive relationships* of retail areas. Hence the use of distance as the only criterion for establishing the extent of a trade area is not reliable. But in terms of distance, the quoted study found that on the average a person will travel: 1-1½ miles for food; 3-5 miles for apparel and household items when selection is not important; 8-20 miles when wide ranges of selection and price are important. According to Larry Smith, "It is quite likely that 80% of the business for even a large regional center will be developed within a distance of seven to eight miles of the location regardless of driving time. A limited amount of business can be expected from more distant population which may be close to the access point of a high-speed expressway by which a distance of 15 or 18 miles could be covered in 20 minutes." Hence the trade area will extend in one direction farther than in others.

Travel times should be set by actual trial runs over access routes—the runs based on an off-peak hour and under conditions of climate typical of the geographic region. For theoretical trade area distances, the following are rules of thumb only:

Neighborhood center—draws from a radius of 1½ miles, depending on density and character of the residential use.

Community center—draws from a radius of 3-4 miles.

Regional center—draws from a radius of 7-8 miles.

The trade area will not assume a regular size or shape by reason of its determining factors.

After studying these factors, a map of the trade area can be prepared. It should show the relationship of the site under consideration to major traffic arterials and to other strong competitive facilities, including the central business district.

b. Population. Within the limits of the trade area as mapped out, characteristics of the population must be studied, including its present numbers, future growth, and characteristics. Racial composition, income levels, age brackets, family size, etc., have bearing upon the types of retail outlets to plan for.

The Census data on population gives basic statistics. (See the discussion about Census data, pages 7 to 23.) These figures pertain generally for several post-census years. In mid-decade periods, such as between 1965 and 1970, Census figures should be up-dated by special enumerations or recourse to other sources of general data.

One of the procedures for doing this is by an up-to-date air photo. Another is to secure from building permit records the number of new dwelling units constructed in each small area since the Census period. A further check can be made with utility companies for new meter installations. These increase in proportion to the increase in new dwelling units. To these figures adjustments can be made to allow for known absorption of vacancies or demolitions. By these devices, fairly accurate estimates for population and family numbers can be made in post-Census years. (See also page 10 to obtain special enumerations and unpublished data by the U. S. Census Bureau.)

c. Buying Power. The income level within the trade area is important, not only in terms of total number of dollars available but also in relation to expenditures by store types and price lines. Income figures for the trade area are derived from the Census. Other Bureau of Labor Statistics figures indicate how much people by family income ranges spend for categories of goods and services—such as food, general merchandise, apparel, furniture and home furnishings, and automotive parts and accessories.[182] From the purchasing power in the segments of the trade area, consumer expenditures can be estimated. When the

[182] See 1958 Census of Business. Data will be included in publications as they are published in 1960. Scheduled reports are as follows: Area Reports on sales and receipts of retail, wholesale and service trades. These will include number of establishments, sales, payroll and person-

number of expected customers is multiplied by averages of annual expenditures for consumer items, the sales potential of the trade area comes into focus. Another factor, the variation in expenditures for the different income groups should be applied also.[183]

Other methods for measuring the buying power of the trade area are possible. Income can be estimated by taking the normal ratio of income to home value. There is a fairly close relationship between value of homes owned and family income (the usual ratio is 2 to 2.5 times the amount of annual income as the price to be afforded for a home). In the 1960 U. S. Census of Housing, the rentals and value of houses are available for every block in cities with a population of 50,000 or more. For suburban areas outside of cities, the U. S. Bureau of the Census, on request, will furnish at nominal cost, photostat sheets of unpublished data showing rentals and homes in 1960 by enumeration districts. Where there is a state income tax, it may be possible to secure the total number of families by income groups in a city or county. State income tax returns can indicate the number of high-income families in the trade area.

d. Measuring Competition. A new shopping center will not, of course, attract all the business in its trade area. Basically, it will draw volume from two sources—from new population growth, and from other stores now serving the same population. The development of a new shopping center will not generate more purchasing power than already exists within the trade area. Instead, it will bring about a redistribution of expendi-

---

nel for the U. S. geographical divisions: states, standard metropolitan areas, counties and cities.

See also Sales Management's *Survey of Buying Power,* issued annually on May 10, for population, buying power and retail purchases for all counties of the U. S. and Canada and for leading cities and towns. Sales Management, 386 Fourth Ave., New York 16, N. Y.

[183] The proportion of total family income spent for food increases rapidly as income declines. As a result, in a trade area with low average family income compared to the average for the city as a whole, the proportion of the total expenditures available for nonfood stores is much less than in an area of medium or high income families. Under circumstances where all the families resident within a given trade area have similar average incomes, the store composition will be quite different from that in a trade area with the same mathematical average income but in which there is a large proportion of high income families counterbalanced by a large proportion of low income families. (Larry Smith, "Economic Potential of Proposed Shopping Center," referred to in Footnote 180.)

tures by way of transfer. For this reason, an important step in the market analysis is a study of the retail facilities which already exist and which will be in competition for the spendable income of the trading area.

In estimating the share of the buying power that can be attracted, no formula exists. Each case depends on its own circumstances. But in evaluating the pulling power for the new center to be derived from the trade area, consideration must be given to the strength and effectiveness of other retail shopping facilities with which the center will have to compete—both existing and proposed. The competition that will influence the potential sales volume of a location consists of three separate types: other existing suburban shopping facilities within and beyond the trade area; the central business district, which exercises a strong though varying influence on residents throughout the entire metropolitan area; shopping facilities that do not exist but are likely to come into being.

Accordingly, having determined earlier the income of each segment of the trade area, it is possible to calculate how much families in that trade area spend in the aggregate at all shopping areas that are the center's existing competition. The surplus in buying power remaining after having subtracted the volume of competition is the figure that is assignable to the new center.

Then the anticipated volume of business and the types of merchandise for the new center can be calculated on the assumption that the center will capture a reasonable percentage of the actual buying power in its logical trade area. What this percentage may be is derived from evaluating known data on the proportion of family incomes spent in each major category (food, clothing, apparel, furniture—department store type merchandise). The unknown quantity is the weight to be given to the new center because of its attractions as a convenient shopping place plus its provision of easy parking and appeal to customers.

It is also necessary to take into account the future population and buying power of the trade area. A new center can more easily secure trade growing out of increased purchasing power resulting from population growth than it can break existing shopping habits. So it is necessary to take into account future growth and its potentials. The direction that future growth may take and the study of the community's economic base are two basic types of analysis needed.

As mentioned, estimates of the potential of the contemplated shopping center must allow for composite pulls of competing retail areas. According to some analysts there is a breaking point between competing retail districts where the natural pull of one is equal to that of the other. This is somewhat like the formula method of analysis evolved by an adaptation of Reilly's Law of Retail Gravitation. Proponents of the formula-judgment method find a reformulation of Reilly's Law useful in predicting sales potentials, particularly for shopping goods presentations such as those at regional centers.[184]

e. Kind of Center. With the trade area and the sales potential determined, the kind of center that can be built begins to emerge. The decision calls for accurate judgment of the potential. Exploitation of this potential depends then on site selection and skillful arrangement plus the choice of good merchandisers as tenants and the creation of strong customer attractions.

At the time a market survey is made, the names of probable tenants are very seldom known. But in most places there is a strong or weak position occupied by merchants locally. For example, most local customers prefer one supermarket chain over another; hence, the relative standing of a merchant locally should be considered because preferred merchants will draw patronage to a new center and should be represented to strengthen customer appeal.

From the sales volume estimate of the market analysis, the store types and the approximate square footage of building can be determined, in a preliminary way, to meet the merchandising potential. With the store area determined, cost and income factors can be set up. From the area of building and the type of stores, parking needs can be estimated. With the parking demand gauged, the total required for the site area can be measured. This determination allows site evaluation and plans for the site layout to begin.

---

[184] See "Estimating Productivity for Planned Regional Shopping Centers" by James W. Rouse, mentioned in Footnote 180, and "Estimating the Potential of Shopping Centers" by L. W. Ellwood, *The Appraisal Journal*, October 1954.

Reilly's Law of Retail Gravitation is: "Two cities competing for retail trade from the immediate rural areas attract such trade from areas in the vicinity of the breaking point approximately in direct proportion to the population of the two cities and in inverse proportion to the square of the distance from the immediate area of each city."

Reilly's Law, as developed in 1929 by Dr. William J. Reilly, University of Texas, is available as a reprint in pamphlet form, 1959. Bureau of Business Research, University of Texas, Austin.

f. Summary. What you can do with the site you have, or what choice is to be made among several possible sites, depends upon how an accurate economic appraisal of the project's possibilities and potentials measures against the cost factors of site acquisition, building construction, parking areas, landscaping, maintenance and operation.

A recommendation on the evaluation of the market is a job for the expert in that field, but the developer should know the items listed below as background for his own knowledge for beginning the project. Your own judgment and common sense will temper the analysis, which naturally should be in terms that are understandable to you. As Larry Smith has said: "It is a tool to assist *you* in making your judgment and should not be taken as a substitute for judgment itself."

The following rudiments of a market analysis are recapitulated:

1. Determination of the trade area tributary to the shopping center. Analysis of the area's population changes, both numerically and in percentages for present and future growth, translated into maps and figures. Analysis of the area's basic employment and economy. Analysis of access —present highway patterns or future ones, traffic counts and street capacities, travel times, translated into maps and data.

2. Purchasing power for primary, secondary, and remote trade areas. Disposable income in amounts or percentages after standard deductions for Federal income and local taxes, housing costs (in terms of mortgage or rental payments), insurance and savings, and transportation costs have been estimated.

3. Measurement of competition—discount for composite pull of other competing retail outlets.

4. Sales potential—deductions from analysis in items 2 and 3. Includes investigation of total retail expenditures, sales capacity of existing stores by types of merchandise, and surplus available to the center.

5. Analysis for the center by type of stores and volume of business; recommended merchants, size of store, rental income through minimum guarantees and percentage leases

obtainable, estimated per annum volume of business, taxes, insurance, depreciation, operational expenses, etc. Parking index.

A final word about the market analysis: "Too many developers have made an economic survey in order to convince prospective tenants that the trading area affords and needs the center. Instead, the survey should be made to find out whether or not the area can support a new shopping center."

Disposition of Personal Income in 1958

	Total (in millions)	Percent
Personal Income	360,312	100
Personal Tax and Nontax Payments	42,440	12
Disposable Personal Income	317,872	88
Personal Consumption Expenditure	293,495	81
Durable goods	37,297	10
Nondurable goods	141,963	40
Services	114,235	31
Personal Saving	24,377	7

Source: *Statistical Abstract of the United States 1960.* U. S. Dept. of Commerce.

Personal Consumption Expenditures by Type of Product 1958

Product	Total (in millions)	% of Disposable Income	% of Total Personal Consumption Expenditure
Food and tobacco	83,210	26.2	28.3
Clothing, accessories and jewelry	31,044	9.7	10.7
Personal care	4,370	1.3	1.5
Housing	38,015	12.0	13.0
Household operation	41,305	13.0	14.1
Medical and death expenses	18,088	5.7	6.1
Personal business	16,724	5.3	5.6
Transportation	33,707	10.6	11.5
Recreation	16,825	5.3	5.8
Private education and research	3,589	1.1	1.2
Religious and welfare activities	3,997	1.2	1.3
Foreign travel and remittances—net	2,621	.8	.9

Source: *Survey of Current Business*—National Income Number, July 1960, U. S. Dept. of Commerce, Washington 25, D. C.

Total Retail Sales by Kinds of Business 1958

Kind of Business	Sales (in millions)	% of Total Retail Trade [1]	% of Disposable Income [1]
Food stores	49,022	25	16
Eating and drinking places	15,201	8	5
General merchandise stores	21,879	11	7
Apparel stores	12,525	6	4
Furniture and appliance stores	10,074	5	3
Automotive dealers	31,808	16	10
Gasoline service stations	14,241	7	4
Lumber, building, and hardware stores	14,304	7	4
Drug and proprietary stores	6,779	3	2
Other retail stores	18,468	9	6
Non-store retailers	5,401	3	2

[1] Rounded to nearest whole number.

SOURCE: *Retail Trade Preliminary Area Report.* 1958 Census of Business. U. S. Dept. of Commerce. April 1960.

C. SITE EVALUATION

With the market analysis to substantiate justification for the project, the development can move forward to its next preliminary stage—site evaluation and selection. In evaluating the suitability of a site for shopping center development, the findings from the market analysis must be tied in closely. Care must be taken to assure that the location is the best possible from all points of view. In most cases though, the site is already owned. In this case, the problem is to evaluate the site and to justify its use as being suitable for the shopping center type and purpose.

In site selection or evaluation, if you already own a site, the same principles hold but in varying degrees—whether the center is to be a small neighborhood one or a regional giant. The following points must be weighed in making the site evaluation:

1. Site Selection Factors in Outline

a. Location and Access—a first consideration. There must be free flow of traffic throughout the feeder area. It is essential that the site be in an impregnable economic position—at least from the standpoint of location.

b. Shape—a prime requirement. The property must be shaped so that the ultimate development is all in one piece, undivided by highways or important through traffic streets. (This principle is often violated.)

c. Size—a basic element. There must be sufficient site area for the initial development intended, with room for expansion and for buffer strips.

d. Topography—a factor in construction. A fairly level or gently sloping piece of ground is easily adaptable to the center. With steep slopes, heavy grading or deep piling an ingenious arrangement is necessary. Low-lying or swampy ground conditions add to complications in construction.

e. Utilities—another element in construction. A location close to or easily accessible to utilities—water, sewer, gas, electricity—cuts down on off-site improvements.

f. Favorable Zoning—a climate for good public relations.

g. Adjacent Land Use—another factor for eventual retail volume. A meadow may be pretty to look at but it doesn't generate walk-in trade. No competitive developments should be present or allowed to crop up later.

h. Land Cost—a variable. The cost of the land must be compatible with the overall economics of the development. Land costs, building costs and volume of sales vary so widely in different sections of the country that any given set of figures can be shot full of holes in so far as any particular citation is concerned.

Only rarely will a site incorporate all these requirements. In most cases compromises will have to be weighed for balancing advantages with shortcomings. The requirements are covered in more detail.

2. Location and Access

Location—A shopping center project must be in an impregnable economic position—at least from the standpoint of location. It must be impossible for another project similar in type and size, but better located, more convenient and protected to be

Illustration No. 70. Location: A Major Factor in Shopping Center Development

"A center must fit its trading area; a center too small for the purchasing potential invites later development of a competing center." University Hills, a regional shopping center in Southeast Denver, Colorado, became vulnerable to the later development of a close-by neighborhood center.

Photo: Courtesy, Harman, O'Donnell & Henninger Associates, Inc., Denver

introduced and, because of its improved services, to compete successfully with your center.

As pronounced by the Council, there are several other maxims about location: "Be sure that your site is located near a well populated residential area or one that is growing so rapidly that it gives promise of soon being able to support the sized shopping center you contemplate building." "The side of the street on which the center is located can spell profit or loss. The right-hand side of an outbound route is preferable where shopping is done largely by the going-home shopper. Where shopping is done by the housewife, as is the case with most neighborhood centers, the center should be city-ward of the tributary population."

There is no rule of thumb applicable to location of shopping centers. Walking distance is no longer any criterion, particularly in suburban locations. But in urban renewal areas where high density, multi-family housing would be part of the redevelopment plan, walking distance plus transportation, and the type and relation to commercial area outside the project would be important factors to consider.

In new residential subdivisions, where a shopping center for that community can be justified, the shopping center should be located so that the site is on the main thoroughfare offering access to the subdivision. The interior streets of the subdivision should be planned to lead to the shopping center from the directly tributary area.

In new large-scale residential developments such as would be contemplated by the developer of a satellite community or new town on several thousand acres of land, the shopping center location should be selected and area allocated while the general development plan of the community is in its preliminary planning stage. In these cases, site selection becomes part of the over-all master planning procedure. The developer and his planners have the opportunity of choosing the most advantageous shopping center site in accordance with the principles of site selection, thus creating a nearly ideal shopping center location.

Access—should be easy and convenient. It should be possible to turn off the highway directly into the site. Easy access means free-flowing traffic to reach the site. Left turns require specially constructed lanes for turning movement. Right turns on a heavy traffic way require deceleration lanes for easy entrance and exit. If cars moving into or out of a center create traffic bottlenecks, resentment rises. Congestion at entrances or back-ups on a major traffic route can be fatal to a center. Redesigning traffic flow at the entrances to a center requires cooperation with the traffic engineers and local highway departments. If the access road system cannot carry the additional traffic and turning movements generated by the center, the cost of improvements must be investigated. This includes whether costs will be borne by the highway construction authorities, by the developer, or shared—and in what proportion.

Adequate access may add to the traffic load, but it must not add to the traffic problem. (Because of heavy, usual night shopping habits, shopping center peak hour traffic flow need not coincide with ordinary rush-hour traffic.) Even for small centers, major customer traffic from outside the immediate neighborhood must not filter through nearby residential streets, creating nuisances and irritations for the local residents and neighbors.

Entrances into and out of a center must be well away from a major street intersection (at least 100 to 150 feet from the corner). At neighborhood centers it is possible for access to be on only one side of the site. (In other words, the site may front on one important access street only.) As mentioned above, locations directly on major expressways carrying high-speed traffic are desirable only when adequate provision is made for safe and convenient access into and out of the parking areas without interfering with the travelled way.

The Council finds that a site accessible only from a ramp at a cloverleaf grade separation for two intersecting highways is not good for convenience in access to a center. Because the grade separational treatment in itself is complicated and confusing to drivers, a psychological resistance to the location is created. This mental hazard acts against a center located where complicated directional turning movements are needed on the part of the driver.

This means that persons not familiar with the access into a center will take a wrong turn. Highway authorities should recognize that the shopping center is in the category of a public service facility and they should cooperate to facilitate patrons' getting to the center through the erection of directional signs. But usually there are so many route markers at grade separations and traffic circles that additional directional signs will add to a driver's confusion. From the access standpoint, a traffic circle is a secondary choice for a shopping center location.

The Council's observations about access can be pinpointed: A location at the intersection of two heavily travelled expressways is not the best.

"Entrances to and exits from the parking areas too close to a major intersection can create a traffic congestion problem. If the location is adjacent to a high-speed expressway, the turn-in facilities for traffic movement are important."

"It is better for the location to be accessible from a major highway. The ability to see the center from a controlled access freeway is important from the advertising value to be derived from the site's unobstructed visibility."

"To achieve the maximum accessibility, the site should be at, near, or readily convenient to at least two main highways."

If there is a choice available, the site for a regional center should be selected where it has access from a radial highway leading to the city and from a circumferential highway that taps the urbanized residential periphery of the metropolitan area.

3. Shape

A site must be all in one piece. A site divided by a traffic way divides the continuity for shopping, complicates the customer car movement within the site, destroys the basic principle of unity for the shopping facility. Once a site is unified, never dedicate any streets within a center. As David Bohannon, the astute developer of Hillsdale, advises, "Keep the shopping area intact, do not cut up the site with any dedicated roads."

However, a minor street through an otherwise suitable site does not always interfere with successful operation of shopping centers. As examples of successful centers with dedicated streets through the property: Cameron Village in Raleigh, North Carolina; The Village Market in LaGrange Park, Illinois; and Hillsdale in San Mateo, California, are cited. These are exceptions that prove the rule. But do not deliberately set out to develop a shopping center on both sides of a heavy traffic way. To do so creates unsafe traffic conditions, interferes with patronage, and violates all principles of good shopping center planning.

A regularly shaped property without acute angles, odd projections or indentations is best for efficient layout even though faults in the shape can be corrected by adjustments and ingenuity. But without extensive frontage, the center cannot enjoy the advantages of being viewed from access thoroughfares. Site depths should approximate 400 feet or more. Greater site depths distinguish shopping center developments from the old standard strip commercial areas which were usually zoned only 100 or 150 feet in depth.

Any awkward, very irregular shape to the property (even though the total site area is sufficient) should be avoided in site selection because portions of the site may be unusable, or if used would result in excessive walking distances, poor parking arrangements or forced, expensive solutions. Sometimes an irregular site can result in an ingenious solution for the placing of the elements—though this is an exception.

4. Size

The area necessary for the type of center is important. There must be sufficient site area for the initial development indicated by the trade area analysis with room for expansion and for buffer strips where needed. As a rule of thumb to gauge site adequacy, an acre of ground can be counted as providing 10,000 square feet of building coverage and 30,000 square feet of parking space. So, as an indication for site area, a neighborhood center having 50,000 square feet of building area requires a 5-acre site area—

—a community center having 150,000 square feet of building area requires a 15-acre site area.

—a regional center having 400,000 square feet of building area requires a 40-acre site area.

The site needs at least the minimum acreage set up by the preliminary estimates from the market analysis. If the site is too small for the parking area needed, then double-deck parking structures may have to be resorted to.

Where there is strong possibility for growth within the trade area, the size of the site should provide for the initial development plus space for growth. In suburban locations, ordinarily the initial price of the land will be low enough to permit acquisition of sufficient site area to avoid later expense for double-decking the parking area or for a parking structure. Allowing enough space to grow is a safeguard for the future, particularly for a neighborhood center in a mushrooming suburb. Frequently, a successful center has been built without reserving extra land for future growth—for increased parking and for additional sales area. For example, Highland Park Shopping Village, that prototype of shopping centers, to remedy the original limitation on its site area as its trade area and the prestige of its retail outlets grew, had to resort to the expensive solution of building an underground garage for additional parking spaces and first floor shops.

A site that is too large for the immediate development contemplated has the advantage of land to be held in reserve. An interim use can be introduced; or the unneeded commercial land can be developed for uses compatible with the shopping center, such as apartments, motel, medical clinic, or suburban office building. No reserve land or lack of sufficient land means the development is static.

However, no more retail selling space should be constructed than is needed for the original development. But, as the Council points out, where a shopping center experiences a full measure of success by meeting its potential sales volume through its ability to draw the ultimate in purchasing power from its trade area, then some one will inevitably try to tap this success by building competition nearby—if land is available and the zoning situation will allow the additional use. The possibility that open land zoned for residential uses across the street from a shopping center may be changed to permit additional business use is always present.

This possibility should be kept in mind by the initial developer. Frequently the developer can afford to buy extra land in order to protect his location from undesirable encroachment or undue competition subsequently. But it should be understood that this observation should not be interpreted as a recommendation to buy up land just to starve off competition in the future. Your center and its operations should be so successful that it would be unwise for another to establish competition close by. In other words, build a center to fit its trade area and its potential.

5. Topography and Physical Characteristics

Topography of the site is another important factor. A steeply sloping site may require excessive filling or cutting for the parking expanse. Even if the cuts and fills can be balanced, the earth moving operation adds to costs in site preparation. If the land cost is low, then perhaps this extra site preparation work can be absorbed into the overall economics of the construction.

If the slope across the site corresponds to grades on surrounding roads, then an opportunity for a two-level arrangement of buildings and parking might exist. However, a two-level merchandising scheme poses planning and leasing complications and requires skillful solutions. The chances for succeeding in taking advantage of sloping site conditions is greater in large projects than it is in small neighborhood ones. Stores in a neighborhood center are more easily arranged in a one-level layout. In a large regional center there is some opportunity for taking advantages of the sloping site conditions by introducing vertical circulation for customers within the larger store spaces.

At The Village Market in LaGrange Park, Illinois, the change in grade of the sloping site was taken up by introducing a medical office unit at the lower level. Access to these offices and their specially assigned parking area is separated from the retail shopping level of the building. Similarly, at Cameron Village in Raleigh, N.C., the sloping site allowed a medical unit to be introduced on an upper level of a building. From the opposite side, this office area appears as a second story above the shops as seen from their general customer parking area. The office and retail uses are thus separated yet integrated into the overall site development. In 1959, to provide additional parking spaces occasioned by an expansion in gross leasable area, J. W. York, the developer, was forced to build a multi-level garage at the change in site grades. But in this case the cost of the parking structure per car space was less than the cost of buying additional land, which could only have been acquired by crossing an important arterial street. Besides the cost of the structure could be amortized through depreciation, whereas the cost of additional land could not. This situation illustrates another factor in site selection—the bearing that finances and taxes for the developer may have on the solution of site development problems.

Clearly, a nearly level site is the most easily adaptable to the arrangement of shopping center elements. Nearly level parking areas can be readily prepared. Multi-level parking is neither simple to lay out nor to operate. Costs mount with the structure involved.

6. Utilities

Availability of utilities at or close to the site is a positive factor in site selection. Long runs to reach available utility connections are a development cost to be avoided. Off-site development costs usually can be adjusted with the municipality and customarily with the private utility company. To minimize time-consuming negotiations with officials, make sure the site is at least within easy reach of required water supply and sewage disposal facilities.

No precise policy for a shopping center's off-site improvements has been established even though in some cities a policy is evolving for residential development.[185]

7. Favorable Zoning

Favorable zoning conditions for the site are needed.

Ordinarily, suitable shopping center sites are not zoned for retail use—nor should they be so zoned in advance of development. Hence the developer must obtain commercial zoning. He must feel assured that a favorable attitude prevails before his planning work is finalized.

Unless a municipal jurisdiction has recently revised and updated its zoning ordinance, the developer will not find a "shopping center district" or "planned development district" as one of the zone classifications for permitted land use. In older standard zoning ordinances, commercial zones were designated as narrow 100-foot or 200-foot strips along both sides of major thoroughfares—usually those that originally had trolley car lines. *Strip business zoning by map designation is not today's shopping center zoning.*

The shopping center concept and its development has advanced ahead of the provisions for commercial use under standard zoning procedures. Under the shopping center concept, off-street parking is an adjunct to the commercial use; hence, the parking which is voluntarily provided by the owner requires acreage areas having depth and breadth, not narrow strips and lengthy ribbons. So it is important that up-to-date zoning ordinances provide for a "planned shopping center district" not through map indication for location but through

---

[185] See *Utilities and Facilities for New Residential Development,* Technical Bulletin No. 27. Urban Land Institute, December 1955.

planning commission review and board of appeals procedures (so-called "floating zones", in city planners' technical parlance).

In zoning there is confusion in the distinction between the new "planned shopping center" and the usual "strip" types of business use area. Most zoning ordinances as prepared in the past have set up provisions for business use that are geared to the pattern of areas described as "downtown," the "satellite shopping district," "the scattered four corner street intersection" and the "strips along major streets." These types of business use areas are all founded on the basis of separated holdings with varying ownerships and with individual buildings on individual lots. The older zoning maps and ordinances pertain to this single lot pattern of city growth and development.

Now the planned shopping center (with its acreage site, unified building, selected tenancy and integrated off-street parking—all under one ownership) does not fit the pattern on which zoning regulations have been based. Accordingly, in zoning ordinances it is desirable to introduce a new classification for the "planned center" type of retail business use.

Because of the market analysis research required on the part of the developer for the proper location or selection of shopping center sites, it is not recommended that zoning maps indicate *shopping center* sites in advance of development or granting of a zoning permit. But it is recommended that the ordinance contain a provision for flexibility in its use provisions to cover the pre-planned shopping center concept in development. The flexibility asked for can be covered by case review under planning commission approval before board of appeals review.

The importance of the market analysis for justifying a new shopping center development is emphasized in cases where the developer must prove the need for increased retail selling space. Too often, applications for a zone change, from residence to business, for example, have no relationship to the need for more business area. In cities and towns already overzoned for business, the solution lies in restudying and revising the zoning ordinance and map. In communities where no provision for shopping center development exists under the zoning ordinance in effect, the solution lies in instituting special provisions to incorporate a "shopping center district"—the district being defined perhaps as "a tract of land developed as a shopping center unit under single ownership." This provision for a planned commercial district is similar in concept to the provisions for a "planned community district." Both these "districts" are ways to allow for large-scale or acreage development geared to an overall master plan. All of these attempts are commendable in that the objective being sought is the giving of an alternative to the provisions of conventional zoning which have been geared to the single lot and single building and which only indifferently promote—and frequently prevent—good, large-scale, unified land and building development.[186]

Providing for a "shopping center district" in a zoning ordinance implies the need to restrict further enlargements or extensions of existing business areas unless the principles of shopping center building are applied—that is, greater than the usual depth and with integral off-street parking in proper ratio. The provision of a new "planned shopping center district" should carefully define what is meant by a "planned shopping center." Then, the provision should require submission of a development plan so that there is "evidence of interest" as a basis for approval by the planning commission and for its recommendation to the board of appeals. Certain other basic stipulations for the new provision—such as items to cover any possible adverse effect on adjacent street traffic movements and on abutting residential areas—could be written in to guide decisions by the approving authority.[187]

In this connection, zoning and planning bodies should not try to zone the business aspects of a shopping center. The

---

[186] See "Zoning of Planned Residential Development" by Eli Goldston and James H. Scheuer. *Urban Land,* March 1960. Urban Land Institute.

"Zoning for the Planned Community" by Fred H. Tuemmler. *Urban Land,* April 1954.

[187] As a guide to planning commissions or to boards of appeal in making decisions about granting permission for shopping center development when the existing zoning ordinance has no special provision for a "shopping center district," the following points are those which should be satisfied in establishing a new zone for shopping center development purposes:

Substantiation of the need

A site arrangement that prevents undue interference with through traffic

An integrated parking area

An insulation against any adverse effect on adjacent residences, if any

A building group that looks like a unified center and not a miscellaneous collection of stores.

Omitted are interpretations that adapt principles of shopping center development to *the particular* site and to local customs.

shopping center as a specially permitted zoning use need not include the specifications for the parking index. The parking is provided as a matter of course in sufficient amount and as an adjunct to the retail selling space for the convenience of the customer. Parking provision is one of the development principles of the shopping center concept. It is sufficient for planners to establish policies and principles under which shopping centers may be generally permitted.

Even so, there are valid reasons in the public interest for granting permissive zoning for shopping centers. Shoppers like shopping centers because their varied shopping needs are satisfied in a limited area. The general community is relieved of traffic and parking space problems by the shopping center's private provision of adequate off-street parking and loading space. Rightly located, the center produces a net income to the community far in excess of land uses allowable in a residential zone.

Location is an important factor in shopping center zoning. As applications for shopping center zoning increase, approval may be rejected because the community either cannot support more retail space or because it cannot support a commercial site too close to an existing business area.

Advantages to the community tax-wise and traffic-wise may overcome objections from existing business areas, but the presence of a nearby school or residential area can be overcome only by the design factors of the shopping center project itself.

An advantage to the developer comes through shopping center zoning which is related to comprehensive community planning and retail demand instead of map designation. By knowing the minimum and maximum size of shopping center for an approved location, the developer can own or control the land needed for the ultimate development. If he wants to reap the full benefit of his enterprise, he must know the future prospect for adjacent land which might be logically promoted as alternative sites for shopping center expansion.

The matter of expanding shopping center zones resolves itself when the primary consideration is assurance that additional zoning will subject neither the existing businesses nor the community's tax base to the hazards of overdevelopment. It is not a proper practice in zoning to direct that additional business area be forestalled to prevent competition. The proper approach comes from comprehensive community planning studies which indicate approximate size of shopping areas necessary to serve existing and future populations involved, supplemented by studies related to the proper timing for the development.[188]

Sometimes there may be local opposition to rezoning a tract of land for shopping center development, particularly if the center is to be built on a site close to a built-up, single-family residential subdivision. (Where a developer reserves a tract of land for a shopping center and obtains the required commercial zoning for this tract, then proceeds to develop the residential portion of his community in accordance with his street and lot plan; the nearby residents know in advance that eventually there may be a shopping center close to their homes. In this case, objections on the part of nearby residents should not arise. Because in this case the developer must build his shopping center to minimize any adverse effect on the residential property that he originally created.) However, in an atmosphere where resentment against "intrusion" by a new shopping center may prevail, then the developer must sell his idea to the community and to the authorities. He must judge the local temper before he goes too far in firming his plans. And if there is a tone of resentment continuing against his project even before it is started, he must be doubly sure that he meets all the criteria for good shopping center development. Where the center is to be located close to existing residences, buffer planting strips or protective screening walls or well-designed fences within the site area are an essential requirement to prevent any adverse effect on the residential values.

---

[188] See "Public Policy and the Shopping Center" by Edgar M. Horwood. *Journal of The American Institute of Planners,* Vol. XXIV, No. 4, 1958. American Institute of Planners, Washington 9, D. C. In this first-class review of policy for comprehensive planning and zoning for shopping centers, Mr. Horwood concludes in part: (1) The comprehensive plan, in its customary mapped form, cannot provide an adequate basis for the public interest in and regulation of outlying shopping center development. (2) The treatment of the outlying shopping center in the zoning ordinance poses many problems for which few advances toward solution have been made. The problems relate mainly to control over the timing of the facility as well as to selection of the precise location. (3) There is serious doubt that public agencies can prezone for outlying shopping centers. These facilities may have to be treated entirely as conditional or special uses upon application by the developer. This raises policy questions regarding the scope of shopping center developments, their general locations and standards for development and operation.

See also *Shopping Center Zoning: Part I,* Information Report No. 128, November 1959, and *Shopping Center Zoning: Part II,* Information Report No. 129, December 1959. Planning Advisory Service, American Society of Planning Officials, Chicago 37, Ill.

Objections to shopping center zoning can be overcome through the manner of shopping center operation—a unit, not a miscellaneous aggregation of stores, integrated parking privately policed and maintained for public benefit, controlled truck delivery arrangement, etc. Buffer or screen planting along the street across from residences can minimize any adverse effects from night lighting and noise.

The use of walls, solid fences, or narrow but dense plantings of hedge or evergreen material should be provided. Failure to insure permanent and effective physical separations between business and single-family residential uses can detract greatly from the value and desirability of the nearby houses.

8. Adjacent Land Use

A site that is too large for the immediate development that is contemplated has the advantage of holding land in reserve. Or if the zoning has been granted for commercial use over the entire tract, compatible uses such as single-tenant office buildings, medical clinics, motels, apartments, and non-competitive commercial facilities can be introduced.

Apartment development adjacent to a shopping center site is an excellent transition between a shopping center location and a single-family residential area.

It is important for the shopping center site not to be vulnerable to adverse influence from adjacent uses outside the control of the developer. If an area across the road is open for sporadic development, then it is possible for parasite business uses, such as drive-ins and discount operations, to come in and trade on the drawing power of the shopping center. The possibility of fringe development which could offer competition must be considered in site selection.

9. Land Acquisition and Cost

The site must be possible to acquire with reasonable negotiation. Sites in single ownership in large parcels are not often found. A higher cost for a good location is preferable to low land cost in a poor or less desirable spot. It is impossible to generalize on land cost except to point out that this cost factor is important in the economic calculations before beginning. Obviously, the lowest cost commercial land will be that which is developed by the developer of a large-scale residential project tributary to the site. In this case the initial cost is no more than that of the surrounding residential land.

10. Summary of Site Selection Factors

If your site does not measure up in favorable factors, then it may be better to find one that does. For a regional center, a few more minutes driving time may not make too much difference in accessibility, or maybe the purchase of a few more acres of additional land will make the site measure up favorably.

For a neighborhood center, the site must be selected, or reserved as it would be in the case of an entirely new community, for its ready access from the supporting residential area.

In the case of a wholly new community, the shopping center site selection is part of the overal master planning required for the whole development.

In setting up criteria for selecting the location of a shopping center, particularly regional ones, Larry Smith uses a rating scale. As an indication of the weight assigned to factors in site evaluation, the following table is quoted.

Criteria for Location of Shopping Centers

Site Factors		Values Assigned
a. *Location*		50
1. Population within 1 mile—Quantity	5	
2. Population within 1 mile—Quality	3	
3. Population within 5 miles—Quantity	7	
4. Population within 5 miles—Quality	4	
5. Population from rural area—Quantity	2	
6. Population from rural area—Quality	1	
7. Pedestrian traffic shopping at competing stores	5	
8. Pedestrian traffic nearby for other purposes	3	
9. Public transportation	5	
10. Automobile traffic—Quantity	4	
11. Automobile traffic—Availability	4	
12. Direction of growth	7	
b. *Area*		20
13. Size of site	20	
c. *Physical Characteristics*		20
14. Shape of site, for design	4	
15. Site not divided by traffic arteries	8	
16. Location on arterials for ease of traffic control	4	
17. Cost of clearing and grading	2	
18. Cost of utilities and drainage	2	
d. *Availability*		10
19. Ease of acquisition and time required	6	
20. Cost	4	
Total		100

This list first appeared in the 1954 Members Edition of the *Community Builders Handbook.* It indicates the relative importance the several factors might assume in decisions about site evaluation. A slight reassignment of values for area and physical characteristics has taken place in the list as later published in *Shopping Towns—USA*, cited previously. In that publication of the table, factors of site visibility and surrounding area have been added to give "Physical Characteristics" a weight of 25, thereby reducing the factor of "Area" to 15.

SECTION TWO

PART II

Planning the Shopping Center Site

The goal in site planning is making the most productive use of the site. To obtain this efficiently requires arranging retail selling spaces with non-commercial facilities, such as customer parking. The best order results when the structures with their tenant spaces and services and the auxiliary parking are integrated by design. Overall, the specific manner of arrangement separates pedestrian traffic from auto traffic and truck traffic within the site. The ingredients produce the market place for selling which is the shopping center.

As noted earlier faults in size and shape of a shopping center site can be solved by ingenuity, but nothing much can be done if the shortcoming is mislocation or miscalculation of the market. Building and parking arrangements can be adapted to awkward shapes by skillful planning. A site too small can resort to double-level parking and building structures, though this is an expensive alternative. If the site is too large for full immediate use, land can be held in reserve or put to some interim use.[189]

A well located site can be adapted to the principles of good shopping center development even if it is deficient in some physical respects. When skillful site arrangement is backed by practical experience, the combination goes a long way toward a successful center. In addition to skillful site planning, there must be sound construction, careful leasing and tenant selection, shrewd promotion and inviting atmosphere to overcome any site handicaps.

With the site decided upon, the next order of procedure is planning the site use. This stage becomes one of studying the layout of the buildings and parking areas. In making the most of the site, the eventual arrangement must offer customers a pleasant place to shop in an atmosphere combining beauty and comfort with convenience and safety. The layout must incor-

[189] An example of interim use is commercial recreation. In other cases, the spare land can be developed in compatible uses, such as a motel or corporation office.

porate adequate and easy parking at short distances from the cars to the stores. The service facilities must be unobtrusive and out of the customers' way. There must be efficient and economical operation for both tenant and landlord. Arranging all these elements calls for study and design.

A. BUILDING LAYOUT

Planning the site begins with allocating areas for the retail structure and its pedestrian circulation, the areas for automobile parking and movement, and for related auxiliary uses.

The building layout, with its tenant grouping and arrangement of stores, starts with thinking about key tenants and customer circulation. "The important thing is to locate the key tenants to distribute their pull and to lead customers past the smaller tenants as they are drawn to the pullers." The strongest magnets are placed at anchor points which are located in a manner to draw pedestrian shoppers throughout the center. In between the big magnets, the customers pass the complementary stores.

In arranging tenant locations it should be kept in mind that each store must have an equal chance. The ultimate success of the center comes from the income derived from rents plus percentages of gross sales. Hence the owner's revenue depends on the total sales volume of the project, which is the sum of all its parts. This fact emphasizes the reality of the shopping center as a merchandising complex. The architectural skin, the store fronts, the furnishings of planting and lighting, the services provided—the convenient parking—are supplementary features to reinforce the appeal of "one stop shopping."

1. Tenant Selection

There is no sharp demarcation for the timing of phases between tenant selection, lease negotiation, and plan finalizing. Each step and stage melds with the other. But usually the

lustration No. 71. Shopping Center Site Planning
The Shopping Center that shows the changes in Shopping Center Planning.
Hillsdale Shopping Center, San Mateo, Calif.
Developer/Owner—David D. Bohannon Organization
Architect/Engineer—Welton Becket & Associates
Economic Analyst—Larry Smith and Company

Photo: Moulin Studios; Courtesy, David D. Bohannon Organization

developer must assure himself that in his portfolio he has enough firm leases to secure financing commitments before proceeding with final site and building plans.

Occasionally a developer will feel that he must have A-1 rated national chains for the success of his center or for assuring its construction financing. From longer range experience, a good shopping center project need have no more than 50 per cent of its tenants representing national chains.[190] In the Community

Illustration No. 72. Plan One—Hillsdale Shopping Center

Strip building plan with parking lumped in rear of stores. Plan as proposed in 1947.

Builders' Council's opinion, local independent merchants with strong customer followings can form the majority of tenants, particularly in a neighborhood center.

But from another's viewpoint, which reflects the centers not having a strong position in relation to competition, "The competition for key chain tenants is so great today that it is largely a matter of the key tenants selecting the center, rather than the developer selecting the tenant."

Once the key tenants are committed and announcements publicized, other tenants are not too hard to obtain. But all

---

[190] The practice has become prevalent during the past few years on the part of lending institutions to require that shopping center developers have sufficient guaranteed rent from national chain tenants to cover the cost of debt charges, taxes, and operating expenses. This policy has frozen out many local merchants from obtaining locations in new centers. However there are indications that this practice is changing. See "What's Ahead for Shopping Center Financing." by Bruce P. Hayden, *Buildings,* August 1960.

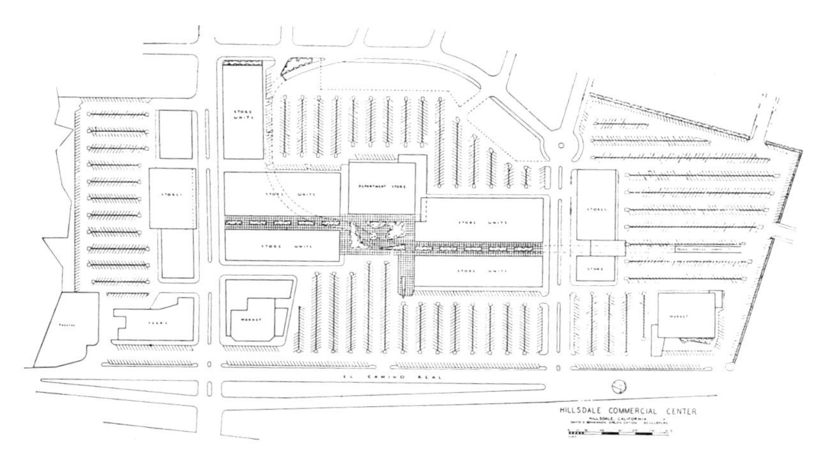

Illustration No. 73. Plan Two—Hillsdale Shopping Center

Mall has been evolved with truck tunnel for separation of deliveries and services from customers. Parking introduced on all four sides to reduce walking distances. Site plan as proposed 1949.

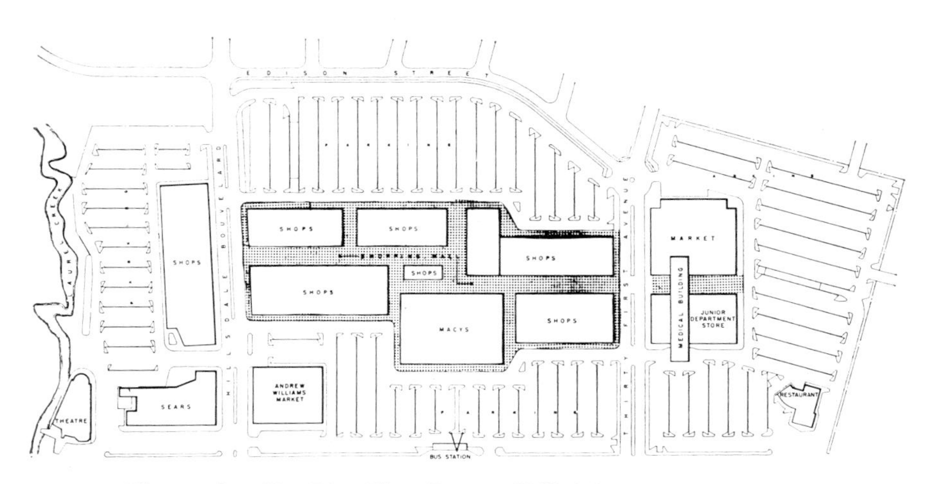

Illustration No. 74. Plan Three—Hillsdale Shopping Center

Plan as constructed 1954. Better use of mall frontages. More careful store grouping. Better arrangement of parking areas and improved interior circulation. Bus stop incorporated for mass transportation. Hillsdale Boulevard and Thirty First Avenue are two dedicated streets in existence before construction began—an exception which proves the rule about a shopping center site being in one piece **not** bisected by access street.

tenants, whether major or minor, national or local, want to know certain facts. Negotiation for shopping center occupancy is a two-way deal. The developer wants certain stores to round out his presentation of merchandise and to make his financing feasible. The merchants want to be sure space in the new shopping center will be profitable to them. Prospective tenants want to know the very things that the developer's market analysis uncovers: The quality of the market, the volume to be expected, the growth of the trade area, the parking available, and the competition to be expected. They also want to know who the other tenants will be.

2. The Number One Tenant

The number one tenant is the key in shopping center development. Once the leading tenant is known, the preliminary plans can proceed even while lease negotiations are continuing. With the key tenant in hand, the developer can set up his program for lease negotiations with the other supplementary stores which will fill in the building area.

In *neighborhood centers*, the supermarket is the key; the drugstore is the next most needed tenant. Other tenant types most frequently found in neighborhood centers are the service food stores, personal service shops—barber, beauty, shoe repair, laundry, dry cleaning, and notions. A variety store (the old 5 and 10 kind) is not ruled out of neighborhood convenience stores.

For a more complete listing of types of shops by location and size of center, see the listings shown on pages 275 and 282.

In *community centers*, the variety store or the junior department store is the leading tenant. Supplementary stores range through apparel and accessories to appliances and toys.

(In this type of center, more than in the other two, the tenant selection depends heavily on the relative bargaining strength of the developer and the prospective tenants. A strong location for the center gives the developer a better position for having tenants come to him asking for space, rather than his having to search for prospects.)

The variety or junior department store and the supermarket should be offered prominent anchor spots in the building layout.

In *regional centers*, the department store is the key tenant. For greater depth of shopping, two department stores are not unusual and there are cases where three department stores are represented. Other tenants can range through the full roster of retail types. "In a regional center follow the Noah's Ark idea, have two of everything," as James B. Douglas, president of Northgate in Seattle, suggests.

Tenant selection needs to proceed along with the site planning because numerous adjustments in building arrangement will take place to meet tenant desires and requirements. These arrangements should be firmed before getting into the final architectural planning and construction working drawings phase of the development. At least, the tenants should be identifiable in the preliminary site planning stage.

Tenant Classifications

The following classifications include not only current types of retail outlets but also services and non-retail activities which can be drawn upon to round out the tenant types in shopping centers.

Definition of Tenant Types:

NATIONAL CHAIN STORE is defined as: A business operating in four or more metropolitan areas located in three or more separate states.

INDEPENDENT STORE is defined as: A business operating in not more than two outlets located in only one metropolitan area.

LOCAL CHAIN STORE is defined as: A business which does not fall into the category of either of the two above.

Food

Supermarket
Meat, Poultry, Fish
Specialty Foods
Delicatessen
Bakery
Hot Bakery
Candy, Nuts
Dairy Products

Food Service

Restaurant
Cafeteria
Sandwich Shop or Snack Bar
Caterer
Restaurant—Liquor
Carry Out
Doughnut Shop

Clothing and Apparel

Department Store
Junior Department Store
Variety Store
Ladies' Specialty
Ladies' Wear
Bridal Shop
Maternity
Hosiery
Millinery
Children's Wear
Men's Wear
Family Wear
Family Shoe
Ladies' Shoe
Men's and Boys' Shoe
Children's Shoe
Furs

Dry Goods

Yard Goods
Curtains & Drapes
Linen
Fabrics
Imports
Luggage & Leather Goods

Furniture and Home Furnishings

Furniture
Lamps
Appliances
Floor Coverings
Radio, TV, Hi-Fi
Children's Furniture
Interior Decorator
Upholstering
China & Glassware

Hardware and Lumber

Hardware
Lumber
Automotive
Auto Dealers
Paint & Wallpaper
Garden Shops

Other Retail

Pet Shops
Music & Records
Hobby Shop
Books & Stationery
Flowers
Tobacco & News
Drugs
Pharmacy
Sporting Goods
Credit Jewelry
Costume Jewelry
Jewelry
Liquors & Wine
Sewing Machines
Key Shop
Cosmetics
Cards & Gifts
Toys
Cameras

Financial

Banks
Savings & Loan
Finance Company
Small Loans
Post Office
Insurance
Brokerage

Offices

Medical & Dental
Legal
Accounting
Architect
Real Estate
Contractor
General
Other

Personal Services

Beauty Shop
Barber Shop
Watch Repair
Shoe Repair
Cleaners & Dyers
Laundries
Travel Agents
Music Studio
Signs
Coin Operated Laundry
Photographer
Optometrist
Slenderizing Salon
Osteopath
Chiropractor

Other Tenants

Service Stations
Bowling Alleys
Theaters
Kiddielands

3. The Building Pattern

With the number one tenant in view or selected, the site can be better studied for the building arrangement. There are typical patterns for shopping center buildings, each susceptible to variations to suit the particular characteristics of the site.

Essentially, the patterns are the strip, the L, the U, the cluster. (The mall is a pedestrian circulation pattern. A "mall center" is a term used to convey the fact that the building pattern includes a pedestrian shopping concourse, enclosed or open air).

The *strip* is a straight line of stores tied together by a canopy protecting the pedestrian walk which extends along the

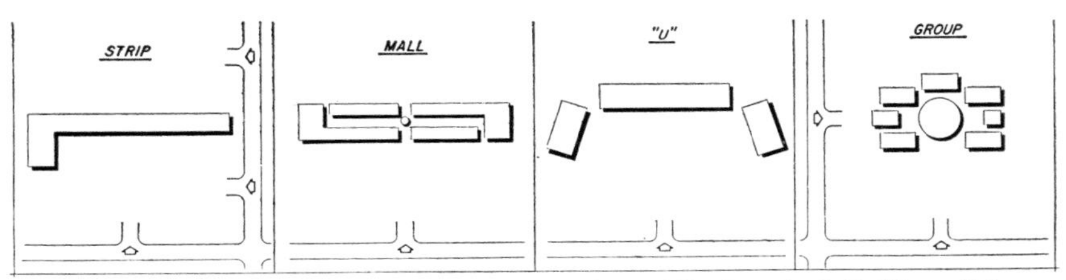

Source: p. 74 October, 1953—*Practical Builder*—Chicago.

Basic Shopping Center Patterns.

Strip. . . . . . simple lines of stores most economical for small centers; as size increases becomes too long, hard to merchandise and service, results in long walking distances.

Mall. . . . . . essentially consists of 2 strips facing each other; service access to stores is solved by a truck tunnel under the mall. This type results in better equalization in store locations, is good for centralized utility service such as air conditioning.

"U" Type. . . . . . sometimes called "Court"; this creates natural key store locations at end and center. Adapts to rectangular, square or corner plots with minimum walking distances.

Group or Cluster. . . . . . used essentially for larger regional centers. The group or cluster pattern can produce, with careful planning, an integrated center on nearly any property.

entrance fronts to the stores. The parking is usually placed between the access street and the building.

The strip is best adapted to the neighborhood center. Care must be taken to avoid elongating the strip beyond a distance that people can comfortably walk. (About 400 feet is a maximum length for a strip.) However, the simplicity of the strip layout makes it adaptable to many site conditions. As one developer expresses his preference: "Due to the shape of the property, we decided the strip to be the most desirable building layout. After considerable discussion with some of the large national chains, we learned that it is preferred in most instances by these chains. We have not had any objection over using the strip. Apparently shoppers will walk considerably more in a center than they are willing to downtown. Also, we find that with ample parking within the center people will drive back and forth to the stores or sections of the center where they wish to shop."

The L—is an adaptation to shorten the frontage length of a strip. The shape lends itself to variations for tenant locations and for site conditions, particularly for a site located at two important intersecting roads. The L can be turned in any direction for site orientation.

Illustration No. 75. A Strip Type Center

Swanway Plaza, Tucson, Arizona—a neighborhood center.

Photo: Courtesy, Roy P. Drachman

The U—creates natural key store locations at its ends and in its center. The pattern adapts to rectangular or square shaped sites and to sites having single road frontage only. The shape is suitable for neighborhood and community type centers.

The cluster—is a group of buildings separated by pedestrian malls or courts. The cluster arrangement is most suitable for the large regional center where parking surrounds the buildings to minimize distances between the farthermost parking space and the building group.

The mall—is the pattern for pedestrian circulation between two strips facing each other. It corresponds to a street for back and forth shopping without interference by automobile traffic. The mall is usual in regional centers. Without underground servicing through a truck tunnel, a mall makes separation of truck deliveries from customer circulation hard to achieve except by the introduction of service courts. The problem, then, is to screen effectively these service areas from the customer approaches from the parking area. Malls also entail double frontage stores in most instances. (See also page 325.)

Malls are not needed in neighborhood centers. "Do not consider using a mall in any center having less than 100,000 square feet gross floor area. But in larger, regional centers malls offer great advantages." "With a mall there is no such thing as a '100 per cent corner' nor 'a good side of the street'." "A mall creates an atmosphere which women like." A mall also offers the place in a large center for outdoor displays and space for special events useful in promotions of the center. The appeals of architectural features, statuary, landscaping, floral displays and casual strolling are advantages of malls which make them powerful customer attractors in large centers. The mall is adaptable to enclosure for complete air-conditioning and complete all-weather protection for customer comfort in shopping.

Of all the building patterns in shopping centers, the strip is most commonly used. In fact, from an Urban Land Institute

Illustration No. 76. An L-Type Center

Dorval Gardens Shopping Center, Montreal, Canada. The L-type of plan is adaptable to both neighborhood and community type shopping centers. In this case a strong, customer-pulling tenant is placed at either end of the L.

Photo: Courtesy, Steinberg's Limited, Owners/Developers

Illustration No. 77. A Cluster Type of Regional Center

Hillsdale Shopping Center, San Mateo, Calif. In this case special tenant types, such as drive-in bank, gasoline filling station, farmers market, and second department store are placed outside the buildings of the mall cluster.

Photo: Courtesy, David D. Bohannon Organization, Owners/Developers

survey[191] it was learned that over 40 per cent of the shopping center buildings are of the strip kind. While the L and the cluster with the mall are used about equally (24 per cent of the centers are L-shaped), the U is seldom used even though it offers a form having advantages for interior service courts, providing the court is wide enough for truck turning. Another shape seldom used is the T.

Irrespective of the buildings' basic pattern, store frontages should be continuous. "Setbacks just look pretty on paper. Tenants in stores set back from the continuous frontage ex-

---

[191] A special survey of Urban Land Institute members who own and operate shopping centers, conducted in 1957 as the basis for findings reported in Part II of its Technical Bulletin No. 30, *Shopping Centers Re-Studied.*

perience customer-resistance to their location," in the Council's experience.

4. Tenant Locations, Types and Groupings—In General

In designating stores within a building, the first consideration is proper selection and arrangement to draw more customers to all the participating stores. It is difficult to overestimate the importance of locating the "puller" stores in such a manner that pedestrian traffic is routed past the smaller stores handling items that are bought on impulse. This makes for the success of the entire center.

Another principle in store grouping is taking care that all convenience goods stores are as close as possible to the parking. As John C. Taylor remarks, "The grouping of stores in a successful center will be more often than not the result of careful planning of store locations so that the relationship of one to another will be of most benefit to all."

The Council has said repeatedly that stores that complement each other should be located together. For example, shops catering to women should be close together; service and repair shops may be grouped; groceries, services and 5 and 10 cent stores complement each other. Such types as hardware, electrical repair and house furnishings are supplementary. In the large regional center, complementary store groups should be located with reference to so-called "hot-spots."

Another set of general considerations in locating tenant types (not necessarily in order of rank) is: (1) rental income; (2) suitability of the tenant for the location; (3) pulling power or customer acceptance by reason of local preference for the merchant; (4) merchandising policy; (5) compatibility and complementary status of adjoining stores; (6) parking needs.

A listing of *tenant types by kind of center* is inadvisable because shopping centers must not only be designed to fit their individual trade area characteristics but also to include the circumstances of leasing, financing and tenant availability. Comparisons between centers can be misleading because a particular tenant could be successful in one center and a total loss to another. The selection of store types must be left to the individual case because the income range and character of tributary population, the expectancy for walk-in trade, local customs, store sizes, merchandising methods, etc., vary greatly for different site conditions and sections of the country. But there is a distinct pattern for the occurrence of certain store types. For example, a supermarket and drugstore will be found in practically all centers (an exception for the supermarket would be a high-fashion specialty type of center catering to an upper income area). (See Tenant Classifications, page 275.)

a. Neighborhood Centers. Tenant types are apt to be grouped in a single multi-tenant building, unless a free-standing, single-tenant structure, such as a supermarket, is introduced for a special reason. The Council, after consideration based on years of experience in the development and operation of centers of varying sizes and types, has developed a list of tenant types in the *general* order in which they should be established for the neighborhood center assuming the developer is able to obtain good lease terms and strong drawing power for each tenant type:

Tenant Types for the Neighborhood Center

First rank in selection

Supermarket
Drugstore (local druggist or chain)
Dry cleaner—laundry agency
Beauty parlor
Bakery (might depend on quality of baked goods offered by the supermarket)
Variety store (once classified as a 5 and 10)
Barber shop
Shoe repair

Filling station—in free-standing structure

Next order of selection to round out neighborhood conveniences

Service grocery (with phone order and delivery service, depending on whether it is a higher-income trade area)
Florist
Women's apparel
Radio, television—music and records
Gifts—stationery and books
Infants' and children's wear
Candy and nut shop
Lingerie and hosiery
Liquor store

Further development of the center would call for the following tenant types as the most important stores to include in a neighborhood center:

Jewelry, including watch repair
Haberdashery
Restaurant, cafe, or "fountain" type of snack shop
Sporting goods and camera supplies
Hardware and paints—including "fix-it" services

At this point in the planning procedures it is well to point out that as any center develops, without doubt, shifts will be needed in tenant locations; some tenants will outgrow their original space, others may need to be shifted to strengthen the whole center's operations. "Many merchants fail or never make progress because of their initial burden of too large a space and too much overhead. Ability to fit space to the changing needs of the tenant cannot be overemphasized."

b. Regional Centers. Tenant types are dependent somewhat on lease negotiations with the department store. Without the department store, or until there is a department store, the center is not a regional shopping center.

The matter of proper tenant location in a regional center is complicated, and essential. As mentioned earlier, in the big center the merchandising plan must place small tenants in the path of pedestrian circulation between the larger magnets—the department store, the junior department or specialty store, the variety store, the quality restaurant. The supermarket in a regional center takes a secondary position. (In fact, some Council members consider the supermarket non-essential in a regional center.)

But as Larry Smith points out: "It behooves the shopping center developer to be sure that the center is laid out in such a way that he will get the maximum benefit from the pedestrian traffic that the department store creates. If the department store is not located so that other stores will benefit from the foot traffic to and from the department store, the owner has lost the very thing for which he pays in negotiating the department store lease. The owner must be sure that the physical plan for the shopping center is such that there will be maximum benefit to all stores from the pedestrian traffic created by the department store's drawing power."[192]

A regional center must be all inclusive and self-sufficient. This characteristic underlines the importance in store grouping. To create "self-sufficiency" means that in addition to the "big pullers," there must be full range of merchandise available to the shopper—including everything found downtown. This completeness also means competition within the center. Competition between merchants is good for the center and good for the merchants. It keeps the merchants on their toes and, besides, gives people the comparison they want to find when shopping. James B. Douglas says: "Women just love to shop. Put in two markets, two dress shops, two drug stores—because a single tenant gets too independent."

To put it another way, the regional center should approximate, if possible, another downtown when it comes to completeness. Therefore, it is important that the size of the selling space depend upon the estimated volume determined by the market analysis. It is also important to remember how many people it takes to support a center of the size that is being contemplated.

Minimum Population Needed to Support Classes of Shopping Centers

Regional (with a department store as largest tenant) 250,000 to 1,000,000 people

Community (with junior department store as major tenant) 100,000 people

Neighborhood-Community (with variety store as major tenant) 10,000-20,000 families; 35,000-70,000 people

Neighborhood (with supermarket as major tenant) 2,000 families; 7,500 people

c. Tenant Grouping. In arranging store locations within a multi-tenant building or in allocating tenant types to the several buildings of a cluster or mall type of center, the experts sometimes don't agree on the theoretical aspect of grouping or separating competing tenants. Whether to bring stores of one

[192] For philosophies of department stores and other merchandising enterprises as entrepreneurs in shopping centers, see *Shopping Towns-USA* by Victor Gruen and Larry Smith, cited earlier. See also, "Department Store Trends in the Development of Shopping Centers" by Larry Smith. *Urban Land,* March 1952. Urban Land Institute.

kind into close relationship for convenience and competition or whether to separate them to spread pedestrian traffic and the demands on car parking spaces are unresolved differences of opinion. (Competitive stores adjacent to each other strengthen downtown, but this widely accepted principle is sometimes lost sight of in shopping center layouts.) In successful shopping center merchandising plans, the large attractors are placed first. Then nearby comes a grouping of stores featuring similar merchandise with respect to type, quality and price. In between the major pullers are the stores needing exposure to foot traffic and those which offer impulse buying items. Service shops seem to thrive in supplementary locations, *provided the parking is close.*

When two supermarkets are placed in adjoining locations, their demand for parking spaces is concentrated and the problem of truck unloading is more complicated. These are two good reasons for separating two supermarkets in the same center. But placed together, comparison shopping is strengthened.

Council members' experience speaks for grouping the supermarket and supplementary food service stores: "The grouping of food stores is important. They complement each other." "We put a supermarket and a service grocery next to each other and both tenants are happy." "We have a food center in our shopping center. Most of the food shopping is done at one time, while shopping for a new dress is done at another. Women buy groceries while wearing slacks. They come to the dress shops with hats and gloves." "In our regional center we group fashion shops and have the less expensive types of women's apparel in another section."

Mr. Douglas, from his Northgate experience, is in favor of grouping competitive store types: "A housewife likes to compare prices. If she sees some lettuce in one market, she likes to go over to the other market and examine its lettuce too. The one that has fresher, crisper and cheaper lettuce she buys. This keeps both markets on their toes and makes for better stores."

Mr. Bohannon favors separation of food stores. "At Hillsdale, we don't want to put food stores together even though it may be a service to the public to do so. The parking required for a food market is more than for any kind of soft line store. We have one big supermarket on either end of the mall and a Sears and Penney's on either side. I think women won't go to two supermarkets on the same day. One-day-a-week food shopping is the trend. We want to encourage other shopping on the same trip."

Even though surveys have been made of the store types and groupings in existing shopping centers,[193] their findings are not conclusive enough to establish any firm guidelines, other than the experiences just cited, for the types of tenants which work well together and which do not. One missing ingredient in store locational studies is the effect of proper interrelated store grouping on the prosperity of the center as a whole. Another is the ability of the merchant to work as a member of the merchandising team which ultimately becomes the shopping center. The Council has studied the matter of store grouping and in Appendix J sets out in four alphabetical arrangements stores that go well when grouped together.

In choosing stores of the right type in starting a center in a new growth area, the developer must consider his ability to secure shops of the right type for rendering service to the trade area and tenants who have credit ratings to weather the pioneering period.

As a final note about selecting the tenants, the special points to consider are:

The tenant's credit rating, his profit and loss experience, his advertising policy, the type of merchandise he sells, the class of customers he caters to, his housekeeping practices, and his long term operational record and merchandising policy, his integrity.

Certain axioms about store grouping have grown out of shopping center experience. A statement that needs no proof is, "Arrange the tenants to provide the greatest amount of interplay between the stores." Another basic principle in tenant placement is, "Be careful where you put the supermarket because of its heavy demand for parking spaces. If you don't have parking for the supermarket, you don't have customers."

Seasoned leasing brokers, Realtors, landlords, and shopping center operators have learned many things about grouping certain kinds of businesses:

Men's stores—shoes, clothing and haberdashery, sporting goods all tend to swell each other's volume.

---

[193] See *Shopping Centers Re-Studied,* Part II. Technical Bulletin No. 30. Urban Land Institute.

For the "Principle of Compatibility" among retail businesses in selecting tenant types, see *The Selection of Retail Locations* by Richard Lawrence Nelson. F. W. Dodge Corp., New York.

Similarly, women's apparel, shoes, millinery, and children's clothes and toys prosper in close proximity—the soft lines.

Food products do well when grouped together—groceries, meat and fish markets, delicatessens, bakeries, doughnut shops, confectioners are related—the food lines.

Businesses which sell many small items to many customers are generally more successful when grouped together—variety stores and drugstores.

Merchants selling hardware, appliances, radio and television sets, musical instruments, and items of this character—the hard lines—group well.

The stores selling personal services and conveniences naturally go together, but in shopping centers they should be as close as possible to the parking, as mentioned before.

There are other sets of considerations in store grouping: Suitability of the shop for the location, convenience to the customer, and the amount of rent. "In any center, the architectural plan must place small tenants in the path of pedestrian traffic moving between the larger tenants—the variety store, the drugstore, and the supermarket." Supermarkets do not pay high rentals (see page 363); therefore a supermarket should be

Illustration No. 78. The Department Store

The leading tenant of the regional type shopping center. Unless a center has a full-line department store it is not a regional center.

Seven Corners Shopping Center, Fairfax County, Virginia
(Washington, D. C., Metropolitan Area)

put at the least expensive part of the center and where people walk past other stores to get to it. The only objection is that in most cases this increases the walking distance to the parked car.

In a large regional center the department store generates pedestrian traffic. So a second department store or a junior department store should be placed at separated locations to distribute the customer pull.

Merchandising factors and pedestrian traffic determine tenant placement in site planning. The building should be placed so maximum walking distance from the parking area is 300 feet. Centralized location of the building on the property is emerging as a pattern for regional center development. Such placement minimizes walking distances, equitably distributes parking, and simplifies traffic circulation on the site. In large centers, a circumferential or ring road should be provided completely on the property, insulated, and removed from the public access highways. This circumferential should connect parking with points of ingress and egress thereby distributing traffic to all the parking areas and equalizing the accessibility of all sides of the center.

5. Tenant Types—In Particular

a. Department Stores. Department stores are the dominant tenants of regional shopping centers. The location of the store determines the placing of other tenants. These units want to benefit from the flow of customers between the parking area and the building. The department store wants the parking area directly accessible to it. The resolving of this dilemma is the crux in the site planning of a regional shopping center.

One form of solution is readily found when there are two department stores. Two equally sized stores can be separated by intervening frontage filled with the auxiliary shops. Cross County Center, Yonkers, N. Y., illustrates this arrangement with Gimbel Bros. at the west end of the mall which extends to John Wanamaker's at the east end. Glendale in Indianapolis uses a similar scheme for the location of L. S. Ayres & Co. separated from Wm. H. Block Co.

Actually, the pivot is the strongest position in a circle—spokes revolve around a hub. When there is one dominating department store for the shopping array, the midpoint location in a cluster arrangement is good. Northland, with its J. L.

Hudson store occupying the hub of the center proves the success of this framework. Westroads in St. Louis represents a simplified version—something like a T formation. A hinge arrangement for the department store location is represented by the L-type plan. The department store occurs at the elbow of the L. Capitol Court in Milwaukee represents a sound version of the elbow action. A department store at the end of a strip building pattern is apt to create imbalance in the customer pull for the full length of the frontage. Mostly this unbalanced arrangement happens when a department store is added to an existing community center to round out or to make complete the presentation of shopping goods for the strengthening of the entire center (thus raising its community status to regional).

Before adding a department store to an existing center, the developer must analyze carefully what will be its real advantage to him. It is true that a department store does anchor the development. This advantage may come from the store as it affects the permanency of the developer's investment. But with a department store added later, the developer must be sure of the kind of deal which he works out. The capital cost of the department store's construction must be justified against the rent obtainable (see also pages 360 and 362). Perhaps as one solution, the developer can lease the ground and have the store build its own building and negotiate for the parking space adjustment.

In negotiating for a department store tenant, the developer should be aware of customer loyalties to the store under consideration. Within the trade area there may be two department stores, each doing about the same volume. In a suburban shopping center location, neither of the stores could hope for as much as 50 per cent of the potential volume anticipated for a branch store because customer loyalty to the other store will cause shoppers to go to the other store regardless of any inconvenience. Thus, if there is reason for a department store at this center, there may be reason for the other, or a second regional center may spring up.

"A full-line department store cannot be housed in less than 125,000 square feet, but more often 300,000 to 400,000 square feet may be required to do justice both to the market and to the name of the store involved. In a well-balanced regional center the department store space should approximate one-third of the total rentable building area in the development."

To illustrate distribution of space for a regional center of 475,000 to 500,000 square feet gross floor area, the following measurements are listed (without reference to volume or other qualifications of the market).

Department Store—	200,000 sq. ft.
Apparel Shops (men's & women's)—	75,000 " "
*Variety Store—	20,000 " "
**Food—	40,000 " "
Furniture, appliances, floor coverings, etc.—	40,000 " "
Drugs—	12,000 " "
Gifts, jewelry, stationery, etc.—	15,000 " "
Eating places—	15,000 " "
Service Shops, and other—	the remainder

* As some variety stores approach junior department store type merchandise, an owner might then want a junior department store of 40,000 sq. ft. or two 20,000 sq. ft. variety stores.

** Supermarket of 25,000 sq. ft. with 15,000 sq. ft. in bakery and other food lines.

As indicated by footnote 192, page 284, department stores themselves are often shopping center entrepreneurs. There are advantages to the store from this kind of operation. For one, the store itself controls the tenant selection. In this way it avoids a risk of having its branch or full operation surrounded by lower grade supporting stores. Then too, some part of any income realized from the development of the center will accrue to the department store. If the center is successful, the department store enjoys what amounts to a very favorable rent condition. The store in this way obtains the degree of control which it thinks necessary and proper for it to retain. On the other hand, few department stores by their complexion as merchandisers are equipped to handle all of the planning, construction, and leasing details involved with shopping center development.

b. Junior Department Stores. A junior department store and a specialty store are similar in that neither carry hard goods or household furnishings—other than a token representation of the line—nor furniture. In this they differ from department stores. (In many cases, the expanding lines carried by variety stores—once the old 5 and 10's—are such that these stores are approaching the status of junior department stores.)

The junior department store is often the second strongest tenant in regional centers.

c. Variety Stores. Variety stores (the old 5 and 10's) are good neighbors for supermarkets in a shopping center. From the variety stores' point of view, a central location is the most prominent. In a regional center, the variety store wants to benefit from the pedestrian traffic moving to the department store. Double store entrances are good, but one national chain's representative reports: "We have no store in a center of the mall type. This confines our selection of sites to the straight strip, L- or U-shaped centers."

To indicate points of view about shopping centers by representatives of chain-operated variety stores, the following quotes are offered for the developer's planning purposes:

"If you are going into a shopping center, you should have enough confidence in the center's prospects to pay the owner enough guaranteed rent to permit him to do proper financing—

Illustration No. 79. The Variety Store

Together with the supermarket, the principal tenant of community type of shopping center. Frequently the **junior** department store displaces the variety store as the major tenant in community centers.

The Meadows Center, Terre Haute, Indiana

the minimum rent per square foot should be tied into the minimum expected sales volume."

"We like to be in centers where the minimum square footage of sales area is 100,000 square feet. We avoid the smaller neighborhood centers. The cumulative pulling power of small centers is not enough for the rigid requirements in our specifications for a shopping center's location with respect to anticipated sales volume."

"In small centers we want to avoid a situation where another, larger center a mile or so away from our successful operation can come in with competition and pull business from our location. We always want to know where competition can also build."

"In several instances we have found the proposed center too small and have encouraged the builder to enlarge his original scheme to avoid future competition. In others, we have eliminated ourselves from the project."

For example: "In a neighborhood center of 40,000 square feet you need about 25,000 square feet for the soft goods, apparel, etc. to pull people," as J. W. York analyzes the size of a center. "This amount of space shouldn't be merchandised by one type of tenant in a center of that relative size."

Another look into location of and size of variety stores in shopping centers comes from an official's statement: "We propose to open stores containing not less than 30,000 square feet and expect to confine our new activity to regional centers or centers containing not less than 200,000 square feet of merchandising area."

d. Drugstores. For the developer, the drugstore is a key tenant in any type of shopping center. He need not wonder whether to include a drugstore. He will have one. He need only choose between a chain operation or a strong independent merchant. According to a current survey made by *American Druggist*, the drugstore ranks ahead of the supermarket in the respect that shopping center operators do not feel that a center is complete without at least one drugstore.

The *American Druggist's* survey reveals that the overall average size of drugstores in shopping centers is 3,576 square feet of *selling area.* In neighborhood centers the average square feet of *selling area* is 3,092 square feet; in community centers, the average *selling area* is 4,210 square feet; in regional centers, it is 5,528 square feet. So it would seem that the larger the center, the larger the selling area occupied by drugstores.

The preferred location for drugstores in shopping centers is a corner. The *American Druggist* survey also showed a corner spot for the drugstore is usual in 51 per cent of the shopping centers, while middle locations are assigned in 45 per cent of the cases and side locations in only 3 per cent. The same survey revealed that shopping center locations have advantages for drugstores because of the traffic drawn by parking and by other stores.

e. Supermarkets. The supermarket is the common denominator of shopping centers. In neighborhood centers, the supermarket is the biggest single attraction. The Council advises: "Do not give the supermarket so much space that it will sell non-food items and compete in these with your other tenants." (The Council has in mind stores having over 15,000 square feet of retail sales area.) A supermarket of 20,000 or 30,000 square feet is out of proportion for a neighborhood center of 40,000 square feet. "Two smaller markets at 12,000 square feet each are better than one supermarket because the supersized ones break into non-food lines." Supermarket operators have upped

Illustration No. 80. The Supermarket

The principal tenant of a neighborhood type of shopping center.

Cherry Chase Center, Sunnyvale, Calif.

their space needs from 10,000 square feet to 22,000 and 37,500 square feet of gross floor area.

In community centers the supermarket is one of the key tenants, but in regional centers the supermarket loses its number one position to the department store. The regional center's function in offerings of shopping goods in depth and variety subordinates the sale of food items (convenience goods). For this reason, most regional centers include one supermarket only to round out their status for "one-stop shopping." The supermarket is not a primary puller in a regional center. (Supermarkets seldom pull customers from distances farther away than 5 or 6 minutes driving time.) But in a regional center a supermarket is a worthwhile convenience for the customers who come to buy things other than food. For example, a large regional center can fill its food item sales need by having a quality food market with small auxiliary food shops occupying less than 5 per cent of the total gross floor area of an 800,000 square foot center.

A supermarket is often served by 6 or 7 trucks at a time, so "a supermarket needs plenty of service delivery space around it." Supermarkets have a heavy parking space demand even though turnover is high. A parking index of 6 to 8 car spaces for each 1,000 square feet of gross leasable area is needed. The variation depends on turnover and availability of duplicate use parking spaces. Remember too that a supermarket has a long, lifeless exterior wall unless this wall is put to use (about 125 feet is perhaps a standard supermarket depth). "When you have a supermarket with dimensions 200 feet by 100 feet, make the frontage 100 feet, not 200 feet."[194]

f. Service Shops. These personal service types of tenants—typified by the barber, beauty parlor, laundry, shoe repair—occupy small unit areas. They are characteristically parts of neighborhood centers. They offer daily conveniences to the population of the close-by trade area—the people within 5 or 6 minutes driving time. As mentioned earlier, service shops should be close to, or easily accessible from, short time, in-and-out parking.

In a regional center, the total area devoted to these units will not take up more than 2 per cent of the gross leasable area.

[194] For facts about supermarkets, particularly averages for new stores built each year, see *The Super Market Industry Speaks*—the annual report issued by Super Market Institute, Inc., Research Division, 500 North Dearborn St., Chicago 10, Ill.

The location of small stores having 500 to 1,000 square feet of leasable area is important. These small shops pay higher rentals on a square foot basis, add interest for the shopper, and contribute to the completeness of the center. One suggestion for a frontage location of small service shops is along the pedestrian passageways between the parking area and the mall. In this way, blank walls are avoided and good spots are provided for service shops. These and other smaller tenant types—such as yarn, dress pattern, costume jewelry—generally receive stock shipments by parcel post and do not need to be directly accessible to a truck service facility.

g. Other Tenant Types and Special Uses. Of course, supermarkets, drugstores, variety stores, and department stores are not the only kind of tenant with which a developer must be familiar. Based on quotations from Community Builders' Council experiences, the following notations indicate some information apart from leasing and architectural planning data, which may be helpful in tenant selection and in *site planning*: (For a tabulation of current percentage rents, guaranteed rent levels and typical sales volumes insofar as these can be indicated, see pages 360 through 369 and Appendix I.)

Auto Supplies. Ordinarily, automobile accessories and services do not belong in the main unit of a shopping center. If provided, such tenants are suitable only in a secondary location where parking space can be specially assigned without interference with general customer parking. An auto laundry—drive-in car wash—is not compatible with a shopping center and could only be possible at an isolated location on the site, providing there is generous site area.

Banks. A bank is a convenience to customers and tenants in any center. A bank with windows for drive-in should be located at the end of a building where you can have space for cars to line up without interference with other parking arrangement and circulation. A free standing drive-in should be located in a corner of the site close to the major access point. Interior bank location should not interrupt continuous retail frontage.[195]

---

[195] For a full discussion of banks and drive-in banks in shopping centers, see "Recent Developments in Branch Banking," *Urban Land*, January 1956; and "Measuring Deposit Potentials When Establishing Branch Banks," *Urban Land*, September 1955—Urban Land Institute. Also *Banking Expansion—New Frontiers Ahead*, Technical Bulletin No. 35, Urban Land Institute. All three references are by Robert H. Armstrong, banking consultant.

Bowling Alleys. In a neighborhood center and where there is basement or other space for secondary, non-shopping use, a bowling alley can be a profitable tenant. Bowling is a popular pastime, stimulated by the existence of leagues and the simplicity of its playability and lack of outlay for participation.[196] Ordinarily, a free-standing, single tenant structure is a preferable solution for operations as hours do not coincide with shopping hours.

Community Rooms. Although such facility is a public relations device for the operational aspects of a center, it should be planned for early in the development. The community room can be part of the department store space, or in other types of center, it can be placed in a basement or other secondary location.

Furniture Stores. Full-line furniture stores are not good as tenants in neighborhood centers. Purchases by the average shopper are infrequent and are made after a long-planned trip. Furniture stores fit into suburban locations and the pattern of evening shopping, *but* characteristically they require large display and storage spaces which can only return low volumes per square foot. Basement areas are easily merchandised by furniture stores with a token reception space on the main shopping level. Interior decorators' shops with token furniture and fabric lines can be substituted for full-line furniture stores.

Filling Stations. A gasoline service station is good in any center. The station must be in a prominent place along the access to the center. A corner location is good if it does not interfere with traffic at the intersection. "Take care to assign a specific area to the station so that it does not infringe on your parking area." Hugh Potter's experienced advice is requoted, "In order to put a filling station in a prominent place, you have to have a nice looking structure consistent with your center's architecture. You have to insist on its being kept clean and you have to segregate its traffic. Housekeeping is the major problem."

Kiddielands and Nurseries. Such space uses in a community or regional center are attractions for children and draw mothers

[196] See "Anyone for Bowling?" by Robert A. Hoffman. *The Mortgage Banker,* January 1960, pp. 22-24. The following excerpt is pertinent: Supporting population per lane—1,500; minimum proximity to competition—2 miles; optimum required parking spaces—number of lanes x 10 x 80%.

to a center. The developer can assign the space and buy the equipment, but he is better off to operate it on a concession basis. In any case insurance against accident claims is a necessity. A nursery can be leased to a profit-making organization, just as any store or operation in a center. An adjacent outdoor playground is an asset to a nursery.

Hardware Stores. Hardware stores are taking to supermarket ways with self-service. The "do-it-yourself" market has changed hardware stores into building equipment and materials supermarkets. Shelf displays eliminate the clerk's aisles. Garden shops require space for outdoor display. The paint and wallpaper store typically occupies less area than the hardware store, usually less than 3,000 square feet.

Medical Clinics. Instead of second story offices for doctors and dentists, a separate medical clinic type of building is preferable for a shopping center. Special wiring, plumbing, cleaning, and construction required by doctors indicate a different kind of building for this purpose. The clinic should be located where special parking can be assigned. A medical building should be placed away from the main shopping section of the center.

Motels. Motels are suitable adjuncts to a shopping center, but only where a special area can be devoted to the motel. A motel generates business for a shopping center's restaurant. A motel is a suitable use for land which a developer may have acquired in excess of the acreage needed for the actual center.

Suburban Offices. Office buildings are suitable as adjuncts to shopping centers and where the office use and its parking are separated from but accessible to the shops.

Restaurants. Do not put a restaurant in the middle of the shopping frontage. It places too much demand on the parking area needed close to the shops. A corner of the site where space for specially assigned parking can be arranged and for direct drive-in purposes is better. A good restaurant has pulling power, but the good restaurant takes a skillful operator. "If you are only a builder, don't get into the restaurant business—It takes special know-how." "A big, brassy restaurant with a night club is too expensive a risk for a shopping center operation." On the other hand, a good restaurant in the center can be an asset and can draw customers from all over the trade area.

Theaters. The movie goers take space needed by night shoppers. Desirability of a theater depends on local habits, patronage customs, and the presence of open air movies in the trade area. Night shopping hours and theater hours conflict. Only rarely today is a theater being built in a shopping center; but when local conditions are such to indicate a demand, a first-run theater can prove to be a profitable tenant.

The Community Builders' Council also emphasizes that developers in selecting stores for a center must consider the service the center is to render to the neighborhood. In considering the revenue to be derived, it must be remembered that all types of stores cannot and should not pay the same rental per square foot. The tenant should be made aware of the fact that his rent is to be based upon the probable volume and profit of his particular type of business. Certain types of service establishments, such as banks, post offices, usually pay low rentals and may even lose money for the developer. These are, however, extremely valuable to high-rent tenants in drawing power and round out the service to the community, which is essential in maintaining continued patronage and good will.

6. Store Sizes

In the discussion on tenant grouping, the Council stressed the need to plan and construct multi-tenant buildings for flexibility in store locations to permit later shifting of tenants as may be needed for space expansions or for improved merchandising.

Buildings for single tenant occupancy are planned in accordance with specific requirements of the specific tenant but in harmony with the overall character of the shopping center's architecture. Single tenancy buildings follow well-established principles of interior store design and tenant practices.

As noted, multiple-tenant structures have to allow for flexibility. In considering ceiling heights, some tenants may want mezzanines for expansion or for non-selling activities. Attic space between a hung ceiling and the roof structure will economize on electrical and mechanical work for heating and air-conditioning.

a. Width. Even though standard widths are commonly cited in multiples of 10, 15, or 20 feet, this spacing does not readily conform to merchandising layouts. Study of proper widths to accommodate counters, display cases, racks and aisles reveals that economies can be realized both in initial store layout and later alteration if columns and wall spacing are moduled on fixturing measurements rather than on round numbers.

Council members have studied store widths and they recommend the following:

(1) If a small store is to have cases and counters only on one side, the width should be 11 or 12 feet.

(2) If the store is to have counter and wall cases on one side with display in the aisle, then not less than 14 to 15 feet should be provided.

(3) If the store is to have counters and wall cases on both sides and an ample customer aisle in the center, 16 to 17 feet should be provided.

(4) If the room is to have cases and counters on both sides and one center line of display tables, the width should be 21 to 22 feet.

(5) If the room is to have counters and wall cases on both sides and a center sales island without central vertical cases, the width should be 26 to 28 feet.

(6) If the room is to have cases and counters on both sides, and an island with vertical central cases as well as counters and service space, then the width should be 29 to 31 feet.

The Council recommends a column spacing of 17 or 34 feet. This permits division into 17 foot stores or variations from the multiple by placing the partition on either side of the column. This arrangement permits store widths of 10 to 11 feet with wall cases on one side with one counter, 17 feet for wall cases on two sides with a counter, or 22 to 23 feet for wall cases with two counters and a center case.

Column spacing must be carefully considered because it determines the manner in which the total leasable area may be divided into individual stores. Twenty-foot column spacing is a usual standard, but the 34-foot spacing, as mentioned above, is more practical.

b. Depth. The ability to provide stores of varying depths is an asset to any center. Depths from 40 to 150 feet are required in many cases. It is advisable to use curtain walls in the rear where possible, to permit future deepening at minimum cost.

Where it is necessary to construct the buildings with the same depth throughout, small stores may be "carved out" of deeper space having rear overlaps or be placed on either side of a through pedestrian walk. Excessive depths from which an adequate return cannot be obtained should be avoided. Where shopper traffic moves on two frontages greater store depth is needed. Deep stores are needed if there are no basements. Where delivery is at the back of the store and storage facilities have to be provided on ground level, greater depth is needed. Lesser depth is possible where service facilities are in the basement and pedestrian traffic is on one side of the structure only.

Stores should be 100 feet to 150 feet deep. A depth of 120 feet is shallow for major stores. Many of the big chains want stores of 150 feet in depth and self-service drugstores now want 160 feet of depth. Where there are no basements, such stores require almost as much storage as they do sales space.

B. THE NECESSARY PARKING

The space for parking customers' cars is a basic requirement in shopping center site planning. After all, it was the automobile that brought about the still evolving planned shopping center. The layout of the parking space must assist in making the center serve its prime function—that of an attractive and profitable market place. In providing the indispensable parking, the only questions are how much area to provide and how best to arrange the space to be so laid out. The parking so provided then becomes an auxiliary to the commercial use and not a commercial use in itself.

1. How Much Parking

From a land use area standpoint, parking takes up more space than all other physical features of the shopping center. The parking for each project must be given careful consideration.

The number of parking spaces needed for any shopping center depends upon factors affecting the demand. These are:

The size and type of center.
The composition of the tenancy.
The amount of walk-in trade generated from nearby areas.
The amount of customer traffic from public transportation.

The local parking habits and the rate of turnover in the parking spaces.

The size and shape of the property; the peak loads encountered.

By taking the above factors into consideration, the size of the parking area can be gauged for the parking of cars and the movement of cars on the site.

There are two terms used to describe the measurement of parking in its relationship to the shopping center structure: The parking index; and the parking ratio.

a. The Parking Index. *Parking need is generated by the area devoted to retail sales.* Hence, the relationship between the number of car parking spaces and the area of retail selling space is the parking index. The area in retail selling space varies according to the tenant type, the display of goods, the method of selling; the number, size, and variety of items, etc. For this reason, *selling space* as a unit against which to make comparisons is too variable for reliable computation. But *the gross leasable area*—i.e. the total gross floor area within buildings which is occupied exclusively by individual tenants and upon which the tenants pay rent—is measurable (see definitions, page 217). Each tenant's gross leasable or rental area is described in the lease document. Gross leasable area (abbreviated GLA) becomes, then, a known factor for measuring parking *spaces* in relationship to tenant area for making statistical analyses.

The parking index is the number of car parking spaces per 1,000 square feet of gross leasable area.[197]

As a unit to indicate the number of parking spaces provided in relation to tenant occupancy, the parking index has the advantage of not needing adjustments or explanations to show the assignments made for area per car, arrangement of the spaces, provisions for car circulation, size and shape of the site, etc.

"The larger the center, the lower the parking index." For a regional center, a parking index of 6 parking spaces per 1,000 square feet GLA is ample provision.

"The smaller the center, the higher the parking index." For a neighborhood center a parking index of 8 parking spaces per 1,000 square feet GLA is satisfactory.

---

[197] Leasable area and rentable area are synonymous terms here.

Illustration No. 81

Parking Lot Layout

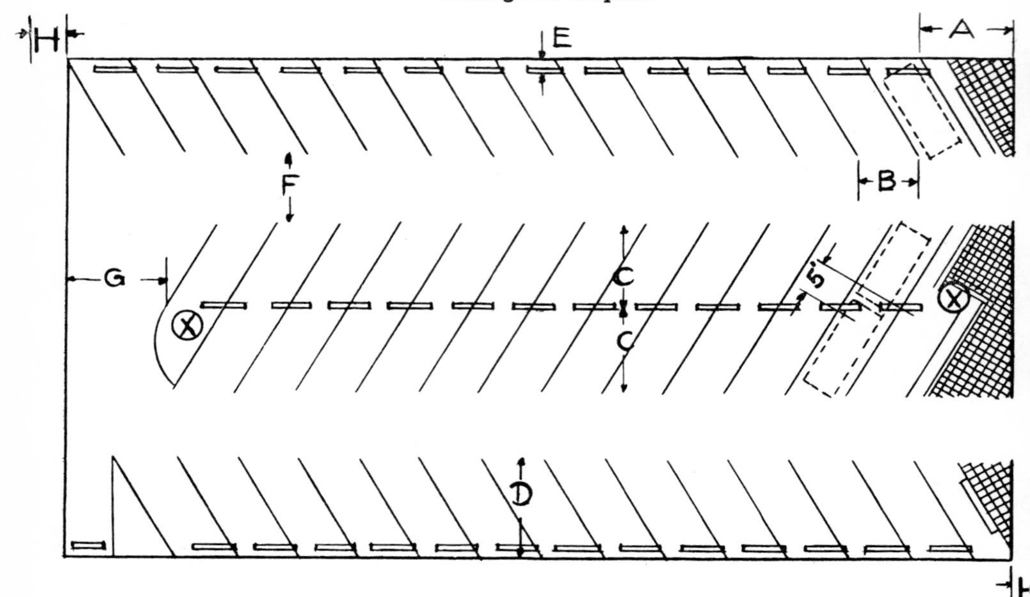

Dimension Table

Dimensions when parking at any of these angles

		45°	50°	55°	60°	90°
Offset	A	18′	15′8″	13′4″	11′	1′6″
Car Space	B	12′	11′4″	10′8″	10′	8′7″
Stall Depth	C	16′	16′8″	17′4″	18′	18′6″
Stall Depth	D	18′	18′4″	18′8″	19′	19′
Overhang	E	2′	2′1″	2′2″	2′3″	2′9″
Driveway	F	13′	14′6″	16′	17′6″	25′
Turnaround	G	17′	16′	15′	14′	14′
Extra	H	6′	5′	4′	3′	0

The schematic drawing above illustrates 60-degree diagonal parking on a lot approximately 100′ x 150′. The table above shows the dimensions for 45, 55, 60, and 90-degree parking which are those most used.

To determine the number of cars that can be parked in each of the four banks:

1. Deduct the area lost in parking the first car. (Dimension "A" in the above sketch)
2. Then divide the car space, (dimension "B") into the total length of each bank of cars, plus the extra factor "H", if there is any extra space.

The shaded space may be used for planting. Dotted lines illustrate two large cars in parking position with alternate wheels against block—bumpers separated. Light standards are represented by "X."

Source: Buildings, The Magazine of Building Management, November, 1959.

The parking index is the factor to apply in comparing provisions at centers in *operation*.[198] The type of tenancy has much to do with the number of parking spaces needed—for example a supermarket requires more spaces than does a furniture store. Ordinarily there is overlap and turnover of space from one tenant's use to another.

b. The Parking Ratio. For *planning purposes* and for estimating adequacy of site area, the parking ratio may be used. The ratio is not a mathematical formula applied with finality, but it is a practical method for estimating parking area requirements in site planning. (Only after a center is leased and in operation is the rentable area and its sales area actually known and accurately measurable.)

The parking ratio is the relationship between the area devoted to parking and the area devoted to building. This ratio is best expressed in terms of gross floor area. (Gross floor area, abbreviated GFA, is the total floor area of all buildings in the project, including basements, mezzanines and upper floors, if any. It excludes separate service facilities outside the stores, such as boiler houses and maintenance shops.)

Based on its long period of experimentation and experience in shopping center *planning*, the Community Builders' Council recommends a ratio of 3 square feet of parking area to 1 square foot of gross floor area be used for *planning* calculations. This method provides a workable measurement for the site's parking capacity. It takes into account the area allocation for the car stall, the moving aisles, access drives, planting spaces, pedestrian walkways—the appurtenances of parking.

At 400 square feet per car. In determining the site's parking capacity by the ratio method, it is now best to allow 400 square feet of area per car. This allowance includes access drives, storage spaces and incidental areas such as landscape plots and unusable corners.[199]

---

[198]

Regional Centers Parking Index	5 to 6 cars per 1,000 sq. ft. GLA
Community Centers Parking Index	7 cars per 1,000 sq. ft. GLA
Neighborhood Centers Parking Index	8 cars per 1,000 sq. ft. GLA

[199] In 1949, when the ratio method was first evolved by the Council, 300 sq. ft. per car was the standard for car storage and movement, but with the change in car design to longer, wider, lower models, greater spacing for self-parking is required. In 1960, compact cars and small foreign cars are coming into use—particularly as a family's second car. Until we know the eventual outcome of compact car use, 400 sq. ft. per car—not 300 sq. ft.—remains a safer unit of area per car.

Illustration No. 81—Continued

60° Parking

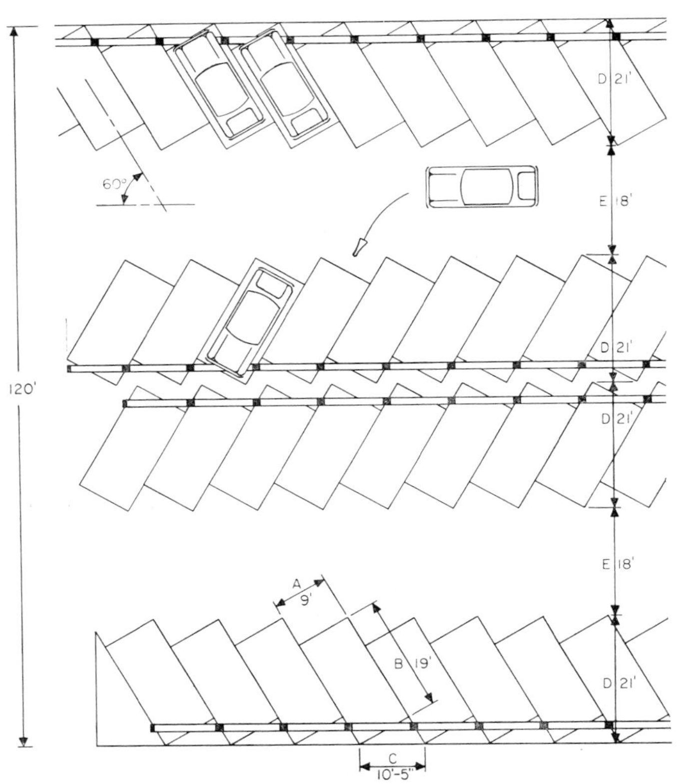

Layout Based on 9' Wide Stalls

		60° PARKING				
STALL WIDTH	A	8'-0"	8'-6"	9'-0"	9'-6"	10'-0"
STALL LENGTH	B	19'-0"	19'-0"	19'-0"	19'-0"	19'-0"
CURB LENGTH PER CAR	C	9'-3"	9'-10"	10'-5"	11'-0"	11'-6"
STALL DEPTH	D	20'-5"	20'-9"	21'-0"	21'-3"	21'-6"
DRIVEWAY WIDTH	E	19'-0"	18'-6"	18'-0"	18'-0"	18'-0"

Source: Adapted from *How to Lay Out a Parking Lot*—a booklet by Western Industries, Inc., Chicago 32, Ill.

To illustrate the conversion suggested above, let us assume that you have an acre of land approximately 40,000 square feet net. A 3 to 1 parking ratio would be 30,000 square feet of parking area to 10,000 square feet of gross floor area. To find the number of cars that can be parked in this area, divide 30,000 square feet by 400 square feet. The answer is 75 cars. In the same way, the ratio of cars per 1,000 square feet of gross floor area (GFA) is 7.5. A center with 100,000 square feet gross floor area would have parking space for 750 cars which would require 300,000 square feet of parking area including car stalls and access aisles. This is a 3 to 1 ratio, or 3 square feet of parking area to 1 square foot of gross floor area. It also becomes a parking index of 7.

(In the same way a 2 to 1 ratio translates to 5 cars per 1,000 sq. ft. of gross floor area.)

At 300 square feet per car. If 300 square feet per car space is used for calculating the number of cars in relation to gross floor area, a 3 to 1 ratio becomes 10 cars for each 1,000 square feet of building area; a 2 to 1 ratio translates to 6.7 cars for each 1,000 square feet GFA. *On this basis, the 3 to 1 ratio,* or 10 cars per 1,000 square feet GFA *becomes an unnecessary provision* for any but a neighborhood center. It also represents providing parking space for a peak seasonal demand such as at Christmas periods, which is not a good thing to do.

Peak demand. It is impractical to design the parking provision for the peak load—the Saturday before Christmas, for example. At other times the parking area will have a deserted look. Barren parking lots react on people unfavorably. In addition, an excessive parking space allocation cannot be justified by the economics involved. Variations in shopping hours, types of tenancy, and rates of turnover help level peak parking demands.[200]

The supermarket will generate the greatest need for parking space at any location. For example, a supermarket with 15,000 square feet of retail selling area might have 300 customers

[200] Parking space demand at a shopping center is tempered by the fact that a shopper buys in several stores while parking his car only once—"one stop shopping," while at a single detached store the parking serves only a single transaction. This shopping characteristic differentiates parking space requirements for shopping centers from parking provisions at free-standing commercial enterprises—a difference not accounted for in most zoning ordinances which set parking for business on a single unit relationship.

Illustration No. 81—Continued

90° Parking

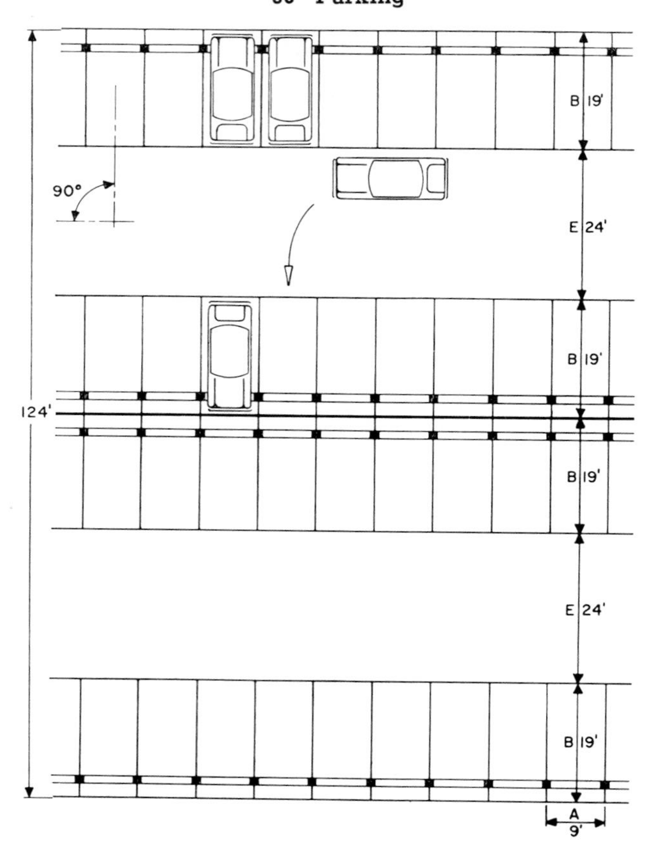

90° PARKING					
STALL WIDTH	A	8'–6"	**9'–0"**	9'–6"	10'–0"
STALL LENGTH	B	19'–0"	**19'–0"**	19'–0"	19'–0"
DRIVEWAY WIDTH	E	25'–0"	**24'–0"**	24'–0"	24'–0"

Layout Based on 9' Wide Stalls

Source: Adapted from *How to Lay Out a Parking Lot*—a booklet by Western Industries, Inc., Chicago 32, Ill.

accumulated at the peak hour. This means 200 to 250 cars would be parked outside. If it takes 400 square feet per car, then the food store alone would take up 100,000 square feet of parking. This is over a 6 to 1 ratio. Obviously, the supermarket's parking spreads over the full parking area. A 6 to 1 ratio for one tenant in a shopping center can't possibly be met. See page 364, footnote 217, for a supermarket parking index.

2. The Parking Layout

The aim of the parking lot layout for a shopping center is to achieve the greatest possible turnover of cars during the shopping period. The act of parking at a shopping center must be simple, trouble-free and convenient. The shopper should be able to find her way without any previous knowledge of the site. Complicated arrangements confuse the driver and often require attendant direction — not compatible with suburban shopping center character or operational practices.

Parking at a shopping center is a "do-it-yourself" performance. For this reason alone "ease of parking" is the criterion for laying out the spaces. Besides *easy parking,* other yardsticks for measuring a parking layout are the area dimensions and topography of the ground, the entrance and exit arrangements, the method for circulation through the whole center, and the walking distances between the cars and the stores.

a. Arrangement. Parking space is made up by the storage stall and the movement aisle. Both must be generous enough in size to provide for the "ease of parking." Aisles can serve as pedestrian walkways leading directly to the stores. Raised walks between two rows of parking stalls (sometimes called bays) are unnecessary and expensive. Besides, these platforms interfere with snow removal where that is a factor to contend with. From experience, it has been learned that shoppers prefer the wide aisle pavement rather than the narrow walkway between automobile bumpers in walking from the car to the shops.

Parking stalls and their access aisles should be oriented to the stores so that customers need not walk farther than necessary nor cross any but other slow-moving traffic interior access roadways. The walking distance between a car parked at the outer fringe of the parking area and the shops should be 400 feet maximum—300 feet is a better walking distance standard.

"Bring the parking close to the stores" is good advice. After parking, "customers should be able to look between the rows of parked cars and see the storefronts." Saying this differently, "It is advisable, where possible, to orient the tiers at right angles to the stores rather than parallel, as this makes for better accessibility to the stores by the shopper after leaving her car."

b. Circulation. Circulation for cars within the center should be continuous. As mentioned previously, it should be possible to maneuver within the site without having to move the car onto the public highways giving access to the center. At a large regional center, interior circulation within the property and to the several sections of the parking area is a study needing the advice of a traffic engineer. About 800 cars per lot is about right for each section of a several thousand car parking facility at a regional center. In these cases the solution requires a belt roadway around the edge of the site and another around the building cluster. Here the main traffic movement aisles are of two types: The entrance and exit lanes and the belt lanes. Major aisles should allow for two-way movement. If the minor aisles are one-way, careful directional indicators are used—arrows painted on the pavement plus standing identification signs. Also, in a large center where there are several thousand car spaces, parking stalls along the main aisles leading to the store cluster should not be provided. This restriction prevents backing into a main aisle and eliminates possible congestion in the aisles leading directly to the stores where the inner belt roadway provides for unloading and pick-up of passengers.

In a smaller, neighborhood center, an aisle along the front of the stores is a good arrangement for circulation. J. W. York's advice from his practical experience is: "Have parking immediately in front of the stores," (i.e. curb-parking along the front canopied pedestrian sidewalk) "so that people can run in and out of the small shops."

3. Parking Patterns

There are two preferred patterns for parking stall arrangements—perpendicular or angular.

Perpendicular or 90-degree parking combines economy of space with ease of circulation. Ninety-degree parking offers the advantage of two-way movement through the aisles. It allows for elimination of expensive curbing; better sight lines and greater safety. Advantages attributable to 90-degree parking include:

Greater parking capacity
Two-way movement without enforcement problems and with less misdirection of parking
No need for barriers between aisles
Shorter cruising distances.

Where 90-degree parking is used, the central aisle should always be wide enough to permit two cars to pass as well as to enter and leave the parking space in one operation. The required width is 65 feet for the entire unit, including a 25-foot center aisle with stalls 20 feet deep on either side. (In a pinch, the unit can be reduced to 60 feet wide with the center aisle narrowed to 20 feet, but this is not recommended). The minimum desirable aisle width for 2-way circulation is 24 feet.

Angle parking is considered as being somewhat easier for entering a stall and does allow for narrower aisles but requires one-way circulation. The angle adopted depends upon the space that is available. Where 45-degree diagonal parking is used, the minimum width of the units can be 50 feet with one-way movement. With 2-way movement within the aisle, the width has to be increased to 60 feet.

Advantages attributable to angle or diagonal parking:

Greater ease (good parkers can swing in with one motion)
Greater safety through minimizing potential head-on conflicts
Safer use of aisles as pedestrian walkways for reaching the stores.

Use of angle parking, or various other schemes such as the herringbone or interlocking and overlapping pattern, is advisable only for areas where space is at a premium.

The dilemma over perpendicular parking and diagonal parking is best solved by using the pattern which is customarily used in your community and best adapted to your site conditions.

The Community Builders' Council has never gone on record as preferring 90-degree parking over angle parking because at each shopping center the problem takes an individual solution. Each parking layout must be evaluated in terms of circulation of

Illustration No. 82. Parking

This successful center has a parking index of 4.1 cars per 1,000 sq. ft. of gross leasable area and a parking ratio of 2 to 1 based on 132,000 sq. ft. of gross floor area, space for 550 customer cars and 50 employee spaces at 400 sq. ft. per car.

Uptown Plaza, a Community Center, Phoenix, Arizona

Photo: Courtesy, Roy P. Drachman, Developer

Illustration No. 83. Parking

Painted lines indicate traffic movement and direction. Shown here is angle parking with two-way movement through the parking aisles.

Los Altos Shopping Center, Long Beach, Calif.

Photo: Courtesy, L. S. Whaley Co., Owners/Developers

pedestrians between cars and stores; circulation for convenience of drivers moving in and out of the parking area and in looking for a parking space; and for the use of space.

4. Stalls

Parking stalls with ample width will ease the act of parking, will avoid space-wasting straddling, and will allow car doors to be opened without damaging the neighboring car.

With the older car models an eight-foot stall was satisfactory, but the latest models require at least an 8½ foot stall; 9 feet is even better. Parking stalls have gradually been upped from 7½ feet to 9 feet in width. Some centers are going to 9½ feet for the car stall measured to the center of "hairpin" markers. Unit parking widths (stall plus aisle plus stall) have increased from 58 feet to 65 feet.

Stalls marked out by a 2-inch wide double or "hairpin" looped line painted on the pavement are the best type of parking space marker. This loop or hairpin type of marker-line acts as a psychological help in keeping the parking public within each space and prevents a tendency to straddle space dividers. As Angus Wynne, Texas shopping center owner-developer, says: "Do not lay out a parking area with permanent dividers, because cars are changing all the time. Make it so that the parking pattern can be altered at any future time."

The following stall widths are suggested:

Angle	Minimum	Maximum
90°	8′ — 6″	9′ — 0″
60°	8′ — 4″	8′ — 10″
45°	8′ — 2″	8′ — 8″

With 9 feet for each stall width, 90° parking requires 20 feet for the stall length and 45 feet for the aisle. The total width for the parking unit is 65 feet. Diagonal parking with two-way movement takes 56 feet for the two stalls and the aisle between for 60° degree parking. To adapt parking needs to space limitations, some centers mix combinations of angle and 90° parking patterns—not a recommended practice.

For dimensions to use in laying out parking patterns, see illustrations pages 302, 304 and 306 and the table, page 312.

Parking Space Dimensions

Angle of Parking at Base Line	Width of Aisle Used Up When Parked	Width Needed for Parking Plus Maneuvering	Length of Base Line Used Per Car	Cars Parked Per 100 Ft.
Parallel	7	19	22.0	4.6
45 degrees	17	29	11.3	8.8
60 degrees	18	36	9.2	10.8
90 degrees	17	40	8.0	12.5

5. Pedestrian Strips

Walkways between cars are favored by some developers. These pedestrian strips have the advantage of taking the shopper away from the rear of parked cars and also provide space for light standards and tree plantings. To be effective, however, the strips should lead toward the store groups. These walkways require additional space and to be usable they should be at least seven feet wide to provide for walking and for bumper overhang. As car doors usually swing to the front, people are in the habit of walking to the rear in parking areas and along the wider car driveways. "Where you have plenty of cheap land," states Hugh Potter, "we favor putting in a wide enough

Illustration No. 84. Parking

The parking area must be well drained, well paved and well lighted. Hairpin-loop lines, 2½" wide, painted on the pavement surface are good parking space indicators.

Seven Corners Shopping Center, Fairfax Co., Va.

strip to permit pedestrian traffic between cars. But where land is tight, the pedestrian strip can be eliminated. But usually some bumper protection is provided."

There is considerable question about the practical value of the walkways in parking areas because of their additional cost and the use of space involved. Besides, in the North these pedestrian strips are an obstacle to snow removal.

6. Appearance

Parking areas must be paved and well drained. Concrete is expensive. Paving should be of a material which reflects a minimum of glare and heat, is easily repaired and is attractive in appearance. Blacktop has been preferred. Parking stalls should be clearly marked. Solidly painted lines or raised metal buttons are satisfactory. To discourage straddling, an oval button 8 inches in diameter and 5 inches high has been used by the J. C. Nichols Company at Kansas City.

In cases where there are great expanses of blacktop pavement, trees and planted areas should be introduced to take away the otherwise barren and unsightly appearance. Tree planting is desirable where the trees are given bumper protection. Screen planting for rear parking areas should be provided, especially where this use is abutting residential property. Highland Park Shopping Village in Dallas is especially noteworthy in this respect. In the Country Club District, Kansas City, the parking areas prove that these utilitarian places need not be eyesores. Here the parking level is depressed about 2 feet in order to bring the car tops below eye level, to increase the feeling of openness and to permit vision across to the store fronts. A low wall helps further to screen the cars from abutting property.

Proper maintenance of parking areas is essential if they are to attract customers. Items of policing, clean-up, night lighting and orderly use cannot be ignored. Maintenance involves insuring proper care either by the developer himself or through the merchants association.

7. Employee Parking

Employees are all-day parkers. All-day parkers can't be allowed to usurp space needed for short-time customer parkers. When employees are allowed to park indiscriminately in a center, they will use up customer spaces that should be turning over 4 or 5 times during opening hours. In a strip center, employee parking might well be located at the rear of the stores. In other types of center, a special area should be assigned and the requirement for parking there enforced. The employee parking area should be located on a part of the site that does not usurp space more useful for customer space.

If employees park their cars in conveniently located customer spaces, they preempt stalls which should be generating retail sales. For example, 163 employee cars parked in customers' spaces loses a sales potential of $3,000,000 a year. This figure is based on the owner's knowledge that each parking space at his center generates $18,400 in sales. He also analyzes the employee parking problem this way: "At our average sales percentage of 4 per cent, an additional $120,000 in net rent could be produced from these spaces. At 6 per cent return, this would produce $2,000,000 valuation. Each employee car space capitalized at 6 per cent is $12,266. Any way you figure it, employee parking is big business."

So if you have a center with 500 employees, one out of three will probably drive his car to work. In a strip center, for example, employee parking can be taken care of by a band of parking along the rear service drive. A minimum width for a combination rear service and parking area is 40 feet. This will provide for one row of cars along the rear property line. A better arrangement is to provide in the rear a minimum width of 60 feet. This permits the service area to function better as a truck delivery drive and parking area.

The rear setback must be increased where space along the back property line is needed for planting as a buffer between the stores and adjacent residences. Failing to provide space for employee parking, a center will find its employees usurping customer spaces or spilling onto surrounding streets and annoying the neighbors.

Naturally, the number of employee parking spaces will depend on the number of employees who drive to work. At Northland, for example, there are over 5,000 employees among the 101 tenants. These people are required to park in the outer reaches of the 9 separated lots. Compliance is accomplished about 90 per cent of the time. Experience there indicates that checking car registrations (on file with the Center's management) is a method more practical to enforce than any sticker or other special area type of designation for regulating employee parking. Employee parking regulation is a lease provision.

Other problems prevail for shopping center parking. Things like maintenance, policing, assessment, and contribution to the whole of the community's off-street parking provision are not in themselves site planning matters, but rather managerial considerations to be included in the lease.

8. Value of a Parking Stall

It may be useful to find a value for each parking stall to indicate its relationship to the sales volume of the center *after it is in operation.*

The value of a parking space can be determined by taking the average unit sale and multiplying it by the average number of passengers arriving per car, times the number of turnovers per stall per day. The result will give the dollar amount sold to the people who park in a stall each day. By multiplying this amount by the number of shopping days per year, you know the value of the stall in terms of annual sales volume. For example, take this hypothetical case:

A — average unit sale (in dollars)	$5.10
C — customers per car	1.5
M — minimum daily turnover per space	3.1
P — per cent of customers arriving by car	60%
N — number of shopping days per year	300

A (5.10) x C (1.5) x M (3.1) = $23.72, the hypothetical value per day of each stall. N (300) x $23.72 = $7,116.00—the value of one parking stall per annum in retail volume.

Even if we use modest figures for turnover and average sale, we find that a parking space is valuable. A turnover of 3 and an average sale per customer of $5 produces $11,000 retail sales per parking stall per year.

a. Policy on Assessment. In some cities where the assessor values land used exclusively for parking purposes at the same rate as land used for business, the parking areas at shopping centers bear an inequitable tax load. Where commitments are made for the continued use of designated areas for parking, such as at shopping centers, it is the Council's opinion that the valuation for tax purposes should be adjusted to the restricted use to which the parking area is put as parking.

While it is true that the parking areas contribute substantially to the success of any single business in the center, it is equally true that this is reflected in the higher taxable value of the land and structure occupied by the business as well as the business itself. As the shopping center's parking area *of itself* is usually neither an existing nor potential revenue producer, its valuation for tax purposes should be adjusted to its use as parking, not as a business use. Municipalities can follow this practice with good results. Valuation of large areas as acreage rather than on a square foot basis is suggested.

For Urban Land Institute's policy statement on the assessment and taxation of shopping centers, see Appendix M.

9. Parking Summary

There are a number of items to consider and weigh in providing parking for the shopping center. They vary in degree and extent according to the type of center, its location, its tenancy, its trade area characteristics. In general, after studying centers that are in existence, the parking arrangement depends on the following:

1. Site potential—parking area needed in relation to the gross leasable area of the retail tenant types.
2. Number of spaces and rate of turnover expected.
3. Direction of traffic flow to the site, volume, and peak loads (not seasonal peaks).
4. Entrance and exit points.
5. Circulation within the site—outer perimeter and along the store frontage—for autos, buses, pedestrians.
6. Separation of customer and truck service traffic.
7. Walking distance from the parking stall to the store (400 feet is the recommended maximum).
8. Balance of the load on the parking area according to tenant occupancy needs.
9. Width and angle of the parking stall; direction of movement through the aisles; "ease of parking."
10. Planned employee parking.
11. Economic factors—such as overflow space for peak parking demands.

To summarize the debatable issue of parking ratio: "The ratio depends on the type of trade and number of customers each tenant attracts daily. Tenants who do most of their business on a quick turnover basis (a laundry-dry cleaning pick-up station, for example) need less parking space than do tenants whose business depends on slower turnover because of the longer time a customer needs for buying (food markets, for example). In general, a 3 to 1 ratio is acceptable measurement for parking demand for *preliminary planning purposes.*

The parking index of car spaces per 1,000 square feet of gross leasable area is the eventual measurement for parking provided.

SECTION TWO

PART III

Architectural and Structural Design of Shopping Centers

Even though the step-by-step process in developing a shopping center leads from its first analysis to its site planning and leasing stages before reaching the period when structural and architectural working drawings are prepared, these later aspects are discussed out of sequence here because of the technical relationship between site engineering and architecture. Leasing and other negotiations are considered with management and operations.

A. ARCHITECTURAL DESIGNING

Shopping centers *are* a special building type: the structure has to house the business of selling; the site has to provide for the parking of automobiles; both elements have to stimulate customer attraction even while satisfying the tenant and rewarding the owner. As in no other type of building, the concept calls for unified design and suitability of treatment for its site and location. Blending these ingredients melds the principles of good site planning with taste in architecture, landscaping, and advertising. In reality, whatever compromises are made between what is afforded and what is left out, the final product must be a pleasant and profitable place in which to shop.

1. The Architect's Task

The architect's task is a special one. It calls for his conceiving a unified treatment which permits variations for individual shop fronts yet results in a general uniformity for the benefit of the whole project.

These specifications require the architect-planner to combine the skills of his profession with those of the team of experts needed, particularly for the large regional center. For the smaller center, the same coordination holds but varies in degree.

In looking at shopping centers that have been erected, their achitecture falls short when scale is neglected, taste is

Illustration No. 85

A Neighborhood Shopping Center

The Boardwalk, Belvedere-Tiburon, Calif.

A 42,800 sq. ft. GFA neighborhood convenience shopping center which eminently suits its suburban locale.

Illustration No. 86

The Boardwalk

Court Shops, View of the shops fronting on the court (see site plan), an unusual feature in a neighborhood center.

Illustration No. 87

Site Plan, The Boardwalk, a Neighborhood Shopping Center

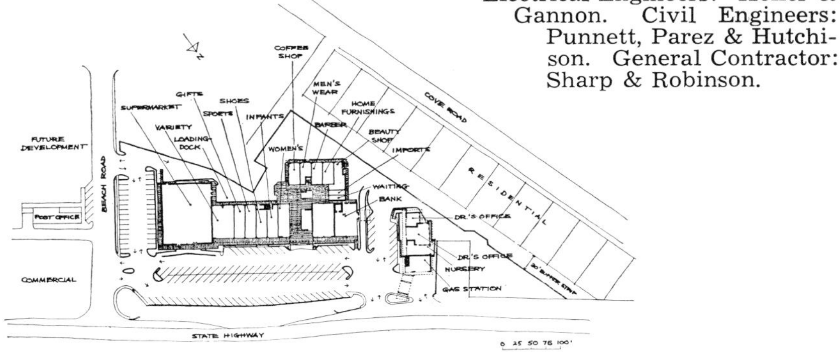

The Team of Experts for the Boardwalk, Belvedere-Tiburon, Calif. Owner: Belvedere-Tiburon Development Co., David W. Allen, President. Architect: John Lord King. Landscape Architect: Thomas D. Church. Structural Engineer: Isadore Thompson. Mechanical and Electrical Engineers: Keller & Gannon. Civil Engineers: Punnett, Parez & Hutchison. General Contractor: Sharp & Robinson.

Source of Site Plan: Architectural Forum, October 1957.

omitted, and materials are disregarded. The style of architecture should be fitting to the character of its suburban location. Contemporary style is good when the selection and combination of materials harmonizes with regional climatic characteristics. Traditional architecture is suitable when it is adapted to modern merchandising concepts.

2. Designing the Structure

The design of shopping center buildings is quite often dictated by the size and shape of the property—even though the arrangement and grouping of tenants within the structures is based upon a merchandising plan. The gross floor area of the buildings is scaled to fit space requirements for the type of center as indicated by market analysis and lease negotiations.

Decisions about basements, structural framing and mechanical equipment can be made before the exterior architectural treatment is decided upon. If there is any choice for building orientation on the site, "face the store fronts north and east." In establishing a framing module, "Use 35 foot column spacing instead of 60 foot widths for bays." "Store widths can be then based on a 17½ foot module. Store depths vary from 100 feet to 150 feet or more, and modules for depth can be given greater spacing between columns." "Use steel column supports. Have as few bearing walls as possible."

a. Flexibility. Whatever width is used for span dimensions, the design should allow for flexibility in store partitioning. Never build a multi-tenant building without using steel supported construction. Try to have no bearing walls.

Partitions between tenant spaces should not be used as bearing walls and should be built of materials and by methods which can assure easy removal. The design should provide for future store space re-allocations and for allowing readjustments in fixturing as tenants expand or shift their locations in the center. To allow for flexibility in operations, such structural features as plumbing and heating stacks, air-conditioning ducts, toilets, and stairways should be placed on end walls rather than side partitions between tenants or in cores as permitted by building codes.

In the structural design of the buildings, the Council urges that the architectural layout be such that flexibility is possible. Then too, all the space may not be leased before the center gets under construction, so changes in designated tenancy may alter the preliminary plans for treatment of the space.

To recall the previous discussion about store grouping, John McC. Mowbray has said: "As a center grows in size, you should shift the locations of various types of businesses in order to improve the groupings of related shops and to free the 'hot spot' locations for higher rental shops and more intensive uses." By shifting division walls, tenants can be moved from space to space. In this way, a good location with a poor tenant does not need to remain as a mistake in leasing.

This feature cannot be over-emphasized as adjustment of space for existing tenants to meet their changing needs can then be provided without undue structural alteration.

Other methods which promote flexibility include stair wells, electric control boxes, plumbing, heating pipes, and cooling ducts, placed in walls least likely to be removed in enlarging a store. If it is necessary to have them in such walls, they should, if possible, be placed at the extreme rear or extreme front and close together. To provide for future building deepening, avoid using the rear wall for this purpose. Where sidewalk grades do not exceed 1¼ per cent, the first floor can be sloped with the grade to permit two or three stores to be combined later without making changes in floor levels. Store fixtures can readily be adjusted to this slope. Avoid the use of heavy masonry piers between store fronts which reduces window space because they are expensive and often difficult to remove at a later date. Front columns should be set back of the front wall from 4 to 6 feet. Small steel columns with curtain walls of gypsum block or exposed painted concrete block are recommended. For one-story buildings, steel beam and column construction with steel truss or bar joist roof members carrying light precast concrete slab roof deck, and monolithic concrete floors covered with mastic, terracotta or asphalt tile, permits quick installation, saves labor costs and provides an incombustible and vermin proof structure.

b. Store Sizes. Do not get stores too big. There is an old saying, "Any store size is all right if it is not too big." "In my experience," John C. Taylor remarks, "a tenant is never making money for us or himself unless he is crying for more space. Our policy is to expand his space only when his need is genuine. This is usually long after the tenant thinks he has an urgent need." In other words, a merchant on a long term percentage lease wants the biggest store possible, if for nothing more than to take care of his expansion. The owner should be interested in giving the merchant no more space than he needs, but the owner should have structural flexibility in the building and a flexible leasing agreement so the tenant can be moved or expanded if and when more space is needed.

c. Ceiling Heights. There is a trend toward lower ceiling heights. Modern lighting and air-conditioning are factors, together with the savings effected initially and in the operation of mechanical equipment.

Clear ceiling height depends somewhat on the exterior architectural treatment for the space over entrances to stores. Lower finished ceilings cut maintenance costs. Hung ceilings should be of the dry-built type in order to permit changes in height, easy access to attic space and re-use of materials. "In these days of air-conditioning and designed interior lighting you do not need high ceilings for store ventilation." Low ceiling heights are used particularly where the center has full basements—either for storage or for merchandising. However, if the locality does not require air-conditioning as a basic facility, then ceiling heights of 16-18 feet are acceptable as they allow for later introduction of mezzanines which are useful when the tenant wants to expand. Where mezzanines are constructed, a minimum ceiling height of 16 feet is necessary. Large store areas require relatively high ceilings for the sake of appearance. Ten feet to clear ceiling height has been found satisfactory in shops ranging in width to 17 feet and from 40 to 60 feet in depth.

d. Basements. Where site conditions permit, experience has found that basements are warranted. "Put basement space under all stores; space under stores not needing basements can be used for bowling alleys, storage, future merchandising areas."

Experience has shown that the omission of basements has often been a mistake. They have proved their value not only for storage, heating and cooling equipment, but even to a greater extent as space for store expansion. The additional cost of providing basement space is relatively low, especially in colder sections of the country requiring foundation footings 3 to 4 feet below grade. It has been found in many cases that basements are superior to mezzanines for merchandising and store offices. Thus the extra store height necessary for mezzanines can be eliminated. This has the further advantage where a second floor is provided of making it more easily accessible to the public. It is advisable in providing basements to anticipate their future use as merchandising space. Pipes and ducts should be located with this in mind and clear basement ceiling heights of about 9 feet could be used satisfactorily.

Cost saving features in basement construction include the use of concrete block foundations where subsurface conditions permit, and supporting the first floor on transverse beams. This eliminates the need for basement stair headers and permits future basement stairs to be relocated and widened without undue expense. This is an important contribution in providing the maximum amount of flexibility in revising store space and arrangement. Another feature that will provide for flexibility is avoiding interior bearing walls wherever possible. Use concrete block partitions to act as fire walls and for rodent control. Fire walls that run from basement to roof are barriers to flexibility and the savings in insurance rates may not justify their additional cost. Fire walls spaced at intervals of 100 feet or more are not too far apart. Stairways leading to basement space should be constructed of concrete or steel. Where the basement is to be used for merchandising, a 5 foot width should be provided.

If basements are not provided, then it is desirable to build a balcony (which makes the main ceiling height greater) or to build deeper stores. Another arrangement for storage where there are no basements is to provide, in some secondary location on the site, a storage building in which space can be leased to individual tenants according to their needs.

Some stores, such as furniture and variety chains, want basement areas for display and merchandising space. Basements, like second story space, seldom bring an economic rental. Basement space, generally, rents for between ¼ and ⅓ of the square foot rental charged for first floor space.

In a big regional center, basements are a required part of the construction. The basements can be scooped out at the same time that a truck tunnel is dug.

e. Second Stories. In small centers, two-story buildings are seldom advisable. Second floors do not necessarily increase earnings. Extra costs are involved for construction, plumbing, heat, light, and maintenance. A two-story commercial building does not pay. It is uneconomical to provide elevators to reach a second floor.

Second floor tenants are all-day parkers and their visitors generally are long-time parkers who are not shoppers. In fact, doctors and dentists don't make good second floor tenants. Such offices require special plumbing, wiring and maintenance.

If second floor space is provided, suitable tenants are those that: pull people to the center at regular and frequent intervals (doctors and dentists do, but their visitors aren't in a shopping mood; besides, the doctors prefer clinic-type buildings); have visitors who will not park longer than an hour during shopping hours; and require no display space on the ground floor. Some of the tenants suitable for second floor locations are beauty parlors, photographers, dance studios, etc. Stairs to second floors should be easy to climb, with intermediate landings.

B. SPECIAL ARCHITECTURAL FEATURES

1. Malls

The elements of separation of foot traffic from automobile traffic and from service traffic in shopping centers has brought about the placing of stores along a pedestrian way or central open space, generally in elongated form. A mall is essentially a pedestrian street with strips of stores face to face. As the Council says: "When you make a mall you create a business street. The mall has certain advantages, particularly for the large regional center.

"First of all, it creates a pleasant shopping atmosphere. When decorated with planting and bits of landscaping, the attractiveness is multiplied immeasurably. The volume of foot traffic passing along in front of stores is increased. This creates many strong store locations through encouragement of impulse buying. On a mall there is no 'best side of the street.' "

For regional centers, a mall is a must. Generally speaking, the mall is preferred for reasons of compactness, simplicity of servicing tenants, overall economy, greater merchandising impact and customer attraction. Some designers advocate a single, somewhat narrow pedestrian mall with stores on both sides and with important tenants, having strong customer-drawing power, at both ends. This is essentially the pattern required when two department stores of nearly equal prestige or of differing merchandising price ranges are within the same

Illustration No. 88. An Enclosed Mall Type of Neighborhood Shopping Center

An enclosed mall type of neighborhood shopping center having a main building, completely air-conditioned under one roof.

Market Center, Pasadena, Texas
Doughtie & Porterfield, A.I.A., Architects

Photo: Courtesy, Carl Detering, Houston

The Market Center, Pasadena, Texas

The following is a list of items of interest for this enclosed mall type of neighborhood center:

General Construction

Concrete slab with drilled footings; steel frame with bar joists—lightweight concrete roof fill on steel deck; masonry exterior walls and masonry, wood stud and sheetrock interior walls; aluminum and glass storefronts; terrazzo floors in malls and supermarket—remainder of floors vinyl asbestos tile; lay-in type mineral fiber acoustical tile ceilings; 7 acre site area; 75,000 sq. ft. gross floor area, including the enclosed mall areas; parking for 480 cars.

Total Cost

Total cost was approximately eight dollars and fifty cents a square foot. This includes all site work and paving, all lighting fixtures to tenants, all air conditioning except units for supermarket, variety store and drug store. The duct work for these areas was furnished by the owner. All interior partitions, storefronts, finish flooring and all landscaping was in the base contract.

Leases

All leases are percentage leases. The air conditioning operating cost is on a pro-rata basis. The low building cost of eight dollars and fifty cents a square foot can be partially attributed to compactness, low ratio of exterior wall area to store area. By using very little exterior glass area total air conditioning tonnage and operating cost were reduced. The store fronts were less expensive to install because they were interior rather than exterior.

Acceptance of this type center by the merchants has been very good. It has been observed that customers tend to shop more leisurely and visit more stores when they are protected from the weather.

Each store is a show case. Window reflection so common to exterior storefronts is non-existent.

The maximum distance from store entrance to store entrance is two hundred feet (supermarket to drug store and variety store) compared to at least twice that distance for a strip center.

The washateria, drive-in grocery, etc., were placed in a separate building due to their functions and store hours. The drug store is the only store within the main building with an exterior store entrance. This was provided due to its store hours. See Plot Plan, page 328.

center. As a design pattern, when a single department store is the principal magnet, the center of one side or the other of the mall is customary, with the next strongest tenants at the ends. By using the cluster plan, the department store magnet can be placed in the center surrounded by smaller stores and pedestrian malls having stores of secondary pulling power to strengthen the customer circulation for exposing pedestrians to smaller units.[201] This essentially is the Northland mall pattern.

a. Truck Service Facility. Another strong point favoring the use of a mall in a regional center is the possibility of complete separation of pedestrian shoppers from truck servicing. This is accomplished by construction of a truck tunnel under the mall, as has been done at Northgate in Seattle, at Stonestown in San Francisco, at Northland in Detroit, at Hillsdale in San Mateo and at most prominent regional centers.[202]

An underground truck service tunnel costing from three to five percent of the project's overall cost may well be justified even though its construction cost tag may cause serious weighing of the investment. The economics of the situation will tell whether or not an underground truck service facility can be afforded. But a truck tunnel built as part of the basement area improves the project's prestige and helps with its architectural attractiveness. For these latter reasons, the facility lends prestige to the center and promotes a higher rent schedule, including basement space. Where underground service roads enter buildings the clearance height must be 14 feet.

There is a growing reluctance to spend the money for truck tunnels in large centers; their cost is considered out of proportion to their contribution. Two basic principles of shopping center development cause the truck tunnel dilemma: One principle being that proper separation of customer and service traffic is essential; the other, that overall costs must be held to a reasonable level if the center is to be financially successful.

---

[201] See "Shopping Center Design" by Lathrop Douglass. *Traffic Quarterly*, July 1958. The Eno Foundation, Saugatuck, Conn.

[202] "In the future more large centers are going to be built without a truck tunnel, but most top notch regional centers will have them." Bruce P. Hayden, from "A Quick Look at Shopping Centers." *Urban Land*, February 1959. Urban Land Institute.

Illustration No. 89. Mall Shops

The Market Center, Pasadena, Texas

Photo: Courtesy, Carl Detering

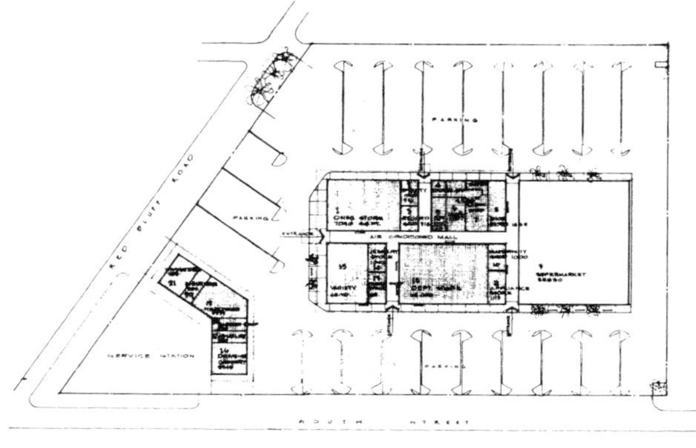

Illustration No. 90. Plot Plan

The Market Center, Pasadena, Texas

Tenant Types, The Market Center

	Sq.
1. Drug Store	7
2. Beauty Shop	
3. Record Shop	
4. Camera & Photography	
5. Gift Shop	
6. Men's Shop	1
7. Dress Shop	3
8. Shoe Store	1
9. Supermarket	25
10. Maternity Shop	1
11. Appliance Store	1
12. Department Store	10
13. Fabric Shop	1
14. Jewelry Store	1,
15. Variety	4,
16. Drive-in Grocery	2,
17. Jewelry	
18. Barber Shop	
19. Hardware Store	3
20. Insurance	
21. Washateria	1

Without an underground service tunnel, a mall requires the introduction of service courts. By the substitution of service courts, the problem becomes one of design for the screening of the court and for determining its adequate size. Such service courts for supermarkets and department stores have to be large enough to allow for maneuvering the 50 foot length of over-the-road tractor-trailers within the court. Unless these courts are properly designed, they give a "backyard" appearance. Old Orchard at Skokie, Illinois, and Stanford Center at Palo Alto, California, are examples of two regional shopping centers operated successfully with screened service courts.

In a smaller community or neighborhood type of center, the difficulty in separating shoppers from service deliveries suggests that a mall is not worth the trouble to achieve it. If the building takes the form of a strip; then, most likely, service will be provided at the rear of stores by means of a service drive and truck dock. Customer circulation is confined to the covered walkway along the fronts of the stores, which face the parking area. A difficulty arises if customer parking must also be placed at the rear. In this situation, customers and truck service get mixed unless, again, screened service courts are introduced. Otherwise, customers are exposed to the old "backyard" approach to the store fronts. As Waverly Taylor points out, "The problem resolves into how to service the stores. It becomes necessary then to introduce a service court which has to be large enough for truck movement. This width may interfere with pedestrian traffic. Certainly trucks shouldn't cross a mall."

b. Width. In the regional center the mall readily provides the atmosphere for pleasant shopping. With fountains, flowers, benches and banners, the mall is the setting for promotional events and pedestrian passage along and through the stores.

From its discussion of malls and their treatment, the Council finds that 65 feet is the *maximum* desirable width for an open, uncovered mall. The best aesthetic effect results when the width is related to the height and length of the structures. The mall at Northgate is 48 feet between face of buildings, perhaps too narrow for its length. The mall at Shoppers World was an opposite extreme. Its 120 feet of width made back-and-forth shopping difficult. This excessive width has been remedied by extending store depths into the mall. At

Stonestown in San Francisco, the mall is 50 feet which, with its relatively short length, gives good proportions. Essentially, as the mall is a pedestrian street, its width must be based on easy view of show windows and store fronts on either side.

c. Mall Treatment. Planting beds spaced through the length of the mall add to its attractiveness. The pleasantness of the mall is a major drawing card for customers and a hold on keeping them longer. The landscaping touches, the inviting benches and the protection from sun and rain invite shoppers to linger, to look and to buy. But remember, as one Council member discovered in the treatment of malls: "Benches, for shopper comfort located at bus stops, main entrances and along the mall are good features, but should be used sparingly. A dirty wooden bench is worse than no place to sit and maintenance cost is high."

On the walking surface of open malls, the Council makes this observation: "Pave malls, but not with blacktop surfacing. This surface becomes rough and uneven. It allows puddles to form after a rainstorm, and absorbs too much of the illumination during night openings."

2. Covered Malls

The mall has the possibility of being covered. This allows for complete weather-conditioning. In the Minneapolis suburb of Edina where "there are only 120 days a year of good outdoor weather," the Dayton Company built its Southdale Center as the first example of the central court, or mall, as a completely covered, air-conditioned central pedestrian circulation space.

Since Southdale's success, other smaller centers such as Harundale at Glen Burnie, Maryland, and Charlottetown at Charlotte, North Carolina, have been built by Community Planning and Research, Inc. of Baltimore. In warm or humid climates such as prevail in the South and West, the covered mall provides customer comfort and appeal.

The dimensions of the central mall determine whether it can be enclosed by long-span elements leaving the space uninterrupted by columns, or whether the enclosure should purposely introduce columns as an architectural element. Where it is desirable to introduce natural lighting into a central mall by means of skylights and clerestories, the structural covering is generally raised above the level of the typical roof framing, thus offering potentials for imaginative and fresh design. Thin shell forms, geodesic dome structures, or other types of special framing may be adapted to the central mall enclosure.[203]

An advantage of the enclosed mall is that stores entered from the climate-controlled space can be partly or completely open, thereby cutting costs on installation of fronts. Gates can be substituted for closed fronts for security during hours when the stores are not open for business, though dust control may be a factor in this decision.

The concept of shopping centers having completely enclosed malls or central courts, such as is represented by Southdale, is basically a return to the scheme used about 1900 in the mammoth department store buildings of the period, such as Marshall Field's in Chicago and Wanamaker's in Philadelphia. In these, the store has a central court several stories high, from street floor to roof. From this court the store's departments open. In adapting the enclosed mall scheme to modern shopping centers, the developer, in effect, is asking independent tenants to act as "departments" in the center.

In lieu of an enclosed mall and as an adaptation of the air-conditioned enclosure for shopper comfort while going from one store to another, a glass enclosed, air-conditioned covered sidewalk can be introduced. This treatment is particularly adaptable to a strip type neighborhood or community center in a climate having either too hot or too cold weather for shopping comfort. North Towne Plaza, a community type center in the North San Pedro area of San Antonio, uses an air-conditioned sidewalk for shoppers as they move along under the canopy connecting the stores' doors.

In Tucson, the same principle has been used in a strip type community center of 132,000 square feet. The sidewalk is 15 feet wide and 750 feet long, enclosed by gray glass, completely air-conditioned to a temperature of 76 degrees.

3. Offsets

Offsets or recessed stores are business barriers. Store fronts should be continuous. Frequently a designer will submit a shopping center plan that has architectural setbacks in order to offer variation in the architectural plan or elevation of the

[203] See *Shopping Towns—USA* by Victor Gruen and Larry Smith, referred to previously.

Illustration No. 91

Enclosed Mall Shopping Center

View of interior planting and clerestory lighting—Charlottetown Mall Shopping Center, Charlotte, North Carolina, opened in October, 1959.

Photo: Courtesy, Community Research and Development, Inc., Owners/Developers

Illustration No. 92

Harundale Mall Shopping Center

Glen Burnie, Maryland. Department store entrances from the enclosed mall.

Photo: Courtesy, Community Research and Development, Inc., Owners/Developer

Illustration No. 93. View—Harundale Mall Shopping Center

This 350,000 sq. ft. GFA regional shopping center is an example of the enclosed, air-conditioned, weather protected mall type of center.

Photo: Courtesy, Community Research and Development, Inc., Owners/Developers
Architects: Rogers, Taliaferro & Lamb

Illustration No. 94

Harundale Mall Shopping Center

Glen Burnie, Maryland. View of the air-conditioned, enclosed mall looking south along center-mall shop spaces from department store stairway.

Photo: Courtesy, Community Research and Development, Inc., Owners/Developers

Illustration No. 95

Store Fronts—Open front stores are possible in enclosed mall centers.

Charlottetown Mall Shopping Center, Charlotte, N. C.

Photo: Courtesy, Community Research and Development, Inc., Owners/Developers

Illustration No. 96

Store Fronts—Expensive store fronts and display windows can be eliminated in an enclosed, air-conditioned mall shopping center.

Charlottetown Mall Shopping Center, Charlotte, N. C.

Photo: Courtesy, Community Research and Development, Inc., Owners/Developers

The Tweed Shop
distinctive
casual
clothes

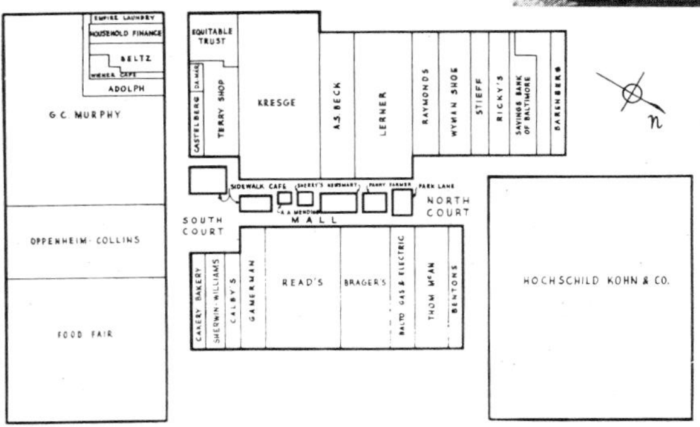

Illustration No. 97

Merchandising Plan

Harundale Mall Shopping Center

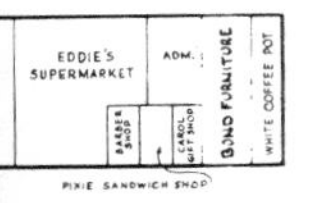

center. These concepts are not practical from a merchandising viewpoint.

A curved facade may offer visual appeal for sightline conditions at a corner location, but the semicircular treatment isn't very practical for merchandising. The wedge shapes resulting from a circular plan treatment are unduly complicated structurally and do not offer good store spaces. The odd shapes cannot be fixtured easily or inexpensively. Tenants resist leasing such stores.

Keep the fronts of stores in one straight line. With off-sets in the building form, there are a number of projections to block the view of stores. If different store depths are needed, the slack can be taken out in the rear line.

4. Combinations of Materials

In the design of exteriors, brick, stone and wood facing in proper proportion and combination are good materials for introducing variety and interest in the facades. Unrelieved concrete gives a monotonous look that is depressing. The use of glazed tile in well chosen patterns adds a note of color and makes an attractive point of interest when a blank wall might occur in a building facade.

5. Show Windows

Good modern shopping center design calls for the maximum of glass front on the first floor with low bulkheads, especially where large items are to be displayed. Mullioned or divided windows should be avoided. Bulkheads as low as 6 to 8 inches have been found desirable for some types of merchandise. This type of front gives a maximum of flexibility as it permits maximum window displays, but is equally adaptable to "spot light" displays for small items, such as jewelry, by painting out or screening the unused glass area with the minimum of interior alteration. This avoids the excessive costs of bulkhead removal, new glass, etc., involved in heavy masonry construction and will save the developer unnecessary expense in the future. Exterior bulkheads of granite veneer require less maintenance than other materials. Aluminum or stainless steel window trim is recommended instead of brass and copper for the same reason. Care should be taken to minimize intensity of outside reflections on plate glass. A new type of glass has been developed to protect displays from the effects of direct sunlight. But canopies along store fronts are helpful in cutting down confusing reflections.

6. Canopies

The colonnaded walk or arcade is an age-old device to shelter shoppers and to protect store fronts. These covered walkways are very desirable in shopping centers to promote shopping in inclement weather and to help make shopping generally more enjoyable in any kind of weather. The Council considers that covered walks along store fronts are a required design feature of shopping centers.

Canopies are either cantilevered from the building wall or supported by free standing columns. Width and height of these covered walks varies according to proportions proper for the architectural style. At Northland, the canopies are high, allowing shop signs to be placed on the building wall below the canopy. This arrangement advances architectural uniformity and controls placement of signs.

In describing features of Cameron Village in Raleigh, J. W. York said this: "The cost of cantilevered canopies was so great that I discarded them in favor of column supported ones."

7. Signs

Even though signs are an essential part of a shopping center, their use must be restrained. One of the things that disgraces the business districts of American cities, along with poor architecture, is the indiscriminate use of projecting colored neon signs. The original intention of directing people's attention to a particular business has been lost in the effort of shops to outdo each other. The result is chaotic, confusing and self-defeating. In this respect, the shopping center—a group of stores under single management—has great advantage over a single store on a street downtown.

For identification, it is better for one sign announcing the center itself to be seen from the access highway than for an assortment of individual store signs to vie for attention. A neatly designed pylon can distinguish the center, but a number of tenants displaying colored trade-marks causes competition in confusion.

The Council favors strongly a reasonable control over signs in shopping centers as to size, design, location and single color of illumination. The J. C. Nichols Company limits signs to a maximum of 12 inch letters and, where illuminated, only white lighting is permitted. Waverly Taylor limits signs in his centers to a belt course above the canopy with an overall letter height of 2 feet and a length of ⅔ of the shop front. Hugh Potter restricts signs to an area under the canopy and directly above the show window. J. W. York at Cameron Village requires uniform sign design on all shops with small name signs under the canopies.

Regarding the problem of signs, the Council adopted the following resolution: WHEREAS *the indiscriminate use of signs and bill boards in suburban commercial areas, and particularly on the main approaches to our cities, is ugly, unsightly, and objectionable; creates an unfavorable opinion of the city in the minds of visitors; and is injurious to all urban property values: Therefore, be it* RESOLVED *that developers of suburban shopping centers be urged to exercise reasonable and proper controls of all signs placed on properties which they control.*

Sign control is an important feature in management policy. Every merchant wants to indicate his presence in the center and to announce his wares. But nothing makes for unsightliness like miscellaneous placement and disorder in sign design. Overhanging, roof, and projecting signs should be prohibited, as should the use of paper signs attached to the show windows. Elimination of such signs will enhance the character and attractiveness of the center. Experience with sign controls has shown that neat signing is appreciated by the public and eventually is supported by the merchants who operate within the center, although they often are opposed to the controls in the beginning. The requirement of uniformity poses problems with trade-mark signs. But usually some modification of these can be worked out for compatibility with the others.

The problem is minimized when the design for the center incorporates style, size and location of signs. In addition, sign approval can be incorporated in leases. Trade-mark signs (there are some good ones, F. W. Woolworth, for example) can be sanctioned if controlled by specifications such as is done at Northland where three rigid requirements are in effect: signs must be placed flat against the facade with a 12-inch limitation on letter projection; signs must be placed under the canopy; signs must have no moving or flashing parts.

Paper paste-ons as window signs are liked by merchants, but nothing so ruins the "atmosphere" of a shopping center. These window stickers are usually prohibited by lease provisions, but the ban is very hard to enforce except when there are continued or flagrant violations.

For visibility from pedestrian walkways, a good place for individual store signs is beneath the covering canopy at right angle to the store entrance. With this arrangement, people can see the location of the stores as they walk along under the canopy.

8. Interiors

The design of store interiors in shopping centers is no different from store design anywhere. Though in a new shopping center under current leasing practices, the developer should not provide a "turn key" job, nor should he install interior finishing and fixturing, unless he does so under an allowance system. This system is one whereby the landlord lists expenditures for store fronts, finished ceiling, primary electrical conduits, secondary wiring, etc. The allowables might include floor covering. By this system the developer protects himself against excessive tenant demands which can unbalance construction estimates. When the stipulated amount for an item has been reached, it is up to the tenant to carry on from that point or accept construction within the stated allowance.

The location of store entrances is an important item that should not be left to an architect's caprice. This is illustrated by a hardware store that occupied a corner location in a midwestern shopping center. The entrance was moved from its original side location to a location on the front along the path of pedestrian travel. The shift of the front door resulted in doubling the merchant's business volume in the first six months.

Terrazzo or tile floors are desirable and economical, particularly for drugstores and food stores. Wood flooring is not recommended for stores in any case. Non-skid floors in halls and stairways are a protection against damage suits.

Generally, too much attention is given to lighting the store interior rather than lighting the merchandise.

Good shopping center development now has maturity comparable with downtown. Tenants pay for air-conditioning. They fixture their stores to suit their own needs. They receive

Illustration No. 98. Northland Center—A Regional Shopping Center

The J. L. Hudson Company, the dynamic store of Detroit, occupies the central unit of four floors and basement with 534,446 square feet of floor space, the largest branch department store in America. The 104 associated stores and services occupy 5 surrounding buildings with an additional 532,739 square feet of floor space. Total gross area that is occupied by all stores and service buildings is 1,261,954 square feet. (The Northland Center buildings and facilities occupy 161 acres of what was originally a 409 acre tract secured for future development. A portion of which has been disposed of to others for the development of office buildings. They are Allstate Insurance Company, Aurora Gasoline Company, General American Life Insurance Company, Reynolds Metals Company, Standard Oil Company, and Providence Hospital.)

Parking spaces for 9,600 cars are provided with subsequent car increase to 12,000 possible. Parking is provided on a ratio of one space to 131 square feet of gross building area. The parking area has 9 sections with over 9,600 spaces including an area for over 1,000 employee cars. The Center is accessible from two main highways with connecting roads on the site for access to the parking areas.

Northland occupies 161 acres in the City of Southfield on the northern outskirts of Detroit.

Photo: Courtesy, Northland Center, Inc.

Illustration No. 99. Northland Center, Site Plan

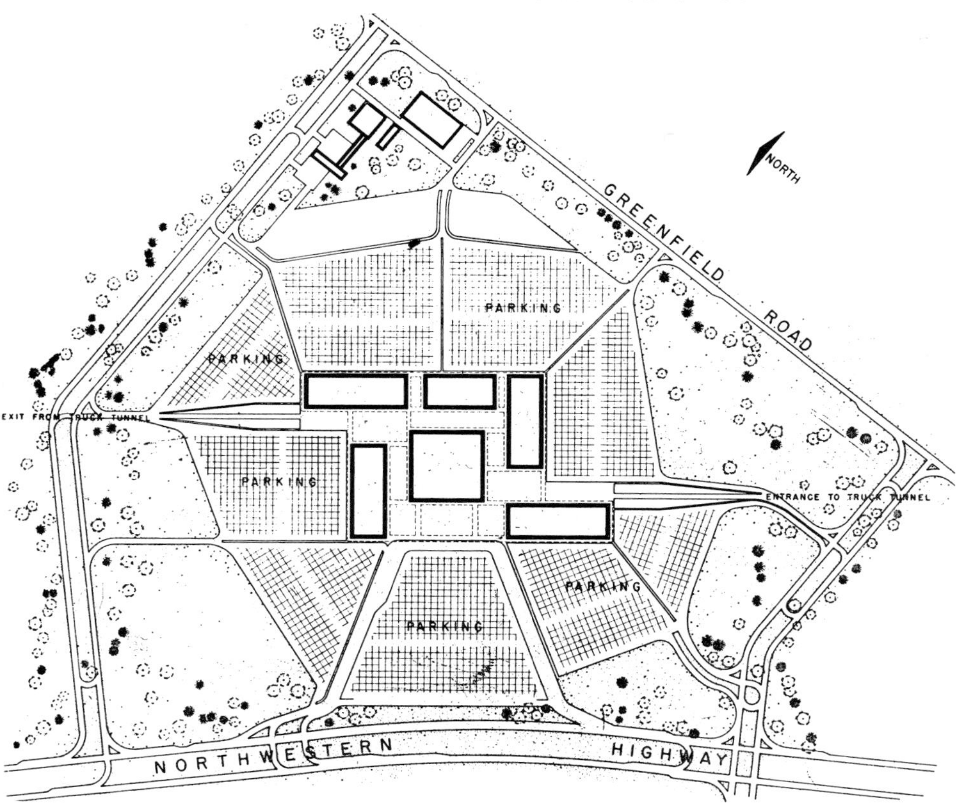

allowances for store fronts, floor covering, ceiling treatment, etc.—a percentage of the cost. Tenants pay completely for light fixtures, counters, shelving, painting, etc. Basically, the owner furnishes the bare space. Where stores are leased before construction, the work that the landlord is to do is plainly shown on working drawings and specifications, and spelled out in the lease.

C. SPECIAL FEATURES AND VARIATIONS

In the preparation of architectural plans and during the several stages of leasing and other negotiations, there are special features which frequently have to be considered. These are variations from the normal tenant types, or are innovations in planning for the development of the center. Other variations crop up as operational and managerial detail. Some of these features and variations are cited for special notice:

1. Buffers

Sometimes the shopping center site is a tract of land surrounded by an existing built-up area. In such cases, the shopping center has to be fitted into existing street and neighboring development patterns even though the advantage of having built-in buying potential accrues to the center. It is necessary to insulate adjacent residential values against any adverse effect of commercial use, even though a shopping center carries with it the built-in protection features of off-street parking and loading.

Where a shopping center—usually of the neighborhood type—is to be located on a site close to a built-up residential area, certain buffers should be introduced. For example, a planting strip of some width, perhaps 20 feet, should be used to insulate adjacent residential use. Where such vegetative planting is not practical, masonry walls, solid fences or high dense foliage planting should be provided. This strip is part of the landscaping treatment of the center and can be so featured.

For a regional center, the buffer should be extensive. It can be a wide grass area, usable at peak seasonal parking periods for overflow parking. Northland, the J. L. Hudson Company's shopping center in the Detroit metropolitan area is an outstanding example of the use of buffer areas.

2. Landscaping

Planting and seasonable floral displays in appropriate places within the center add greatly to customer appeal. In a mall arrangement, planting and water display are essential features. However, landscaping and seasonal floral displays are operating expenses which must be weighed by management. Even so, the enhancement of the center by trees and flowers is an asset reflected intangibly in sales volumes. The best advice of the Council is to select plant materials which require minimum maintenance—but have some.

Where wide expanses of paved parking areas occur, it is well to break up the eyesore of barren asphalt by well placed trees in wells.

3. Expansion

A center built in advance of its trade area's maturity must take expansion into account. Perhaps for the time being the trade area potential justifies only a neighborhood type center of 40,000 square feet, but growth predictions indicate a potential expansion to a community type center of 150,000 square feet retail selling area. In such case, the design for the present center must be incorporated with the design for an ultimate center—in other words, "Master plan your whole development." With enough site area and a plan for ultimate expansion, it is possible to start small. J. W. York started Cameron Village in Raleigh with 30,000 square feet and now has over 400,000 square feet of gross leasable area.

A center that has the mistake of inadequate site area for its required parking and building area may resolve its difficulties by introducing two-level merchandising to lessen the ground coverage of the structure. Or, if the parking area is inadequate for the size of the building, a double deck parking structure can be built. But this solution is expensive, even though its cost per car space so provided might be less than the land cost for an equivalent parking area. As mentioned earlier the parking structure can be a tax write-off whereas the land cannot.

4. Office Buildings

Offices as a unit on a second floor in shopping centers are not good rental propositions. Vertical circulation and service complications are reasons for eliminating this type of rental office space in the shopping center building. A special purpose-type office building is a better solution when the structure can be designed as a separate unit within the shopping center property.

In a small neighborhood center, a practical location for an office unit is the corner of an L-shaped shopping center building where both "legs" of the L are devoted to stores. The corner of the L can introduce an open well with covered skylight for a small office grouping. This arrangement is used at Hillside in Dallas and is known locally as Hillside Professional Corner.

An office building for a corporation or for a combination of tenants brings people to a center. It generates volume for the shops and restaurants. But, if provided, the building must have its own parking space apart from the shoppers' parking and must be capable of taking care of all-day parkers. Accordingly, sufficient site area must be available for handling the special parking and traffic movement to the office building.

In connection with office use within a shopping center, it is found that 3,000 square feet of office space is equivalent to 1,000 square feet of retail space in parking demand. Accordingly, a parking index of 7 car spaces per every 3,000 square feet of office space is practical.

Experience with doctors' and dentists' offices also indicates special clinic-type buildings within or adjacent to the shopping center site are preferable. There is a trend toward building a professional building in today's shopping center. This includes space for doctors and dentists, plus a prescription pharmacy. When the building is placed apart from the retail stores, special parking space, separate from shopper parking can be provided and regulated. A one-story clinic type of building eliminates the elevator problem of the several story professional building. A separate medical building, either clinic or office building type, is good because the medical practitioners' needs are so special that higher rentals must be asked.

A medical building requires 6 parking spaces per doctor including one space for each doctor and technician. See also footnote 221, page 376.

5. Filling Stations

The Council believes that filling stations in shopping centers are fitting and proper if their location doesn't interfere with circulation to the parking lot. The station must be in a prominent place.

"You must segregate the filling station area from the store parking area. In order to put a filling station in a prominent place, you have to have a nice looking structure; you have to keep it clean and you have to segregate its traffic. If you can accomplish those things, I think you can do it. You must have harmony with the architecture of the center. There is no reason why a filling station can't be attractive.

"If you are uncertain about the filling station, you can make a 10 year, or so, lease. Lease the ground and take a percentage of gallonage sales (about 1¢ per gallon) and other revenues. If the station goes in for servicing, it should have some place to store cars afterward."

6. Special Tenants and Innovations

a. Department Stores. The design quality in architectural treatment for a department store in a shopping center must be closely related to the quality of the trade area. A luxury store rightfully demands that the tone of the center be in keeping with its own traditions in merchandising techniques and quality, as well as design.[204]

b. Discount Houses. A discount house in a shopping center is an unwelcome tenant. The Council is less than enthusiastic about including a discount house in a shopping center development. Its practices and policies in merchandising are not compatible with those of valid tenants, or with policies in management and sign control. A discount house represents parasitical commercial use which frequently springs up near or opposite a shopping center, thus trading on the customer attraction to the center. The inclusion of a discount house represents an admission of defeat in obtaining compatible tenants within the center.

c. Farmers' Market. Instead of a second supermarket, Hillsdale Shopping Center in San Mateo, California, has introduced a Farmers' Market of 60,000 square feet—44,000 on the sales floor and 25,000 in the basement. "These Farmers' Markets in California are really just big restaurants, which are very valuable in pulling power." The selling space is divided into departments—dry groceries, meats, exotic foods, etc. To maintain the quality of the produce, such market needs large washing and cold storage facilities. All tenants in the "market" are on separate percentage leases which add up to better returns than a straight percentage lease, as would be the case with a supermarket. Customer eating space is a feature of such markets.

d. Supermarkets. The supermarkets' flight into non-food items and their growth to giant sizes introduce new problems of design. To incorporate the structure for these large areas into the design for smaller space spans requires special skill. Interior design of these supermarkets often incorporates entrances into supplementary tenant spaces such as bakery, toys, gifts, liquor—as is done at Swanway in Tucson. With the disappearance of the meat counter, the supermarkets tear out a wall and put in a glass partition so the housewife can see some of the

---

[204] For special considerations in department store design and construction see *Shopping Towns—USA* by Victor Gruen and Larry Smith, cited previously.

cutting and wrapping taking place. The stores are adding piped music, color, gay murals, and even "kiddielands."

For suggested ways of controlling non-food departments and for obtaining comparable percentage rents in supermarkets, see page 364.

D. ENGINEERING FEATURES

The structural framing system for the multi-tenant and special tenant buildings is part of the engineering of the shopping center. The selection of the structural system is closely related to the site planning and architectural design of the center. In this, collaboration between the architect and the engineer is essential. The matter of local building codes and fire walls may cause some sacrifice in flexibility of tenant spaces.

Mechanical and electrical equipment are essentials in the engineering design of shopping centers. "Since design and construction costs related to mechanical and electrical systems can add up to approximately 30 per cent of the total project cost, it is obvious that this work demands more and more attention from developers and designers of all centers, particularly regional centers." [205]

1. Heating and Air-Conditioning

Historically, commercial space tenants are provided with heating for the leased premises. The tenant includes the cost of operation as part of his expenses in doing business. When air-conditioning first entered the retail field, it was added by the tenant and operated by him. Shopping center leasing follows this pattern; although certain parts like ducts and outlets may be common to both heating and air-conditioning under modern engineering developments, an attempt is made to separate their costs. The tenant is expected to pay a charge over and above the rent as amortization of that part applicable to air-conditioning. In certain cases he may pay a pro rata share of the cost of operation, particularly where there is a central plant.

Air-conditioning is now a feature of all new shopping centers even where hot weather lasts only a short time. Lack of air-conditioning is detrimental to customer attraction and without doubt affects sales volume.

There are two alternative methods for air-conditioning the shopping center: Individual units for each store or central plant

---

[205] See *Shopping Towns—USA* by Victor Gruen and Larry Smith, cited previously.

for serving all stores. "Individual units are tenant responsibilities, important in bad times," as John C. Taylor says. The central plant is the most efficient as a center-wide convenience. The pros and cons of individual units versus cooling and heating from a central plant are essentially a cost and income study.

In air-conditioning, the system of individual package units is one to which most tenants are already accustomed by experience in older downtown stores. The tonnage per square foot required by the individual store cannot be determined satisfactorily by any rule-of-thumb method. Individual units are available in 3, 5, 7½ and 10 ton capacities. The number of units in any given store will depend upon economics, area, special conditions, type of merchandise and importance of cooling for customers' and employees' comfort. This measurement is a job for the air-conditioning engineer.

For individual units, the landlord provides the electrical, water and drainage outlets at the time of building, and the tenant installs the equipment. If the landlord also were to provide the air-conditioning equipment, he would be forced to assume the cost and to pass this cost to the tenant in increased rent. As the landlord likes to quote the lowest rent, the air-conditioning charge should be "an extra."

If the landlord is to pay for the air-conditioning, it is cheaper and more satisfactory for him to provide heating and cooling from a central plant. This eliminates servicing problems and separate, tenant-operated equipment. The disadvantages are that tenants may wish to operate at different hours, but these finer points can be negotiated in the leasing.

Even on an individual unit basis, uniform equipment throughout the center means economy in purchase, maintenance and repair. However, this would practically force the landlord into assuming all costs of air-conditioning which would be translated into a rent increase. Theoretically, if the landlord is to pay for the capital cost of air-conditioning, it should be cheaper and more satisfactory for him to provide heating and cooling from a central plant. The capital cost can be amortized through charges to the tenant.[206]

---

[206] For further discussion of shopping center air-conditioning, especially for package units and the central plant, methods of balancing air-heating and air-cooling and charging for operating costs; see pages 182-185, *Shopping Towns—USA* by Victor Gruen and Larry Smith, cited previously.

Then, too, central versus individual tenant utilities is not just a simple problem of determining the cost and the other advantages of unit or central systems to the owner and to the tenant, nor is it the simple matter of determining whether advantages of a central system justify the capital outlay. As a practical matter, the decision must be resolved entirely apart from the questions of cost or advantage. The crux of the decision is the financing and the operating problems involved, particularly when mortgage financing is based on constructing the shopping center in stages rather than all at one time.

2. Plumbing

Plumbing requirements in a shopping center are essentially the same as those for individual store construction. Facilities for heating water, if required by the tenant, are generally provided by the tenant. Major stores will provide toilet facilities for customers. Groups of small tenants can benefit from combined toilet facilities provided by the developer and maintained by the group. The lease should specify the responsibility for providing vents and drains for those tenants which require large plumbing installations such as supermarkets, restaurants, dry cleaners. Without basements, under floor installations should be deferred because the tenants' requirements will lag behind the developer's construction schedule.

Sprinklers may or may not be installed, depending on local fire insurance rates.

E. CAPITAL COST

Capital cost is the total investment in the project. The expected gross income of a shopping center must be related to this figure. The construction cost for the gross floor area of all the buildings, including basements, is only one item entering capital cost. So variable are the items included in capital cost that citing figures of total or per square foot cost is meaningless. A quotation of $15 per square foot as the cost of a project must specify on what basis it is made. For valid comparison, the cost figure must also identify the type and character of the center, its location, etc. For these reasons, the Council makes no pronouncements about construction figures for typical shopping centers. When the Council may cite building costs, it does so on the basis of gross floor area as the unit which includes everything you have to build, pay for and maintain.

On the other hand, the Council can act as a bibliographer and point out the items that must be taken into account in arriving at a valid estimate of the capital investment against which the arithmetic of anticipated rental income can be applied to gauge whether or not the project is feasible. Such composite items in capital cost are:

Land cost; on-site improvements including grading, underground utilities (storm drainage, water, sanitary sewer, electrical and telephone conduit, etc.); parking lot paving, lighting, curbing and marking, landscaping; off-site improvements (such as any share in bringing utilities to the site); additional road or traffic access improvements; basic gross building cost including allowances to tenants; professional fees for economic, legal, planning, designing, engineering and tax consultant services; expenditures for taxes, insurance, and temporary heating and lighting during construction; expenditures for leasing, management and promotion during the development period.

The developer must be certain that the return on the investment can justify his expenditure. In these days of high construction costs and increased competition, it is important to evaluate the economics and to carry out the arithmetic of shopping centers carefully.

The Council cannot make capital budgets nor offer measurements other than benchmarks for comparison purposes.[207]

The Council, on the other hand, has advanced its views on maintenance versus capital costs: "Do not consider second-rate construction for shopping centers in order to provide for annual maintenance expenditures rather than for initial or capital costs. The solution is not to sacrifice quality but to seek quality in planning and construction. Even though the geographic and physical surroundings of a project influence the amount of money per square foot that you can invest in the building, we believe in the best character of building under all conditions.

"Think of maintenance as maintenance and not as capital expenditures. Build your shopping center in line with common sense for getting a return but not with the idea of beating the present tax picture.

---

[207] One of the important needs in the shopping center industry is the establishment of valid "benchmarks" on capital costs and income from tenants. By such guideposts a developer could then compare his figures for his own project to decide whether or not he has a good deal. In its current (1960) "Cost and Income" research study, Urban Land Institute hopes to arrive at such benchmarks.

"The important point in this discussion is not to confuse good judgment with dangerous philosophy. For somebody to throw out a philosophy to build cheap is ridiculous. Good judgment is another thing and one to be subscribed to by architects and builders."

This far, the Council's presentation has been primarily on the planning aspect of shopping centers. But the matter of capital costs and financing are essentially parts of the planning phase. And the financing is tied so directly to the leasing as to be almost inseparable.

In its financial aspect a mortgage is based normally on the sum of the minimum rent schedules as set up by the leases. It is the income expected, rather than the construction cost which establishes the amount of the loan. So the budget for construction cost becomes geared to income from the guaranteed rent expectancy.[208] By using earning power of the project, the developer can establish his construction budget realistically. Otherwise, the careful planning for stores, malls, parking and planting can turn out to be just another hopeful prospect.

F. FINANCING

As noted above, shopping center finances rest heavily on the rental return anticipated. It is difficult to get financing for shopping center construction before major leases have been negotiated. There is no set formula but the requirements for obtaining a loan will vary, depending upon the lender, the borrower, the money market at the time, the strength of the project—its location, quality of planning—and the rent scale for leases negotiated up to the application for a loan. "Get 70 per cent leased before you ask for mortgage commitments," is one Council member's advice.

Under the circumstances of the tie between financing and leasing, the practice has become prevalent lately on the part of lending institutions, such as insurance companies, to require that shopping center developers have sufficient guaranteed rent from the highest credit rated national tenants to cover the cost of debt charges, taxes, and operating expenses. Under this turn of

[208] The rent schedules include minimum guarantees plus percentages of gross sales. In the operational phase of shopping center development, it behooves the developer-owner to do everything practical to bolster the earning capacity of his tenants by not only planning wisely but by promoting his center well. See pages 371 to 391.

events, the lender has been prone to discount local tenants. To secure the "blue chip" credit rated tenants, the developer has frequently made unprofitable deals. To this, the Council has said: "More respect is due leases from good local merchants. Leases from national chains should not be the sole basis for shopping center financing." This condition is improving.[209]

In the matter of securing financing even with the key tenant's signature on the lease, there is a pertinent comment to be noted as offered by a prominent mortgage-lender: "I find that in a number of instances, house builders who reserve a portion of their subdivision for a shopping center are not so clever or capable in dealing with commercial tenants, such as chains both local and national, as they are in dealing with material suppliers. As a general rule, in this territory, at least, I find that in most shopping center deals, the blue-chip tenants out-trade the developers and obtain some very low rentals and favorable leases, all out of line with current building costs. It is the old story that the developer is so anxious to get a blue-chip tenant as a drawing card for the shopping center that in his anxiety he gives away more than he receives."

"We found on analysis that the developer had been committed to build this store to specifications which we think will run his costs close to $18.00 a square foot. The store will pay him approximately $1.10 a square foot rental and will allow him 2% on sales to a point well below coverage of the $1.10 minimum, 1½% to a point slightly above the minimum coverage, and 1% thereafter. The store will contribute nothing to promotion; nor will it pay a cent for maintenance of common areas.

"We are in this instance asked to loan $14.00 a square foot on the center as a whole, with debt service at 8½% constant. Applying these figures to the department store section, we find that whereas the minimum rent is $1.10, the debt service alone will be $1.19 a square foot. In addition, the owner has to pay taxes, insurance, common area and promotional expenses.

"On minimum rents the owner will be out of pocket by at least 50 cents a square foot and will, of course, have no return on his equity investment. If the store is so outstandingly suc-

---

[209] See "What Financial Institutions Look For in Shopping Centers" by Hubert D. Eller, cited previously, footnote 179, page 241.

See also "What's Ahead for Shopping Center Financing?" by Bruce P. Hayden in *Buildings,* August 1960, pp. 44-46.

See also "Chain Store Leasing in Shopping Centers" by Roy P. Drachman. *Urban Land,* February 1959. Urban Land Institute.

cessful that volume reaches $114 a square foot of gross area, the owner will cover his out-of-pocket costs. If he is to recover 10% return on his equity as well, the store sales will have to exceed $144 a square foot of gross area.

"In this instance, we felt the proposed lease was so burdensome to the operation as a whole that the financial success of the entire shopping center was seriously jeopardized. We did not approve the loan."—From "What's Ahead for Shopping Center Financing?" by Bruce P. Hayden, footnote 209, page 349.

SECTION TWO

PART IV

Management, Maintenance and Operation of Shopping Centers

A. LEASES

A lease is the contract by which a landlord gives a tenant the use and possession of demised premises for a specified time and for fixed payments. Such conveyance is "leasing." The conveying party is the lessor and the party to whom the terminable use right is conveyed is a lessee. The terminable use right in real estate conveyed to the lessee is a leasehold. Rents are estimates of the value of future use possibilities. Space does not permit going into the many possible and probable causes which operate to increase or decrease the value of future use possibilities. This Handbook can not be a leasing manual, it can only indicate what is actually being done to equalize the risk and the profits of lessor and lessee through the employment of a "participating" lease arrangement, in the form of what is known as a "percentage lease."

1. The Percentage Lease

In the retail field, the percentage lease has become the fairest kind of rental contract for both the tenant and the landlord. The percentage lease is an instrument wherein it is agreed that the tenant shall pay as rent a stipulated percentage of the gross dollar volume from his sales and services.

For shopping centers, the most commonly accepted type of percentage lease is the one in which the tenant agrees to pay a specified minimum rent even if the agreed percentage when applied to gross sales produces an amount less than the agreed minimum. In this way there are two factors of fairness, the minimum rent and the percentage of gross sales. The guaranteed minimum specification protects the shopping center owner in case his tenant's sales are not enough in dollar volume to produce the necessary rental income. The owner receives more as the tenant's business prospers; conversely, he gets less when times are tough. The rental fluctuates with the volume of business produced.

The percentage first applies against the base minimum or guaranteed rental. The excess rental applies after the base volume of gross sales is reached. Once the rate of percentage and the minimum rental are agreed on, the breaking point follows mathematically. To illustrate: If the owner knows his minimum rental should be $6,000 and the agreed upon percentage rate is 6 per cent, gross sales of $100,000 would be the break even point. But if gross sales were to fall below this figure, say to $50,000, the owner would still be entitled to his $6,000. Without the guaranteed minimum, he would only get $3,000 as rent.

A shopping center owner is confronted with two basic economic problems in his leasing: One, to assure himself an adequate income to enable him to meet fixed expenses; the other, to secure a reasonable return on his equity which will reflect the value of his property. The percentage lease, if properly administered, answers both needs.

Besides giving some return on the investment, the minimum rents should cover the fixed expenses—principal and interest on the mortgage, taxes, insurance, upkeep, and promotion. The percentage rental, when added, should produce a satisfactory return on the investment.[210]

Percentage leases are based upon the ability of the merchant to pay, the kind of business, the volume of business per square foot of leased space, the profit made on the merchandise, the importance of the location, absence of too much competition, and similar factors. There are several types of percentage leases. Probably the one most commonly used provides for a minimum guaranteed rental from which the owner will derive enough to cover amortization and operating costs, plus a small return on his investment as above noted. This protects both the owner

---

[210] See *The Percentage Lease.* The Building Managers' Association of Chicago, 38 S. Dearborn St., Chicago. 1955. This 20-page booklet is a complete manual of principles and practices.

For a textbook discussion of leases and percentage leases, see *Leases, Percentage, Short and Long Term,* 4th ed., by Stanley L. McMichael. Prentice-Hall, Inc., New York.

See also, *Principles of Real Estate* by Weimer and Hoyt. Ronald Press, New York.

For information about current ranges in percentage rates, see page 360. See also *Percentage Leases,* 9th ed., National Association of Real Estate Brokers, 36 S. Wabash St., Chicago.

and tenant during possible depression periods. During normal periods of business activity, both parties participate in the increased business, again to their mutual advantage. The usual method is to arrive at the additional rental to be received by the owner by agreeing on a specified percentage of the gross sales.

While various percentage ranges and contract forms have been established for different types of stores in shopping centers, they should be considered only as guides. Each case should be considered on its merits, taking into account all of the factors which involve the particular store in question. For this reason, it is inadvisable to recommend any particular form of lease contract which would be adaptable to all cases.

The lease document itself is primarily a legal instrument and should be so drafted by a lawyer. There is no standard shopping center lease form because there is no universal situation applicable to all shopping centers, to all tenant types, and to all jurisdictions; but as a guide see Appendix K.

The lawyer should draft the document, but the developer should delineate the specifications upon which the lease document is based. The legal instrument then becomes the end product of all the factors which make up an intelligent planning job. A well constructed, well drawn-up lease is also a management tool. "The Council can indicate the factors to consider in formulating a lease and point out the guides to successful practices based upon experience. But there is no magic formula to cover all cases in all places.

"A sample copy of a printed lease form for a shopping center should not be used without changing the form by additions and deletions to conform to the varying requirements of the different lessees. Caution is offered against using any form based on other jurisdictions. It is unsafe to enter into important transactions such as long term leases for commercial properties without the aid of legal counsel resident in your state and in your city and familiar with statutes, ordinances, and decisions of the Court applicable to the many different points which will arise. The same may be said of the percentages in varying types of businesses, as there are a great many factors which prevent the formation of any reliable formula applicable to the different cities of the United States."

Perhaps the most reliable compendium of percentage ranges is that published by the National Institute of Real Estate Brokers, see footnote 210, page 352; and the Percentage Lease Table, page 360. But even these do not apply to local practices.

2. Some Highlights of Lease Provisions

The leasing document establishes the financial arrangements, the obligations and responsibilities as the basis for working relationships between landlord and tenants. The lease also incorporates the means for insuring that the shopping center will preserve its long range character and appearance as a merchandising complex.

Again, the Council points out that the lease document is a legal instrument to be drafted by legal counsel. The comments and opinions below are those items which tend to establish beneficial relationships between the developer and the tenant and which should be taken into consideration in a well planned operation.[211]

Lease clauses should cover all types of agreement for the operation of the shopping center, such as description and use of the premises; rental terms including minimum guaranteed rent, percentage rent with no guaranteed minimum, and payments under escalator charges; definition of gross sales; auditing of tenants' accounts; monthly sales figures; how rents are paid; security deposit; term of lease; occupancy conditions; maintenance of the premises on the part of both the landlord and the tenant including such tenant operations as trash removal, window displays, advertising signs, painting of interiors; conditioning by landlord for tenant occupancy; changes in site plan; parking index; such "standard" commercial clauses as insurance, tax escalator, continued occupancy, default under the lease, surrender of possession, change in tenant corporation, and miscellaneous items such as notices, and waiver of claims.

Shopping center leases include other operating provisions such as the merchants association, utility services, types of merchandise to be sold, location of nearest competing business outlet of the same tenant, and hours of operation. In fact, the entire operating and promotional policy of the center can be outlined. (Such policy is not necessarily incorporated in the lease except

---

[211] The Handbook is not a leasing manual. For such see footnote 210. However, for those who are anxious to refer to a "standard" lease form, one such form is published by International Council of Shopping Centers, available to its members; another is found in Appendix K.

for a spelling out of the basis and scale of assessment for participation in the merchants association.)

It is desirable to provide lease clauses covering the following points of possible conflict:

a. Premises and Terms. The premises are identified as a portion of the shopping center which in turn is given a property description. The gross leased area is described. Usually exhibits are attached showing the leased space and the site plan of the center.

The lease's duration is stated in months or years with separate clauses for commencement of the term and for establishing the tenant's sales reports on a fiscal basis.

Other clauses will include provisions for both landlord's and tenant's work in construction and acceptance of the premises. In these the allowance system, mentioned on page 337, is part of the division of responsibility between developer and tenant.

Percentage leases should always give the owner the constant right to check the tenant's books. Accounting should be arranged on a monthly basis if possible. Where tenants have other stores at lower percentage rates or at fixed rentals, the possibility of tenants running sales through those stores must be considered. As J. W. York says: "Use an outside accountant for tenant auditing, especially during the first two years of operation. The tenant's monthly statement should show daily sales. For this, insist on cash registers with locked totals."

Require monthly reports on volume of business done, although settlements of percentage rent may be quarterly. Usually guaranteed rent is paid monthly, in advance.

Provide that percentages apply to all sales in and from the premises. This will take care of mail orders not accounted for otherwise. No deductions are normally allowed for uncollectable accounts. Among items commonly deductible from gross sales are cash refunds to customers, sales taxes, and allowances for goods returned to shippers.

b. Renewal Option. Leases should not be made for too long a period; some developers go so far as to say, "Educate your tenants to no long-term leases." "Do not give small tenants more than a five year lease." This allows for flexibility to permit changes of tenant location within the center. With local tenants, you are better off having short term leases. However, special tenant buildings such as a department store or supermarket must be on a long-term basis, 15 to 20 years or longer.

There are many compromises in renewal options: Some developers give a renewal only with leases standing for 20 years or longer; others give a renewal if the tenant reaches a certain productivity in overage payments on his percentage rent.

Options theoretically help the tenant so he is not obligated for a long term period. In the case of untried tenants, the landlord should have the right to terminate should the tenant be unproductive in percentage rent payment. In the case of a long term tenant, such as 10 or 20 years, providing the tenant's volume has been satisfactory, a renewal option is practical.

Each case is individual and should be treated as such.

c. Use Clause. Reasonable protection should be given to merchants from undue competition. (Customers like competitive shops and more than one dress shop, one food market, etc., is desirable for completeness of the center.) However, to protect merchants against undue competition by other tenants who may take on new lines of merchandise, it is therefore necessary to designate in leases the general types of merchandise each will be permitted to sell.

Stipulate the lines of merchandise to be carried; require the tenant to carry stocks comparable with competitive lines. A use clause should be so worded that the developer knows that the tenant will be doing the same type of retailing for the length of the lease.

Vending machines should be covered in the business use clause with provisions that the tenant report gross sales—not net to him; that the machines be limited either to lines similar to the principal merchandise, to space occupied, or to employee use.

For provisions to cover supermarkets which increasingly enter non-food lines, see page 364.

d. Exclusives. The stimulant in downtown retailing is competition. The same principle applies in shopping centers. Hence, the consensus is *"Do not put exclusives in a lease."* Sometimes tenants request the right to be the sole outlet for a type of merchandise. The solution depends on negotiation and size of center. From experience, it is evident that where two candy stores, for example, are in a center, each does a better volume of business than where there is just one. You may give a tenant an exclusive clause for the type of store, but certainly not as to the lines tenants may handle.

e. Change of Control of Tenant Corporation. A clause to protect the developer against change in type of tenancy by reason of change in that tenant's stock control is necessary. Despite a use clause, change in a tenant's corporate control can affect that tenant's operation. Hence, in event of such happenings due notice to the owner for his protection or for cancellation of the lease under these circumstances is a safeguard.

f. Site Plan. Under the site plan exhibit which accompanies the lease document, the developer should reserve the right to change the plan for expansion or other purposes without objections from the tenants or cancellation of the lease by either party. The developer reserves the right to change the site plan without tenant approval of the change. At the same time, the tenant wants assurance that the parking index will be guaranteed. The developer may reserve the right to encroach upon the area as much as 10 per cent, perhaps, without jeopardizing the parking index.

g. Condemnation. Such clauses are legal and technical, but necessary to protect against conditions arising by the event of a land or premises condemnation by eminent domain. Generally, the clause applies to the lease of a larger tenant having a parking index guarantee.

h. Common Areas. Common areas are everything outside the gross leasable area. Common areas include parking lots, service roads and loading areas, delivery passages, pedestrian malls and canopied sidewalks, public restrooms, community rooms, landscaped areas and all access roads not owned by a municipality. The clause includes the requirement that the tenant pay his share of the cost of operation and maintenance of these areas, and the basis on which charges are made.

There are several ways of prorating the charge among the tenants. The three most common are: (1) A prorata charge based on the tenant's leased area as a portion of the total rented area of the center; (2) a fixed charge stated as a dollar charge for a stated period; (3) a variable charge based on a percentage of sales. The fixed charge method places a ceiling on expenditures, which tenants like but which, with rising costs, landlords find prevents satisfactory maintenance.[212] Common area charges should never be looked upon by a tenant as a rent deductible from overages.

The clause provides for the developer's control of the parking and other common areas and to enforce compliance with these rules—such as restriction of employee and tenant parking to specified areas and specification of conditions for enforcement such as default of lease, if the provision is not adhered to.

i. Merchants Association. In fairness to all tenants, you should have—and must have—a merchants association in your lease. This clause in shopping center leases is the important provision for solution of operational problems. Provide for the association and for membership in the group.

The clause sets up the basis for participation under separate by-laws. The clause also sets the formula for assessment and for fund contributions to the continuing advertising and promotional program and for the pre-opening and opening expenses. For more complete discussion, see pages 371 to 391. The matter of store hours can be omitted from lease specifications and be regulated by vote of the merchants association. The matter of agreeing to window display and store lighting during night opening hours should be covered by this lease clause, however.

j. Sign Control. Exterior signs should be regulated in the lease contract. Put a definite restriction on signs and their use, specify sign approval by the landlord and provide for such matters as projection, placement, size and color.

No roof or projecting signs should be permitted. Chains won't give up trade mark signs, but they will go along with proper placements and color control. Size of lettering, color and placement should be subject to approval by the developer. Window advertising by paper paste-ons should be regulated so that gaudy paper posters and masses of placards will not cheapen the entire shopping center. Prohibit sidewalk display of merchandise.

---

[212] This contribution must cover all common area maintenance. It's dangerous to put a ceiling on costs. As Larry Smith points out, the lease usually specifies the type of cost items allocable to maintenance of the common area. Normally, these can include cleaning, snow removal, fire protection, cost of liability and property damage insurance, workmen's compensation insurance, and supervision.

k. Radius. Prohibit the tenant from owning and operating another store in the same locality. A protective clause should be inserted that the tenant will not open another store within whatever distance fits the conditions.

l. Assignment and Subletting. Limit the tenant's right to assign his lease or to sublet without the landlord's consent.

m. Care and Maintenance. Provide certain specifications for cleanliness and regularity of cleaning windows and doors. Provide for strict measures of rodent control in leases to all tenant types selling food items.

n. Tax Escalator. It is desirable to have a clause which would require the tenant to pay his prorated share of any increase in real estate taxes over the average of the first two or three years, allowing him to deduct it from the percentage rent.

o. Other Clauses. Apart from the above clauses which are unique perhaps to shopping centers and which are for the purpose of continuing operations in tenant and landlord relationships, the shopping center lease will provide for the usual type of clauses written in commercial real estate leases—such as contingencies, co-tenancies, maintenance of and repairs to premises, indemnity, insurance, utility services, remedies and defaults, surrender of premises, etc.

Naturally, there will be objections to parts of lease provisions by some tenants. *There will be compromises.*[213] The extent of this give-and-take will depend on the strength of the bargaining position or negotiating skill of the two parties. The important things for the developer are the percentage rents, contributions for common area maintenance, control of the parking area, and tenant participation in the merchants association and in its advertising and promotion programs.

Lease clauses presented here are notations only, to aid a developer's planning and negotiation. They are not to be considered as full discussions nor as coverage of the items in clauses, nor are they presented in precise order for a lease document.

---

[213] See "Lease Negotiations for Small Centers" by Frederick C. Arpke; "Chain Store Leasing in Shopping Centers" by Roy P. Drachman. *Urban Land*, February 1959. Urban Land Institute.

Percentage Lease Table, 1960

The percentage lease table below is adapted from the table compiled annually and published by Stamats Publishing Company, 427 Sixth Ave., S.E., Cedar Rapids, Iowa, in its magazine, *Buildings*—The Magazine of Building Management, is reproduced only for negotiation and guidance. The figures are originally given to *Buildings* by its "Board of Experts," who report these average ranges for their sections of the country. Remember that these are averages. Rates vary with stipulations in the lease.

	West Coast	Mid-West	East Coast	South
Art Shops	5-9	6-10	7-10	—
Auto Accessories	3-7	3-6	3-6	3-5
Auto Agencies	1¼-3	1½-4	2-4	—
Bakeries	4-7	4-8	4-7	4-8
Barber Shops	7-10	8-12	8-12	8-10
Beauty Shops	5-12	8-15	8-15	6-13
Books and Stationery	5-10	6-10	5-10	5-7
Candy	6-10	6-12	6-10	6-10
Children's Clothing	4-8	5-8	5-8	4-10
Cigars and Sundries	5-8	4-8	4-8	8
Cocktail Lounge	5-9	7-9	6-10	6-10
Credit Clothing	5-8	4-8	5-8	4-8
Department Stores	2-4	2-4	2-3	2½-6
Drugstores (Chain)	2-6	3-5	3-5	3-7
Drugstores (Individual)	4-8	4-7	4-8	3-7
Dry Cleaning and Laundry	5-10	7-10	5-10	5-10
Electrical Appliances	3-8	5-8	5-8	2-8
Florists	6-10	6-12	5-10	5-9
Fruit and Vegetable Market	6-8	4-8	5-9	—
Furniture	3-8	3-7	4-7	4-6
Furs	5-8	4-8	5-9	—
Garage (Storage)	30-50	30-65	35-50	35-65
Gas Stations	1-2¢	1-2¢	1-1½¢	½-2¢
Gift Shops	5-10	6-9	6-10	6-10
Grocery Stores (Ordinary)	1½-7	1½-5	1½-4	1-2½
Grocery Stores (Chain)	1-2	1-2	1-1½	.08-2
Hardware	3-6	4-7	4-8	4-6
Hobby Shops	5-8	6-10	5-8	6-8
Hosiery and Knit Goods	6-8	5-10	5-10	5-10
Jewelry (Cheap Costume)	7-12	6-10	7-10	7-10
Jewelry (Expensive)	5-10	6-10	5-10	4-10
Leather Goods	5-10	6-10	6-10	5-10
Liquor Stores	3½-8	3-6	4-8	5-6
Meat Markets	4-6	3-5	3-5	—
Meat Markets (Chain)	3-5	1½-5	2-5	—
Men's Clothing	4-8	4-7	4-7	4-8
Men's Furnishings	4-10	5-10	6-9	4-10
Men's Hats	7-10	6-10	6-10	6-12
Men's Shoes	4-8	5-9	5-8	5-10
Men's Shoes (Volume)	5-7	5-7	5-7	5-8
Men's Tailors	6-8	4-8	6-9	6-8
Millinery	6-15	8-17	10-12	10-12
Motion Picture Theaters	8-12½	10-15	12-15	8-10
Office Supply Stores	3-7	4-8	5-6	6-8
Optical Stores	5-10	4-12½	7-10	4-8
Paint, Wallpaper Supplies	3-8	5-12	4-7	3
Parking Lots	30-60	40-65	35-55	35-50
Photography Shops	6-10	5-10	6-10	4-8
Pianos and Musical Instruments	4-8	5-8	4-7	5
Radio and Television	3-10	3-7	4-7	4-8
Restaurants	3-10	4-8	3-10	3-10

	West Coast	Mid-West	East Coast	South
Shoe Repair	6-10	6-15	8-10	8-10
Specialty Stores	6-10	7-12	6-9	5-8
Sporting Goods	4-7	4-8	6-8	5-8
Taverns	5-6	7-10	5-8	—
Women's Dress Shops	4-8	5-10	4-7	4-8
Women's Furnishings	4-10	5-10	5-9	5-10
Women's Shoes	5-8	5-8	5-8	5-10
Women's Shoes (Volume)	4-7	5-7	4-7	4-7
5-10¢ or 25¢-$2 Stores	3-6	3-6	½-5	3-6

Reprinted from *Buildings*—The Magazine of Building Management, by special permission of Donald W. Hansen, Editor and Manager. The original table appeared in the December 1959 issue of *Buildings,* pages 40-42.

3. Rental Terms

Absolute terms for negotiating the percentages in leases are not practical. But there are some specific leasing experiences and examples of percentage rates and rental terms which the Council considers beneficial in the planning and operation of shopping centers.

Everyone favors percentage leases with a minimum guarantee. In fact, all types of tenancies in shopping centers are being leased on the basis of percentage of the gross volume of business. As with every rule, there is an exception. Exceptions are apt to be service shops and institutional or non-retail tenants such as barber shops, beauty parlors, shoe repair, etc., and banks; and offices which do not keep sales volume records. Where such fixed guarantees are involved, it may be wise for the developer to investigate short term leases. On fixed rentals, the owner is placed disadvantageously. He is not properly provided with incentive income as he proceeds to develop and promote his center. With short term leases, he is better able to protect himself for adjustment of rental income in line with expansion of the center, higher operating costs and changing circumstances.

To indicate some ranges in percentages for rents from various tenant types, the tables on pages 360, 368 and 425 are of interest. Percentages will vary between tenant types. The main function of any "percentage lease table" is to indicate what rates have been found to be fair by many experienced rental brokers and merchants.

In addition to the tables, the following notes indicate in a general way rental terms as gleaned from shopping center experiences. Quoted figures reflect case histories rather than precise levels.

"Get a guaranteed per square foot minimum. The minimum is the important thing." The percentage of gross volume is a cushion. "The minimum rental should total enough for the landlord to meet real estate taxes, interest, amortization, and other fixed charges. *Never put a maximum rental in a lease.*"

a. Department Store. Because of its importance in a regional center, the department store is able to negotiate favorable terms. (The developer is cautioned against "subsidizing" the department store in order to obtain a lease.)

"Guaranteed rents in gross leases which also contain percentage rent terms typically range from a token amount of $1.00 in some cases to $1.50 per square foot in stronger locations, and more in exceptional cases."[214]

Percentage rents range between 2 per cent and 3 per cent of gross sales with a sliding scale as sales volumes increase. Use a sliding scale and cut-off (no further increase after a total covered by percentages).

3% on sales to $5,000,000

2½% on the next $2,500,000

2% on volume beyond $7,500,000: Long term lease—
20 to 30 years.

Department store productivity varies according to its dominance of the trade area. But department stores must obtain at least $60 per square foot volume for profitable operation.

A full line department store must have at least 100,000 square feet of gross leasable area.

As a percentage of the gross leasable area of the center, department store tenancy should approximate no less than one-third of the total leasable area of the center.

b. Junior Department Store. The dominant position of the tenancy in a community center and its importance to a regional center places this store type in a strong negotiating position.

---

[214] *Shopping Towns—USA* by Victor Gruen and Larry Smith, cited previously. This and other citations in quotes are from the above source. Other citations are based on excerpts from Urban Land Institute's Technical Bulletin No. 30 and from Council statements at plan analysis sessions.

Guaranteed rents with percentage terms range from $.75 to $1.50 per square foot, depending upon the project's strength of location.

Percentages range between 2½ and 5 per cent of sales, depending on the type of store. (One prominent chain offers no minimum guarantee despite strength of location.)

Productivity varies widely, between $40 to $75 per square foot.

Store sizes range between 30,000 and 80,000 square feet.

c. Variety Stores.[215] Variety stores contribute to the completeness of any center. "Depending upon the quality of location and dominance in the center, guaranteed rent ranges from $1 to $2 per square foot and percentage rent from 3 to 6 per cent of sales." From the tenant's point of view, occupancy cost is the real measurement of rental charges—between 4 and 5 per cent is a measurement of rent as a percentage of gross sales.

Average yearly gross sales per square foot—$40 to $70.

Store sizes range between 20,000 and 40,000 square feet and occupy between 4 to 10 per cent of the total GLA of regional centers.

d. Supermarkets. Rentals are generally based on a fixed percentage of gross sales with a minimum guarantee.

"Typical supermarket guaranteed rents vary from $1.25 to $2.00 per square foot. Percentage rents usually range between 1 and 2 per cent with occasional sliding scales as sales volumes increase. Supermarkets typically range in size from 15,000 to 35,000 square feet."[216]

While volumes vary, $90 to $150 per square foot of GLA is typical for a strong supermarket in a well located center.[217]

---

[215] See also, *Shopping Centers Re-Studied,* Technical Bulletin No. 30, p. 61. Urban Land Institute.

[216] In its 8th annual report on shopping centers, *Chain Store Age,* Executive Edition, May 1960, offers abstracts from 68 supermarket leases. An analysis of these is as follows:

Average GLA—24,547 sq. ft.

Average minimum rent per sq. ft.—$1.50.

Percentage rates—1½%. (Only 4 of the 68 cases report rates sliding downward from 1½% as volumes increase.)

Terms of lease—range from 10 to 25 years: average about 20 years.

[217] Statistics about supermarkets are presented in its annual report, *The Super Market Industry Speaks—1959* by Super Market Institute, Inc., 500 North Dearborn St., Chicago 10, Ill. As presented in that Institute's

Virtually all supermarkets carry non-food departments, defined to *include* such lines as health and beauty aids, housewares, toys, magazines, glassware, stationery, soft goods, etc.; to *exclude* items commonly carried in the grocery department as cigarettes, paper goods, household cleaners, matches, etc. The proportion of non-food sales to total sales varies from 1.5 to 25 per cent in individual stores. The non-food departments occupy an average of 10 per cent of total *selling* area. The non-food department is most significant in larger store sizes, averaging 7 per cent of total sales in supermarkets with *selling* area above 15,000 square feet, as reported by Super Market Institute in its annual report (1959), see footnote 217.

The supermarket's departure into non-food departments has bearing upon lease negotiations. As suggested by the Council, three approaches to the leasing problem of percentage rents for supermarkets can be taken.

1. Limit the supermarket to food items and such items normally associated with food sales. (This provision can be modified to limit the lessee to the sale of those items which he is merchandising in other stores. This approach would be effective only where the prospective tenant is now limiting his merchandising to conventional food items. It would not be effective where he has already branched out into a series of non-food departments.)

2. Limit the floor area devoted to non-food items to a percentage of the total square footage of sales area or to a specified

---

annual report (1959), the following facts about *new* supermarkets opened in 1959 are offered: (The basic report includes many more facts.)

Sales Volume—$38,000 a week, average (nearly $2,000,000 yearly)
Store Size—20,000 sq. ft. Selling area averages 67% of total store area (when all on one floor)
Parking Index—5 (selling area)
Sales per sq. ft.—$2.91 per week: 53% of new supermarkets were erected as part of new shopping centers.

Type of Location	Average Weekly Sales Per Super	Total Store Area (sq. ft.)	Selling Area (sq. ft.)
New "Large" Shopping Center	$39,900	23,000	13,600
New "Small" Shopping Center	38,300	20,800	13,500

The typical new supermarket in a small shopping center serves a trading area populated by 25,000 people.

Supermarkets in large new shopping centers average 27,500 people in their trading area.

Other facts, particularly trends and comparisons for the super market industry, are presented in the Super Market Institute's annual report.

maximum in square feet. For example, 10 per cent of the total sales area is a reasonable limit to assign to the sale of non-food items. (See the above.)

3. Permit the supermarket to go into non-food lines, but only on a competitive basis with other merchants insofar as percentages are concerned. You would require the lessee to register his departmental sales on housewares, apparel, etc., and apply a percentage to these gross sales comparable to that paid by other tenants in the same lines.

e. Other Food Stores. The small specialty food stores—delicatessens, meats, fish and poultry, candy and nuts, bakeries, etc., when effectively merchandised are valuable tenants in any shopping center.

Such stores pay as much as $5 to $6 per square foot guaranteed rent and percentages ranging between 6 to 10 per cent of gross sales.

They range in size from 500 to 2,000 square feet.

f. Furniture Stores. A furniture store produces low volume per square foot of sales area. Percentage rates average 5 per cent. Frequently, the store can have a limited display area on the main merchandising level of the center with its main selling space in a secondary location such as a basement. Store sizes vary from a few hundred feet where the store carries only token items such as decorator fabric and furnishings, up to as much as 40,000 square feet for a full-line furniture store.

g. Apparel Stores. These are the stores in men's, women's and children's clothing lines, which provide strong attractions for comparison shopping. Independent merchants and national chains, custom shops and ready-to-wear outlets, millinery, shoes of all grades, and other specialties are among the tenant types in this category. Store size is another factor, the smaller store normally paying a higher guaranteed rent per square foot. The lease table, page 360, indicates ranges in percentages which are applied typically.

h. Service Shops. For the most part, barbers and beauty shops, like other service shops, yield a high guaranteed rent on a square foot basis. Percentage rates range up to 10 per cent. Some service shops are difficult to check on gross sales, hence a higher guaranteed minimum rent per square foot can be substituted for the percentage of sales arrangement.

Illustration No. 100. Eastland—A Regional Shopping Center

Photo: Courtesy, Eastland Center, Inc.

Eastland is situated on 105 acres of land bounded on three sides by Kelly Road, Eight Mile-Vernier and Beaconsfield and on the west by a new 4-lane road, Eastland Drive, and is located 12 miles northeast of downtown Detroit. Paved parking areas and circulating roads occupy 80 acres of the site. No less than 8,460 family cars find free parking space at Eastland Center. Seven large lots, clearly marked, engineered for easy single-turn parking at 52°, flood lighted at night, cluster on all sides around the Center. No car is parked more than 600 feet away from the nearest store. All circulating roads around the Center enable the driver to get to any lot from any of the 17 entrances.

Largest of the buildings is Hudson's branch department store with 478,644 square feet of space, four floors above ground and a complete basement store below. Five one-story multiple store buildings are clustered on three sides of Hudson's, each with complete basements. Siegel's store occupies a separate 2-story and basement building on the east side of the Center; Stouffer's Restaurant adjoins the Siegel store on the east end. Other buildings include a Special Events Building for community services and Center activities, and Hudson's separate package pick-up building. Half of one multiple-store building on the west end is occupied by the power house and maintenance and protection services.

How completely Eastland qualifies as a shopping town will be evident from these facts: It has a large department store, 15 apparel stores for men, women, and children, 7 shoe stores, two millinery stores, two jewelry stores, two home furnishings stores, an electrical appliance store, a huge supermarket, a fruit juice bar, two candy stores, two bakeries, a bank, barber shop, three beauty parlors, dry cleaner, a book store, key shop, florist, music center, bird store, toy shop, stationery, jewelry repair shop, travel service, utility service center, a public auditorium, a slenderizing salon, an exhibit center, a United States post office, and even a radio program booth—totaling 1,085,416 square feet.

The architects of Eastland Center were Victor Gruen and Associates who also designed Northland. The economc analyst for both centers was Larry Smith & Co. All-weather shelter has been created for customer comfort by the introduction of a colonnade around all the buildings, including the department store, and by covered walkways which connect all of the buildings to one at logical and convenient points.

The Team of Experts for Eastland Regional Shopping Center, Harper Woods, Mich. was, Owner: Eastland Center, Inc. Architects and Engineers: Victor Gruen Associates. Partner in Charge: Karl O. Van Leuven, Jr. Project Director: Raymond O. Brinker. Landscape Architect: Edward A. Eichstedt. Electrical and Mechanical Engineers: Hyde & Bobbio, Inc. Civil Engineers: Hubbell, Roth & Clark. Economic Consultants: Larry Smith & Co. Traffic Consultant: Lloyd B. Reid. Sculptors: Morris Brose, Joseph Bullone, Marshall Fredericks, Louise Kruger, Mary Callery, Lindsey Decker, Thomas McClure and William McVey. General Contractors: O. W. Burke Co. and A. A. Smith Co. Mechanical Contractor: Donald Miller Co. Electrical Contractors: John H. Busby Co. and F. J. O'Toole Co.

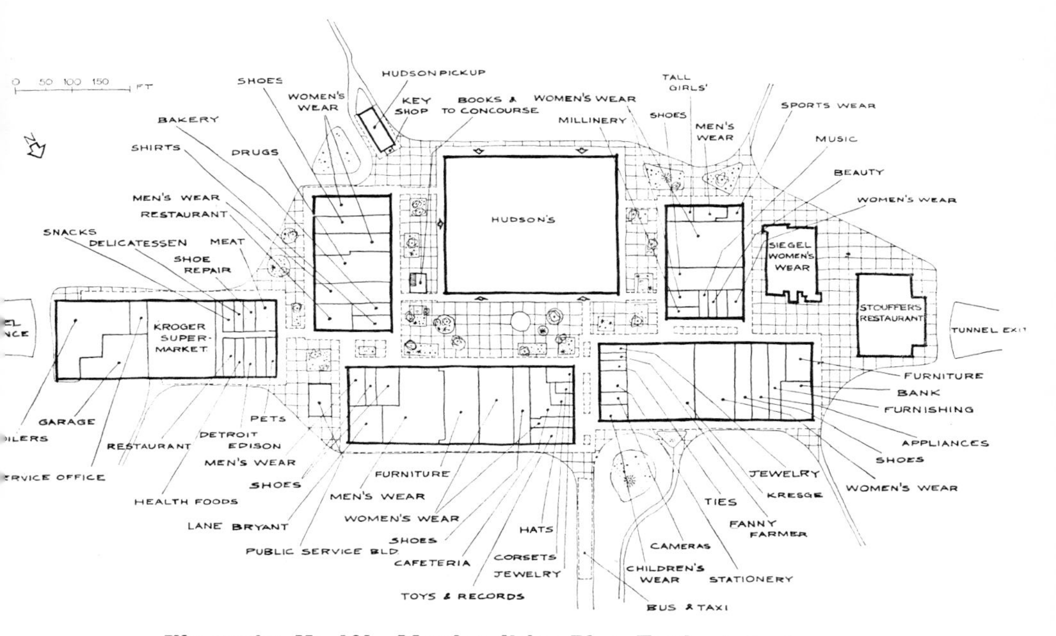

Illustration No. 101. Merchandising Plan, Eastland Center

Source: Architectural Forum, October 1957

i. Other Tenant Types. Apart from the major categories of tenant types, the others such as jewelry, gifts, sporting goods, camera shops, etc. are valuable tenants because of their ability to pay guaranteed and percentage rents which are higher than those paid by users of large space.

Banks. Banks prefer establishing minimum rents with a percentage overage ranging from 1/10th of 1 per cent to 2/10ths of 1 per cent, based on the volume of deposits over a set period of years. The guaranteed rent ranges from $1.75 to $5.00 a square foot. Banking leases are similar to other commercial leases in that the rental paid must be arrived at through agreement and negotiation.[218]

Typical Percentage Rents in a Shopping Center

Drug Store	4½%
Drug Store	5% first $500,000 4% next $100,000 3% over $600,000
Supermarket	1%
Service Grocery	2½%
Women's Apparel	
Store No. 1	6%
Store No. 2	6%
Store No. 3	5%
Store No. 4	6% first $80,000 5% next $40,000 4% over $120,000
Men's Apparel	
Store No. 1	5%
Store No. 2	6%
Beauty Shop	
Shop No. 1	10%—2nd floor
Shop No. 2	10%—1st floor
Variety	
Store No. 1	5%
Store No. 2	5%
Stationery & Book Store	5%
Photographer	5% Educational 10% All other business } 2nd floor
Restaurant	
No. 1	5%
No. 2	5%

[218] For a fuller explanation of banks and banking leases see *Banking Expansion—New Frontiers Ahead* by Robert H. Armstrong. Technical Bulletin No. 35. Urban Land Institute.

Cafeteria	5%
Bakery	6%
Barber Shop	10%
Shoe Repair	12½%
Cleaners & Laundry	10% dry cleaning 5% finished laundry
Florist	8%
Motion Picture Theatre	15% ticket sales 5% confections
Gift Shop	7½%
Children's Apparel	
Store No. 1	4%
Store No. 2	6%
Shoe Store	
Store No. 1	5%
Store No. 2	7.4% first $100,000 5% next $100,000 4% above $200,000
Jr. Dept.	2½%
Dept. Store	3½%
Toy Shop	5%
Music Store	3½%
Hardware Store	5% first $250,000 4% next $50,000 3% above $300,000 2% wholesale sales

4. Leasing Policies

In the matter of leasing policy from the shopping center developer's point of view, the following statements by Council members are offered:

"Do not make too many low-price percentage leases."

"Use split percentage clauses; do not over-work the straight percentage arrangement."

"We do not install show cases, floor covering or light fixtures for the lessee. In some locations, however, where the shopping center and its merchants have not become established, some one or all of these things may be furnished by the lessor in order to secure a more capable and experienced lessee than could be obtained otherwise.

"We prefer a fixed rent where the lessee is a small shop, where bookkeeping and accounting methods are not on some standardized basis and where it is difficult for the lessor to check up on the lessee's volume. Moreover, certain types of shops and certain lessees need to be tested out in a particular locality as to their adaptability, and a short term percentage lease would be indicated in such cases. On the other hand, where you have a large concern, well established, with orthodox bookkeeping methods and where the prospect is for the building up over a period of years of a large volume of business; the percentage lease, if well drawn by an experienced lawyer, is desirable."

"Our leases extend from one year to twenty years, dependent upon many varying conditions and some of our ground leases extend for ninety-nine years."

"Our monthly rent does not include light, heat, gas or water for first-floor shops. In the first floor shops, the lessee pays for air-conditioning installation and upkeep. On the second floor, in offices, the rental includes all of these charges together with year round air-conditioning and janitor service."

"In this section of the country we do not have basements. Our second floors will rent for about 15 per cent less than the first floor unless the second floor is air-conditioned. In this case, and with the paying of utilities and janitor service by the lessor, the rental on the second floor is from 40 to 60 per cent higher than that on the first floor without air-conditioning, utilities or janitor service."

"We favor chain operators for some types of stores, such as food, drug and clothing units. But for most small shops in new neighborhoods we prefer independent operators. When the center is large enough and has developed sufficient buying power, there is no objection to a chain cash-and-carry store in addition to a locally owned and operated service grocery."

a. Basements. Basement space rentals often hinge on differences between basement storage area and merchandising area. Typically, the percentages apply against the total volume of business, basements included. Otherwise the landlord is faced with the practical problem of defining storage area. "It isn't practical to expect an initial delineation of storage space to hold for the duration of a 10 or 20 year lease. During such interval, the storage or basement area will be converted to retail space, it is hoped. A hard and fast formula putting different values on portions of the demised premises might conceivably deter a merchant from undertaking a program of expansion."

"Our policy in leasing basement space is to set our rental on the basis of the gross square footage regardless of whether it is used for storage or selling, which seems a sound procedure where a percentage of gross sales is the basis of the lease. This, of course, requires all fixtures and finish at tenant's cost. There is no deduction for space which may be used for storage."

"All tenants are on percentage leases with minimum guarantee; the minimum guarantee is based upon the size of the store and if a basement is provided, this is taken into consideration when fixing the minimum guaranteed rental. If the basement is suitable for merchandising, rental is received from the percentage clause; so it makes no difference to us whether the tenant merchandises the basement or not."

B. MAINTENANCE AND MANAGEMENT

From the preceding discussion of lease clauses and leasing policies, the extent of a lease as a management tool is readily discernible, even though the lease in itself is a legal document. From its scope, the lease can ease the problems of maintenance and management.

With authority through the provisions of the lease, management has control of such things as completeness of merchandise which the center offers; control of common areas; and assessments for operating such items as parking lot lighting, sweeping, snow removal, marking; and enforcement of measures such as sign control, hours of opening, employee parking, tenant housekeeping and maintenance of interiors of premises.

One of the most workable ways of clearly defining the responsibility between landlord and tenant is to insert in the lease a clause providing for that which the lessor is obliged to maintain and that which the lessee is required to perform. Ordinary maintenance costs should be charged to tenants. Structural maintenance of the buildings is the owner's responsibility as is the repair of outside walls, the roof, and repair of sidewalks, canopies, parking lots and landscaping. The tenants should have responsibility for maintenance inside their leased premises. Experience indicates that they should have separate meters and pay for their own utilities—light, water, gas. Air-conditioning charges depend on whether the system is from a central plant or whether from individual package units. In either case, capital costs and operating charges are divided between landlord and tenant as provided for in the lease clause. Tenants should contribute to common area charges for maintenance and cleaning.

Most shopping center owners prefer to separate the income from rent from the pro rata charges received for maintenance of common areas. Lighting of the parking areas, for example, is considered a maintenance cost and should be so charged to the tenants by the lease. But, as the Council has so often summarized, "Whatever the arrangements are for maintenance, they should be enforceable as a legal obligation."

l. Operational Expenses and Accounting

As with building costs, the Community Builders' Council is reluctant to present dollar figures. As with other aspects of shopping center management, the operational phases are so filled with variables that any quotation of costs could be misinterpreted. Any citation of what it costs to operate a shopping center has to be modified by an explanation of what the figure includes and how it is measured. Accordingly, the Council offers only an itemization of costs included in operational expenses in realistic cost accounting.

Operational expenses vary according to what services and performances are included in the lease and how these costs are allocated between payments by the landlord and charges to the tenants. Regional differences—for example, costs for snow removal—affect operational cost figures. Elements of costs vary according to accounting systems used by owners, even though *items* to be included can be fairly uniform. Insurance, mortgage interest and amortization, real estate taxes are common to all centers, but inherent lack of comparability in several of the other elements in operating costs such as depreciation of buildings (where tax considerations are important) and financing costs (where the extent of equity capital is a dominant factor) makes it difficult to arrive at uniform cost accounting. Even so, there are elements of cost which can be useful in developing comparative data on a reasonably consistent basis.[219]

---

[219] It is hoped that through Urban Land Institute's current (1960) research study on cost and income of shopping centers, enough comparable data on a consistent basis can be compiled so that there will be benchmarks dealing with sales, income, operating expenses, and capital costs in regional, community, and neighborhood centers. A ULI *Manual on Standard Accounts for Shopping Centers* will be released December 1960.

These natural divisions of expense are:

Operating Expenses

Building maintenance—such items as exterior painting, repairs and alterations to structures (not capitalized), etc.

Parking lot, mall, and other common areas—such items include maintenance and repair of paving, striping, cleaning, lighting, guard or police service, heating and ventilating of enclosed malls, servicing of public toilets, power used for and maintenance of signs which are responsibility of landlord, snow removal, trash removal, maintenance of landscaping and grounds, etc.

Office services—such items as janitor service of office buildings (if any), lighting, etc.

Advertising and Promotion

Contribution to merchants association—including contributions in kind such as salaries and office expense as well as cash.

Other promotional costs to landlord—including services furnished, net of any reimbursements such as cost of furnishing a meeting place for public use.

Real Estate Taxes

Real Estate Insurance

Fire and other damage, public liability, plate glass and rental value (use and occupancy).

General and Administrative

Expenses not otherwise classified, such as management of center, communications, office staff, etc.

Not all centers, particularly neighborhood ones, keep accounting records detailed according to functional divisions, as above, but the following natural divisions of expense are proper for any center's accounting purposes:

Payroll, including payroll taxes and supplementary benefits—all salaries and wages of officers and employees. The cost of company-furnished insurance and other employee benefits, such as pension or retirement plans as well as vacation pay, overtime, etc., are included.

Management fees—purchase of a service to manage the center (if that is the method of the center's management). Wide variation exists in the type of service rendered by management agencies, but the intent here is to limit this classification to the promotion and the general and administrative categories of functional divisions of expenses, outlined above.

Other contracted expenses—purchase of service from others in lieu of the center's own staff, to perform work such as guard or police services, snow removal, trash removal, cleaning, etc.

Professional services—legal, accounting, etc.

Leasing fees and commissions—expense incurred for outside services in lieu of own staff work after initial occupancy by tenants.

Materials and supplies—operating expense items such as paint, oil, cleaning compound, and the general and administrative items such as forms and office supplies.

Utilities—water, gas, electricity, etc.

Equipment expenses (including depreciation)—autos, trucks, cleaning equipment, common area equipment, etc.

Travel and entertainment—transportation, hotels, meals, taxi fares, etc.

Communications—telephone, postage, etc.

Taxes and licenses (exclusive of payroll tax)—real estate, personal property, business licenses, etc.

Insurance (exclusive of supplementary benefits)—fire and other damage, plate glass, public liability, rental value (use and occupancy), bonding of employees, etc.

Other—not provided for otherwise.

By totaling operating expenses under the above natural classifications and by computing these elements of expense by square footage of gross leasable area for each tenant, the shopping center owner can compare his expenses with his total rental and other shopping center income on the same basis. His total rental and other income for this purpose would be accounted for by each tenant classification with the income sources subdivided by payments according to lease arrangements on percentage rent—no minimum guarantee, minimum guaranteed yearly rent, overage rental earned for the year plus income from common area charges to tenants, tax and insurance charges under escalator clauses. By this accounting, the owner can compare his costs and income on a logical basis.

2. Management Arrangements

Depending on the size of the center and the arrangements worked out earlier by lease negotiation, the shopping center owner-developer provides for maintenance and management in the following ways or in combinations thereof:

(a) The owner-developer acts as his own manager and supervises his own maintenance and management force, including promotions and advertising—either by outside contract or by his own staff's work. This is the usual practice in regional and community centers.

(b) The owner-developer acts as the agent for the merchants association, collecting the funds that the association raises and disburses.

(c) The owner-developer turns over the center's operations to a management firm. This practice is more common in neighborhood centers.

In the latter case, fees are involved; for these there are no set standards. Usually the management fee is determined by negotiation. The fee depends on the extent of services rendered. A higher fee would be charged when advertising, promotions, and work with the merchants association is included in the contract. A leasing agreement and a management agreement should be considered as two separate functions. If only leases are secured, and no other management functions are performed, then a leasing fee might be 5 per cent for the first year and 2½ per cent for the succeeding nine years of a ten year lease, for example. In shopping center leasing, commissions paid to the broker who secures a tenant lease do not vary much from those which he would obtain for a commercial lease downtown, even though the shopping center's lease clauses would vary from clauses which would be in a downtown commercial lease. For straight management, the fees are generally based on a percentage of the gross rentals collected.

3. Management Problems

Apart from the maintenance and other operations which are the landlord's responsibilities, there are some specific problems in shopping center operation which are usually troublesome:

a. Sign Control. In today's merchandising methods many tenants, chain stores particularly, resort to the practice of pasting paper posters on display windows, hoping to promote items or to announce special sales. In shopping centers, the practice is not effective; besides, it gives a shabby appearance to the center as a whole. As mentioned earlier the Council frowns on the practice and urges no concessions on sign control.

Size and location of all signs is a matter over which the owner should maintain rigid control. Lease clauses usually limit the amount of space which the tenant's sign may occupy. They require that no signs be placed on the roof; that any lettering on plate glass windows or doors must have the landlord's prior approval. But frequently the sign control clause will not be so rigid as to prevent the lessee from mounting paper posters if he so wishes. However, the owner-developers who most carefully manage their centers undertake very rigid sign control over paper posters on display windows. "Its prevention has to be put into your lease in a vigorous and enforceable form and be backed up by management directive if you are going to get results."

b. Parking Enforcement. Power to enforce regulations designating where employees are to park is a lease provision. Management must continuously check and enforce this regulation—otherwise employees will usurp prime parking spaces for customer parking.[220]

The number of employee cars is sizable. For example: "In our shopping center we have 460,536 square feet of GFA; we have a gross *selling* area of 311,092 square feet. For this retail selling part of the center we have 1,057 employees, 592 cars and 10 trucks. In our office building section next to the shopping center, we have a total gross floor area of 263,610 square feet. For this space we have 1,196 employees and 714 cars."[221] From

[220] The value of a parking space as it relates to sales volume has been estimated at existing shopping centers. These estimates show that $10,000-$15,000 in sales is related to one parking space.

[221] This center has 1 car for each 1.78 retail selling employees and 1 car for each 1.67 office employees. In another relationship, this center has 1 employee for each 505 sq. ft. of GFA, or 1 for each 300 sq. ft. of selling area.

these statistics the importance of controlling employee parking is obvious, as mentioned on pages 313-315.

Shopping center parking areas are private property, hence enforcing regulations does not have the force of public police power. Employee parking regulations and action against flagrant violations are best handled through management and merchants association enforcement.

Parking violations by the public, who may also be customers, is a matter for diplomacy and finesse. Problems generally arise where commuters find a shopping center to be a convenient place for leaving their cars all day. In this case, enforcement requires a municipal ordinance permitting police enforcement of parking regulations on private parking lots, such as is in effect in Kansas City, Missouri.

c. Night Openings. A major movement in retailing is night shopping. The custom allows the family to shop together (a reason for considering children's play areas in shopping centers). Night shopping is changing the times of peak hours and customary shopping schedules. After dark, business volumes mean better night lighting of parking areas, store windows and pedestrian walks. With night shopping there is less interference with evening rush-hour traffic on the highways.

Centers that stay open only two nights a week are becoming conservative. Shopping center operators also report that theirs is a weekend business even to a greater degree than for downtown areas. The real business in a center starts building up from Thursday, reaching its peak on Saturday afternoon. Then too, with night operations, two, three or four evenings a week, merchants are closing more mornings. This change affects the center's operations, particularly the early demand on the parking area. Management's problem is to achieve volumes in the off-peak hours through effective advertising and promotions.

Emphasis on night shopping also means that store illumination is an important factor in both interior and exterior design. Incandescent and fluorescent lights must be mixed to get a balance between warm and cold light. Fluorescent lights alone are not suitable for fashion goods and are unflattering to women's complexions.

Store hours are best handled by agreement through the merchants association rather than as a specification in the lease. An added precaution in the lease to avoid unlighted stores would provide for night window lighting by a tenant which did not remain open during night shopping and at other times.

d. Package Pick-Up Stations. The way of handling the arrival of goods at the center is a problem in itself, usually solvable by planned arrangements of service courts, a truck tunnel, or a rear service road; but the carrying away of their purchases by the customers is a separate problem. It is far more satisfactory for both the seller and the buyer if the articles can be taken home at the time of purchase. But a shopper burdened with bundles isn't going to stroll past stores to do even some window shopping.

Supermarkets have pioneered with "carry-out" service. But this is an expensive operation. The answer lies in providing some form of package pick-up station. The customer checks her bundles, goes to her car, then drives up to the special station where an attendant loads the car in return for the claim check. The mechanics are variable, but a system can be worked to solve the bundle carrying problem. The real solution is to have the parking lot laid out for minimum walking distances.

e. Real Estate Taxes. The problem of real estate taxes and assessments is another special one for the shopping center owner. Taxes are often estimated too low. To be on the safe side, taxes should be figured at the local rate and to nearly full value as represented by whatever method the local assessor uses as his basis for assessment. Assessments do get changed frequently and the trend is ever upward.

There is a difference in value in land used for *building* and in land used for *parking*. This acknowledgment is in accord with the statement that the Community Builders' Council propounds on the matter of providing the necessary parking in a shopping center. See page 315. Support for the thesis that reasonable valuations are needed for shopping centers can be seen when assessment practices recognize the contribution to public benefit made by the shopping center parking area.

A new attitude and approach to shopping center assessments will also recognize that such standard factors used customarily as front foot values, corner influences, standards of depth, etc., do not apply to a commercial concept wherein the whole property is used roughly in the proportion of 20 per cent for building and 80 per cent for free parking. Principles used for assessing downtown commercial real estate are not directly applicable to the suburban shopping center concept.

While it is a fact that parking makes the shopping center, it is also a fact that it is provided at private expense (the owner's). "The land has been purchased and paved. There is an annual charge to interest on capital invested, taxes, and maintenance, none of which is borne by competing business areas. Were the developers of a mind to adopt a policy of dedicating the parking areas for public use, it would cost them control but save them the expense of maintenance and taxes." As the chief land appraiser of San Mateo County, California, who is quoted here, says: "I believe, and without fear of being accused of subsidizing, that some preferential treatment should be allowed the area used for parking."

The Community Builders' Council, through its Committee on Assessment Practices, has studied the matter of shopping center assessment for real estate tax purposes. The Council's statement of policy is presented as Appendix M. As a report, this statement of policy is not designed to assist a shopping center owner in escaping his fair tax responsibility in the community. Rather, it is a resumé of the criteria which the Community Builders' Council of Urban Land Institute feels should be used in properly assessing shopping center property so that it will pay a fair share of the tax load, but will not be taxed out of existence.[222]

C. MERCHANTS ASSOCIATION

An association of merchants for the promotion of a shopping center of any size is *the prime requirement in shopping center operations*. Experience indicates that the merchants association and membership in the association must be a requirement of the lease and that assessments for the association's activities should be collected at the same time as the rent. Experience also indicates that the merchants' contributions to the advertising and promotional fund on the basis of a percentage of their gross sales is an equitable method of assessment.

Even before construction scaffolding has been removed, the shopping center owner-developer organizes his tenants for pre-

[222] See also, *Assessment and Appraisal of Shopping Centers*, and *Shopping Centers—Analysis and Appraisal for Assessment Purposes*. Both publications by National Association of Assessing Officers, 1313 East 60th St., Chicago 37, Ill.

EATON'S of CANADA
NOVACK'S
HARDWARE

Opening and Opening Day activities and for the daily operations which follow. With the period of operations at hand, he is involved with his problems of management and promotion. As owner, he must produce a program for team play among his merchants. He must resolve any conflicting self-interests in the group. He must bring about cooperation among individuals representing large tenants, small tenants, national chain stores and parent companies, and local independents. He must prepare for doing business in an environment which invites customers to come to the center and not just to one store. An atmosphere for mutual benefit through tenant and landlord cooperation is the key to successfully reaching the full sales volume potential of the center. The degree of success depends upon the effectiveness of the merchants association.

1. Membership

Recommended procedure is the establishment of a merchants association as a lease clause. The next problem confronting the developer is whether membership in the association shall be mandatory or voluntary. Experience dictates mandatory membership. But there are difficulties in securing mandatory membership in the association as a lease requirement. Chain stores, though not all the leading ones, resist the inclusion of any clause which makes membership mandatory. If the chain store happens to be the leading tenant, then it is hard to get other tenants to agree to the clause. So the solution becomes one of setting up provisions for the association and obtaining membership on a voluntary basis. This places the burden on management to keep the association alive and active.

Once the leading tenant agrees to belong to the merchants association and to contribute a percentage toward the advertising program, then you can say to other tenants, locals and chains, "Well, you have to do it or you can't go into the center because the leading tenant insists upon it."

Illustration No. 102. The Shopping Center in Urban Redevelopment
Aerial view of Wellington Square in London, Ontario, with the Wellington Street facade of the new downtown retailing center in the foreground. Wellington Square is a commercial redevelopment project built and financed by private enterprise. The project represents a large-scale shopping center built in a central business district. The project opened August 10, 1960. It includes a weather-conditioned enclosed mall and off-street parking spaces for 840 cars.

Photo: Courtesy, Webb & Knapp (Canada) Ltd.

Illustration No. 103.

Wellington Square in Downtown London, Ontario, Canada

Wellington Square is the first large downtown shopping center with an enclosed mall built as a private enterprise, central business district, commercial redevelopment project in a Canadian city. The project is built on a 6-acre site area; 840 car parking spaces are provided in a multi-level garage. The T. Eaton Company is a full-line department store of 250,000 sq. ft., GFA on 5 levels.

Photo: Courtesy, The T. Eaton Co., Limited

In other cases, tenants who will not sign a lease with a mandatory membership clause will agree to formation of a merchants association and will belong and will support it because the principle of the association and its activities have become so fully successful. "The formation of a merchants association comprised of tenants with an owner's representative included is the only answer to proper and well directed advertising and promotional activity."

2. Operations and Activities

Apart from stipulating in the lease that the tenant shall be a member of the merchants association, experience indicates that the organization and operation of the association should be left largely to the merchants. To make the most of the association, the owner can rely on either of two policies: He can act as a mere agent for the association, relying on the members' interest and organization to operate the association (in this case an executive secretary or promotions director paid for by the association is necessary); or he can actively run the association, relying on the members' officers and committees to acquiesce to the advertising and promotional programs. But the better way is "Try hard to have the merchants run the association and *you,* the *owner,* try hard to stay out of it."

An association should be organized as a non-profit corporation. It should have a constitution and by-laws. These set forth all pertinent information and rules—how officers are to be elected; what is a quorum; when the annual meeting is; what committees are appointed as regular standing committees (usually there is a board of directors including the president, vice-president, secretary and treasurer; the normal committees are finance, advertising, special events and publicity); duties of

Illustration No. 104. Wellington Square

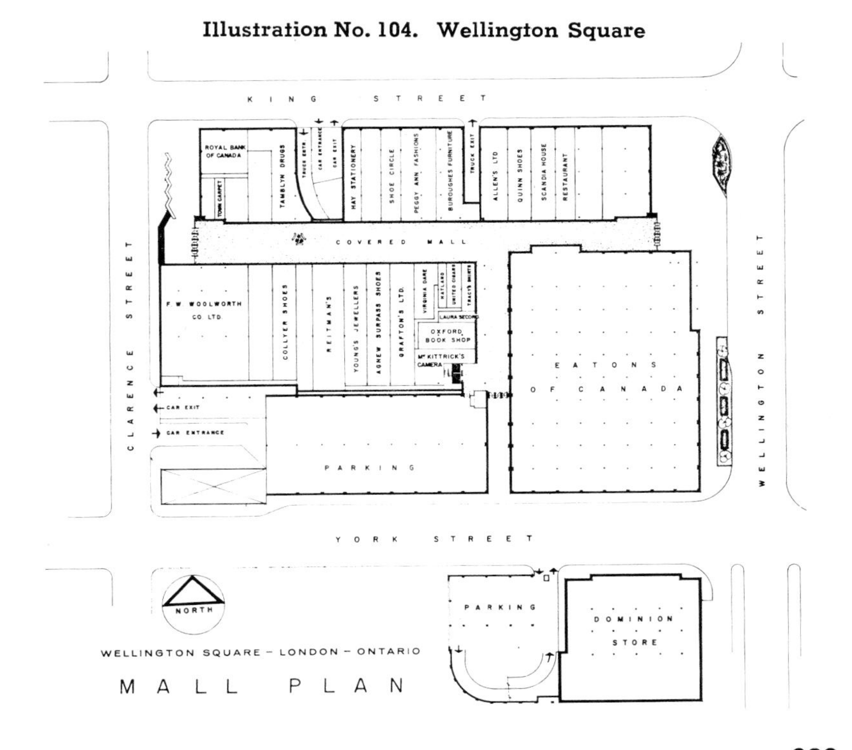

officers; order of business for monthly meetings. The authority to assess dues and fees for advertising, promotion, seasonal decoration, etc., is spelled out in the formal lease document.

A paid part- or full-time secretary is a necessity for successful operation. There are too many items of correspondence, newsletters, notices, billing, etc., to be assumed by any one member whose main effort must always be to make his own store pay. In small centers, it is not always possible for the association to maintain a staff. Such staff work as is needed may be part of the owner's contribution to the association.

The merchants association can be charged with a wide range of activities: Joint advertising of the center, including the use of the center's name on advertising mastheads, letterheads and statements; center-wide special promotions, seasonal events and decorations; enforcement of parking lot regulations, particularly problems of employee parking; business referrals and credit systems; store hours and night openings; merchants' directory and center-wide news bulletin or special newspaper for trade area distribution. In some cases, the association can be charged with parking lot maintenance and lighting, trash collection, snow removal, etc.; but "what is everybody's business is nobody's business." It is better for management to perform the maintenance services and charge back the pro rata share to each merchant.

The association acts as the clearinghouse for suggestions, ideas, programming of merchandising events, and quasi-court for sifting complaints and irritations.

3. Basis for Assessment and Voting

The basis for assessment for contributions to the cost of the association's activities varies widely.

The *most equitable method* for all tenants to contribute to *the advertising fund*—regardless of their store size—is the basis of a percentage of their gross sales. The most frequently used basis is the gross leased area occupied by each tenant; or combinations of the two basic formulas.

Less usual methods used in solving the problem of contributions to the advertising and promotional activities of the association are: A sales volume percentage added to the basic formula of "square feet occupied"; front footage occupied; a per cent of the tenant's annual rent in relation to the total annual rent of the center; arbitrary assessments regardless of the merchant's size or volume; combinations of these methods. Complicated formulas combining some or all of these methods are difficult to administer. The best method in the opinion of many Council members is a percentage of gross sales.

A typical schedule on the latter method as contained in a lease clause could be as follows:

"The ____________ Shopping Center Company agrees to organize a merchants association. The purpose of said merchants association shall be the general furtherance of the business interests of the shopping center as a whole, including advertising, promotion, special events calculated to benefit the shopping center and the business of all the tenants located therein.

"Membership in the association shall be limited to the ____________ Shopping Center Company and to all tenants of the center. Contributions to such merchants association shall be required of all tenants in the shopping center and shall be on the following basis:

"A: One-tenth of one per cent on all gross income from all tenants who pay less than three per cent.

"B: One-fourth of one per cent on all gross income to be paid by all tenants whose percentage rent schedule provides for rental of three per cent of their gross income.

"C: One-half of one per cent on all gross income for those tenants whose percentage rent schedule provides for rental of more than three per cent up to and including four per cent.

"D: One per cent of all gross income for all tenants whose percentage rent schedule provides for rental of more than four per cent for rent."

In the clause which is cited[223] the shopping center also inserts a maximum on payments (thereby creating an exception to the rule—"Never put a maximum in a lease.").

"E: Maximum of twenty cents per square foot per year for tenants with 10,000 square feet or more.

"F: Maximum of forty cents per square foot per year for tenants with less than 10,000 square feet, but more than 5,000 square feet.

"G: Maximum of sixty cents per square foot per year for tenants with less than 5,000 square feet, but more than 2,500 square feet.

---

[223] From Roy P. Drachman, Roy Drachman Realty Co., Tucson, Ariz., shopping center owner-developer and co-vice chairman, Executive Group, Community Builders' Council.

"H: No maximum for tenants with less than 2,500 square feet.

"I: The ____________ Shopping Center agrees to pay 25 per cent of the total of all contributions paid by tenants for advertising and promotion."

The developer agrees to pay one-fourth of the total amount raised. For every $4,000 that the merchants association raises, the developer contributes $1,000.

"The ____________ Shopping Center Company agrees to require by lease or other agreement that every tenant in the shopping center join said merchants association and pay its share of contribution as herein provided. ____________ Shopping Center Company agrees to formulate reasonable by-laws or other articles of association for their merchants association, which will provide a workable basis for effective operation by the association."

Distribution of votes in this lease clause reads:

"Voting among the members of such association shall be on a basis of contribution to the fund. Each member shall have one vote and an additional vote for every $1,000 of contribution to the merchants association in excess of $1,000 except during the first year of the lease term each member shall have one vote for each 1,000 square feet of floor area in the center."

The above formula is used for the first year because, obviously, the developer does not know what the tenant's volume is going to be. This formula is changeable so that the figure can be cut to one vote for each $500 or each $100 contributed.[224] The developer also retains votes for his own contribution; while this does not give him control of the association, his 25 per cent of the votes enables him to vote with the major tenants and in this way he can control the activities of the association.

The point made in the above is that unless the method of contributing to the association is spelled out by a lease clause, the lease and the association are apt to be weak. In fact, a strong lease can specify the amount to be contributed for pre-opening and opening promotions and for the first year of operations, provided the lease also carries a merchants association clause.

[224] Another adaptation of the percentage of gross sales volume as a basis for contribution to the merchants association is: "One-twentieth of one per cent for stores which are on percentages up to three per cent; a quarter of one per cent for those paying from three to six per cent; and one per cent for those paying a rental of over six per cent on their gross sales."

4. Owner Participation

Experience also dictates that the owner-developer must not only organize the merchants association, he must participate in and guide its activities; *and* he must contribute to the fund. The basis for the owner-developer's contribution is normally 25 to 30 per cent of the total of the association's annual budget. Unless there is the active and energetic assistance of the owner in stimulating interest, originating and launching promotions, preparing budgets and coordinating all activities; there will be no active association.[225]

Developers and tenants are becoming more and more convinced that an effective merchants association is of great mutual benefit. The association's advertising and promotional program increases traffic and increases sales. As the merchants increase their profits, they become more competitive and better serve their customers. As the sales volumes go up the owner-developer receives greater overages from the percentage rent scale. So the owner's participation in programs for increasing sales is highly important to him and to the tenants. The owner has every reason to be interested in the volume of business done by each tenant and in the aggregate by all stores. The owner should therefore be very interested in furnishing the leadership, the talent, the skills for having the merchants properly organized for center-wide effective promotion of merchandise, public events and community service.

D. PROMOTION

"A successful center is a promoted center." The promotion of a center is important. It is important for owners of small centers to use promotional techniques. They, too, receive percentage rents.

---

[225] See also: *Merchandising and Promotions, Shopping Center Operations.* A special report to sustaining members, Urban Land Institute. 1958. Urban Land Institute.

Special Report on Shopping Center Promotions, including such items as "Why Shopping Centers Need Good Merchants Associations" by David D. Bohannon, "Raising Promotional Funds through Merchants Associations" by Roy P. Drachman, "Advertising and Promotion" by Donald L. Curtiss, "Pre-Opening Plans and Activities" by Edwin A. Daniels, Jr., "Showmanship in Promoting Your Shopping Center" by William Callahan; a multilithed report, February 1960 by Urban Land Institute.

Shopping Center Merchants Associations by Robert S. Nyburg. Published by The International Council of Shopping Centers, 54 Park Ave., New York 16, N. Y.

Generally speaking, the amount of money spent for promotions should be higher in the first few years of operation or until the center has the fullest acceptance throughout its trade area. "To accomplish this, you must have clearly defined, workable campaigns and top-level cooperation among the center's retailers."

The type of promotion undertaken by the center is important for its growth. The purpose of a promotion is the attraction of customers and not just curious crowds. "Pack the stores, not the parking lots" is a maxim that applies to promotional events. Carnival-type promotions have their purpose, but their limit should be the offering of attractive merchandise and sound values during the events.

The larger the center, the more it must be promoted. The first job is to build customer attraction based on the public's knowing that the center offers competitive merchandise as well as convenient parking. To build this appeal, shopping centers can make a present-day approach to retailing and can depart from many formal methods followed by downtown stores.

Shopping center promotional activities vary greatly. However, cooperative advertising heads the list of activities in the frequency of cases in which it is used. Newspaper and radio advertising are the media relied upon primarily. Constant bulletins to merchants to be sure that they understand the scheme of a forthcoming promotion and that they will cooperate on all promotions is extremely important.

1. Seasonal Decorations and Events

Christmas, Easter, Hallowe'en, etc.—decorations followed by special events which highlight the decorations are the most fre-

Illustration No. 105. Shopping Center Promotions—A Style Show

View of style show held periodically in the weather-condi tioned mall, Southdale, a regional center, Edina, Minn.

"The shopping center promotion program must create medi if such media is not already available. The individual ten ant or the collection of all individual tenants will hav advertising budgets much greater than the Merchants Asso ciation's budget for the Center. How this large fund o advertising money is spent, and if it is spent, will have tremendous impact on the success of the center. The avail ability of and the effectiveness of this advertising fund i largely determined by the tenants who are brought into th merchants association through the leasing program."

Southdale Shopping Center, Edina, Min
Photo: Courtesy, J. Martel Rud, Publicity Manage

W. WOOLWORTH CO.

Illustration No. 106.

Shopping Center Promotions—Opening Day

Pre-opening and Opening Day promotions are the beginning of a continuous series of programs and events which all tenants through the center's Merchants Association must support and participate in. The Merchants Association, its assessment formula and basis of membership are part of the leasing program for successful operation of any shopping center.

Los Altos Shopping Center, Long Beach, Calif.
Photo: Courtesy, L. S. Whaley Company, Owners/Developers

quent promotional activity engaged in by merchants associations and shopping center managers. Other promotional schemes worth noting are give-aways, children's attractions, and special sales, such as birthday or anniversary events. A "Suburban Living Fair" can replace the old midsummer clearance affairs. Northgate finds that style promotion events are always benefited by using live models in show windows to illustrate such things as patio cooking, children playing with children's play equipment, etc.

Whatever promotional activities are used, the wider the participation by the tenants, the greater will be the force and success of the promotion. Joint participation enables small tenants to bid for business through methods ordinarily limited to the field of large merchandising enterprises.

2. Group Advertising

It is important to advertise the center. In the public's mind the individual shops within the center must be associated with the center itself.

Northgate uses a lot of daytime radio advertising and finds these spot announcements a very helpful way to reach the public. Northgate's method of weekly full-page newspaper advertising is worth noting. The Northgate Company contracts with the paper for the page ad in its own name. Then space is sold to the Center's individual merchants at a lower rate than they would have to pay on small linage contracts were they to advertise separately. In this way the advertising is identified with the Northgate masthead. Filling up the full page ad each week may not be an easy job for management, but the results in building sales volumes are worth the effort.

In summary, there are several prerequisites for a successful shopping center operation: A strong, enthusiastic merchants association; a general manager provided by the owner, who has a free hand, promotional know-how, and a knowledge of mer-

Illustration No. 107.

Shopping Center Promotions—Pack the Stores, Not the Parking Lots

In considering promotional events it is important to use those things which will pack the stores and not just the parking lots.

Photo: Courtesy, Roy P. Drachman

chandising; a developer-owner who is keenly interested in promoting the center.[226]

E. A FINAL NOTE

Shopping centers have emerged in the decade of the 1950's to the point of being an accepted building type and merchandising complex. Principles for their planning, development and operation have grown out of successful practices and experiences—and some unfortunate failures. During the 1960's as more and more shopping centers open their doors for business, the matter of sound management grows in importance. The extent to which an operation turns out to be as was hoped for depends largely upon the degree to which consideration is given to these development high points: Good location with respect to access from the trading area; proper relation of the stores with respect to their size and their merchandising ability for serving the trade area; proper site planning; sound leasing; adequate and suitable promotional activities on the part of tenants in behalf of the center; and sound operating procedures.

---

[226] As a complete guide to shopping center management and promotion, see *Operation Shopping Centers: Guidebook to Effective Management and Promotion,* compiled by Donald L. Curtiss. This guide is scheduled for publication by Urban Land Institute on or about March 1961.

Concluding Statement for the Handbook

In this volume, the Community Builders' Council has attempted to record the conclusions and suggestions which have been developed collectively through its deliberations on the subject of community development, and which, in turn, are the result of the extensive individual experience of its members in this field. The Council is convinced that through the application of these principles to community development, more permanent, attractive, and stable residential and commercial areas will result in our cities which will be directly reflected in sounder, more durable health, social, financial, and civic values.

In this process, the Council urges the greatest cooperation and consultation with the public officials and departments of the local governments who represent the community. In turn, it is urged that these officials and departments give serious attention to the multitude of problems which confront the community builder in his undertaking, and with which obviously they cannot always be fully acquainted. It is the hope of the Council that many of the practical considerations which must govern new community development have been pointed out. Community building as a cooperative undertaking cannot be solved by unduly rigid, extravagant, and drastic public regulations without greatly hampering the potentialities of the development itself and the city as a whole. It is through this kind of reciprocal cooperation that the fullest extent of enduring values can be realized.

American cities have been notorious for the vast losses which occur each decade in large segments of our urban areas through the building up and tearing down process. Sound community development, built in terms of generations instead of decades, will go far toward helping to remove this destructive process through providing better living environment for our citizens, preventing future slums, and maintaining the stable and reliable taxable values which are so necessary to the financial support of the governmental unit of which the community is a part.

This edition of the *Community Builders Handbook* is devoted to the challenge of creating new communities through intelligent and realistic planning and building for an environment which offers people what they need and want in their daily lives consistent with the American principles of private enterprise.

Appendices

APPENDICES

Appendix A

PROTECTIVE COVENANTS

For Developments of Single-Family Detached Dwellings Recommended by the Federal Housing Administration

This information is offered as a general guide to sponsors who desire to obtain for individual properties maximum protection against inharmonious land uses.

(SOURCE: FHA Land Planning Bulletin No. 3—Protective Covenants Data Sheet 40, Rev. 4/59)

SAMPLE CLAUSES

PART A. PREAMBLE

(Include the date, purposes, names and addresses of all parties and legal descriptions of all lands involved.)

PART B. AREA OF APPLICATION

B-1. FULLY-PROTECTED RESIDENTIAL AREA. The residential area covenants in Part C in their entirety shall apply to ______________________
(Include entire subdivision or suitable portion of it. Include any adjoining land in other ownership to which all residential covenants are to apply.)

B-2. PARTIALLY-PROTECTED ADJOINING RESIDENTIAL AREA. The residential area covenants numbered ____________ and ____________ in Part C shall apply to ____

B-3. PARK AREA. The park area covenants in Part D shall apply to ___
____

B-4. CIVIC AREA. The civic area covenants in Part E shall apply to ___
____
(Areas, if any, for churches, community buildings, schools, etc.)

B-5. BUSINESS AREA. The business area covenants in Part F shall apply to ____

PART C. RESIDENTIAL AREA COVENANTS

C-1. LAND USE AND BUILDING TYPE. No lot shall be used except for residential purposes. No building shall be erected, altered, placed, or permitted to remain on any lot other than one detached single-family dwelling not to exceed two and one-half stories in height and a private garage for not more than two cars.

C-2. ARCHITECTURAL CONTROL. No building shall be erected, placed, or altered on any lot until the construction plans and specifications and a plan showing the location of the structure have been approved by the Architectural Control Committee as to quality of workmanship and materials, harmony of external design with existing structures, and as to location with respect to topography and finish grade elevation. No fence or wall shall be erected, placed or altered on any lot nearer to any street than the minimum building setback line unless similarly approved. Approval shall be as provided in part G.

C-3. DWELLING COST, QUALITY AND SIZE. No dwelling shall be permitted on any lot at a cost of less than $_____________ based upon cost levels prevailing on the date these covenants are recorded, it being the intention and purpose of the covenant to assure that all dwellings shall be of a quality of workmanship and materials substantially the same or better than that which can be produced on the date these covenants are recorded at the minimum cost stated herein for the minimum permitted dwelling size. The ground floor area of the main structure, exclusive of one-story open porches and garages, shall be not less than __________ square feet for a one-story dwelling, nor less than ____________ square feet for a dwelling of more than one story.

C-4. Building Location.

(a) No building shall be located on any lot nearer to the front lot line or nearer to the side street line than the minimum building setback lines shown on the recorded plat. In any event no building shall be located on any lot nearer than __________ feet to the front lot line, or nearer than __________ feet to any side street line, except that on all lots abutting ____________________ (*collector and arterial streets*) no building shall be located nearer than ____________ and __________ feet respectively to the street property lines of said streets.

(b) No building shall be located nearer than __________ feet to an interior lot line, except that no side yard shall be required for a garage or other permitted accessory building located __________ feet or more from the minimum building setback line. No dwelling shall be located on any interior lot nearer than __________ feet to the rear lot line.

(c) For the purposes of this covenant, eaves, steps, and open porches shall not be considered as a part of a building, provided, however, than this shall not be construed to permit any portion of a building, on a lot to encroach upon another lot.

(d) (*Include any exceptions by lot number and permitted minimum.*)

(e) (*Use of the following clause permits greater flexibility necessary in controlling house locations on steep topography.*)

With written approval of the Architectural Control Committee, a one-story attached garage may be located nearer to a street than above provided, but not nearer than __________ feet to any street line, where the natural elevation of the lot along the established minimum building setback line is more than either eight feet above or four feet below the established roadway level along the abutting street and where in the opinion of said committee the location and architectural design of such proposed garage will not detract materially from the appearance and value of other properties. Furthermore, under similar conditions and approval, a dwelling may be located nearer to a street than above provided, but not nearer than __________ feet to any street line.

C-5. Lot Area and Width. No dwelling shall be erected or placed on any lot having a width of less than __________ feet at the minimum building setback line nor shall any dwelling be erected or placed on any lot having an area of less than __________ square feet, except that a dwelling may be erected or placed on lots numbered ________________ as shown on the recorded plat.

C-6. Easements. Easements for installation and maintenance of utilities and drainage facilities are reserved as shown on the recorded plat and over the rear five feet of each lot. Within these easements, no structure, planting or other material shall be placed or permitted to remain which may damage or interfere with the installation and maintenance of utilities, or which may change the direction of flow of drainage channels in the easements, or which may obstruct or retard the flow of water through drainage channels in the easements. The easement area of each lot and all improvements in it shall be maintained continuously by the owner of the lot, except for those improvements for which a public authority or utility company is responsible.

C-7. NUISANCES. No noxious or offensive activity shall be carried on upon any lot, nor shall anything be done thereon which may be or may become an annoyance or nuisance to the neighborhood.

C-8. TEMPORARY STRUCTURES. No structure of a temporary character, trailer, basement, tent, shack, garage, barn, or other outbuilding shall be used on any lot at any time as a residence either temporarily or permanently.

C-9. SIGNS. No sign of any kind shall be displayed to the public view on any lot except one professional sign of not more than one square foot, one sign of not more than five square feet advertising the property for sale or rent, or signs used by a builder to advertise the property during the construction and sales period.

C-10. OIL AND MINING OPERATIONS. No oil drilling, oil development operations, oil refining, quarrying or mining operations of any kind shall be permitted upon or in any lot, nor shall oil wells, tanks, tunnels, mineral excavations or shafts be permitted upon or in any lot. No derrick or other structure designed for use in boring for oil or natural gas shall be erected, maintained or permitted upon any lot.

C-11. LIVESTOCK AND POULTRY. No animals, livestock, or poultry of any kind shall be raised, bred or kept on any lot, except that dogs, cats or other household pets may be kept provided that they are not kept, bred, or maintained for any commercial purpose.

C-12. GARBAGE AND REFUSE DISPOSAL. No lot shall be used or maintained as a dumping ground for rubbish. Trash, garbage or other waste shall not be kept except in sanitary containers. All incinerators or other equipment for the storage or disposal of such material shall be kept in a clean and sanitary condition.

C-13. WATER SUPPLY. No individual water-supply system shall be permitted on any lot unless such system is located, constructed and equipped in accordance with the requirements, standards and recommendations of ____________________ (*state or local public health authority*). Approval of such system as installed shall be obtained from such authority.

C-14. SEWAGE DISPOSAL. No individual sewage-disposal system shall be permitted on any lot unless such system is designed, located and constructed in accordance with the requirements, standards and recommendations of __________________________ (*state or local public health authority*). Approval of such system as installed shall be obtained from such authority.

C-15. PROTECTIVE SCREENING. Protective screening areas are established as shown on the recorded plat, including a ________ foot strip of land on the residential lots along the property lines of ______________________ _________________________ (*arterial streets, other streets having adverse influences, business areas, etc.*). Except as otherwise provided herein regarding street intersections under "Sight Distance at Intersections", planting, fences or walls shall be maintained throughout the entire length of such areas by the owner or owners of the lots at their own expense to form an effective screen for the protection of the residential area. No building or structure except a screen fence or wall or utilities or drainage facilities shall be placed or permitted to remain in such areas. No vehicular access over the area shall be permitted except for the purpose of installation and maintenance of screening, utilities and drainage facilities.

C-16. SLOPE CONTROL AREAS. Slope control areas are reserved as shown on the plan titled "____________", dated " ____________", and recorded as a part of these covenants. Affected lots are ________________ and ______________, as shown on the recorded subdivision plat. Within these slope control areas no structure, planting or other material shall be placed or permitted to remain or other activities undertaken which may damage or interfere with established slope ratios, create erosion or sliding problems, or which may change the direction of flow of drainage channels or obstruct or retard the flow of water through drainage channels. The slope control areas of each lot and all improvements in them shall be maintained continuously by the owner of the lot, except for those improvements for which a public authority or utility company is responsible.

C-17. SIGHT DISTANCE AT INTERSECTIONS. No fence, wall, hedge or shrub planting which obstructs sight lines at elevations between 2 and 6 feet above the roadways shall be placed or permitted to remain on any corner lot within the triangular area formed by the street property lines and a line connecting them at points 25 feet from the intersection of the street lines, or the case of a rounded property corner from the intersection of the street property lines extended. The same sight-line limitations shall apply on any lot within 10 feet from the intersection of a street property line with the edge of a driveway or alley pavement. No tree shall be permitted to remain within such distances of such intersections unless the foliage line is maintained at sufficient height to prevent obstruction of such sight lines.

C-18. LAND NEAR PARKS AND WATER COURSES. No building shall be placed nor shall any material or refuse be placed or stored on any lot within 20 feet of the property line of any park or edge of any open water course, except that clean fill may be placed nearer provided that the natural water course is not altered or blocked by such fill.

PART D. PARK AREA COVENANTS

(Include appropriate covenants for any designated area.)

PART E. CIVIC AREA COVENANTS

(Include appropriate covenants for any designated area.)

PART F. BUSINESS AREA COVENANTS

(Include appropriate covenants for any designated area.)

PART G. ARCHITECTURAL CONTROL COMMITTEE

G-1. MEMBERSHIP. The Architectural Control Committee is composed of

----

(Names and addresses of three members)

A majority of the committee may designate a representative to act for it. In the event of death or resignation of any member of the committee, the remaining members shall have full authority to designate a successor. Neither the members of the committee, nor its designated representative shall be entitled to any compensation for services performed pursuant to this covenant. At any time, the then record owners of a majority of the lots shall have the power through a duly recorded written instrument to change the membership of the committee or to withdraw from the committee or restore to it any of its powers and duties.

G-2. PROCEDURE. The committee's approval or disapproval as required in these covenants shall be in writing. In the event the committee, or its designated representative, fails to approve or disapprove within 30 days after plans and specifications have been submitted to it, or in any event, if no suit to enjoin the construction has been commenced prior to the completion thereof, approval will not be required and the related covenants shall be deemed to have been fully complied with.

PART H. GENERAL PROVISIONS

H-1. Term. These covenants are to run with the land and shall be binding on all parties and all persons claiming under them for a period of thirty years from the date these covenants are recorded, after which time said covenants shall be automatically extended for successive periods of 10 years unless an instrument signed by a majority of the then owners of the lots has been recorded, agreeing to change said covenants in whole or in part.

H-2. Enforcement. Enforcement shall be by proceedings at law or in equity against any person or persons violating or attempting to violate any covenant either to restrain violation or to recover damages.

H-3. Severability. Invalidation of any one of these covenants by judgment or court order shall in no wise affect any of the other provisions which shall remain in full force and effect.

PART J. ATTEST

(Include the date and signature of all parties. Include signatures of prior lien holders to evidence consent to subordination of existing lien to covenants.)

REQUIREMENTS REGARDING PROTECTIVE COVENANTS

These requirements are a part of FHA Neighborhood Requirements. They apply in residential developments in which properties are offered or are to be offered as security for FHA insured mortgages. They apply in their entirety to developments proposed on unimproved land under centralized control. For other developments they apply to the extent determined by the local FHA office.

Area of Application. Protective covenants shall apply to the entire area of development and, to the extent necessary for adequate protection, to adjacent areas which may affect properties in the development. If a tract is to be developed progressively by sections, complete protective covenants shall be applied initially for the entire development or progressively for the protection of each section.

Land Use. The covenants shall provide adequate protection of neighborhood quality and property values by appropriate regulation in both residential areas and any non-residential areas of:

a. Land use and building type.
b. Size, quality, design and location of structures.
c. Lot size.
d. Easements.
e. Nuisances.
f. Other objectionable uses.

Property-Owners' Association. The covenants shall establish an appropriate property-owners' committee or association as necessary for architectural control, for maintenance of any neighborhood improvements not otherwise provided with suitable maintenance, and for any other appropriate neighborhood services.

Recordation. The protective covenants shall be effective for an appropriate stated period of time, properly executed and recorded in the public land records.

Appendix B

Sample Form

PROTECTIVE COVENANTS

Conditions, Covenants, Restrictions, and Easements Affecting Property of the ____________________________ Corporation.

THIS DECLARATION, made this _____ day of ______________, by the ______________________ Corporation, hereinafter called the Declarant,

WITNESSETH:

WHEREAS, Declarant is the owner of the real property described in Clause I of this Declaration, and is desirous of subjecting the real property described in said Clause I to the restrictions, covenants, reservations, easements, liens and charges hereinafter set forth, each and all of which is and are for the benefit of said property and for each owner thereof, and shall inure to the benefit of and pass with said property, and each and every parcel thereof, and shall apply to and bind the successors in interest, and any owner thereof;

NOW, THEREFORE, ______ Corporation hereby declares that the real property described in and referred to in Clause I hereof is, and shall be, held, transferred, sold and conveyed subject to the conditions, restrictions, covenants, reservations, easements, liens and charges hereinafter set forth.

Definition of Terms

Building Site shall mean any lot, or portion thereof, or any two or more contiguous lots, or a parcel of land of record and in a single ownership and upon which a dwelling may be erected in conformance with the requirements of these Covenants.

Corporation shall mean the ____________________________ Corporation.

Association shall refer to the Homes Association of the tract covered by these Covenants or any extension thereof as herein provided.

CLAUSE I.

Property Subject to This Declaration

The real property which is, and shall be, held and shall be conveyed, transferred and sold subject to the conditions, restrictions, covenants, reservations, easements, liens and charges with respect to the various portions thereof set forth in the various clauses and subdivisions of this Declaration is located in the County of ______________, State of __________________, and is more particularly described as follows, to-wit: (Insert legal description.)

No property other than that described above shall be deemed subject to this Declaration, unless and until specifically made subject thereto.

The declarant may, from time to time, subject additional real property to the conditions, restrictions, covenants, reservations, liens and charges herein set forth by appropriate reference hereto.

CLAUSE II.

General Purposes of Conditions

The real property described in Clause I hereof is subjected to the covenants, restrictions, conditions, reservations, liens and charges hereby declared to insure the best use and the most appropriate development and improvement of each building site thereof; to protect the owners of building sites against such improper use of surrounding building sites as will depreciate the value of their property; to preserve, so far as practicable, the natural beauty of said property; to guard against the erection thereon of poorly designed or proportioned structures, and structures built of improper or unsuitable materials; to obtain harmonious color schemes; to insure the highest and best development of said property; to encourage and secure the erection of attractive homes thereon, with appropriate locations thereof on building sites; to prevent haphazard and inharmonious improvement of building sites; to secure and maintain proper setbacks from streets, and adequate free spaces between structures; and in general to provide adequately for a high type and quality of improvement in said property, and thereby to enhance the values of investments made by purchasers of building sites therein.

A All Building sites in the tract shall be known and described as residential building sites, except ______________________________
(Describe areas to be designated
______________________________ No
in separate covenant for retail business, schools, churches, etc.)
structures shall be erected, altered, placed, or permitted to remain on any building site other than one detached single-family dwelling not to exceed two and one-half stories in height, a private garage for not more than three cars, guest house, servants' quarters, and other outbuildings incidental to residential use of the premises.

B No building shall be erected, placed, or altered on any premises in said development until the building plans, specifications, and plot plan showing the location of such building have been approved in writing as to conformity and harmony of external design with existing structures in the development, and as to location of the building with respect to topography and finished ground elevation, by an architectural committee composed of ____________, ____________, and ____________, or by a representative designated by a majority of the members of said committee. In the event of death or resignation of any member of said committee, the remaining member, or members, shall have full authority to approve or disapprove such design and location, or to designate a representative with like authority. In the event said committee, or its designated representative, fails to approve or disapprove such design and location within 30 days after said plans and specifications have been submitted to it or, in any event, if no suit to enjoin the erection of such building or the making of such alterations has been commenced prior to the completion thereof, such approval will not be required and this Covenant will be deemed to have been fully complied with. Neither the members of such committee, nor its designated representative shall be entitled to any compensation for services performed pursuant to this Covenant.

C No building shall be located on any building site less than ______ feet from the front lot line for all sites covered by these covenants, nor less than ______ feet from any side street line. No building shall be located less than _____ feet from any side lot line or _____ feet from any building on the same site, except a detached garage or other outbuilding located in the rear yard may be placed _____ feet from the side line. No residence shall be so located as to reduce the rear yard of the plot on which it is located to less than _____ feet.

D No residential structure shall be erected or placed on any building site, which has an area of less than ______ square feet or a width of less than ______ feet at the front building setback line for interior lots, and less than ______ feet for corner lots.

E No noxious or offensive trade or activity shall be carried on upon any building site nor shall anything be done thereon which may be or become an annoyance or nuisance to the neighborhood.

F No trailer, basement, tent, shack, garage, barn, or other outbuilding other than guest houses and servants' quarters erected on a building site covered by these Covenants shall at any time be used for human habitation temporarily or permanently, nor shall any structure of a temporary character be used for human habitation.

The keeping of a mobile home or travel trailer, either with or without wheels, on any parcel of property covered by these covenants is prohibited. A motor boat, house boat or other similar water borne vehicle may be maintained, stored, or kept on any parcel of property covered by these covenants only if housed completely within a structure which has been architecturally approved by provisions of paragraph B hereof.

G No main residential structure shall be permitted on any building site covered by these covenants, the habitable floor area of which, exclusive of basements, porches, and garages, is less than ______ square feet in the case of a one-story structure or less than ______ square feet in the case of a one and one-half, two, or two and one-half story structure.

H Where no alleys are provided, an easement is hereby reserved over the rear five feet of each building site for utility installation and maintenance.

I No animals or poultry of any kind other than house pets shall be kept or maintained on any part of said property.

J The premises hereby conveyed shall not be occupied, leased, rented, conveyed or otherwise alienated, nor shall the title or possession thereof pass to another without the written consent of the Grantor, except that the Grantor shall not withhold such consent if and after a written consent is given to permit such occupation, leasing, renting, conveyance or alienation by a majority of the owners of the fifteen (15) building sites included within these covenants most immediately adjacent to the said premises, and which adjoin or face said premises for a distance of five (5) building sites from the respective side lines of said premises, and also the five (5) building sites which are most immediately adjacent thereto and across any street upon which said premises front; except transfer of title by way of devise or inheritance, in which case the devisee or heir shall take such property subject to the restrictions herein imposed, and except that said property may be mortgaged or subjected to judicial sale, provided, in any such case, that no purchaser of said premises at judicial sale shall have the right to occupy, lease, rent, convey or otherwise alienate said premises without the written consent of the Grantor first had and obtained in the manner above stated.

In the event there is a total of less than fifteen (15) building sites which meet the consent requirements of this Section, then a sufficient number of the most immediately adjacent building sites included within these covenants and lying to the rear of said premises shall be included to obtain the required fifteen (15) building sites.

It is understood, however, that the rights hereby reserved to the Grantor shall apply with equal force and effect to its successors and assigns; but in the event the ownership and control of the rights hereby reserved, pass from the hands of the Corporation, either by reason of the appointment of a Receiver, assignment for the benefit of creditors, bankruptcy, by sale under legal process of any kind, by the transfer of the ownership of a majority stock to other than the Corporation's interests, or otherwise, the provision for consents by the Grantor in this Section J, provided for, shall be deemed to be sufficiently obtained when obtained only from a majority of the owners of the said adjoining and facing building sites, as specified in Section J herein, and thenceforth the right to enforce the restrictions in this Section J of this deed contained shall immediately pass to the said owners of the said adjoining and facing building sites.

K No fence, wall, hedge, or mass planting shall be permitted to extend beyond the minimum building setback line established herein except upon approval by the architectural committee as provided in Section B.

L Oil drilling, oil development operations; refining, mining operations of any kind, or quarrying shall not be permitted upon or in any of the building sites in the tract described herein, nor shall oil wells, tanks, tunnels, mineral excavations or shafts be permitted upon or in any of the building sites covered by these Covenants.

M The owner of each building site to which these covenants apply shall be entitled to one membership in a Homes Association and to participate in the operation of the Association in accordance with the bylaws of said Association filed herewith.[1]

[1] The paragraph as here written provides for an optional membership in the Association. Some developers prefer to provide that the owner of each building site "automatically becomes a member" of the Association otherwise anyone who wishes could decline membership in the Association and thus avoid payment of the Association's assessments.

N These Covenants are to run with the land and shall be binding on all parties and all persons claiming under them until January 1, 19___, (twenty-five year period), at which time said Covenants shall be automatically extended for successive periods of 10[2] years unless by vote of a majority of the then owners of the building sites covered by these covenants it is agreed to change said covenants in whole or in part.

If the parties hereto, or any of them, or their heirs or assigns, shall violate or attempt to violate any of the Covenants herein, it shall be lawful for any other person or persons owning any real property situated in said tract, or the Homes Association as provided in Section M, to prosecute any proceedings at law or in equity against the person or persons violating or attempting to violate any such Covenant, and either to prevent him or them from so doing or to recover damages or other dues for such violation.

O Invalidation of any one of these Covenants or any part thereof by judgments or court order shall in no wise affect any of the other provisions which shall remain in full force and effect.

---

[2] Some developers recommend as high as a 40 year initial period with successive extensions of 25 years.

Appendix C

Sample Form

DECLARATION OF INCORPORATION OF ________________________ HOMES ASSOCIATION

This declaration made on this _______ day of ________________, 19__, by ____________________________________, a corporation of the State of ___________________________, the owner of property set opposite its name below, and those individuals whose names are subscribed hereto as the owners of the lots set opposite their respective names.

WITNESSETH: That whereas, ________________________ Corporation is now developing parts of said _________________ (Subdivision) for high class residential purposes, and it is the desire to continue the development of certain parts of such land and other land in this vicinity for such purposes, and for the creation and maintenance of a residential community possessing features of more than ordinary value to a residential community, and

WHEREAS, In order to assist it and its grantees in providing the necessary means to better enable it and its grantees to bring this about, the parties hereto do now and hereby subject all of the property, described below to the following covenants, charges and assessments.

KNOW ALL MEN BY THESE PRESENTS:

That we, the undersigned, have this day voluntarily associated ourselves together for the purpose of forming a non-profit corporation under the laws of the State of ________________, and we do hereby certify:

SECTION 1. That the name of this corporation is:

"____________________" HOMES ASSOCIATION

SECTION 2. That this corporation, hereafter referred to as the Association, is a corporation which does not contemplate pecuniary gain or profit to the members thereof, and that the purposes for which it is formed are:

(a) To exercise its powers and functions on the following described real property situated in the Town of ________________, ______________ County, State of __________________, and more particularly described as follows:

All of the real property shown on that certain map entitled, "____________________", ____________________ County, ________________, filed in the office of the Town Clerk of the Town of _________________ on ____________________ (Date) ____, ____.

Together with any and all other real property which may hereafter, through the operation of conditions, covenants, restrictions, easements, reservations or charges pertaining to the same, be placed under or submitted to the jurisdiction of this Association, and be accepted as within the jurisdiction of this Association by resolution of the Board of Directors of this Association (which said real property hereinabove specifically described, together with the property hereafter within the jurisdiction of this Association as above provided, is referred to as "said property").

(b) To care for vacant, unimproved and unkempt lots in said property, remove and destroy grass, weeds and rodents therefrom, and any unsightly and obnoxious thing therefrom, and to do any other things, and perform any labor necessary or desirable in the judgment of this Association to keep the property, and the land contiguous and adjacent thereto neat and in good order.

(c) To pay the taxes and assessments, if any, which may be levied by any governmental authority upon roads and parks in said property, and any other open spaces maintained, and lands used or acquired for the general use of the owners of lots or building sites within said property, and on any property of this Association, or which may be held in trust for this Association.

(d) To enforce charges, restrictions, conditions and covenants existing upon and created for the benefit of said property over which this Association has jurisdiction; to pay all expenses incidental thereto; to enforce the decisions and rulings of this Association having jurisdiction over any of said property; to pay all of the expenses in connection therewith; and to reimburse any declarant under any declaration of conditions, covenants, restrictions, assessments or charges affecting said property, or any part thereof, for all costs and expenses incurred or paid by it in connection with the enforcement, or attempted enforcement, of any of the conditions, covenants, restrictions, charges, assessments or terms set forth in any declaration.

(e) To provide for the maintenance of tennis courts, playgrounds, water areas and other community features on land set aside for the general use of the members of said Association, and to maintain and operate the country club and golf course in proportion to its percentage of membership therein.

(f) To do any and all lawful things and acts which this Association at any time, and from time to time, shall, in its discretion, deem to be to the best interests of said property and the owners of the building sites thereon, and to pay all costs and expenses in connection therewith.

(g) Any powers and duties exercised by said Association relating to maintenance, operation, construction or reconstruction of any facility provided for herein may be contracted for with the ________________ Corporation or other qualified contractor as agent.

(h) To fix the rate per square foot of the annual charges or assessments to which said property shall be made subject; to collect the charges or assessments affecting said property; to pay all expenses in connection therewith, and all office and other expenses incident to the conduct of the business of this Association, and all licenses, franchise taxes, and governmental charges levied or imposed against said property of this Association; such charges or assessments shall become a lien on said property as soon as due and payable. Settlement of such lien shall be made as determined by the Directors of this Association.

(i) To acquire by gift, purchase, or otherwise to own, hold, enjoy, lease, operate, maintain, and to convey, sell, lease, transfer, mortgage, or otherwise encumber, dedicate for public use, or otherwise dispose of real or personal property in connection with the business of this Association.

(j) To expend the money's collected by this Association from assessments or charges and other sums received by this Association for the payment and discharge of all proper costs, expenses and obligations incurred by this Association in carrying out any or all of the purposes for which this Association is formed.

(k) To borrow money; to mortgage, pledge, deed in trust, or hypothecate any or all of its real or personal property as security for money borrowed or debts incurred, and to do any and all things that an association organized under said laws of the State of ________________ may lawfully do, and generally to do and perform any and all other acts which may be either necessary for, or proper or incidental to the exercise of any of the foregoing powers, and such powers as are granted by the provisions of the laws of the State of _______________ to a non-profit corporation.

(l) To do any and all lawful things which may be advisable, proper, authorized or permitted to be done by this Association under and by virtue of any condition, covenant, restriction, reservation, charge, or assessment affecting said property, or any portion thereof, and to do and perform any and all acts which may be either necessary for or incidental to the exercise of any of the foregoing powers, or for the peace, health, comfort, safety, or general welfare of the owners of said property, or any portion thereof, or residents thereon.[1]

SECTION 3. That the town in this state where the principal office for the transaction of the business of this Association is to be located is the Town of ________________, ________________ County, ________________.

SECTION 4. That the number of directors of this Association shall be five; that the names and addresses of the persons who are to act in the capacity of directors until the selection of their successors are as follows:

NAMES ADDRESSES

That the number of directors, as hereinabove set forth, may be changed by a by-law duly adopted pursuant to authority contained in this Declaration of Incorporation, and authority is hereby granted to change the number of directors by an amendment to the by-laws of this Association which by-laws shall be adopted in accordance with the terms of this declaration.

[1] An additional clause may be added giving the Association general authority to cover other matters as the need may arise.

SECTION 5. The members of this Association shall be:

(a) All persons who are owners of record of any building site in said property, provided that no person or corporation taking title as security for the payment of money or the performance of any obligation shall thereby become entitled to membership.

(b) All persons who reside on a building site in said property, and who are purchasing such building site under a contract or agreement of purchase.

Such ownership or such residence and the purchasing of such building site under a contract or agreement of purchase shall be the only qualifications for membership in this Association.

When a building site is owned of record in joint tenancy or tenancy in common, or when two or more residents are purchasing a building site under a contract or agreement of purchase, the membership as to such building site shall be joint and the right of such membership (including the voting power arising therefrom) shall be exercised only by the joint action of all owners of record of such building site, or of all purchasers under said contract or agreement of purchase, respectively.

Membership in this Association shall lapse and terminate when any member shall cease to be the owner of record of a building site, or upon any member ceasing to be a resident on a building site in said property or a purchaser thereof under a contract or agreement of purchase.

A building site for the purpose of this Declaration of Incorporation shall be taken to be and mean a building site as defined in the protective covenants covering the portion of said property in which the building site is located.

The voting power of members of this Association shall be limited to one vote for each building site, as defined in the covenants covering said property, owned or under purchase contract by such members.[1]

The owner or contract purchaser of any building site which is or may hereafter be included within the jurisdiction of this Association shall be automatically eligible for membership in the _______________ Country Club to the extent of two persons for each building site so owned or under contract, without the payment of an initiation fee and including all usual membership privileges. Such owner or contract purchaser shall, however, be personally responsible for any subsequent annual dues, greens fees, or other fees which may be charged in addition to the general assessments levied by said Association. Membership eligibility without payment of an initiation fee shall lapse and terminate when any person or persons shall cease to be an owner of record or a contract purchaser of a building site within the jurisdiction of said Association.[2]

Each member of this Association shall have such interest in all the property owned by this Association as is represented by the ratio of the number of votes in this Association. Such interest is and shall be ap-

[1] Certain difficulties may arise from this method of representation. Some developers advocate giving only one vote to each owner, including the developer, regardless of the amount of land or number of sites he may hold. This is probably a more democratic method and subject to less misinterpretation. Each developer should decide this question on the basis of his own project and experience.

[2] Clauses referring to the country club should be included only where it is desired that this facility, if provided in the development, be under the Homes Association.

purtenant to the building sites which qualify such person for membership in this Association.

IN WITNESS WHEREOF, for the purpose of forming this Association under the laws of the State of _______________, we, the undersigned, constituting the incorporators of this Association, including the persons hereinabove named as the first directors of this Association, have executed this Declaration of Incorporation this ______ day of ___________, 19___.

Signed: ______________________________
____
____
____
____

The above clauses are designed to fit areas in which municipal authority furnishes most or all of the municipal services. If the development lies in an area where municipal services are not provided, or plan approval is to be included, additional clauses similar to the following should be added under Section 2:

(1) To improve, light, provide for, beautify, and maintain streets, parks, and other open spaces, including all grass plots, park strips, other planted areas and trees and shrubs within the lines of said streets in and bordering upon said property as shall be maintained for public use, or for the general use of the owners of lots or building sites in said property, but only until such time as such services are adequately provided by public authority.

(2) To sweep, clean and sprinkle the streets within and bordering upon and adjacent to said property; to collect and dispose of street sweepings, garbage, rubbish, and the like from said property; to provide for community police and fire protection of said property, and to construct, maintain and keep in repair fire hydrants and mains, sewers, and any sewage disposal systems, but only until such time as such services are adequately provided for by public authority.

(3) To pay for the examination and approval, or disapproval, of plans, specifications, color schemes, block plans and grading plans for any building, outhouse, garage, stable, fence, wall, retaining wall, or other structure of any kind which shall be erected, constructed, placed or maintained on said property, or any part thereof, and for any alteration, condition, changing, repairing, remodeling, or adding to the exterior thereof, and for such supervision of construction and inspection as may be required to insure compliance therewith, including the services of architects and other persons employed to examine and advise upon such plans, specifications, color schemes, block plans, and grading plans.

If it is desired to define the voting and property rights and interests of members of the association in more detail, clauses should be added similar to those in Article III of Association By-Laws, page 411.

Appendix D

Sample Form

BY-LAWS
OF
________________________ HOMES ASSOCIATION

ARTICLE I

Definitions

Section 1—The words "said property" as used in these By-Laws shall be deemed to mean the following described real property situated in the County of ____________________, State of ___________________, and more particularly described as follows:

All of the real property shown on that certain map entitled, "____" filed in the office of the County Recorder of the County of ______________, State of _________________, on _________________ ______, ______, in (Date) Map Book ________.

Together with any and all other real property which may hereafter, through the operation of conditions, covenants, restrictions, easements, reservations or charges pertaining to the same, be placed under or submitted to the jurisdiction of this Corporation and be accepted as within the jurisdiction of this corporation by resolution of the Board of Directors of this corporation.

Section 2—The words "building site" wherever used in these By-Laws shall be deemed to mean a building site as defined in any declaration of conditions, covenants, restrictions, easements, reservations or charges affecting the portion of said property in which the building site is located.

ARTICLE II

Membership

Section 1—The members of this corporation shall be:

(a) All persons who are owners of record of any building site in said property, provided that no person or corporation taking title as security for the payment of money or the performance of any obligation shall thereby become entitled to membership.

(b) All persons who reside on a building site in said property, and who are purchasing such building site under a contract or agreement of purchase.

Such ownership or such residence and the purchasing of such building site under a contract or agreement of purchase shall be the only qualifications for membership in this corporation.

When a building site is owned of record in joint tenancy or tenancy in common, or when two or more residents are purchasing a building site under a contract or agreement of purchase, the membership as to such building site shall be joint and the right of such membership (including the voting power arising therefrom) shall be exercised only by the joint action of all owners of record of such building site, or of all purchasers under said contract or agreement of purchase, respectively.

Any person claiming to be a member in this corporation shall establish his right to membership to the satisfaction of the Secretary of this corporation. No membership or initiation fee shall be charged, nor shall members be required to pay at any time any amount to carry on the business of this corporation, except to pay annually the charges or assessments set forth in the declaration of conditions, covenants, restrictions, easements and charges dated the ________ day of ______________, ______, executed by __________________________________ Company, and recorded on the ________ day of _________________, ______, in the office of the County Recorder of the County of ___________________, State of __________________, in Volume ______ of Official Records at page ______ thereof, or as set forth in any other declaration affecting any portion of said property.

Membership in this corporation shall lapse and terminate when any member shall cease to be the owner of record of a building site, or upon any member ceasing to be a resident on a building site in said property and a purchaser thereof under a contract or agreement of purchase.

ARTICLE III

Voting Rights

Section 1—In all matters which shall come before the members of this corporation, and in all corporate matters, the voting power of the members of this corporation shall be unequal, according to the following rules:

(a) Except as provided in (d) of this section, each member of this corporation shall have at least one vote.

(b) Except as provided in (d) of this section, each member of this corporation owning of record one or more building sites shall have the right to the number of votes equal to the total number of building sites of which he is the owner of record.[1]

(c) Except as provided in (d) of this section, each purchaser who is a resident on a building site and is purchasing it under a contract or agreement of purchase shall be entitled to one vote.

(d) When a building site is owned of record in joint tenancy or tenancy in common, or when two or more residents are purchasing a building site under a contract or agreement of purchase and residing thereon, the several owners or purchasers of said building site shall collectively be entitled to one vote only therefor.

ARTICLE IV

Property Rights

Section 1—Each member of this corporation shall have such an interest in all of the property owned by this corporation as is represented by the ratio of the number of votes to which said member is entitled to

[1] See footnote 1 on page 408.

the total number of votes in this corporation. Such interest is and shall be appurtenant to the building sites in all said property which qualify such person for membership in this corporation.

ARTICLE V

Corporate Powers

Section 1—The corporate powers of this corporation shall be vested in, exercised by, and under the authority of, and the business and affairs of this corporation shall be controlled by a board of five directors. The directors, other than those named in the Articles of Incorporation shall be members of the corporation. Three of said directors shall constitute a quorum for the transaction of business.

ARTICLE VI

Election of Directors

Section 1—The directors named in the Articles of Incorporation of this corporation shall hold office until the next annual meeting thereafter and until their successors are elected, either at an annual meeting or at a special meeting called for that purpose, unless otherwise provided by the By-Laws of this corporation.

Section 2—Unless otherwise provided by the By-Laws of this corporation, the Directors, other than those named in the Articles of Incorporation, shall be elected at the annual meeting of the members, and shall hold office until their successors are elected.

Section 3—Unless otherwise provided by the By-Laws of this corporation, the term of office of any director shall begin immediately after election. The term of office of members of the Board of Directors of this corporation may be determined by a majority of the members of this corporation and may, from time to time, be changed if demanded in writing by a majority of the members of this corporation.

Section 4—Upon the sale of fifty-one per cent (51%) of the building sites shown on that certain map entitled, ______________________________ ____________________________________ filed in the office of the County Recorder of the County of ________________, State of ________________ on ______________________________, in Map Book ______ at pages ________
(Date)

inclusive, as said building sites are defined in that certain Declaration of conditions, covenants, restrictions, easements and charges dated the ________ day of ____________________, executed by ____________________ Company as Declarant, and recorded in the office of the County Recorder of the County of __________________, State of __________________, on the ________ day of __________________, in Volume ______ of Official Records at page ______ thereof, the terms of office of all members of the Board of Directors of this corporation shall cease and terminate at the date of the first annual meeting of the members thereafter, and thereupon a new board of directors shall be elected by the members of this corporation at a special meeting of the members called for that purpose.

ARTICLE VII

Vacancies

Section 1—Vacancies in the Board of Directors shall be filled by a majority of the remaining directors though less than a quorum, and each director so elected shall hold office until his successor is elected at an annual meeting or at a special meeting called for that purpose. If any director at any time tenders his resignation to the Board of Directors, the Board of Directors shall have power to elect his successor to take effect at such time as the resignation becomes effective.

ARTICLE VIII

Powers of Directors

Section 1—The Board of Directors shall have power:

(a) To call special meetings of the members whenever it deems it necessary, and it shall call a meeting at any time upon written request of the members who have the right to vote at least one-third of all of the votes of the entire membership.

(b) To appoint and remove at pleasure all officers, agents and employees of the corporation, prescribe their duties, fix their compensation, and require from them security or a fidelity bond for faithful performance of the duties to be prescribed for them.

(c) To conduct, manage and control the affairs and business of this corporation, and to make rules and regulations not inconsistent with the laws of the State of ____________________ or the By-Laws of this corporation for the guidance of the officers and management of the affairs of the corporation.

(d) To establish, levy and assess, and collect the charges or assessments referred to in Article II hereof, and to fix the rate per square foot for such charges or assessments within any proper limitation.

(e) To exercise for the corporation all powers, duties and authorities vested in or delegated to this corporation or which it may lawfully exercise.

ARTICLE IX

Duties of Directors

Section 1—It shall be the duty of the Board of Directors:

(a) To cause to be kept a complete record of all of their minutes and acts, and of the proceedings of the members, and present a full statement at the regular annual meeting of the members, showing in detail the assets and liabilities of this corporation, and generally the condition of its affairs. A similar statement shall be presented at any other meeting of the members when required by members who have the right to vote at least one-third of all the votes of the entire membership.

(b) To supervise all officers, agents and employees of this corporation, and to see that their duties are properly performed.

ARTICLE X

Directors' Meetings

Section 1—The annual meeting of the Board of Directors shall be held on the second Monday in February of each year at the hour of 9:00 o'clock P.M.

Section 2—A regular meeting of the Board of Directors shall be held on the second Monday of each month at 2:30 o'clock P.M., provided that the Board of Directors may, by resolution, change the day and hour of holding such regular meetings.

Section 3—Notice of such annual meeting and such regular meeting is hereby dispensed with. If the day for the annual or regular meeting shall fall upon a holiday, the meeting shall be held at the same hour on the first day following which is not a holiday, and no notice thereof need be given.

Section 4—Special meetings of the Board of Directors shall be held when called by the President, the Vice-President, or Secretary or Treasurer, or upon the written request of any two directors. Written notice of each special meeting of the Board of Directors shall be delivered personally to the directors, or given or sent to each director, at least three days before the time for holding said meeting, by letter, postage thereon fully prepaid addressed to the director. Each director shall register his address with the Secretary, and notices of meetings shall be mailed to him at such address.

Section 5—The transactions of any meetings of the Board of Directors, however called and noticed, or wherever held, shall be as valid as though had at a meeting duly held after regular call and notice if a quorum be present, and if either before or after the meeting each of the directors not present sign a written waiver of notice, or a consent to holding such meeting, or an approval of the minutes thereof. All such waivers, consents or approvals shall be filed with the corporate records and made a part of the minutes of the meeting.

Section 6—Every act, or decision, done or made by a majority of the directors present at a meeting duly held at which a quorum is present shall be regarded as the act of the Board of Directors. In the absence of a quorum, the majority of the directors present may adjourn from time to time until the time fixed for the next regular meeting of the Board.

ARTICLE XI

Meetings of Members

Section 1—The regular annual meeting of the members shall be held on the second Monday of the month of February in each year, at the hour of 8:00 o'clock P.M. If the day for the annual meeting of the members shall fall upon a holiday, the meeting shall be held at the same hour on the first day following which is not a holiday.

Section 2—Special meetings of the members for any purpose may be called at any time by the President, the Vice-President, the Secretary, the Treasurer, or by the Board of Directors, or by any two or more members thereof, or upon written request of the members who have the right to vote at least one-third of all of the votes of the entire membership.

Section 3—Notices of annual and special meetings shall be given in writing to the members by the Secretary. Notice may be given to the members either personally, or by sending a copy of the notice through the mail, postage thereon fully prepaid to his address appearing on the books of the corporation. Each member shall register his address with the Secretary and notices of meetings shall be mailed to him at such address. Written notice of each meeting shall, at least three days before the time for holding said meeting, be given or sent to each member by letter, postage thereon fully prepaid addressed to the member. Notice of each annual or special meeting of the members shall specify the place, the date, and the hour of the meeting, and the general nature of the business to be transacted.

Section 4—The transactions at any meeting of the members however called or noticed shall be as valid as though had at a meeting duly held after regular call and notice if a quorum be present, in person or by proxy, if either before or after the meeting each member entitled to vote not present signs a written waiver of notice, or a consent to the holding of such meeting, or approval of the minutes thereof. All such waivers, consents or approvals shall be filed with the corporate records and made a part of the minutes of the meeting. The presence in person or by proxy of a majority of the members of this corporation shall constitute a quorum for the transaction of business. In the absence of a quorum any meeting of the members may be adjourned from time to time by a vote of a majority of the members present, but no other business may be transacted. Members present at any duly called or held meeting at which a quorum is present in person or by proxy may continue to do business notwithstanding the withdrawal of enough members to leave less than a quorum.

ARTICLE XII

Officers

Section 1—The officers of this corporation shall be a President, a Vice-President, who shall at all times be members of the Board of Directors, and a Secretary, and a Treasurer, and such other officers as the Board of Directors may, from time to time, by resolution, create.

Section 2—The officers of this corporation, except such officers as may be appointed in accordance with Sections 3 or 5 of this Article, shall be chosen annually by the Board of Directors, and each shall hold his office for one year unless he shall sooner resign or shall be removed, or otherwise disqualified to serve.

Section 3—The Board of Directors may appoint such other officers as the business of the corporation may require, each of whom shall hold office for such period, have such authority, and perform such duties as the Board of Directors may, from time to time, determine.

Section 4—Any officer may be removed from office either with or without cause by a majority of the Directors at time in office at any annual, regular or special meeting of the Board. Any officer may resign at any time by giving a written notice to the Board of Directors, or to the President, or the Secretary of the corporation. Any such resignation shall take effect at the date of receipt of such notice, or at any later time specified therein, and unless otherwise specified therein the acceptance of such resignation shall not be necessary to make it effective.

Section 5—A vacancy in any office because of death, resignation, removal, disqualification, or other cause shall be filled in the manner prescribed in the By-Laws for regular appointment to such office.

Section 6—The offices of Secretary or Assistant-Secretary, and Treasurer may be held by the same person.

ARTICLE XIII

President

Section 1—The Board of Directors shall at their first regular meeting elect one of their number to act as President, and shall also at said meeting elect a Vice-President.

Section 2—If at any time the President shall be unable to act, the Vice-President shall take his place and perform his duties. If the Vice-President, for any cause, shall be unable to act the Board of Directors shall appoint some member of the Board to act, in whom shall be vested for the time being all the duties and functions of the President.

Section 3—The President, or the Vice-President, or in the absence or inability to act of both the President and the Vice-President, the Director appointed as above provided

(a) Shall preside over all meetings of the members and of the Board of Directors.

(b) Shall sign as President all deeds, contracts and other instruments in writing which have been first approved by the Board of Directors.

(c) Shall call the Directors together whenever he deems it necessary and shall have, subject to the advice of the Board of Directors, general supervision, direction and control of the business affairs of the corporation, and generally shall discharge such other duties as may be required of him by the Board of Directors.

ARTICLE XIV

Vice-President

Section 1—All duties and powers required by law, or by these By-Laws of, and all powers conferred by law or by these By-Laws upon, the President shall, in his absence, inability or refusal to act be performed by the Vice-President.

ARTICLE XV

Secretary and Assistant-Secretary

Section 1—The Board of Directors shall elect a Secretary, and it shall be the duty of the Secretary

(a) To keep a record of all meetings and proceedings of the Board of Directors, and of the members.

(b) To keep the corporate seal of the corporation, and to affix it on all papers requiring the seal of the corporation.

(c) To keep proper books.

(d) To serve notices of meetings of the Board of Directors and the members required either by law or by the By-Laws of this corporation.

(e) To keep appropriate records showing the members of this corporation together with their addresses as furnished him by such members.

Section 2—The Board of Directors may appoint an Assistant Secretary who, in case of the absence, inability or refusal to act of the Secretary shall perform the duties of the Secretary.

Section 3—The Assistant-Secretary shall also perform such other duties as may be required of him by the Board of Directors.

ARTICLE XVI

Treasurer

Section 1—The Treasurer shall receive and deposit in such bank or banks as the Board of Directors may, from time to time, direct, all of the funds of the corporation, which funds shall be withdrawn by such officer or officers as the Board of Directors shall, from time to time, designate.

ARTICLE XVII

Books and Papers

Section 1—The books, records and such papers as may be placed on file by the vote of the members or the Board of Directors shall at all times, during reasonable business hours, be subject to the inspection of any member.

ARTICLE XVIII

Proxies

Section 1—At all corporate meetings of members, each member may vote in person or by proxy.

Section 2—All proxies shall be in writing, and filed with the Secretary.

ARTICLE XIX

Corporate Seal

Section 1—This corporation shall have a seal in circular form having within its circumference the words

"______________________" HOMES ASSOCIATION
Incorporated ______________________
____
(State)

ARTICLE XX

Amendments

Section 1—By-Laws may be adopted, amended, or repealed

(a) By the Board of Directors, subject always to the power of the members to change or repeal such By-Laws; or

(b) By the vote or written assent of a majority of the members entitled to vote, or the vote of a majority of a quorum at a meeting duly called for such purpose.

Above By-Laws prepared by Mason-McDuffie Company, Inc., Berkeley, California.

Appendix E

Retail Expenditure in Selected Kinds of Retail Stores in 1958

Retail Stores	TOTAL (in millions)	% of Dispos-able Income	% of Total Retail Trade 1958
I. *Food group*			
Grocery stores	43,696	13.8	21.8
Meat markets	2,327	.7	1.2
Fish (seafood) markets	194	.06	.1
Fruit stores, vegetable markets	505	.2	.3
Candy, nut, confectionery stores	528	.2	.3
Retail bakeries	905	.3	.5
II. *Eating and drinking places*			
Restaurants	11,038	3.5	5.5
Cafe	4,164	1.3	2.1
III. *General merchandise group*			
Department stores	13,359	4.2	6.7
Variety stores	3,621	1.1	1.8
General merchandise stores	4,899	1.5	2.4
IV. *Apparel group*			
Men's, boys' apparel stores	2,597	.8	1.3
Women's clothing specialty stores	4,909	1.5	2.5
Shoe stores	2,130	.7	1.1
V. *Furniture, furnishings, appliances group*			
Furniture stores	4,783	1.5	2.4
Floor covering and drapery stores	938	.3	.5
China, glassware, metalware stores	103	.03	.05
Appliance, radio and TV stores	3,500	.1	1.7
Music stores	586	.2	.3
VI. *Automotive group*			
Tire, battery, accessory stores	2,426	.8	1.2
Gasoline stations	14,241	4.5	7.1
VII. *Lumber, building, hardware group*			
Hardware stores	2,717	.9	1.3
Paint, glass, wallpaper stores	740	.2	.4
VIII. *Drug and proprietary group*			
Drugstores	6,531	2.2	3.3
Proprietary stores	248	.8	.1

Appendix E (continued)

Retail Expenditure in Selected Kinds of Retail Stores in 1958

Retail Stores	Total (in millions)	% of Disposable Income	% of Total Retail Trade 1958
IX. *Other retail stores*			
Liquor stores	4,203	1.3	2.1
Book and stationery stores	679	.2	.3
Sporting goods and bicycle stores	624	.2	.3
Garden supply stores	191	.03	.1
Jewelry stores	1,495	.5	.7
Florists	638	.2	.3
Cigar stores	233	.07	.1
Newsstands	285	.09	.1
Camera & photographic supply stores	382	.1	.2
Gift and hobby stores	582	.2	.3
Optical goods stores	188	.06	.1
Typewriter stores	105	.03	.05
Luggage and leather goods stores	82	.03	.04
Pet shops	49	.01	.02
X. *Services*			
Laundries and laundromats	3,300	1.0	
Cleaners	1,357	.4	
Beauty shops	1,028	.3	
Barber shops	783	.2	
Shoe repair	232	.07	
Bowling alleys	433	.1	

Source: 1958 Census of Business: Retail Trade Preliminary Area Report and Selected Services Preliminary Area Report, U. S. Dept. of Commerce.

Appendix I

Schedule of Average Per Foot Gross Sales and Percent of Gross Sales for Rent Paid By Retail Types

Type of Business	Yearly Gross Sales Per Square Foot	Range in % of Gross Sales for Rent
Art goods and gifts	$30-50	5-10
Automobile accessories (retail)	45	3-7
Bakery	45	4-8
Barber	40	7-12
Beauty	40	5-15
Books and stationery	50	5-10
Cameras	55-80	4-10
Candy	35-100	6-12
China and glassware	50-55	6-8
Clothing—children's	65	4-10
Clothing—men's	38-65	4-8
Clothing—women's	34-65	4-10
Delicatessen	85	4-6
Department stores	60	2-6
Drugs (general—independent)	55	3-8
Drugs (super-type)	65-70	2-7
Florists	50-55	6-12
Food (general—independent)	54	1-7
Food (supermarket)	100-125	1-2
Fruits and vegetables	50	5-9
Furniture	40-45	3-8
Gifts	50	5-10
Hardware	40-45	3-7
Hats—men's	45	6-12
Hats—women's	38-50	6-15
Hobby shop	45	5-10
Hosiery	70	5-10
Household appliances	41	5-6
Ice cream, fountain	60	5-6
Jewelry (cheap—costume)	50-70	6-12
Jewelry (credit)	49	6-8
Jewelry (high quality—non-credit)	45-75	4-10
Lingerie	35	6-10
Liquor (packaged goods)	60-100	3-8
Luggage	45-53	5-10
Meat markets (independent)	60	3-6
Motion pictures		8-15
Music	50	4-8
Paints, wallpaper	40	3-12
Radio and TV	41	3-10
Restaurants	40-65	3-10
Shoe-repairing	40	6-15
Shoes—men's (high quality)	50	4-10
Shoes—men's (volume—low-price)	60	5-8
Shoes—women's (high quality)	55	5-10
Shoes—women's (volume—low-price)	65	4-7
Specialty—women's	65	6-12
Sporting goods	50-55	4-8
Taverns	40-65	5-10
Variety (5¢-10¢-25¢)	40-50	3-6

Source: The figures above are data gathered from sources including: National Institute of Real Estate Brokers; National Association of Real Estate Boards; *Buildings;* Frank E. Cox, The Kawneer Company; and Larry Smith.

Appendix J

LIST OF STORES BY LOCATIONS

For reference purposes, the alphabetically arranged lists below represent a check list of stores that the Council considers are suitable for the several categories of real estate location in shopping areas.

NO. 1 LOCATIONS

(100 Percent or "Hot Spot")

1. Bakery
2. Boys' Clothing
3. Candy Store
4. Children's Wear
5. Cosmetics and Perfume
6. Costume Jewelry
7. Department Store
8. Drug Store
9. Five and Ten
10. Florist
11. Gift Shop
12. Girls' Apparel
13. Grocery (cash and carry)
14. Handkerchiefs and Handbags
15. Hosiery Shop
16. Infants' Wear
17. Jewelry
18. Lingerie
19. Leather Goods and Luggage—(Depends on ability to pay high rent)
20. Men's Furnishings
21. Men's Clothing
22. Millinery
23. Novelties
24. Photographic Supplies and Cameras
25. Pop Corn and Nuts
26. Prescriptions (May not be possible because of drug store)
27. Restaurant
28. Shoes, Women's
29. Shoes, Men's
30. Shoes, Children's
31. Sportswear, Women's
32. Tobacconist
33. Toilet Goods
34. Variety Store
35. Women's Wear

The following shops may go equally well in either No. 1 or No. 2 locations:

1. Cafeteria
2. Dry Goods
3. News Stand
4. Service Grocery

No. 1 locations should be held largely for shops that keep open on certain common nights.

NO. 2 LOCATIONS

(Near the 100 percent area)

1. Art Store and Artists' Supplies
2. Athletic Goods
3. Auto Supplies
4. Bank

A bank should not be in a No. 1 location, as it has limited open hours and when closed has a deadening effect on adjacent shops.

5. Bar (Liquor)
6. Barber Shop (Basement in the No. 1 Location)

When deciding on width of a barber shop, consider carefully the number of lines of barber chairs in order that space will not be wasted.

7. Beauty Shop
8. Bookstore
9. China and Silver
10. Cleaners and Dyers (Pick-Up)
11. Cocktail Lounge

12. Corset Shop
13. Delicatessen (Also in No. 1 location in some cases)
14. Electrical Appliances
15. Fruit and Vegetable Market (Should be considered in relation to regular grocer)
16. Glass and China
17. Laundry Agency
18. Linen Shop
19. Liquor Store
20. Maternity Clothes
21. Pen Shop
22. Radio and Television
23. Sewing Machines and Supplies
24. Sporting Goods
25. Stationery and Greeting Cards
26. Telegraph Office
27. Theater (or No. 3 location)
28. Woolens and Yarns

The following shops may go equally well in either No. 2 or No. 3 locations.

1. Gas, Power and Light Company Offices
2. Ticket Offices
3. Toy Shop

NO. 3 LOCATIONS

1. Army Goods Store (or in No. 4 location)
2. Art Needlework Shop
3. Baby Furniture
4. Building and Loan Office
5. Chinese Restaurant
6. Christian Science Reading Room (or 2nd floor in No. 2)
7. Dance Studio (or No. 4 location)
8. Doctors and Dentists

Doctors and dentists are not favored in central locations. Janitorial expense for doctors' and dentists' offices is at least twice as high as for ordinary office space. Also, they are hard tenants to please as to maintenance.

9. Drapery and Curtain Shop
10. Electric Equipment and Repair
11. Express Office (A popular service that helps build up a retail area)
12. Furniture (Pays low rent per square foot)
13. Hardware
14. Health Foods Store
15. Hobby Shop
16. Interior Decoration
17. Ladies' and Men's Tailor (or 2nd floor in No. 1 or No. 2 locations)
18. Mortgage Loan Office (or 2nd floor in No. 2 location)
19. Office Supplies and Office Furniture (Pays low rent per square foot)
20. Optometrist and Optician (or 2nd floor in No. 1 or No. 2)
21. Paint Store
22. Photographers (or 2nd floor in No. 1 or No. 2 locations)
23. Piano Store (Low rent)
24. Pictures and Framing (Low rent)
25. Post Office
26. Power and Light Offices
27. Real Estate Offices (or No. 4)
28. Shoe Repair
29. Tavern
30. Ticket Offices
31. Travel Bureau (or No. 2 location)

NO. 4 LOCATIONS

1. Automatic Family Laundry Service
2. Bowling Alleys
3. Carpets and Rugs, Oriental
4. Diaper Service
5. Dog or Cat Hospital (without outside runs)
6. Drive-In Eating Places
7. Radio and Television Broadcasting Station

Appendix K

A SHOPPING CENTER LEASE FORM

Note: Merely as a quide to wordage for a shopping center lease, this form is included in the Handbook. It is not to be considered applicable to all shopping centers nor to all jurisdictions.

THIS LEASE AGREEMENT, made and entered into the ____________ day of ____________________, 19____, by and between ______________________ ____________________________, a ____________________ corporation, with its principal place of business in the City of ____________________________, County of ________________________, State of ______________________ (hereafter called "LANDLORD"), and ____________________________ ____________________________________ (hereafter called "TENANT").

WITNESSETH:

LANDLORD hereby leases to TENANT and TENANT hereby takes and hires from LANDLORD the PREMISES described, for the TERM set forth, at the RENT stated, and which PREMISES shall be occupied and used by TENANT only for the PURPOSE described in the schedule hereto annexed, made a part hereof, and marked "SCHEDULE A", and in consideration of which LANDLORD and TENANT, except as may be otherwise expressly provided in SCHEDULE A or by other written agreement expressly identified and referred to in SCHEDULE A, covenant and agree as follows:

1. POSSESSION. In the event that by reason of the holding over of a prior occupant or for any other cause beyond the control of LANDLORD the latter shall be unable to give TENANT possession of the PREMISES on the date herein provided then LANDLORD shall not be liable in damages to TENANT by reason thereof and during the period that LANDLORD shall be unable to give TENANT possession all rights and remedies of both parties hereunder shall be suspended.

2. DEFINITIONS. As used herein, except only where the context requires a different meaning, the word "PREMISES" shall mean and refer to the demised premises described or identified in SCHEDULE A; "BUILDING" shall mean and refer to the structure in which such PREMISES are located, and the term "SHOPPING CENTER" shall mean and refer to the land and the improvements located in the City of ____________________, __________________ County, ____________________, described as follows:

(Here insert legal lot description)

3. CONDITIONS PRIOR TO OCCUPANCY. If the BUILDING is non-existing or partially existing and not ready for occupancy by TENANT at the time of execution of this lease, then:

a. LANDLORD, at its own cost and expense, shall erect and/or complete construction of the BUILDING for the use and occupancy of TENANT in conformity with plot plan of the SHOPPING CENTER and in accordance with plans and specifications prepared by the architect of LANDLORD and approved by TENANT, said BUILDING and PREMISES to be of that type and quality of construction and to contain such interior improvements, services, and fixtures as provided in "Description of Landlord's and Tenant's Work", hereto annexed, made a part hereof, and marked "EXHIBIT A." LANDLORD shall use reasonable diligence to have the PREMISES ready for occupancy on or before the __________ day of ______________________, 19____. In the event the PREMISES are not ready for occupancy by TENANT within two (2) years of the above date, TENANT, unless such delay is beyond the reasonable control of LANDLORD, at its option, may terminate this lease by giving written notice thereof to LANDLORD. The right of termination herein provided is separate and independent of any other provision of this lease relative to termination.

b. TENANT, at its own cost and expense, shall do and perform or cause to be done and performed, and shall furnish, provide, and be responsible for the items and things required of TENANT as provided in EXHIBIT A.

4. RENT. RENT for said PREMISES shall be paid by TENANT to LANDLORD in the amounts and at the times stated in SCHEDULE A. TENANT shall pay such RENT to LANDLORD at the latter's office in ______________________________, or upon the prior written direction of LANDLORD to such other person, firm or corporation or at such other place as LANDLORD may from time to time direct.

5. SECURITY DEPOSIT. TENANT, on or before the date the TERM hereof commences, shall deposit in cash with LANDLORD as security for the payment of RENT herein reserved and the faithful performance of the terms, conditions, covenants, and agreements herein contained, a sum equal to one-twelfth (1/12th) of the annual base, fixed, or guaranteed minimum RENT to be paid by TENANT as provided in SCHEDULE A. In the event this lease is terminated as herein provided, but for reasons other than the happening or occurring of an EVENT OF DEFAULT as designated in paragraph 27 of this lease, or upon the assignment or subletting of the PREMISES by TENANT in the manner provided by paragraph 25 of this lease, or upon the expiration of the TERM of this lease, LANDLORD, without being bound or obligated for the payment to TENANT of any interest thereon, shall apply said security deposit to the payment of any RENT due and owing at the time of such termination, assignment, subletting, or expiration of the TERM provided all terms, conditions, covenants, and agreements of this lease have been complied with by TENANT, and the sum remaining, if any, shall be forthwith repaid to TENANT by LANDLORD.

6. PERCENTAGE RENT. If the RENT payable hereunder by TENANT is to be based in whole or in any part upon a computation of a percentage of the gross amount of sales of the business conducted at or from said PREMISES then:

a. GROSS AMOUNT OF SALES. The term "GROSS AMOUNT OF SALES" as used herein is hereby defined to mean and shall be the total amount of the dollar value, exclusive of the amount of ______________ Sales Tax paid or payable thereon, of all sales of merchandise and services and all revenues of every kind and character derived from, arising out of or payable on account of the business and all business transactions conducted at or from said PREMISES by or for the account of TENANT, both for cash and on credit, including all orders for merchandise or services taken or sold at or from said PREMISES and filled or delivered from any other place or location. The amount of the dollar value of bona fide refunds or credit granted for return of merchandise shall be charged as a credit in reduction of the GROSS AMOUNT OF SALES for the period within which such refunds or credits for return of merchandise shall have been made.

b. RECORDS. TENANT, during the TERM of this lease, shall maintain and keep, or cause to be maintained and kept, at said PREMISES, a full, complete, and accurate permanent record and account of all sales of merchandise and services and all sums of money paid or payable for or on account of or arising out of the business, and all business transactions conducted at or from said PREMISES by or for the account of TENANT for each day of the TERM hereof. Such records and accounts and all supporting records at all times shall be open to inspection and audit at said PREMISES by LANDLORD and its duly authorized agents or representatives at all reasonable times during ordinary business hours. The cost of such investigation and audit shall be borne by LANDLORD; provided, however, in the event any written statement or report of GROSS AMOUNT OF SALES herein required to be submitted by TENANT to LANDLORD is determined as the result of such investigation and audit to be incorrect by one per cent (1%), or more, the cost thereof shall be borne by TENANT.

c. REPORTS. On or before the fifth (5th) day of the month following the month in which the TERM hereof commences and on or before the fifth (5th) day of each month thereafter, to and including the month following that in which the TERM hereof shall terminate, TENANT, at the place where the RENT herein reserved shall be payable, shall deliver to LANDLORD, or the person, firm or corporation to whom such RENT shall be payable, a copy of the ____________________ Sales Tax Report for the preceding month, and a complete written statement showing in all reasonable detail the GROSS AMOUNT OF SALES for such preceding month, including therein the number and dollar amount of all refunds and credits for return of merchandise, if any, made during such period. Each such statement shall be signed by the TENANT or if TENANT is a corporation then by one of its principal officers, and if so requested by LANDLORD such statements shall be signed under oath. LANDLORD, if it so elects, may require that any or all of such statements be prepared and submitted by a Certified Public Accountant to be selected by and the cost of which shall be borne by LANDLORD. Within sixty (60) days of the end of the first complete fiscal year of TENANT, occurring during the TERM of this lease and within sixty (60) days of the end of each fiscal year of TENANT thereafter, TENANT, at the place where the RENT herein reserved shall be payable, shall deliver to LANDLORD, or the person, firm, or corporation to whom such RENT shall be payable, a written statement prepared by a Certified Public Accountant showing in all reasonable detail the GROSS AMOUNT OF SALES for the preceding fiscal year and including therein the number and dollar amount of all refunds and credits for return of merchandise, if any, made during such period. Such Certified Public Accountant shall be selected by and the cost thereof shall be borne by TENANT.

7. USE OF PREMISES. The PREMISES during the TERM of this lease shall be used and occupied solely for the PURPOSE stated in SCHEDULE A and TENANT shall not use or permit the same to be used for any other purpose or purposes without the prior written consent of LANDLORD. TENANT at all times shall fully and promptly comply with all laws, ordinances, orders, and regulations of any lawful authority having jurisdiction of said PREMISES, including but not limited to such as shall relate to the cleanliness, safety, occupation, and use of said PREMISES and the nature, character, and manner of operation of the business conducted in or at said PREMISES. Except as otherwise expressly provided herein, TENANT shall cause said business to be conducted and operated on Tuesday, Wednesday, Thursday, and Saturday from the hours of 9:30 a.m. to 5:30 p.m., and on Monday and Friday from the hours of 9:30 a.m. to 9:00 p.m., ____________ Standard Time, or if different hours shall be prescribed by the hereinafter mentioned Merchants' Association and approved by LANDLORD, then during the hours so prescribed and approved, and in good faith and such manner as shall assure the transaction of the maximum volume of business in and at said PREMISES. TENANT shall not permit, allow or cause any public or private auction sales to be conducted in or at said PREMISES or the adoption or use of any sales promotion devices or practices that shall tend to mislead or deceive the public or which directly or indirectly would tend to detract from or impair the reputation or dignity of

said business, said PREMISES, the BUILDING, the SHOPPING CENTER, or the general reputation or dignity of the businesses of others conducted in the SHOPPING CENTER.

8. STREETS, ALLEYS, AND PARKING AREAS. TENANT shall have a non-exclusive right of use of all streets, driveways, and alleys adjoining said PREMISES. Public parking areas provided by LANDLORD in and about the SHOPPING CENTER are acknowledged to be intended primarily for use by customers in said SHOPPING CENTER. TENANT shall not and shall not permit its employees to use said parking areas, the streets, alleys or vacant lands in said SHOPPING CENTER for the parking or storage of any automobiles, trucks, or vehicles owned or used by them except as may be approved and designated in writing by LANDLORD, and TENANT on request of LANDLORD, within five (5) days thereof, shall furnish to LANDLORD a written statement of the names of all employees, agents, and representatives employed in or at the PREMISES by TENANT and the license registration number of all vehicles owned or used by TENANT or by such employees, agents, or representatives. The cost of maintaining and operating the public parking areas, and all other areas in the SHOPPING CENTER provided by LANDLORD for the non-exclusive use of TENANT, shall be borne pro rata by TENANT on the basis which the square footage of BUILDING area in the PREMISES leased by TENANT bears to the total gross square footage of BUILDING area in all PREMISES leased in the SHOPPING CENTER, and such cost to include all expenses incurred by LANDLORD in lighting, repairing, painting, cleaning, and policing (including the removal of snow and ice) the areas herein referred to. LANDLORD shall prepare and submit to TENANT a monthly statement, setting forth in reasonable detail the expenses incurred by LANDLORD in maintaining and operating said areas during the preceding month, and including therein the pro rata share of such expenses to be borne by TENANT. TENANT shall pay to LANDLORD such pro rata share at the time and place, and in the manner provided herein for the payment of RENT.

9. SIGNS AND ADVERTISING. TENANT shall not permit, allow, or cause to be erected, installed maintained, painted, or displayed on, in or at said PREMISES or any part thereof any exterior or interior sign, lettering, placard, announcement, decoration, advertising media or advertising material of any kind whatsoever, visible from the exterior of said PREMISES, without the prior written approval of LANDLORD; provided, however, that, subject to compliance with all other applicable provisions hereof, TENANT may display merchandise and advertising media within said PREMISES but not closer than three (3) inches to the interior side of any store front display window. TENANT shall not permit, allow, or cause to be used in or at said PREMISES any advertising media or device such as phonographs, radios, public address system, sound production or reproduction devices, mechanical or moving display devices, motion pictures, television devices, excessively bright lights, changing, flashing, flickering, or moving lights or lighting devices, or any similar devices, the effect of which shall be visible or audible from the exterior of said PREMISES.

10. EXAMINATION OF PREMISES. TENANT shall examine the said PREMISES before taking possession and TENANT'S entry into possession shall constitute conclusive evidence that as of the date thereof the said PREMISES were in good order and satisfactory condition.

11. MAINTENANCE AND REPAIRS. LANDLORD, at its sole cost and expense, shall maintain and keep in good repair the roof, exterior and supporting walls, the electrical wiring and the plumbing of the BUILDING; provided, however, that the cost of any such repairs required as a result of the negligence or willful act of TENANT, its customers, licensees, agents, servants, or employees, shall be borne by

TENANT. TENANT, at its sole cost and expense, whether the same shall be the property of TENANT or LANDLORD, shall promptly repair and at all times maintain in good condition the interior of said PREMISES, including heating units, store fixtures, store equipment, air conditioning equipment, electrical fixtures and equipment, electrical installations, plumbing, plumbing equipment and fixtures, all machinery, all hardware, all interior painting or decorations of every kind, all door and window screens and replace all broken or damaged glass, including window glass and plate glass, and such repairs and replacements shall be made only by persons approved in advance in writing by LANDLORD.

12. EQUIPMENT AND FIXTURES. TENANT shall not install in or about said PREMISES any interior or exterior lighting or plumbing fixtures, steps, partitions, walls, fences, shades or awnings or make any structural changes or alterations in or to any part of the BUILDING or the PREMISES except upon the prior written consent of LANDLORD. All furnishings, fixtures, and equipment used in said PREMISES supplied and installed at the sole cost and expense of TENANT shall at all times be and remain the property of TENANT and the latter shall have the right to remove the same from the said PREMISES at any time during the TERM hereof or within five (5) days next following the date of termination of this lease, provided TENANT shall not be in default hereunder and provided further that TENANT, at its sole cost and expense, shall repair or reimburse LANDLORD for the cost of repairing any and all damage to said PREMISES resulting from the removal of such furnishings, fixtures, and equipment.

13. CARE OF PREMISES. TENANT shall not permit, allow or cause any act or deed to be performed or any practice to be adopted or followed in or about said PREMISES which shall cause or be likely to cause injury or damage to any person or to said PREMISES or the BUILDING or to the sidewalks and pavements adjoining the PREMISES. TENANT shall not permit, allow or cause any noxious, disturbing or offensive odors, fumes or gases, or any smoke, dust, steam or vapors, or any loud or disturbing noise, sound or vibrations to originate in or to be emitted from said PREMISES. TENANT at all times shall keep said PREMISES in a neat and orderly condition and shall keep the entry ways, sidewalks and delivery areas adjoining the PREMISES clean and free from rubbish, dirt, snow and ice. TENANT shall keep the PREMISES clear and free of rodents, bugs and vermin and at the request of LANDLORD participate and cooperate in carrying out any program of extermination that LANDLORD may direct and TENANT shall bear the cost thereof, or if conducted in cooperation with other tenants then TENANT shall bear its pro rata cost on the basis of floor areas involved. TENANT shall not use or permit the use of any portion of said PREMISES as sleeping or living quarters or as lodging rooms, or keep or harbor therein any live animals, fish, or birds or use the same for any illegal purpose. TENANT shall not permit, allow or cause the sinks, toilets or urinals in the PREMISES or BUILDING to be used for any purpose except that for which they were designed and installed, and the expense of repairing any breakage or damage or removal of any stoppage resulting from a contrary use thereof shall be paid by TENANT. TENANT shall maintain the show windows in a clean, neat and orderly condition and the glass thereof clean, and shall store all trash, rubbish and garbage within said PREMISES, and shall provide for the prompt and regular removal thereof for disposal outside the area of the SHOPPING CENTER, and TENANT shall not burn or otherwise dispose of any trash, waste, rubbish or garbage in or about the PREMISES or said SHOPPING CENTER.

14. MOVING OF FURNITURE, HEAVY ARTICLES. TENANT shall not allow, permit or cause to be taken into or removed from the PREMISES any heavy or bulky articles, furnishings, fixtures or equipment of such size or weight as shall require the use of tackle, carts, dollies or

other moving aids or the services of more than two (2) men, except upon the prior approval of LANDLORD and at such times as the latter shall specify. TENANT shall be liable for the cost of any damage to the PREMISES or the BUILDING or the sidewalks and pavements adjoining the same which shall result from the movement of such articles or objects. TENANT shall not unduly load or overload the floors or any part of said PREMISES and any heavy object or article stored or used therein shall be stored and placed only in such place or location as LANDLORD, if it so elects, shall designate.

15. LOSS OF PROPERTY OR DAMAGE. LANDLORD shall not be liable for any loss of any property of TENANT from said PREMISES or for any damages to any property of TENANT, however occurring, except only such damage in the latter instance as may result directly from the failure of LANDLORD to perform an act required of it under the terms of this agreement. LANDLORD, without liability to TENANT, shall have the right and may at any time close the said PREMISES whenever the same may become necessary in compliance with any law, order, regulation or direction of any lawful authority or the agents, officers or representatives thereof or in the event of any public disturbance or like circumstance which, in the judgment of LANDLORD, may appear proper or advisable.

16. ENTRY OF LANDLORD. LANDLORD, its agents and representatives, at all reasonable times may enter said premises for the purpose of (1) inspection thereof, (2) inspection and examination of TENANT's records pursuant to the provisions of paragraph number 3 hereof, (3) making repairs, replacements, alterations or additions to said PREMISES or said BUILDING, (4) exhibiting the PREMISES to prospective tenants, purchasers or other persons, and (5) during the last ninety (90) days of the term hereof, if during or prior to such ninety (90) day period TENANT shall have vacated the PREMISES, to decorate, remodel, alter and otherwise prepare the PREMISES for reoccupancy and any such entry by or on behalf of LANDLORD shall not be or constitute an eviction, partial eviction or deprivation of any right of TENANT, and shall not alter the obligations of TENANT hereunder or create any right in TENANT adverse to the interests of LANDLORD.

17. USE AND COST OF UTILITIES AND SERVICES. TENANT shall procure for its own account and shall pay the cost of all water, gas, electric power and fuel consumed or used in or at said PREMISES. TENANT shall keep all show windows and display windows visible from or fronting on the street or other public way, and all adjoining walkway and marquee lights and approved exterior electric signs clearly illuminated during the hours from dusk to 11:00 p.m., ________ Standard Time, each day, including Sundays and Holidays. LANDLORD, if it shall so elect, within six (6) months after the date of TENANTS entry into occupancy of said PREMISES, shall furnish and install at such place on the exterior of said BUILDING as LANDLORD shall designate an electrically illuminated sign of such design, content, form and material as shall be selected by LANDLORD for the purpose of designating generally the location of the said business of TENANT and the cost thereof shall be paid by TENANT to LANDLORD within ten (10) days after demand thereof by the latter, and TENANT, at its sole cost and expense, at all times thereafter during the TERM hereof shall promptly repair and at all times maintain such sign in good condition.

18. BUILDING AND SHOPPING CENTER CHANGES. LANDLORD, without liability of any kind to TENANT, at any time may construct additional buildings and change, alter, remodel or remove any of the improvements of the SHOPPING CENTER, or alter, change or add to the said BUILDING, close off, enlarge or decrease the size or change the locations of any skylight, window, door or opening in or about said PREMISES or said BUILDING, provided that at all times there shall be

provided a public entry-way to said PREMISES; alter, remodel or change the store front of said PREMISES and install or emplace in or through said PREMISES wiring, piping, ducts or conduits for service of the PREMISES or other parts of the BUILDING or other buildings.

19. FIRE AND OTHER CASUALTY. If the PREMISES shall be made untenantable by fire or other casualty, LANDLORD, if it so elects, may (a) terminate the term of this lease, effective as of the date of such fire or casualty, by written notice given to TENANT within thirty (30) days after such date, or (b) repair, restore, or rehabilitate said PREMISES at LANDLORD'S expense within ninety (90) days after the date of such fire or casualty, in which event the TERM hereof shall not terminate but any base, fixed, or guaranteed minimum RENT herein reserved shall be abated on a per diem basis while the PREMISES shall remain untenantable. If LANDLORD elects to so repair, restore or rehabilitate said PREMISES and shall fail to substantially complete the same within said ninety (90) day period, due allowance being made for delay due to practical impossibility, either LANDLORD or TENANT, by written notice to the other, given within fifteen (15) days next following the last day of said ninety (90) day period, may terminate the TERM hereof as of the date of such fire or casualty. In the event of termination of the TERM hereof pursuant to this paragraph, base, fixed, or guaranteed minimum RENT, if any, reserved hereunder shall be apportioned on a per diem basis and paid to the date of such fire or casualty, and percentage RENT, if any, shall be paid to the date of termination. The right of termination herein provided is separate and independent of any other provisions of this lease relative to termination.

20. USE OF NAMES AND PICTURES OF PREMISES, BUILDING OR SHOPPING CENTER. TENANT shall not use or permit others on its behalf to use the name of the PREMISES, the BUILDING or the SHOPPING CENTER for any purpose other than as the address of the business to be conducted in or at said PREMISES or to use any picture or likeness of the PREMISES, the BUILDING or the SHOPPING CENTER or any part of any of the same in any advertisement, notice, correspondence or other type of announcement or communication without the prior written consent of LANDLORD. TENANT shall not have or acquire any property right or interest in or to any name or distinctive designation which may become identified or associated with the business to be conducted in or at said PREMISES if such name or distinctive designation shall contain as a part thereof the name or any reference to the PREMISES, the BUILDING, the SHOPPING CENTER, or any part or combination of parts of any of the same, but all property rights and rights of use of such name or distinctive designation shall be and remain the property of LANDLORD.

21. INSURANCE AND TAXES. (a) LANDLORD, during the TERM of this lease, or any extension hereof, at its own sole cost and expense, shall keep the BUILDING and PREMISES insured to the extent of its full insurable value against loss or damage by fire, with extended coverage. TENANT during the TERM hereof, at its own sole cost and expense, shall keep all furniture, fixtures, and equipment, whether supplied or owned by TENANT or by LANDLORD, and, in addition, all glass forming a part of the PREMISES, including, but not limited to, plate glass, insured to the extent of its full insurable value thereof against loss or damage by fire, with extended coverage.

(b) LANDLORD shall promptly pay as and when the same shall become due and payable, all taxes, levies, and assessments levied upon the BUILDING and PREMISES during the TERM of this lease, or any extension hereof, and in the event of default, TENANT, at its election, may pay the same and deduct the amount thereof, together with any penalties and interest which may have been paid by TENANT, from the RENT next accruing hereunder.

(c) It is expressly understood and agreed that the RENT herein reserved is based upon insurance rates, ad valorem tax rates and property valuation prevailing during the first year of occupancy under this lease. In the event that said insurance rates, tax rates or property valuation are thereafter decreased during the TERM of this lease, or any extension hereof, LANDLORD shall credit to the account of TENANT an amount equal to any resulting decrease in cost of insurance or taxes. In the event that said insurance rates, tax rates, or property valuation are thereafter increased during the TERM of this lease, or any extension hereof, TENANT shall pay to LANDLORD, as additional rental, an amount equal to any resulting increase in cost of insurance or taxes. It is further agreed, however, if TENANT shall pay or become bound and obligated to pay to LANDLORD as additional rental for any lease year during which such increase in cost of insurance or taxes shall occur, a percentage RENT over and above the annual base, fixed, or guaranteed minimum RENT herein reserved, LANDLORD shall apply or credit in payment thereof the percentage RENT paid or required to be paid by TENANT.

22. MERCHANTS' ASSOCIATION. There shall be established an association of the merchants engaged in business in the SHOPPING CENTER, and TENANT agrees that it shall maintain membership in said association and make annual contributions thereto in accordance with the schedule of rates set forth in the Merchants' Association Agreement hereto annexed, made a part hereof, and marked "Exhibit B." TENANT shall abide by all decisons made by and will adopt store hours prescribed by said MERCHANTS' ASSOCIATION and approved by LANDLORD. TENANT shall conduct and operate its said business in a manner in keeping with the dignity and reputation of the SHOPPING CENTER and will make all reasonable effort to work harmoniously with other merchants in the SHOPPING CENTER.

23. ALTERATIONS. TENANT may make minor alterations to the interior of the PREMISES so that the same shall conform to the uses of said business, provided such alterations shall be made at the expense of TENANT with the prior approval of and under the supervision of LANDLORD'S architect.

24. EMINENT DOMAIN. In the event that the whole or any part of said PREMISES shall be taken by any public authority under the power of eminent domain or like power, then the TERM hereof shall terminate as to the part of the PREMISES so taken, effective as of the date possession thereof shall be required to be delivered pursuant to the final order, judgment, or decree entered in the proceedings in exercise of such power. All damages awarded for the taking of said PREMISES, or any part thereof, shall be payable in the full amount thereof to and the same shall be the property of LANDLORD, including, but not limited to, any sum paid or payable as compensation for loss of value of the leasehold or loss of the fee or the fee of any part of the PREMISES, and TENANT shall be entitled only to that portion of any award expressly stated to have been made to TENANT for loss of business and the loss of value and cost of removal of stock, furniture, and fixtures owned by TENANT.

25. ASSIGNMENT AND SUBLETTING. TENANT shall not assign or in any manner transfer this lease or any estate, interest or benefit therein or sublet said PREMISES or any part or parts thereof or permit the use of the same or any part thereof by any one other than TENANT without the prior written consent of LANDLORD. Consent by LANDLORD to any assignment or transfer of interest under this lease, or subletting of said PREMISES or any part thereof shall be limited to the instance stated in such written consent and shall not constitute a release, waiver, or consent to any other assignment, transfer of interest, or subletting.

26. HOLDING OVER. In the event TENANT remains in possession of the PREMISES after the expiration of the TERM hereof and without the execution of a new lease, TENANT thereby shall not acquire any right, title or interest in or to said PREMISES, provided, however, that at the option of the LANDLORD, by written notice of the exercise thereof given to TENANT within thirty (30) days next following the last day of the TERM hereof or any extension thereof, TENANT as a result of such holding over thereby shall have renewed this lease for the further period of the TERM herein provided and if LANDLORD shall not exercise the option above described then TENANT as a result of such holding over shall occupy said PREMISES as a tenant from month to month, and in either event subject to all the conditions, provisions, and obligations of this lease insofar as the same shall then be applicable to whichever of such tenancies shall result.

27. DEFAULT. The happening of any one or more of the following listed events (hereafter referred to singly as "EVENT OF DEFAULT" and plurally as "EVENTS OF DEFAULT") shall constitute a breach of this lease agreement on the part of TENANT, namely:

a. The filing by, on behalf of or against TENANT of any petition or pleading to declare TENANT a bankrupt, voluntary or involuntary, under any bankruptcy law or act.

b. The commencement in any court or tribunal of any proceeding, voluntary or involuntary, to declare TENANT insolvent or unable to pay its debts.

c. The failure of TENANT to pay any rent payable under this lease agreement and the continued failure to pay the same for three (3) days or more after written notice of such failure of payment given to TENANT by LANDLORD.

d. The failure of TENANT to fully and promptly perform any act required of it in the performance of this lease or to otherwise comply with any term or provision thereof.

e. The appointment by any court or under any law of a receiver, trustee, or other custodian of the property, assets or business of TENANT.

f. The assignment by TENANT of all or any part of its property or assets for the benefit of creditors.

g. The levy of execution, attachment or other taking of property, assets, or the leasehold interest of TENANT by process of law or otherwise in satisfaction of any judgment, debt or claim.

Upon the happening of any EVENT OF DEFAULT, LANDLORD, if it shall so elect, may (1) terminate the TERM of this lease agreement. or (2) terminate TENANT'S right to possession and occupancy of the PREMISES, without terminating the TERM of this lease agreement and in the event LANDLORD shall exercise such right of election the same shall be effective as of the date of the EVENT OF DEFAULT upon written notice of LANDLORD'S election given by the latter to TENANT at any time after the date of such EVENT OF DEFAULT. Upon any termination of the TERM hereof, whether by lapse of time or otherwise, or upon any termination of TENANT'S right to possession or occupancy of the PREMISES without terminating the term hereof, TENANT shall promptly surrender possession and vacate the PREMISES and deliver possession thereof to LANDLORD and TENANT hereby grants to LANDLORD full and free license to enter into and upon the PREMISES in such event and with or without process of law to repossess the PREMISES as of LANDLORD'S former estate and to expel or remove TENANT and any others who may be occupying the PREMISES and to remove therefrom any and all property, using for such purpose such force as may be necessary without being guilty of or liable for trespass, eviction or forceable entry or detainer and without relinquishing LANDLORD'S right to rent or any other right given to LANDLORD hereunder or by operation of law. Except as otherwise expressly provided in this lease, TENANT hereby expressly waives the service of any demand for the payment of rent or for possession of the PREMISES or to reenter the PREMISES, including any and every form of demand and notice prescribed by any statute or other law.

The phrase "rent payable for the remainder of said TERM," as used in the next following two (2) paragraphs, is hereby defined to be and shall be that sum equal to the number of months of the TERM then unexpired, including the month in which the EVENT OF DEFAULT relied upon by LANDLORD shall occur, multiplied by the average monthly rent payable by TENANT pursuant to this lease agreement during the period of the twelve (12) months next preceding the month in which such EVENT OF DEFAULT shall occur or if TENANT shall have been entitled to occupy said PREMISES during a period of less than said twelve (12) months prior thereto then such lesser number of months.

If LANDLORD shall elect to terminate the term of this lease agreement, LANDLORD, upon such termination, shall be entitled to recover of TENANT damages in an amount equal to the then current value of the rent reserved in this lease agreement for the remainder of the said TERM.

If LANDLORD shall elect to terminate TENANT'S right to possession only, without terminating the term of this lease, LANDLORD at its option may enter into the PREMISES, remove TENANT'S property and other evidences of tenancy and take and hold possession thereof without such entry and possession terminating the term of this lease or otherwise releasing TENANT in whole or in part from its obligation to pay the RENT herein reserved for the full TERM hereof and in any such case TENANT thereupon shall pay to LANDLORD a sum equal to the entire amount of the rent payable for the remainder of said TERM. Upon and after entry into possession without termination of the TERM hereof, LANDLORD may, but need not, relet the PREMISES or any part thereof for the account of TENANT to any person, firm or corporation other than TENANT for such rent, for such time, and upon such terms as LANDLORD in its sole discretion shall determine. If any rental collected by LANDLORD upon such reletting for TENANT'S account is not sufficient to pay monthly the full amount of the rental herein reserved and not theretofore paid by TENANT, together with the costs of any repairs, alterations or redecoration necessary for such reletting, TENANT shall pay to LANDLORD the amount of each monthly deficiency upon demand, and if the RENT so collected from such reletting is more than sufficient to pay the full amount of the rent reserved hereunder, together with the aforementioned costs, LANDLORD, at the end of the stated term hereof, shall apply any surplus to the extent thereof to the discharge of any obligation of TENANT to LANDLORD under the terms of this lease.

28. IDENTITY OF INTEREST. The execution of this lease or the performance of any act pursuant to the provisions thereof shall not be deemed or construed to have the effect of creating between LANDLORD and TENANT the relationship of principal or agent or of partnership or of joint venture and the relationship between them shall be that only of LANDLORD and TENANT.

29. NOTICE. Any notice provided herein shall be deemed sufficient notice and service thereof if the same shall be in writing addressed to the addressee at the last known post office address thereof, mailed postage prepaid.

30. PUBLIC RECORDATION. Neither LANDLORD nor TENANT shall permit, allow, or cause this lease or any amendment hereof to be

recorded in the office of the Register of Deeds, ________ County, ________, or any other office or public registry. In order to effect public recordation, the parties hereto, at the time this lease is executed, agree to execute a short form lease, incorporating therein by reference the terms of this lease, but deleting therefrom any expressed statement or mention of the amount of RENT herein reserved, which short form lease may be recorded by either party in the office of the Register of Deeds, ________ County, ________, or any other office or public registry.

IN TESTIMONY WHEREOF, ____________ Shopping Center, ______, has caused these presents to be signed in its corporate name by its ____________ President, attested by its ____________ Secretary, and its corporate seal to be hereto affixed, all by order of its Board of Directors duly given, and

ATTEST: ____________ SHOPPING CENTER, ____

______________________________ Secretary

By______________________________ President

____

____

(STATE)

____________ COUNTY

This __________ day of ______________, 19__, personally came before me __________________________ who, being by me duly sworn, says that he is the ____________ President of ____________ Shopping Center, ______, and that the seal affixed to the foregoing instrument in writing is the corporate seal of the Company, and that said writing was signed and sealed by him, in behalf of said Corporation, by its authority duly given. And the said ____ acknowledged the said writing to be the act and deed of said Corporation.

WITNESS my hand and notarial seal this ______________ day of ________________, 19__.

My commission expires:

Notary Public

____

____________________ SHOPPING CENTER

(City and State)

EXHIBIT A

Attached to and Forming Part of Lease to

Dated ______________________

DESCRIPTION OF LANDLORD'S AND TENANT'S WORK

DESCRIPTION OF LANDLORD'S WORK

A. STRUCTURE

1. Footings and foundations shall be reinforced concrete.
2. The first floor structure shall be steel frame or concrete and steel frame.
3. Above grade, exterior wall surfaces of structure shall be architectural concrete, cement, plaster, brick, stone or other material

selected by Landlord. Exterior trim and other exterior work normally requiring painting, shall be painted.

4. Canopies shall be of steel frame construction with composition roof, metal soffit, and metal fascia.
5. Roofing shall be built-up composition roofing.
6. Standard ceiling height in first floor shall be 10′ 0″.
7. Partitions of concrete block, structural tile, or other material approved by applicable codes, shall be provided between the demised premises and other leased areas.

B. STORE FRONT

1. Store front shall be designed by Landlord's or Tenant's architect and the design thereof shall be subject to approval by the Landlord.
2. Exterior materials for the store front shall be brick, stone, metal, plaster, or other finish material acceptable to Landlord and Tenant, and in harmony with the project as a whole.
3. Store fronts shall be provided by Landlord, provided that the cost to Landlord shall not exceed $____________ per linear foot of the front wall. If Tenant desires a more costly store front the additional cost shall be paid by the Tenant. Included in store front costs shall be costs of show window platforms.
4. Entrance doors shall be provided in number, size and locations as specified by Landlord's or Tenant's architect in conformity with the National Building Code, and any other applicable laws and ordinances.

C. INTERIOR FINISH

1. Toilet rooms shall have asbestos vinyl floors.
2. The first floor within the demised premises shall be smooth, finished concrete to receive floor coverings by tenant.
3. Interior surfaces of walls enclosing the demised premises shall be plastered or drywall.
4. All areas of the demised premises shall have plastered or drywall ceilings. If Tenant requires special treatment of ceiling including recessing electrical fixtures and acoustical treatment extra costs shall be paid by Tenant.
5. Interior trim in the demised premises shall receive priming coat of paint only.

D. VERTICAL TRANSPORTATION

1. The demised premises where required shall have access to a stairway.

E. SANITARY FACILITIES

1. The demised premises shall be furnished with or have access to toilet rooms in accordance with all applicable code requirements.

F. SIGNS

1. Tenant shall pay for all signs and the installation thereof.
2. Landlord shall provide electrical conduit from panel to junction boxes for sign locations where required to service tenant signs.
3. Any and all signs, including window signs, shall be subject to approval by the Landlord.

G. PARKING AREAS AND WALKS

1. Parking areas on grade shall be surfaced with asphaltic concrete.
2. Walks shall be surfaced with concrete, stone or other hard material as specified by Landlord's architect.
3. Parking areas and walks shall be provided with artificial lighting.

H. UTILITIES

1. Water service shall be brought to the demised premises, if Tenant requires same.
2. Domestic hot water heaters shall be provided in each Tenant space for toilet facilities only.
3. Gas service shall be brought to the demised premises if Tenant requires same.
4. Waste line shall be brought to the demised premises if Tenant requires same, and shall be connected to the public sewer.
5. All plumbing fixtures and connections thereto within the demised premises shall be provided by Tenant, except that the Landlord shall provide toilets and lavatories to the extent required by applicable codes.
6. Interior rest room areas shall be provided with forced ventilation.
7. Electrical service shall be brought to the demised premises.
8. Allowance will be made by Landlord to Tenant for the following items:
   (a) Duct work, heating and registers of $___________ per square foot of gross rentable space.
   (b) Electrical work of $___________ per square foot.
   All of the above work shall be done by Landlord, providing that the expense to the Landlord shall not exceed above allowances. Any cost above these allowances shall be paid for by Tenant.
9. All telephones with service thereto shall be provided by Tenant. All telephone installation charges shall be paid by Tenant directly to the telephone utility company furnishing the service.

I. FIRE PROTECTION

1. Fire hydrants shall be installed as required by applicable codes.
2. Additional fire protection required due to increased fire hazard by reason of Tenant's merchandise or operations, shall be provided by Tenant.

J. LIMITATIONS

1. The work to be done by Landlord shall be limited to that described as Landlord's Work in the foregoing paragraphs.
2. Where requested to do so, Tenant shall promptly furnish to Landlord information regarding construction requirements of the demised premises.

____
____
____
____

DESCRIPTION OF PRINCIPAL ITEMS OF TENANT'S WORK

1. The work to be done by Tenant shall include, but shall not be limited to the purchase and/or installation and/or performance of the following:

   a. Electrical fixtures.
   b. Interior partitions within the demised premises.
   c. Light coves and special hung or furred ceilings.
   d. Floor coverings.
   e. Interior painting.
   f. Store fixtures and furnishings.
   g. Display window enclosures.

h. Plumbing fixtures within the demised premises except as provided in paragraph H-5 of this exhibit.

i. Refrigeration, air conditioning equipment, and ventilating equipment shall be provided by Tenant. (See Section H, Paragraph 8.)

j. Such work as is stated in the foregoing portions of this exhibit to be work or matters to be provided or done by Tenant.

2. All work undertaken by Tenant shall be at Tenant's expense, and shall not damage the building or any part thereof.

3. Work undertaken by Tenant and at Tenant's expense during the general construction, shall be awarded to Landlord's contractor, unless Landlord shall otherwise agree in writing.

4. The design of all work and installations undertaken by Tenant shall be subject to the approval of Landlord's architect.

5. Design costs and other architectural services over and above that which is applicable to Landlord's work shall be paid for by Tenant; likewise, costs involved in changes desired by Tenant after Landlord's architect has incorporated Tenant's design in the overall plans, shall be paid by Tenant.

____
____
____
____

____________________ SHOPPING CENTER

(City and State)

EXHIBIT B

Attached to and Forming Part of Lease to

Dated ______________________

MERCHANTS' ASSOCIATION AGREEMENT

____________ SHOPPING CENTER agrees to organize a Merchants' Association. The purpose of said Merchants' Association shall be the general furtherance of the business interests of the shopping center as a whole, including advertising, promotion, special events calculated to benefit the shopping center and the business of all the tenants located therein.

Membership in the merchants' association shall be limited to the ____________ SHOPPING CENTER and all tenants of the shopping center. Contribution to such merchants' association shall be required of all tenants in the shopping center and shall be on the following basis:

A. One-twentieth of one per cent on all gross income for food markets, or anyone who pays less than three per cent (3%).

B. One-fourth of one per cent on all gross income for those tenants whose percentage rent schedule provides for rental of more than three per cent (3%) up to and including six per cent (6%).

C. One-half of one per cent of all gross income for all tenants whose percentage rent schedule provides for rental of more than six per cent (6%) for rent.

D. Maximum of fifteen cents (15¢) per square foot per year for tenants with 10,000 square feet or more.

E. Maximum of twenty cents (20¢) per square foot per year for tenants with less than 10,000 square feet, but more than 5,000 square feet.

F. Maximum of forty cents (40¢) per square foot per year for tenants with less than 5,000 square feet, but more than 2,500 square feet.

G. No maximum for tenants with less than 2,500 square feet.

H. ____________ SHOPPING CENTER agrees to pay twenty-five per cent (25%) of the total of all contributions paid by tenants to Association for advertising and promotion.

____________ SHOPPING CENTER agrees to require by lease or other agreement that every other tenant in the shopping center join said merchants' association and pay its share of contribution as herein provided. ____________ SHOPPING CENTER agrees to formulate reasonable by-laws or other articles of association for their Merchants' Association, which will provide a workable basis for effective operation by the association.

Voting among the members of such Association shall be on a basis of contribution to the fund. Each member shall have one vote and an additional vote for every $500 of contribution to the Merchants' Association in excess of $500 except during the first year of the lease term each member shall have one vote for each 1,000 gross square feet of floor area which tenant occupies in the center.

Appendix L

Sample Form A

BY-LAWS

OF

__________ MERCHANTS (OR TRADE) ASSOCIATION

(Based on a Shopping Center in Illinois)

ARTICLE I

Purposes

The purposes of the corporation as stated in its certificate of incorporation are "Civic and trade association".

Said purposes shall be accomplished by the promotion, establishment, operation and management of parking areas and facilities and equipment therefore, and by causing to be maintained a clean, orderly and attractive appearance in such parking areas, and in the (name of center) area, all in the __________ of ________________, Illinois, and by other means, and to develop and promote the general welfare of the ____________________ by joint cooperation of tenant members and to establish joint business practices for the advancement of customers' good will and convenience.

For all purposes of these by-laws the __________________ is hereby defined as being those two certain tracts of land, and all improvements from time to time upon the same, legally described as:

(Here insert a legal description of the shopping center property)

The corporation also has such powers as are now or may hereafter be granted by the General Not For Profit Corporation Act of the State of Illinois.

ARTICLE II

Offices

The corporation shall have and continuously maintain in this state a registered office and a registered agent whose office is identical with such registered office, and may have other offices within or without the State of Illinois as the board of directors may from time to time determine.

ARTICLE III

Members

Section 1. Classes of Members. The corporation shall have three classes of members, of which classes, one, the initial members, shall exist only temporarily and in connection with the commencement of operation of the corporation. The designation of said classes and the qualifications of the members of said classes shall be as follows:

Subsection 1. Initial Members. At the date of adoption of the original by-laws, ____________________________________, the incorporators, are initial members. They shall continue to be initial members until there are at least three general members who are general members without or independently of having been designated by other general members to be substitutes for said other general members, respectively.

Subsection 2. General Members. The general members shall be as follows:

Paragraph A. Tenants and Others as General Members. Any person, firm, partnership or corporation who is a tenant or lawfully in possession of any premises within the ____________________ shall, by virtue of being such tenant or so lawfully in possession, be a general member of this corporation; provided that the membership of any such person, firm, partnership or corporation may be terminated for nonpayment of dues in the manner and under the circumstances hereinafter specified in these by-laws; and provided further that only one person, firm, partnership or corporation may be a general member of this corporation by virtue of being a tenant or lawfully in possession of any particular premises or portion thereof, and in each case of a subtenancy or of lawful possession by someone other than a tenant or subtenant, only that person, firm, partnership or corporation which is a tenant or lawfully in possession most directly and immediately under and from the owner of the fee title to said premises or portion thereof shall be a general member by virtue of being a tenant or lawfully in possession. For the purposes of the second proviso of the sentence immediately preceding this sentence, any tenant of premises who becomes such under a lease shall be deemed to be a tenant more directly under the owner of the fee title than any grantee or transferee of the lessor's rights under said lease whether said rights are granted or transferred by another lease, by conveyance of fee title, or in some other manner. For the purposes of these by-laws no person, firm, partnership or corporation is a tenant of any premises until the commencement of his, their or its right to possession to said premises as a tenant, nor after the termination of said right to possession. The words "member" and "members", in each case where used in these by-laws, shall mean respectively, "general member" and "general members" unless the context requires a different meaning.

Paragraph B. Substitutes for Tenants and Others as General Members. Any firm, partnership or corporation which is a general member by reason of Paragraph A of this subsection may, subject to approval by the board of directors, designate any person who alone or with one or more other persons is actively engaged in the management of its business conducted upon and from the premises in the ____________________ of which it, said firm, partnership or corporation is a tenant or lawfully in possession, to be a general member of this corporation as a substitute for or in lieu of said firm, partnership or corporation, and in each such case said person so designated shall be a general member of this corporation as a substitute for or in lieu of said firm, partnership or corporation, but only as to those rights of a general member which by their nature may be exercised only by a natural person, as for example, the right to be a candidate for election as a director, and to be a director if duly elected, and not as to any duties except those duties which are concomitant with said rights, nor as to any rights or duties which by their nature may be exercised and performed by a firm, partnership or corporation, as for example the right to appoint a proxy and the duty to pay dues, as to all of which latter rights and duties said appointing firm, partnership or corporation shall continue to be a general member and shall have the sole right to cast votes or to appoint a proxy in respect of the premises in the ______________________ of which it is a tenant or lawfully in possession;

PROVIDED THAT (1) any such designation shall be in writing duly signed on behalf of the firm, partnership or corporation making the same, shall be filed with the secretary of this corporation, and shall be ineffective until approved by the board of directors of this corporation, and (2) any such designation shall be revocable by a revocation in writing duly signed on behalf of the firm, partnership or corporation making the designation, which revocation shall be ineffective until filed with the secretary of this corporation. If any firm, partnership or corporation which is a general member by reason of Paragraph A of this subsection shall cease to be such general member, then any person who is at that time a general member of this corporation as a substitute for or in lieu of said firm, partnership or corporation, shall immediately cease to be a general member in that capacity.

Subsection 3. Special Members. The board of directors may from time to time at any duly convened meeting of said board, by a resolution in favor of which at least two-thirds of the entire membership of said board votes, create one or more classes of special memberships, giving to each such class such designation and such rights, specifying for each such class such conditions as to eligibility, and imposing upon the members in each such class such, if any, duties, as shall be specified in the resolution creating said class of special membership, provided that membership in any such class of special members shall confer no right to vote. In each case where used in these by-laws neither the word "member" nor "members" shall mean or include, unless the context so requires, any person, firm, partnership or corporation by reason of his, their or its membership in any such class of special members.

Section 2. Voting Rights. The voting rights of the members shall be as follows:

Subsection 1. Initial Members. Each initial member shall be entitled to one vote on each matter submitted or subject to a vote of the initial members.

Subsection 2. General Members. On each matter submitted to the vote of the members, each member shall have one vote for each one hundred square feet of space occupied by said member. The fractional part of each one hundred square feet included in the total square feet occupied by the member shall be calculated to the nearest one hundred square feet in determining the number of votes said member shall have.

Subsection 3. Special Members. Special members shall have no voting rights.

ARTICLE IV

Meetings of Members

Section 1. Annual Meeting. An annual meeting of the members shall be held on the ________________ of the ____ calendar month after the first date on which there shall be at least three general members, at the hour of ____________________, and on the same date at the same hour in each calendar year thereafter, for the purpose of electing a director or directors and officers, and for the purpose of transacting such other business as may come before the meeting. If such day be a legal holiday, the meeting shall be held at the same hour on the next succeeding business day. If the election of directors and/or officers shall not be held on the day designated herein for any annual meeting, or at any adjournment thereof, the board of directors shall cause the election to be held at a special meeting of the members called as soon thereafter as conveniently may be.

Section 2. Special Meeting. Special meetings of the members may be called either by the president, the board of directors, or by members who have not less than one-third of all the votes of all the members as determined at the time when each such respective call of a special meeting is completed.

Section 3. Place of Meeting. The board of directors may designate any place within ___________ County, Illinois, as the place of meeting for any annual meeting or for any special meeting called by the board of directors. If no designation is made or if a special meeting be otherwise called, the place of meeting shall be the registered office of the corporation in the State of Illinois, provided, however, that if all of the members shall meet at any time and place, either within or without the State of Illinois, and consent to the holding of a meeting, such meeting shall be valid without call or notice, and at such meeting any corporate action may be taken.

Section 4. Notice of Meetings. Written or printed notice stating the place, day and hour of any meeting of members shall be delivered, either personally or by mail, to each member entitled to vote at such meeting, not less than five nor more than forty days before the date of such meeting, by or at the direction of the president, or the secretary or the officers or persons calling the meeting. In case of a special meeting or when required by statute or by these by-laws, the purpose for which the meeting is called shall be stated in the notice. If mailed, the notice of a meeting shall be deemed delivered when deposited in the United States mail addressed to the member at his address as it appears on the records of the corporation, with postage thereon prepaid.

Section 5. Quorum. The members holding one-third of the votes which may be cast at any meeting, present in person or by proxy, shall constitute a quorum at such meeting; provided that for the purpose of establishing a quorum members shall be regarded as present by proxy only if their respective proxies are authorized to act and vote for them as said respective members could act and vote if present in person, upon any and every matter which may properly come before the meeting. If a quorum is not present at any meeting of members, a majority of the members present may adjourn the meeting from time to time without further notice.

Section 6. Proxies. At any meeting of members, a member entitled to vote may vote either in person or by proxy executed in writing by the member or by his duly authorized attorney-in-fact. No proxy shall be valid after eleven months from the date of its execution unless otherwise provided in the proxy.

Section 7. Tenants and Others and Substitutes for Tenants and Others. At every meeting of members of this corporation any or all members of each respective firm or partnership which is a member of this corporation, any or all officers of each respective corporation which is a member of this corporation, and any or all persons actively engaged in the management of the business of any such member conducted on or from premises in the ________________, may, either alone or together with any person who may be a member of this corporation as a substitute for or in lieu of said respective firm, partnership or corporation, attend and participate in the meeting, but the right of each respective firm, partnership or corporation to vote may be exercised only by it or its proxy as if there were no members as substitutes for or in lieu of any of said firms, partnerships or corporations.

Section 8. Notices and Communications Between Members and the Corporation. Except insofar as it is specifically provided to the contrary in these by-laws, whenever it is necessary or appropriate for the corporation to give any notice or make a communication to any member or former member, it shall be sufficient to give or make the same by written or printed instrument signed by some officer of the corporation and mailed to said member at his address as it appears on the records of the corporation, by first class United States mail, postage prepaid. Except insofar as it is specifically provided to the contrary in these by-laws, whenever it is necessary or appropriate for any member or former member to give any notice or make any communication to the corporation, it shall be sufficient to give or make the same by written or printed instrument duly signed by or on behalf of the member or former member and mailed to the corporation at the registered office of the corporation in the State of Illinois, by first class United States mail, postage prepaid. Any notice or communication so mailed shall, except insofar as it is specifically provided to the contrary in these by-laws, be deemed to be given or made on the fifth day following the date of mailing, regardless of the time when, if ever, said notice or communication is received by the addressee. It shall be the duty at all times of each member and former member to keep the corporation supplied with information for its records giving an address at which first class United States mail will be received by or on behalf of said member or former member, and to which such mail will in the ordinary course of the mails, be presented for delivery within not more than five days after the date of mailing if mailed in __________ County, Illinois; and it shall be the duty of the secretary at all times to keep the records of the corporation current in accordance with such information.

ARTICLE V

Board of Directors

Section 1. The number of directors shall consist of three directors, and the President, Vice President, Secretary and Treasurer.

Section 2. General Powers. The affairs of the corporation shall be managed by the Board of Directors.

Section 3. Number, Tenure and Qualifications. The number of directors shall be three. Each director elected by the members shall be elected for a term of two years and until his successor is elected and qualified, provided however that one of the first board of directors to be elected shall serve until the first annual meeting of members after his election, another until the second annual meeting of members after his election, and the third until the third annual meeting of members after his election, and each shall serve thereafter until his successor is elected and qualified; and the determination of which ones of the first board of directors to be elected shall serve said respective terms shall be by lot. At each annual meeting of the members after the first, one director shall be elected to serve for two years and until his successor is elected and qualified. Each director shall be a member of the corporation, provided that ________________________, the incorporators, are members and the original directors, and shall continue to be directors until the first board of directors to be elected by the members has been elected and qualified, whether or not said original directors continue to be members until said time. If any director, during the term of office for which he was elected by the members or appointed by the directors to fill a vacancy, shall cease to be a member of this corporation, he shall immediately cease to be a director of this corporation.

Section 4. Election of Directors. Directors shall be elected at meetings as provided in Article IV, Section 1 of these By-Laws. The directors shall be nominated by a committee as selected in accordance with Article VII, Section 1, which committee shall act in accordance with resolution as provided by the Board of Directors at least thirty days prior to the annual meeting. The method of conducting an election shall be provided for by such resolution, and shall be conducted by secret ballot, said ballot being furnished to each member at the time and place at which the election is held.

For all purposes of these by-laws, an election conducted in accordance with any such resolution shall be deemed to be an election at the meeting at which there is the last opportunity for members to vote in said election.

Section 5. Regular Meetings. A regular annual meeting of the board of directors shall be held without other notice than this by-law, immediately after, and at the same place as, the annual meeting of members. The board of directors shall provide by resolution the time and place within ________ County, Illinois, for the holding of additional regular meetings of the board without other notice than such resolution.

Section 6. Special Meetings. Special meetings of the board of directors may be called by or at the request of the president or any two directors. The person or persons authorized to call special meetings of the board may fix any place within ______________ County, Illinois, as the place for holding any special meeting of the board called by them.

Section 7. Notice. Notice of any special meeting of the board of directors shall be given at least three days previously thereto by written notice delivered personally or sent by mail or telegram to each director at his address as shown by the records of the corporation. If mailed, such notice shall be deemed to be delivered when deposited in the United States mail in a sealed envelope so addressed with postage thereon prepaid. If notice be given by telegram, such notice shall be deemed to be delivered when the telegram is delivered to the telegraph company. Any director may waive notice of any meeting. The attendance of a director at any meeting shall constitute a waiver of notice of such meeting, except where a director attends a meeting for the express purpose of objecting to the transaction of any business because the meeting is not lawfully called or convened. Neither the business to be transacted at, nor the purpose of, any regular or special meeting of the board need be specified in the notice or waiver of notice of such meeting, unless specifically required by law or by these by-laws.

Section 8. Quorum. A majority of the board of directors shall constitute a quorum for the transaction of business at any meeting of the board, provided, that if less than a majority of the directors are present at said meeting, a majority of the directors present may adjourn the meeting from time to time without further notice.

Section 9. Manner of Acting. The act of a majority of the directors present at a meeting at which a quorum is present shall be the act of the board of directors, except where otherwise provided by law or by these by-laws.

Section 10. Vacancies. Any vacancy occurring in the Board of Directors shall be filled by the Board of Directors. A director appointed by the directors to fill a vacancy shall be appointed for a term until the next annual meeting, at which time an election shall be held to elect the directorship for the unexpired term of the predecessor in office.

Section 11. Compensation. Directors as such shall not receive any compensation for their services.

ARTICLE VI

Officers

Section 1. Officers. The officers of the corporation shall be a president, vice-president, treasurer, secretary and such other officers as may be elected in accordance with the provisions of this article. The board of directors may elect or appoint such other officers, including one or more assistant secretaries and one or more assistant treasurers, as it shall deem desirable, such officers to have the authority and perform the duties prescribed, from time to time by the board of directors.

Section 2. Election and Term of Office. The officers of the corporation shall be elected annually by the members at the regular annual meeting. If the election of officers shall not be held at such meeting, such election shall be held as soon thereafter as conveniently may be. Each officer shall have office until his successor shall have been duly elected and shall have qualified.

Section 3. Removal. Any officer or agent elected by the members or appointed by the board of directors may be removed by the board of directors whenever in its judgment the best interests of the corporation would be served thereby, but such removal shall be without prejudice to the contract rights, if any, of the person so removed.

Section 4. Vacancies. A vacancy in any office because of death, resignation, removal disqualification or otherwise, may be filled by the board of directors for the unexpired portion of the term.

Section 5. President. The president shall be the principal executive officer of the corporation and shall in general supervise and control all of the business and affairs of the corporation. He shall preside at all meetings of the members and of the board of directors. He may sign, with the secretary or any other proper officer of the corporation authorized by the board of directors, any deeds, mortgages, bonds, contracts, or other instruments which the board of directors have authorized to be executed, except in cases where the signing and execution thereof shall be expressly delegated by the board of directors or by these by-laws or by statute to some other officer or agent of the corporation; and in general shall perform all duties incident to the office of president and such other duties as may be prescribed by the board of directors from time to time.

Section 6. Vice President. In the absence of the president or in the event of his inability or refusal to act, the vice president shall perform the duties of the president and when so acting, shall have all the powers of and be subject to all the restrictions upon the president. The vice president shall perform such other duties as from time to time may be assigned to him by the president or by the board of directors.

Section 7. Treasurer. If required by the board of directors, the treasurer shall give a bond for the faithful discharge of his duties in such sum and with such surety or sureties as the board of directors shall determine. He shall have charge and custody of and be responsible for all funds and securities of the corporation; receive and give receipts for moneys due and payable to the corporation from any source whatsoever, and deposit all such moneys in the name of the corporation in such banks, trust companies or other depositaries as shall be selected in accordance with the provisions of Article VIII of these by-laws; and in general perform all the duties incident to the office of treasurer and such other duties as from time to time may be assigned to him by the president or by the board of directors.

Section 8. Secretary. The secretary shall keep the minutes of the meetings of the members and of the board of directors in one or more books provided for that purpose; see that all notices are duly given in accordance with the provisions of these by-laws, or as required by law; be custodian of the corporate records and of the seal of the corporation and see that the seal of the corporation is affixed to all documents, the execution of which on behalf of the corporation under its seal is duly authorized in accordance with the provisions of these by-laws; keep a register of the postoffice address of each member which shall be furnished to the secretary by such member; and in general perform all duties incident to the office of secretary and such other duties as from time to time may be assigned to him by the president or by the board of directors.

Section 9. Assistant Treasurers and Assistant Secretaries. If required by the board of directors, the assistant treasurers shall give bonds for the faithful discharge of their duties in such sums and with such sureties as the board of directors shall determine. The assistant treasurers and assistant secretaries, in general, shall perform such duties as shall be assigned to them by the treasurer or the secretary or by the president or the board of directors. Compensation for such assistance shall be authorized by resolution of the board of directors.

ARTICLE VII

Committees

Section 1. Committees. Committees may be designated by a resolution setting forth duties, authorities and functions, adopted by a majority of the directors present at a meeting at which a quorum is present. Except as otherwise provided in such resolution, members of each such committee shall be members of the corporation, and shall include a member of the board of directors, and the president of the corporation shall appoint the members thereof. Any member thereof may be removed by the person or persons authorized to appoint such member whenever in their judgment the best interests of the corporation shall be served by such removal.

Section 2. Term of Office. Each member of a committee shall continue as such until the next annual meeting of the members of the corporation and until his successor is appointed, unless the committee shall be sooner terminated, or unless such member be removed from such committee, or unless such member shall cease to qualify as a member thereof.

Section 3. Chairman. One member of each committee shall be appointed chairman.

Section 4. Vacancies. Vacancies in the membership of any committee may be filled by appointments made in the same manner as provided in the case of the original appointments.

Section 5. Quorum. Unless otherwise provided in the resolution of the board of directors designating a committee, a majority of the whole committee shall constitute a quorum and the act of a majority of the members present at a meeting at which a quorum is present shall be the act of the committee.

Section 6. Rules. Each committee may adopt rules for its own government not inconsistent with these by-laws or with rules adopted by the board of directors.

ARTICLE VIII

Contracts, Checks, Deposits and Funds

Section 1. Contracts. The board of directors may authorize any officer or officers, agent or agents of the corporation, in addition to the officers so authorized by these by-laws, to enter into any contract or execute and deliver any instrument in the name of and on behalf of the corporation and such authority may be general or confined to specific instances.

A maximum total expenditure not to exceed ____________ is authorized for the initial temporary budget until such time as an annual budget is presented to the members and approved by the members.

Section 2. Checks, Drafts, Etc. All checks, drafts or other orders for the payment of money, notes or other evidences of indebtedness issued in the name of the corporation, shall be signed by such officer or officers, agent or agents of the corporation and in such manner as shall from time to time be determined by resolution of the board of directors. In the absence of such determination by the board of directors, such instruments shall be signed by the treasurer or an assistant treasurer and countersigned by the president or a vice president of the corporation.

Section 3. Deposits. All funds of the corporation shall be deposited from time to time to the credit of the corporation in such banks, trust companies or other depositaries as the board of directors may select.

Section 4. Gifts. The board of directors may accept on behalf of the corporation any contribution, gift, bequest or devise for the general purposes or for any special purpose of the corporation.

ARTICLE IX

Books and Records

The corporation shall keep, correct and complete books and records of account and shall also keep minutes of the proceedings of its members, board of directors and committees having any of the authority of the board of directors, and shall keep at the registered or principal office a record giving the names and addresses of the members of each class, and of the directors. Each member, each former member who, as such, may have any further business with the corporation, and each director, shall keep the corporation supplied with his, their or its current address. All books and records of the corporation may be inspected by any member, or his agent or attorney for any proper purpose at any reasonable time.

ARTICLE X

Fiscal Year

The fiscal year of the corporation shall begin on the first day of January and end on the last day of December in each year.

ARTICLE XI

Dues

Section 1. Assessment of Dues. Dues to defray the expenses of the corporation may be assessed from time to time in the manner and subject to the restrictions and limitations hereinafter stated. Each assessment shall be made by resolution of the board of directors, which resolution shall: (a) fix and determine the total amount of said assessment; (b) specify the purpose for which said assessment is made; and, (c) specify a period of time, not greater than three months, for which said assessment is made, which said period shall have its beginning not more than three weeks before the time of adoption of said resolution, and its ending not more than twelve weeks after said time. The making of an assessment for a specified purpose and period of time shall not preclude the making of additional assessments for the same or some other purpose and for the same period of time or for some other period of time including all or a part of said first mentioned period of time. Promptly after the adoption of each assessment resolution the secretary shall apportion the total amount of the assessment among those who are members of the corporation at the time of adoption of the resolution, pro rata according to the number of votes which each member, respectively, had and will have in accordance with Article III, Section 2 of these by-laws, upon each of the days, Sundays and holidays included, of the period for which the assessment is made. For the purposes of said apportionment it shall be assumed, unless facts to the contrary shall be established by notice to the corporation, that each person, firm, partnership or corporation which was a tenant or lawfully in possession of any particular premises in the ______________ at the time of adoption of the assessment resolution, will continue to be a tenant or lawfully in possession of the same premises until the expiration of the period for which the assessment was made. It is a purpose and an intent of this by-law that dues shall be assessed upon a current basis so that members shall pay for the services of the corporation approximately as the same are rendered, allowing the corporation only a reasonable operating fund with which to meet current expenses and so that those members ceasing to be such prior to the adoption of any particular assessment resolution, and those members becoming such subsequent to the adoption of said resolution, shall not be given the benefit of the services of the corporation paid for by the assessment made by said resolution, to any extent more than shall be unavoidable consistently with this by-law and the practical requirements which shall be applicable; but the discretion of the board of directors as to assessments shall not be subject to question except for bad faith, and no former member shall have any right, title or interest in or to, or any claim against the corporation in respect of any of its property, or all or any portion of any assessment collected in part from said former member and not expended for the purpose for which the assessment was made, and the amount or portion of any assessment not expended for the purpose for which said assessment was made shall belong to the general funds of the corporation and be applied to its future needs and in minimizing future assessments.

Section 2. Payment and Collection of Dues. Promptly after the secretary makes any apportionment of an assessment of dues the treasurer shall mail to each member to whom any part of said assessment has been so apportioned, by first class United States mail, postage prepaid, a notice of said assessment showing a copy of the assessment resolution and containing a statement of the amount apportioned to said respective member and of the date when the same will become due and payable to the corporation by the member, which date shall be the tenth day after the mailing of said notice, if said tenth day is not a Sunday or holiday, and shall be the first business day after said tenth day if said tenth day is a Sunday or holiday. Each member shall pay the part of each assessment of dues apportioned to him on the day when the same becomes due and payable. In any case in which a member ceases to be a member after the adoption of an assessment resolution but before the making of the apportionment of the assessment, or before the mailing of notice, or before the day when the part of the assessment apportioned to said member becomes due and payable, said member shall nevertheless be liable to the corporation for the part of the assessment apportioned to him.

Section 3. Default and Termination of Membership—Continuing Liability for Dues—Reinstatement of Membership. If any member shall fail to pay in full the part of any assessment apportioned to him before the expiration of the third calendar month after the month in which said part of said assessment became due and payable, then in each such case said member shall cease to be a member of this corporation at the expiration of said third calendar month; provided, however, that the treasurer shall within each of said three calendar months, and at least seven days before the end of each such month, mail to said member, by first class United States mail, postage prepaid, a notice stating the amount of the part of the assesment apportioned to said member, when it became due and payable, how much remains unpaid thereon at the time of mailing of each such notice, respectively, and the date on or before which said member must pay said amount in full or cease to be a member of the corporation; and in default of such notices so given in said three calendar months the membership of said member shall not terminate until the expiration of three consecutive calendar months in which such notices shall have been so given without said member paying said amount in full before the expiration of said last-mentioned three calendar months. After the membership of any member shall have been terminated as above provided:

(a) The former member shall continue liable for all amounts due and payable by him to the corporation at, before, and/or after the termination of his membership, and apportioned or to be apportioned to him on account of assessment resolutions adopted while he was a member, except insofar as he shall have paid said amounts.

(b) The secretary shall apportion to him, as if he were a member, a part of the assessment made by each assessment resolution adopted by the board of directors so long as he continues to be a tenant or lawfully in possession of any premises in the ________________; and for the purpose of making said apportionment, but for no other purpose, he shall be regarded as if he were and would continue to be a member and therefore entitled to vote throughout the entire period subsequent to the termination of his membership until and after the adoption of the assessment resolution, all as would be the case had he made no default or defaults in the payment of dues and had his membership not been terminated. The treasurer shall give said former member notice of each such assessment in all ways as if he were still a member, except that in said notice he shall be referred to as a former member rather than as a member, and he shall be liable as if he were a member to pay to the corporation the amount so apportioned to him.

(c) The former member may be reinstated as a member by his paying to the corporation all amounts which have, at the time of such payment, previously become due and payable from him to the corporation and which have not been, at said time, previously paid.

ARTICLE XII

Seal

The board of directors shall provide a corporate seal which shall be in the form of a circle and shall have inscribed thereon the name of the corporation and the words "Corporate Seal, Illinois".

ARTICLE XIII

Waiver of Notice

Whenever any notice whatever is required to be given under the provisions of the General Not For Profit Corporation Act of Illinois or under the provisions of the articles of incorporation or the by-laws of the corporation, a waiver thereof in writing signed by any one or more of the persons entitled to such notice, whether before or after the time stated therein, shall be deemed equivalent to the giving of such notice to such one or more of said persons.

ARTICLE XIV

Amendments to By-Laws

These by-laws may be altered or amended by a majority of the members present at any regular meeting or at any special meeting, provided that at least ten days' written notice is given of intention to alter or amend at such meeting.

Appendix L

Sample Form B

___________________ MERCHANTS ASSOCIATION, INC.
BY-LAWS

ARTICLE I

Objects, Members and Dues

SECTION 1.01. *Objects.* The object of the Association shall be to promote the general business interests of the merchants in the ________ Shopping Center, and in furtherance of such object to engage in and conduct promotional programs and publicity, special events, decoration, cooperative advertising and other joint endeavors in the general interest and for the general benefit of merchants in the center. The Association shall be conducted as a non-profit organization, and no part of the profits (if any) of the Association shall inure to the benefit of any other member or other person.

SECTION 1.02. *Members.* Each and every business doing business in the _____________ Center as a tenant shall be a member in the Association and shall be entitled to one vote as such a member. ___________, Inc. as the owner of the Center, shall be a full member of the Association and in such capacity shall have the right to attend and participate in all meetings of the members, but shall waive the right to vote thereat. Any other owner of a property doing business as a merchant in the Center, may become a member, entitled to full voting rights, by paying dues in an amount approved by the Board of Directors. Membership in the Association shall continue so long as the respective members continue to conduct merchandising business in the Center as a tenant or, in the case of an owner, so long as such owner desires to continue membership and dues are regularly paid.

SECTION 1.03. *Dues.* Regular monthly dues shall be paid by the members to the Association as provided by lease or other agreement. For the year 19____ said regular monthly dues shall be payable beginning _____________ 1, 19____. Thereafter the regular monthly dues shall be payable monthly as billed for which the same are due and payable. Any new merchant admitted to the Association as a member thereof shall prior to the opening for business by him in the center pay his full regular annual dues pro rated for such year to reflect expenditures theretofore or thereafter made by the Association applicable to its activities during the period such member will be open for business in the center. The regular annual dues for any member whose lease terminates within a calendar year shall in a similar manner be pro rated for such year to reflect estimated expenditures of the Association applicable to its activities during the period prior to termination of such lease.

SECTION 1.04. *Regular and Annual Meetings.* The Association shall hold each year, commencing with the year 19____, an annual meeting of the members for the election of directors and the transaction of any business within the powers of the Association, at 2:00 P.M., on the fourth Wednesday in February in each year if not a legal holiday, and if a legal holiday then on the first day following which is not a Sunday or a legal holiday. The Association shall also hold each month, commencing with the first full calendar month after the opening of the center for business, a regular monthly meeting of the members for the transaction of any business within the powers of the Association. Any business of the Association may be transacted at a regular meeting without being specifically designated in the notice, except such business as is specifically required by statute or by charter to be stated in the notice. Failure to hold an annual meeting at the designated time shall not, however, invalidate the corporate existence of the Association or affect otherwise valid corporate acts.

SECTION 1.05. *Special Meetings.* At any time in the interval between annual meetings, special meetings of the members may be called by the President or by a majority of the Board of Directors or by any ten members by vote at a meeting or in writing with or without a meeting.

SECTION 1.06. *Place of Meeting.* All meetings of the members shall be held at the principal office of the Association in ______________, except in cases in which the notice thereof designates some other place; but all such meetings shall be held within the state of ______________.

SECTION 1.07. *Notice of Meetings.* Not less than ten days nor more than ninety days before the date of every meting of members, the secretary shall give to each member written or printed notice stating the time and place of the meeting, the purpose or purposes for which the meeting is called, either by mail or by presenting it to him personally or by leaving it at his residence or usual place of business. If mailed, such notice shall be deemed to be given when deposited in the United States mail addressed to the member at his post office address as it appears on the records of the Association, with postage thereon prepaid. Notwithstanding the foregoing provision a waiver of notice in writing, signed by the person or persons entitled to such notice and filed with the records of the meeting, whether before or after the holding thereof, or actual attendance at the meeting in person or by proxy, shall be deemed equivalent to the giving of such notice to such persons. Any meeting of members annual or special, may adjourn from time to time to reconvene at the same or some other place, and no notice need be given of any such adjourned meeting other than by announcement.

SECTION 1.08. *Quorum.* Unless otherwise provided in the charter, at any meeting of members, the presence in person or by proxy of members entitled to cast a majority of the votes thereat shall constitute a quorum. In the absence of a quorum the members in person or by proxy, by majority vote and without notice other than by announcement, may adjourn the meeting from time to time when a quorum shall attend. At any such adjourned meeting at which a quorum shall be present, any business may be transacted which might have been transacted at the meeting as originally notified.

SECTION 1.09. *Votes Required.* A majority of the votes cast at a meeting of members, duly called and at which a quorum is present, shall be sufficient to take or authorize action upon any matter which may properly come before the meeting, unless more than a majority of votes cast is required by statute or by the charter.

SECTION 1.10. *Proxies.* Any member may vote either in person or by proxy, or representative designated in writing by such member.

SECTION 1.11. *Voting.* In all elections for directors every member shall have the right to vote, in person or by proxy, or representative, for as many persons as there are directors to be elected and for whose election he has a right to vote. Unless so demanded or ordered by any member, no vote need be by ballot, and voting need not be conducted by inspectors, but all members must vote for as many directors as are to be elected.

ARTICLE II.

Board of Directors

SECTION 2.01. *Powers.* The business and affairs of the Association shall be managed by its Board of Directors. The Board of Directors may exercise all the powers of the Association, except such as are by statute or the charter or the by-laws conferred upon or reserved to the members. The Board of Directors shall keep full and fair accounts of its transactions.

SECTION 2.02. *Number of Directors.* The number of Directors of the Association shall be fifteen until such number be changed as herein provided. By vote of a majority of the entire Board of Directors, the number of directors may be increased or decreased, from time to time, to not exceeding fifteen nor less than three directors, but the tenure of office of a director shall not be affected by any decrease in the numbers of directors so made by the Board.

SECTION 2.03. *Election of Directors.* Until the first annual meeting of members or until successors are duly elected and qualify, the Board shall consist of the persons named as such in the charter. At the first meeting of members and at each annual meeting thereafter, the members shall elect directors to hold office until the next succeeding annual meeting or until their successors are elected and qualify.

SECTION 2.04. *Vacancies.* Any vacancy occurring in the Board of Directors for any cause other than an increase in the number of members of the Board of Directors may be filled by a majority of the remaining members, although such majority is less than a quorum. Any vacancy occurring by reason of an increase in the number of directors may be filled by action of a majority of the entire Board of Directors. A director elected by the Board of Directors to fill a vacancy shall be elected to hold office until the next annual meeting of members or until his successor is elected and qualifies.

SECTION 2.05. *Regular Meetings.* Regular meetings of the Board of Directors shall be held on such dates and at such places within or without the state of ____________ as may be designated from time to time by the Board of Directors.

SECTION 2.06. *Special Meetings.* Special meetings of the Board of Directors may be called at any time by the President or by the Board of Directors by vote at a meeting, or by a majority of the Directors in writing with or without a meeting. Such special meetings shall be held at such place or places within or without the state of ____________ as may be designated from time to time by the Board of Directors. In the absence of such designation such meetings shall be held at such places as may be designated in the calls.

SECTION 2.07. *Notice of Meetings.* Except as provided in Section 2.05, notice of the place, day and hour of every regular and special meeting shall be given to each director two days (or more) before the meeting, by delivering the same to him personally, or by sending the same to him by telegraph, or by leaving same at his residence or usual place of business, or, in the alternative, by mailing such notice three days (or more) before the meeting, postage prepaid, and addressed to him at his last known post office address, according to the records of the Association. Unless required by these by-laws or by resolution of the Board of Directors, no notice of any meeting of the Board of Directors need state the business to be transacted thereat. No notice of any meeting of the Board of Directors need be given to any director who attends, or to any director who, in writing executed and filed with the records of the meeting either before or after the holding thereof, waives such notice. Any meeting of the Board of Directors, regular or special, may adjourn from time to time to reconvene at the same or some other place, and no notice need be given of any such adjourned meeting other than by announcement.

SECTION 2.08. *Quorum.* At all meetings of the Board of Directors, a majority of the entire Board of Directors shall constitute a quorum for the transaction of business. Except in cases in which it is by statute, by the charter or by the by-laws otherwise provided, the vote of a majority of such quorum at a duly constituted meeting shall be sufficient to elect and pass any measure. In the absence of a quorum, the directors present by majority vote and without notice other than by announcement may adjourn the meeting from time to time until a quorum shall attend. At any such adjourned meeting at which a quorum shall be present, any business may be transacted which might have been transacted at the meeting as originally notified.

ARTICLE III.

Officers

SECTION 3.01. *Executive Officers.* The Board of Directors shall choose a President from among the directors, and a Secretary and a Treasurer who need not be directors. The Board of Directors may also choose one or more Vice-Presidents, one or more Assistant Secretaries and one or more Assistant Treasurers, none of whom need be a director but shall be entitled to attend directors' meetings ex-officio. Any two of the above mentioned officers, except those of President and Vice-President, may be held by the same person, but no officer shall execute, acknowledge or verify any instrument in more than one capacity if such instrument be required by statute, by the charter, by the by-laws or by the resolution of the Board of Directors to be executed, acknowledged or verified by two or more officers. Each such officer shall hold office until the first meeting of the Board of Directors after the annual meeting of members next succeeding his election, and until his successor shall have been duly chosen and qualified, or until he shall have resigned or shall have been removed. Any vacancy in any of the above offices may be filled for the unexpired portion of the term by the Board of Directors at any regular or special meeting.

SECTION 3.02. *President.* The President shall preside at all meetings of the members and of the Board of Directors at which he shall be present; he shall have general charge and supervision of the business of the Association; he may sign and execute, in the name of the Association, all authorized deeds, mortgages, bonds, contracts or other instruments, except in cases in which the signing and execution thereof shall have been expressly delegated to some other officer or agent of the Association; and, in general, he shall perform all duties incident to the office of a President of a corporation, and such other duties as, from time to time, may be assigned to him by the Board of Directors.

SECTION 3.03. *Vice-Presidents.* The Vice-President or Vice-Presidents, at the request of the President or in his absence or during his inability to act, shall perform the duties and exercise the functions of the President, and when so acting shall have the powers of the President. The Vice-President or Vice-Presidents shall have such other powers and perform such other duties as may be assigned to him or them by the Board of Directors or the President.

SECTION 3.04. *Secretary.* The Secretary shall keep the minutes of the meetings of the members and of the Board of Directors in books provided for the purpose; he shall see that all notices are duly given in accordance with the provisions of the by-laws or as required by law; he shall be custodian of the records of the Association; he shall see that the corporate seal is affixed to all documents the execution of which, on behalf of the Association, under its name; and in general, he shall perform all duties incident to the office of a secretary of a corporation, and such other duties as, from time to time, may be assigned to him by the Board of Directors or by the President.

SECTION 3.05. *Treasurer.* The Treasurer shall have charge of and be responsible for all funds, securities, receipts and disbursements of the Association, and shall deposit, or cause to be deposited, in the name of the Association, all moneys or other valuable effects in such banks, trust companies or other depositories as shall, from time to time, be selected by the Board of Directors; he shall render to the President and to the Board of Directors, whenever requested, an account of the financial condition of the Association, and in general, he shall perform all the duties incident to the office of a treasurer of a corporation, and such other duties as may be assigned to him by the Board of Directors or the President.

SECTION 3.06. *Assistant Officers.* The Assistant Secretaries shall have such duties as may from time to time be assigned to them by the Board of Directors or the Secretary. The Assistant Treasurers shall have such duties as may from time to time be assigned to them by the Board of Directors or the President.

SECTION 3.07. *Subordinate Officers.* The Board of Directors may from time to time appoint such subordinate officers as it may deem desirable. Each such officer shall hold office for such period and perform such duties as the Board of Directors or the President may prescribe. The Board of Directors may, from time to time, authorize any committee or officer to appoint and remove subordinate officers and prescribe the duties thereof.

SECTION 3.08. *Removal.* Any officer or agent of the Association may be removed by the Board of Directors whenever, in its judgment, the best interests of the Association will be served thereby.

ARTICLE IV.

Sundry Provisions

SECTION 4.01. *Checks, Drafts, Etc.* All checks, drafts and orders for the payment of money, notes and other evidences of indebtedness, issued in the name of the Association, shall, unless otherwise provided by resolution of the Board of Directors, be signed by the President or a Vice-President and countersigned by the Secretary or Treasurer, who shall be bonded to the extent deemed necessary by the Board of Directors.

SECTION 4.02. *Annual Reports.* There shall be prepared annually a full and correct statement of the affairs of the Association, including a balance sheet and a financial statement of operations for the preceding fiscal year, which shall be submitted at the annual meeting of the members and mailed to all members, and filed within twenty days thereafter at the principal office of the Association in the State. Such statement shall be prepared by such executive officer of the Association as may be designated in an additional or supplementary by-law adopted by the Board of Directors. If no other executive officer is so designated, it shall be the duty of the President to prepare such statement.

SECTION 4.03. *Fiscal Year.* The fiscal year of the Corporation shall be the calendar year, unless otherwise provided by the Board of Directors.

SECTION 4.04. *Seal.* The Board of Directors shall provide a suitable seal, bearing the name of the Association, which shall be in charge of the secretary. The Board of Directors may authorize one or more duplicate seals and provide for the custody thereof.

SECTION 4.05. *Bonds.* The Board of Directors may require any officer, agent or employee of the Association to give a bond to the Association, conditioned upon the faithful discharge of his duties, with one or more sureties and in such amount as may be satisfactory to the Board of Directors.

SECTION 4.06. *Amendments.* Any and all provisions of these by-laws may be altered or repealed and new by-laws may be adopted at any annual meeting of the members, or at any special meeting called for that purpose.

Appendix M

TAXATION AND THE SHOPPING CENTER

A Statement of Policy

The modern shopping center is a comparatively recent innovation in the field of retail merchandising. While it is true that certain pioneers in the field, for example, the late J. C. Nichols of Kansas City, Missouri, planned and built shopping centers several decades ago, it required the recent enormous growth pressure of American cities reaching out with their suburbs to stimulate the development of shopping centers in the very great numbers that have been built since the end of World War II.

In keeping abreast of the manifold changes in community developments that have occurred in the last decade or two, the Community Builders' Council of the Urban Land Institute, Washington, D. C., has held many plan analysis sessions in many cities of the United States for the purpose of helping developers solve some of their complex problems by exchanging information among the members. In these sessions the shopping center has held a prominent place.

With the building of these centers throughout the country, the emphasis on problems has shifted from planned layout, market surveys, arrangement of stores, selection of tenants and similar development matters to that of operational costs.

In this process, it has become increasingly apparent that much confusion and difference of opinion exists as to the real role being played by the shopping center in our communities.

One of the major questions that has arisen as a result of this confusion has been the formulation of an equitable approach to the problem of the assessment and appraisal of shopping centers for tax purposes. It has been generally recognized by members of planning commissions, professional planners, tax assessors and other public officials, and the general public that properly planned shopping centers of the neighborhood, community or regional types are a real and tangible asset to the entire community.

The only group who might be expected to be antagonistic to the development of properly planned shopping centers are the merchants and property owners in the central business districts of our cities. Even these merchants and property owners, however, have come to realize that they have an important though changing role to fill and that the outlying shopping center has no less an important role to play in the integrated life of the whole community.

It must be remembered that planned shopping centers did not create the desire on the part of the consumer public to shop in suburban areas. The planned shopping center was the inevitable result in meeting this desire.

OBVIOUS ADVANTAGES

Some of the obvious advantages accorded by properly planned shopping centers are as follows:

Adequate free parking

A selection of merchandise and tenants that offer the possibility of one-stop shopping

The opportunity to create a pleasant park-like environment for the customers

The opportunity to have the cooperation of many merchants as well as the landlord in merchandising promotion

The opportunity to take a more active part in community affairs and activities

The opportunity to control signs and litter; to provide music, places to rest, and other amenities

The opportunity to develop a pleasing and homogeneous architectural appearance.

In brief, the modern shopping center is the best answer we have to the unattractive, inconvenient, string-type commercial districts of the past—with their lack of convenience and unattractive appearance. If retail business is not concentrated in properly planned shopping center developments, then at each major intersection of our new highways and all along the route we will find repeated the same mistakes that we have made in the past—unattractive, scattered, inadequate commercial projects.

These strip developments tend to cause ruinous congestion on the highways almost as quickly as the highways can be built. It is far more costly to the community to supply services to multiple strip developments and to alleviate the congestion caused by them than it is to supply services to a single planned shopping center.

Indeed, we are familiar with some great centers in this country where their beautiful fountains, statuary and greenery provide not only great shopping convenience, but great cultural and esthetic advantages as well.

Large, well-planned shopping centers are known to draw considerable business from people living well beyond the limits of the taxing authority in which the center is located.

Fundamentally, however, the shopping center is an economic machine. From the developers' standpoint, it has proved to be more of a business career than an investment. As an economic machine, it must, of course, carry its fair share of the tax load of the community. The purpose of this report is to attempt to determine what criteria should be used in determining that "fair share."

APPRAISAL METHODS

It is not the purpose of this report to recommend any one of the various methods of appraisal which are used to determine the market value of shopping centers. The most popular methods used in various sections of the country, and a brief description of each, are:

THE COMPARATIVE METHOD:

In this method, a comparison of the new center being assessed is made with the known market value of other commercial properties. These other properties may or may not be other shopping centers.

Residual Land Method:

The net income of the shopping center, before taxes and depreciation, is calculated and then a total value is arrived at through selection and use of a capitalization rate. The buildings are appraised at replacement cost figures. The value arrived at by using the capitalization rate, less the replacement cost of the building, equals, then, the residual value of the land.

Residual Building Method:

The market value of the land is estimated. The net income of the project, before taxes and depreciation, is capitalized at a selected capitalization rate. This capitalized value, less the land value, results in a residual building value.

Replacement Cost Method:

The acquisition cost and improvement cost of the land is determined. This value is sometimes graded upward in various stages to conform to the progress of the center. The value of the building is determined by replacement cost. These two values added together determine the market value for purposes of tax assessment.

There is considerable question in the minds of many people as to the practical life for depreciation purposes of the average shopping center. Regular obsolescence appears to be more accelerated than estimated. This is further accented by the fact that in the early life of a shopping center many changes are often required because of the turnover of tenants resulting in additional costs for new store fronts, partitions, lighting, etc.

A shopping center that becomes very successful is more susceptible to the development of competition than is a downtown store building, because land is more readily available in the suburbs for the construction of competitive stores.

It is the feeling of a growing number of people that we are overdeveloping certain areas of our country with this type of improvement, resulting in the rapid obsolescence of the less efficient and attractive centers. In connection with this, Robert H. Levi, head of The Hecht Company, a department store in Washington, D. C., in a talk before the American Society of Real Estate Counselors on January 12, 1957, in Washington, D. C., stated in speaking of department store locations:

> ". . . it involves a basic, long-term decision requiring considerable capital and the result is going to be very, very permanent. You cannot put a department store on wheels and move it. With the problem of expanding cities, the greatest danger in retailing is that the suburban store can become obsolete a lot faster than the downtown store."

When using the comparative approach in determining the value of shopping centers for assessment purposes, comparisons should be limited to other shopping centers or to retail buildings providing extensive parking. In no case should the value of surrounding small commercially used parcels be considered, as their value is enhanced by the parasitic position they occupy relative to the adjacent shopping center, and any purchase cannot be considered an open-market transaction.

In evaluating the land used for parking purposes, it is not realistic to use the same square footage or front footage approach that is used in the downtown area, because the shopping center parking area is strictly an overhead item serving merely to enhance the value of the land under the store buildings. These parking areas which provide, in many cases, space for public functions, are not fully used except at times of peak activity, and if these facilities were not supplied by private owners on which they pay taxes, they would probably be supplied, as in many downtown areas, by the municipality without the benefit of taxes and at the expense of all the taxpayers of the community.

In providing outdoor lighting, policing, traffic control, landscaping, etc., many shopping center owners are providing at their own expense, services that normally would be supplied and paid for by all the taxpayers of the community.

In appraising improvements, a careful determination should be made as to what is the landlord's property and what is the tenants'. Tenants' improvements are usually of a specific nature and have no intrinsic value to the landlord after that particular tenant is gone.

In determining value by capitalizing net income, the minimum guaranteed rental should be given relatively more importance than overage rentals because buyers and lenders, in establishing the market value of a shopping center, give less weight to the percentage overage rental unless and until it is paid by strong tenants over a period of years. A vacancy factor is also used by lending institutions in determining value because of the relatively high turnover of the smaller tenants.

The capitalization rate used in determining value should be realistic and reflect the rate of net return demanded by purchasers of shopping centers in the general area.

SHOPPING CENTER OWNERSHIP

As ownership of a shopping center is a business activity instead of being a mere investment medium, expenses typical of most businesses must be paid by the developer-owner and should be taken into consideration in determining net income. Such expenses include:

Administration or management
Promotion
Maintenance
Commissions
Renovation costs
Accounting fees
Legal costs
Taxes and insurance

THE APPROACH TO USE

Whatever formula the assessor uses, the approach should be consistent. For instance, there is no justification in applying a number of different formulae and then using the one that results in the highest valuation.

The approach to the determination of value used by the assessor should be tailored to the facts at hand and be consistent throughout the community in assessing the same types of property. In determining the rate of depreciation and, hence, the economic life of a shopping center, it might be wise to segregate such items as:

Heating
Ventilating
Lighting fixtures
Plumbing
Wiring
Paving and similar items

These have a much shorter life, generally speaking, than the building structures themselves.

In this connection, the amortization period for the costs of store fronts and special installations for particular tenants should coincide with the terms of the lease.

It is a false conclusion to assume that all shopping centers, because they are new and in the spotlight of modern merchandising are, per se, profitable. Some are very successful, some are failures.

As real estate taxes make up a very large item in the expenses of any shopping center, we cannot over-emphasize the importance of appraising these projects on a reasonable and equitable basis.

THE PURPOSE OF THIS REPORT

It is not the purpose of this report to help shopping center owners avoid their financial responsibility to the community. Rather, it is our hope to establish certain definable criteria which will assist the assessor and the property owner in arriving at what that financial responsibility should be.

It is generally acknowledged that properly planned and managed shopping centers represent real assets to any community both financially and aesthetically. If we are to encourage their construction and proper operation, we should not penalize them with unfair and unreasonably high tax assessments. Determining a fair or reasonable assessment is not an easy task, but the results should be well worth the effort expended.

Index

A

B

C

D

E

F

G

H

I

N

S

T

U

V

W

Y

Z